Complete Book of
PARENTING

The Parents' Question-and-Answer Book

BEEKMAN HOUSE

CARVAJAL S.A.
Impreso en Colombia
Printed in Colombia

ISBN 0-88176-410-8

Photo Credits:
Comstock: cover, p. 210; FPG International: Michael Nelson, cover, p. 82; G. Steiner, cover, p. 146; International Stock Photography Ltd: cover, p. 8; The Stock Market: Paul Barton, cover.

Illustrations: Chris Horrie

Contributing writers:

ROBERT A. MENDELSON, M.D., F.A.A.P., is the chairman of the Committee on Communications of the American Academy of Pediatrics. He is a clinical professor of pediatrics at Oregon Health Sciences University and is on the pediatric staff of three private hospitals. He has been in private practice in pediatrics since 1964. He is coauthor (with Lottie Mendelson) of a monthly patient newsletter and has appeared on national television as a media spokesperson for the American Academy of Pediatrics. He is also chairman of the editorial advisory board of *Healthy Kids*, a parenting magazine.

LOTTIE M. MENDELSON, R.N., M.S., is a pediatric nurse practitioner. Together with Dr. Robert Mendelson, she teaches family life courses and gives lectures on human sexuality, love and marriage, and general pediatric topics to audiences from the preschool to college level. She is coauthor of a monthly patient newsletter, writes regularly for *Healthy Kids* magazine, and has frequent speaking engagements to parent groups and parent-child groups throughout the Northwest.

MICHAEL K. MEYERHOFF, ED.D., is executive director of The Epicenter, Inc. ("The Education for Parenthood Information Center"), a family advisory and advocacy agency based in Wellesley Hills, Massachusetts. He received his doctorate in human development from the Harvard Graduate School of Education, where he served as a researcher with the Harvard Preschool Project. He has conducted workshops on "Educating the Infant and Toddler" throughout the United States and Canada. He has been instrumental in developing many parent preparation and support programs, most notably the state of Missouri's "New Parents as Teachers" project.

LOUISE BATES AMES, PH.D., is associate director and cofounder of the Gesell Institute of Human Development in New Haven, Connecticut. She has coauthored or collaborated on more than thirty child-care books and more than 200 scientific articles and monographs.

CONTENTS

INTRODUCTION 6

BIRTH TO 6 MONTHS 9

How Your Child Develops
The greatest period of growth in her life
10

Understanding Your Child's Behavior
Orienting himself to life outside the womb
17

Daily Care Basics
Meeting her needs and handling her safely
24

Nutrition and Feeding
Providing proper nutrition—by breast or bottle
36

Safety and Health
Keeping her safe and healthy during this vulnerable period
48

On Being a Parent
Adjusting to your new life together
61

Selecting Toys and Equipment
What she needs, and what she doesn't
72

6 MONTHS TO 1 YEAR 83

How Your Child Develops
Learning how to get around on his own
84

Understanding Your Child's Behavior
Exploring and investigating her wider world
92

Daily Care Basics
Getting him clean, dressed, and on his way
100

Nutrition and Feeding
Giving her a taste of foods to come
107

Safety and Health
Keeping your mobile baby safe and healthy
114

On Being a Parent
Being her "consultant" as she learns how to learn
129

Selecting Toys and Equipment
Making your home a safe and exciting "playground"
137

1 YEAR TO 2½ YEARS 147

How Your Child Develops
From little "baby" to small "child"
148

Understanding Your Child's Behavior
Testing the boundaries and striving toward independence
156

Daily Care Basics
Allowing her to help with her own daily care
164

Nutrition and Feeding
Learning how to feed himself
171

Safety and Health
Staying one step ahead of your adventuresome toddler
177

On Being a Parent
From rituals to rebellion—setting examples and limits
192

Selecting Toys and Equipment
Keeping up with her growing interests and abilities
203

2½ YEARS TO 5 YEARS 211

How Your Child Develops
Becoming a rational, social individual
212

Understanding Your Child's Behavior
Exercising her mind as well as her body
221

Daily Care Basics
Tackling toilet training, and teaching hygiene
230

Nutrition and Feeding
Learning healthy eating habits for now and for the future
237

Safety and Health
Setting safety examples now that will be with him always
244

On Being a Parent
Being her guardian, consultant, disciplinarian—and friend
257

Selecting Toys and Equipment
Opening up new worlds for him to enjoy and explore
269

GLOSSARY 278

INDEX 282

INTRODUCTION

Congratulations—and welcome to the wonderful world of parenting. The day that you have been waiting for has finally arrived—your baby is here. The birth of your child is the culmination of nine months of excitement and anticipation. It is also the start of a new way of life for you. Your journey through parenthood has just begun. It is a journey that will be filled with joys, frustrations, rewards, responsibilities, challenges—and above all, questions. Because you and your child are both individuals, some of what you'll need to know must be learned along the way. That doesn't mean, however, that you have to figure everything out on your own. Within this book, you'll find authoritative, practical answers to hundreds of child care and parenting questions. The book is designed to be a reference and resource for parents like you—parents who want to give their child the best possible start in life but who may not always be sure how to go about that task.

Now that you are a parent, the last thing you have time to do is sift through an entire book to find the advice and information you need. For this reason, *Complete Book of Parenting* is divided into four color-coded age groups: Birth to six months (pink), six months to one year (blue), one year to two and a half years (yellow), and two and a half years to five years (green). This format allows you to turn directly to the questions and answers that refer to your child's age group.

Within each of the four age groups, you'll discover a wealth of information on taking care of your child.

You'll also find a great deal more. After all, there's more to being a parent than knowing how to change a diaper. As your child's caregiver and guide, you need to know who your child is, what she can do and comprehend, and why she behaves the way she does at each stage of development.

To give you the understanding as well as the information you need, each age group contains sections on development, behavior, daily care, feeding and nutrition, safety and health, parenting issues, and toys and equipment. The sections entitled "How Your Child Develops" trace your child's physical, emotional, and intellectual development. You'll get an idea of what kinds of gains in height, weight, and ability you might expect—as well as reassurances about lags and spurts in your child's progress. The "typical" age ranges for the onset of skills like crawling, walking, and talking are discussed, with an emphasis on the wide variability among children and the need for patience on your part.

If you're wondering why your baby puts everything—including his feet—into his mouth, why your toddler seems to refuse every request you make of him, or why your preschooler won't go to bed without his favorite blanket, then "Understanding Your Child's Behavior" is where you'll find the answer. These questions and answers help you see your child's behavior in the context of his abilities at each stage of development. You'll discover that many of the seemingly odd behaviors your child may exhibit are quite common and actually make a good deal of sense when you think about how your child sees the world. With the insights you'll gain from these sections, you'll be able to solve—and perhaps even prevent—some common parenting problems.

In the "Daily Care Basics" sections, you'll get "hands-on" instructions and step-by-step illustrations for tasks like diapering, dressing, and bathing your child. Our experts explore the pros and cons of cloth and disposable diapers. They also give you tips on making bath time easier, getting wiggly arms and legs into shirts and sleepers, and making hygiene fun for your child. In addition, you'll find guidelines for when and how to begin toilet training.

To be sure you're providing your child with the nutrients she needs for proper growth and development, refer to the "Feeding and Nutrition" section in each age group. You'll find discussions of breast-feeding and bottle-feeding as well as step-by-step instructions on burping positions, nursing positions, sterilizing bottles and formula, and preparing your own baby food. The authors provide helpful advice and recommendations on weaning, introducing solids, offering a prudent diet, and encouraging healthy eating habits.

Your concerns and questions about keeping your child from harm and dealing with illness are covered in the extensive "Safety and Health" section in each age group. You'll find practical advice for making your home safe for your child while encouraging him to explore and learn about the world. You'll also find expert advice and guidelines for dealing with common childhood health problems; having your child immunized; taking your child's temperature; knowing when to call the pediatrician; and much more.

In the sections entitled "On Being a Parent," you'll learn how to play the role of your child's "consultant"—by making her environment accessible and interesting, by adding on to the information she is gaining herself, and by using her interests and abilities as your guide. The authors give you advice on what you can do—and what you should try not to do—to help your child learn about the world. The sections cover tough parenting issues like disciplining wisely, dealing with sibling rivalry, and selecting high-quality day care. You'll find advice on coping with your role as a parent, too. You'll discover ways to enjoy your child, handle setbacks and frustrations, and keep worries and guilt from getting out of hand.

The final section in each age group, "Selecting Toys and Equipment," gives you solid advice and recommendations about choosing safe, suitable toys and equipment for your child at each stage of development. You'll even find suggestions for turning common household items into safe, entertaining, and inexpensive playthings for your child.

At the end of the book, you'll find a handy glossary of terms used throughout the text and a detailed index to help you locate the specific information you need quickly and easily.

As you read and refer to this book, you may notice that we alternate, by section, our references to the gender of your baby and the gender of your pediatrician. The exceptions to this are those questions in which the gender of the baby is dictated by the topic being discussed (questions on circumcision, for example). This method was chosen in order to account for the obvious possibilities without making the references confusing. Unless indicated otherwise, the answers apply to children of either gender.

Of course, there is no single source that can answer every parenting question in every situation. Your child will grow, develop, and learn at his own pace. You will need to adjust your parenting strategies—and your expectations—accordingly. This book can, however, make the job of being a parent easier. With the authoritative and practical advice and information presented here, you'll have a good head start on the road to becoming your child's caregiver, protector, disciplinarian, instructor—and friend. Together with your own natural instincts, your love for your child, and the experience you'll pick up along the way, *Complete Book of Parenting* can help you become the best parent you can be.

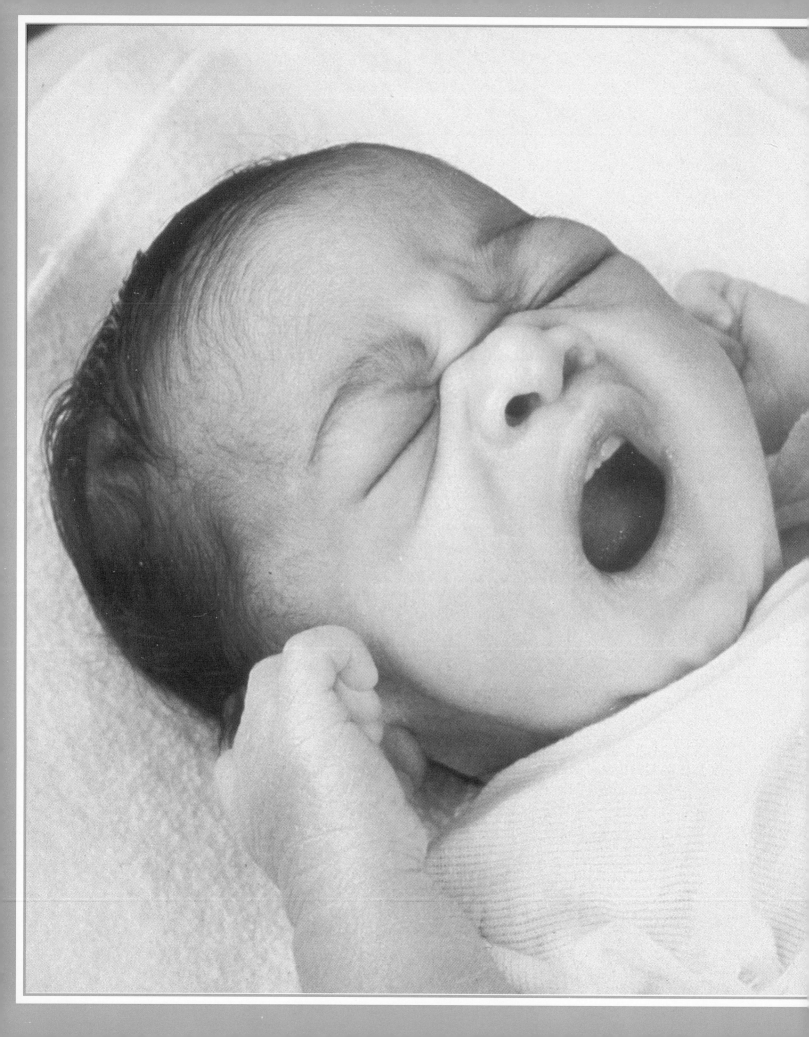

BIRTH
TO
6 MONTHS

The first six months of life can be described as an "orientation" period for you and your baby. After making the transition from womb to outside world, your baby will gradually discover his various body parts and become familiar with their basic movements. He will become adept at using his senses to absorb information from his immediate surroundings. And he will get well-acquainted with the people who care for him. Meanwhile, you will become accustomed to his presence, confident in your ability to make him comfortable and meet his basic needs, and familiar with his characteristics and idiosyncracies. In general, this will be a relatively easy time for you and your baby. Of course, you will need to make a number of adjustments in your lifestyle. You are likely to experience some anxious moments. And you will probably suffer from fatigue occasionally. Still, as long as your baby is healthy and you behave in a naturally concerned and caring manner, chances are he will make optimal progress at this point. In terms of your baby's development, there will be relatively little at risk. With regard to your nurturing role, it will be extremely difficult for you to make major mistakes. The most important thing is that your baby fall in love with you and that you fall in love with him—and that will probably happen with virtually no thought or effort at all.

HOW YOUR CHILD DEVELOPS

Will my baby grow much during the first six months?

She certainly will. In fact, she will grow more rapidly during this period than during any other time in her life. The average newborn weighs between seven and eight pounds and is between 19 and 22 inches long. Of course, many babies are considerably smaller or larger and are still well within the "normal" range. However, from whatever point she starts, your baby will grow almost one inch and gain nearly two pounds each month during her first half-year of life. Again, all babies have unique rates and patterns of growth. Minor "irregularities" are the rule rather than the exception. So, use these figures as approximations.

Although she is beautiful to me, objectively speaking, my newborn is not very attractive. Is something wrong with her?

Nothing that a little time won't cure. The perfectly proportioned, absolutely adorable newborn is a Hollywood illusion. Whenever a "newborn" appears on television or in the movies, the tiny actor is usually at least two or three months old. In reality, babies start out somewhat misshapen because the upper parts of their bodies are more fully developed before birth than the lower parts. In addition, the birthing process can be tough on their physical features. The tight passage through the vaginal canal often results in a temporary overlap of the skull bones, so their heads are typically elongated and melonlike. Their ears may be pushed out of normal position, their feet turned, and other parts slightly squeezed awry, giving them a "windblown" look. What's more, most newborns are covered with a white, waxy material (called the vernix), and many have a complete body coat of fine, dark hair (called the lanugo). Some also may have minor skin rashes. But don't worry. All of these "unattractive features" gradually disappear within a few days to a few weeks.

I like to joke that my baby looks just like her grandpa— bald and toothless. When will she get her hair and teeth?

Although some babies are born with a full head of hair, most come into the world almost totally bald. And many who do

THE "BONDING" PHENOMENON

Bonding refers to the development of a deep emotional attachment between parent and child. The term first appeared several years ago in an early research report. The report indicated that mothers and babies who had skin-to-skin contact during the hours immediately after birth eventually developed a superior relationship compared to those who did not have the benefit of this special experience. However, later and more thorough research revealed that this particular sort of contact during this supposedly "critical" period actually is irrelevant (a nice thing to do, but certainly not necessary). It also showed that the "bond" between parent and child grows slowly and steadily over the course of many months. It has been shown that as long as they provide a significant amount of nurturing as time goes by, mothers who are under anesthesia during delivery and don't get to hold their babies until many hours later have no problem forming a solid "bond" with their babies. The same holds true for adoptive mothers who do not even see their babies until days after birth and fathers who don't get a chance to become involved to a great extent until their babies are brought home from the hospital.

have hair at birth lose it within a few weeks. It is not until several months later that the vast majority of babies begin to grow permanent hair with lasting color and characteristics. By the time the soft spots (fontanels) on your baby's head completely close between ten and 18 months of age, her head will likely have a suitable covering of hair as well. As for teeth, again, some babies are born with one tooth or more. However, the first teeth typically do not appear until about six or eight months of age. The rest come in at regular intervals for many months after that. It may not be until her second birthday or so that your baby has her complete set of "baby" teeth.

My newborn seems to have no control over her head and body—she's like a rag doll. Is that normal?

It certainly is. In the beginning, your baby's body is simply too much for her small and undeveloped muscles to control. Her "floppiness" is most noticeable—and perhaps most alarming—with her disproportionately large head. Therefore, for the first few weeks, whenever you pick her up or otherwise handle your baby, you will have to provide the support that her neck and shoulder muscles can't. By the time she is about six weeks old, she should be able to hold her head steady for a moment or two when she is placed in an upright position—as long as she is kept perfectly still. By three or four months of age, she probably will have fairly good control of her head when she's held upright.

When can I expect my baby to start lifting her head? Rolling over? Sitting up by herself?

Even when your baby is only a day old, she is capable of lifting her head a tiny bit for a split second. However, it will be several weeks before her capacity to lift her head becomes significant. And it will be somewhere between two and four months (typically around three months) before she is capable of lifting her head and chest up a few inches from a prone position and holding it up for more than a few seconds. By three months of age, you may notice her regularly rolling from side to side. It usually isn't until somewhere between four and six months (typically around five months) of age, however, that babies achieve the ability to turn completely from back to stomach and stomach to back (most babies do stomach to back first, but quite a few reverse the order). As for sitting up by herself,

your baby probably won't hit that milestone until sometime between five and eight months (typically at about five and a half months). By the way, it is important to remember that there is wide variability in the specific ages at which "normal" babies achieve these abilities. So don't make too much of it if your baby's progress is somewhat more or less than the "average."

My baby is one month old, and whenever she's on her back, she looks like a fencer—one arm cocked up and the other outstretched. Is this normal?

Roughly between one and three months of age, a baby's head and arm movements are controlled to a large extent by what is

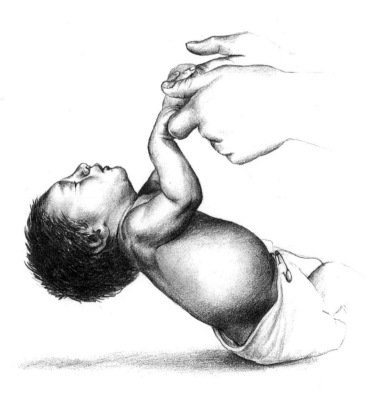

Your newborn's neck and back muscles are not yet strong enough to support her heavy head.

called the tonic neck reflex. When lying on her back, her head will almost always turn to one side, the arm on that side will stretch out, and the other arm will bend up. If you turn her head, the arms will switch position. As odd as this "fencer's pose" may be, rest assured that it is only temporary. You may also notice that from the time she was born, your baby has been holding her fingers in a clenched fist most of the time. Her fingers will gradually start to unfold at about the same time that the tonic neck reflex fades.

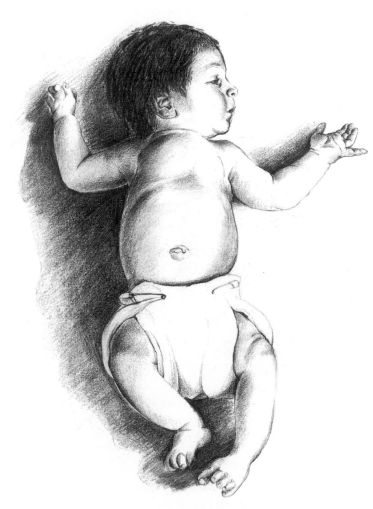

The "fencer's pose" is common during the first weeks of life because of the tonic neck reflex.

I've heard that babies are virtually blind and deaf at birth. Is that true, and if so, when will my newborn's vision and hearing improve? What about her other senses?

Newborns are not blind and deaf. In fact, they are sensitive to light and sound even while they are still in the womb. However, at birth, their senses are far from fully developed. For the first two or three months, the muscles in their eyes do not work very well and often do not work together. As a result, your baby may appear cross-eyed or wall-eyed on occasion. Also, at this stage, she can focus comfortably only on objects that are about eight to 12 inches from her eyes. Her ears have been capable of hearing well right from the start—perhaps too well for her brand-new nervous system. Consequently, she's likely to startle and cry in response to any loud and sudden noises. As for her other senses, they, too, have been in working order right from birth. It will take weeks and even months, however, before your baby has had enough practice and experience with them to make them fully useful. Starting at about three months, and certainly by about six months, you will be able to consider your baby's senses almost totally mature.

Can my newborn do anything by herself, or is she completely helpless?

At birth, babies are not without some ability, but the list of things they can't do is certainly a lot longer than the list of things they can do. Actually, your newborn's "abilities" consist of a small collection of basic "reflexes." These reflexes include rooting (turning the head when the cheek is touched), sucking, swallowing, grasping things that are placed in the hand, crying in response to physical discomfort, and gazing into the eyes of others (especially during feeding). While these basic capacities are obviously useful, it is clear that your baby is totally dependent upon you for her survival at this point. By the end of this period, you will be surprised and delighted by how much she has learned to do for herself. But it takes a very long time for little human beings to achieve a truly significant degree of independence from their parents.

Can my newborn understand anything that is happening to her?

Probably not. According to our best research on how the human mind grows, babies are born with virtually no ability to "think" or "comprehend" at all. They are just beginning to receive information through their senses. They have no experience they can use to process and organize information in a meaningful fashion. As a result, they have no concept of time or space and are unable to distinguish themselves from the world around them. So there really is no way for them to "know" what is going on. Although your baby began gaining experiences and making "sense" of them from birth, it will be many months before she achieves what we refer to as true "understanding."

How does my baby learn during these early months?

Learning takes place through the continuous interaction of two major functions—assimilation and accommodation. On one hand, your baby is constantly taking in, or assimilating, various elements of her environment. In a very basic sense, she is gathering "information." To do this, she uses whatever mental structures she has. On the other hand, she is constantly adjusting, or accommodating, those mental structures so that she can take in even more information about her environment. In the beginning, her only mental structures are those basic reflexes referred to earlier. Although they are rather primitive and uncoordinated, they are the building blocks of intelligence. They allow your baby to begin the process of adapting to her environment. And adaptation to the environment is what early learning is all about. For example, one of your baby's basic reflexes is sucking. At first, your baby will suck vigorously on whatever comes in contact with her lips—whether it's her mother's nipple or her father's little finger. However, after a month or so of experience and practice, she will have refined that basic reflex somewhat. She may still suck on whatever comes near her mouth, but when she is presented with the breast, she will make minor adjustments with her body, head, and lips in order to better participate in the nursing process. In other words, as she exercises the basic sucking reflex, she will "learn" something about her environment. Then, she will use that information to adjust her sucking reflex to make it more useful.

If my baby can't really "think" or "comprehend" at this point, what kind of "intelligence" can she acquire?

The first stage of mental development is referred to as the "sensorimotor" period because intellectual and physical growth

A FEW WORDS ABOUT INDIVIDUAL DIFFERENCES

It is important for parents to realize that the process of charting early human development is not an exact science. Pediatricians, psychologists, and educators can use their experience to establish "normal" ranges and pinpoint "average" ages at which certain abilities are likely to appear. They cannot, however, precisely forecast an individual child's rate and pattern of development. They prepare developmental charts merely to give parents some general guidelines, not specific predictions. Therefore, if your baby hits one milestone directly on the mark, such a phenomenon is likely to be an exception rather than the rule. As strange as it may sound, babies who progress precisely "as expected" are not "typical." What's more, while some babies are routinely "late" or "early," most are early in some areas and late in others, and they often change pace at different ages. So unless your baby is constantly showing up on one extreme of the scale, it is inappropriate to make too much of what she does in any single situation. Many parents get into trouble by making unfair and meaningless comparisons between their baby's progress and another's. Perhaps the most critical thing for parents to keep in mind is that when it comes to early development, "different" does not automatically imply "better" or "worse," and "equal" does not necessarily mean "the same."

are so closely interrelated at this point. Babies begin to learn about the world through their senses and their physical movements. Gradually, they achieve greater control and mastery over their bodies. They also gain greater experience with more aspects of their surroundings by directly exploring and investigating. Thus, at first, the "intelligence" that your baby acquires is extremely "practical." It is limited to getting direct information and results from her immediate environment. However, slowly but surely, the many experiences she obtains through her senses and movements will form the foundations for distinctly "mental" functions such as memory, language, problem solving, imagination, and so on.

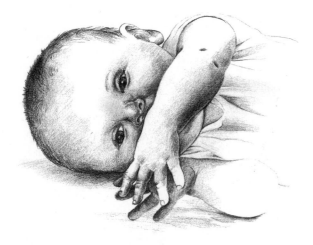

By the end of her third month, she will have discovered that she is connected to her own hand.

When, and how, will my baby begin to realize that her different body parts are connected?

Sometime between the end of the first month and the end of the third month, your baby will make her first major discovery—that she is connected to her own hand. When her random movements bring her hand into contact with her mouth, she will enjoy sucking on it. When those movements bring her hand into her line of vision, she will enjoy looking at it. Gradually, she will come to realize that she can control those movements to a certain extent; she will hold her hand in her mouth or in her line of vision for longer and longer periods of time. Eventually, she will also put the two together. After looking at her hand for a while, she will purposefully bring it to her mouth so she can suck on it. This is the first sign that your baby has learned to actively "do" things in order to bring about specific events that she "wants" to happen.

During this period, she will gradually learn to use her hands under the direction of her eyes.

How coordinated will my baby's actions become during the first six months?

After about three months of age, once she has gained fairly good control over her head, has become free from the tonic neck reflex, and has started unfolding her fingers, your baby will begin to make rapid progress in putting her senses and her movements to work together. Perhaps the most noticeable and most impressive capacity she will achieve during this period is "prehension," or visually directed reaching. Somewhere between four and seven months (typically at about five months), babies become adept at using their hands under the direction of their eyes. This accomplishment, along with the coordination of other senses and movements, allows for some fairly sophisticated activities. So, for example, by the time she is six months old, if your baby hears something, she will look right at it. Once she sees it, she will reach for it and grab it. Once she has grabbed it, she will bring it to her mouth and suck on it. When you consider how basic and uncoordinated her activities were at birth, it is remarkable how far she has come in such a short period of time.

Will my baby be able to remember things that happen to her during this period?

Your baby will "retain" a lot of what happens, but that is not the same as "remembering." She will be using the information she gains through experience to help improve her capacity to take in more information. She will be making more associations, forming habits, and otherwise "learning" on a very basic level. At this point, however, your baby's consciousness will be largely limited to "here and now." It will not be until she is almost two years old that she will be able to "picture" something in her mind when it is not directly in front of her and be able to store that mental image for a substantial length of time. Only when she is able to form, organize, and store such mental images will she be able to recall them for quick and easy reference. Think about it. None of us really remembers anything much prior to our third year of life, and our earliest memories are spotty and incomplete as compared to those from only a year or two later.

Will my baby understand anything I say to her during the first six months?

Probably not a single word. Your baby eventually will respond enthusiastically to the sound of your voice; you may even get a sense that she is responding to changes in the tone and inflection of your voice after a while. But actually understanding the meaning of specific words is a bit beyond your baby's mental abilities at this point. Words are symbols for things, actions, feelings, etc. It takes a while for babies to gain enough experience to associate a symbol with what it stands for, and even longer for them to develop the ability to form and store these symbols in their minds for any length of time. Language and thought are tied closely together. So for the first six months of your baby's life, actions not only speak louder than words, they are the only kind of "words" your baby will truly comprehend.

Will my baby be able to communicate at all with me during this period?

She certainly will, although her communication tactics will range from obvious to subtle, with very little in between. Her main means of giving you a message will be something she was born with—the cry. When she is hungry, cold, in pain, or suffering from any sort of discomfort, your baby won't hesitate to let you know with a loud wail. Unfortunately, while she will be able to let you know something is wrong, she won't be able to tell you exactly what the problem is. Starting at two or three months of age, your baby will add giggling and squealing with delight, but these new forms of communication will be equally unspecific. Therefore, you will have to pay attention to the many forms of nonverbal communication your baby will employ as well. As you try to feed or diaper her, for instance, you may notice that she tenses her body, turns her head away, scrunches up her face, or in some other way tries to inform you that she is not happy about what you are doing at the moment. On the other hand, you may notice that she relaxes her body, waves her arms, smiles, or in some other way tries to inform you that she is content or thrilled with what you are doing.

Our one-month-old baby began smiling at us almost from the day she was born. Does this mean that she knows we are her parents?

We would all like to think that our children feel immediate and significant fondness for us. Unfortunately, this probably is impossible. Although something resembling a smile may appear from time to time during the first few weeks of life, a baby at this point does not have the social awareness to make such episodes meaningful. Starting a little before the second month of life, babies begin to smile fairly regularly, but even then the smile appears to be in response to familiarity rather than people. In other words, babies will smile just as often at their crib rails, mobiles, blankets, etc. as they will at their mothers and fathers. It is not until around the third month of life that babies really get a sense that they are separate and distinct from other people. It is at this time that smiling in direct response to the presence of their parents becomes frequent and reliable. By the way, this is also the time when you can first tickle your baby successfully, because she is now aware that you are the "tickler" and that she is the "ticklee"—a social awareness that must be added to the physical stimulation in order for tickling to work.

SOME "AMAZING" BUT MISLEADING ABILITIES OF NEWBORNS

Every once in a while you may see an article that talks about researchers discovering some "amazing" ability in newborns. This ability is supposed to demonstrate that little babies are far more aware and capable than previously believed. The fact of the matter is that newborns occasionally do some strange things, but what they do is often misinterpreted. A good example is the phenomenon of "neonatal imitation" discovered a few years ago. Some researchers found they could get babies only a couple of days old to stick out their tongues in imitation of an adult doing the same. Since it was previously believed that babies aren't capable of imitative behavior until the end of the first year, news of this discovery spread like wildfire. However, further study revealed that tongue protrusion was the only behavior newborns could imitate, and that they would imitate it only rarely under very special conditions. What's more, after a few days, this "ability" disappears completely until the end of the first year. In other words, what was discovered was a reflexlike response that has little significance. We always have known that if you hold a newborn over a surface so that her feet are lightly touching it, she will move her legs up and down in a "walking" motion. This "walking reflex" goes away shortly, and the baby doesn't start true walking until many months later. No one would be so foolish as to claim that newborns can walk. Therefore, any time you read about some incredible capacity being discovered in newborns, or if you notice your newborn apparently doing something that you would not expect her to be able to do, chances are it is not what it appears to be.

Lately my baby has been looking up when I call her. Does this mean she at least knows her own name?

A lot of parents get fooled here. Starting at about four months of age, babies become capable of orienting accurately to the source of sound. Early on, you may have noticed that when her name was called, something else was said, or any noise was made around her, your baby perked up, but she acted like she didn't know where it was coming from. Now, when a sound is produced, she is likely to look immediately and directly at whatever produced it. Moreover, she is becoming very interested in sounds, particularly human ones. So, now, when she looks, she is likely to smile as well, especially if the sound is familiar. Therefore, when you call her name, she looks up and smiles at you. But if instead you called out "George Burns," you would probably get the same reaction.

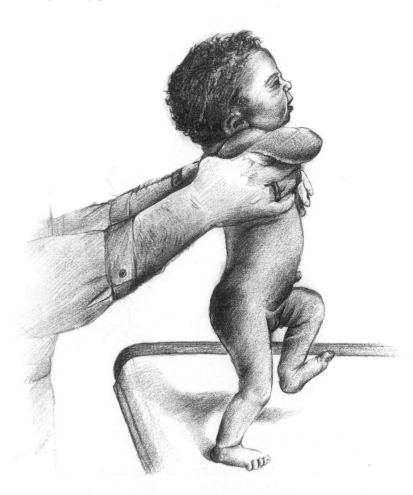

If her feet lightly touch a surface, her legs will move up and down. This "walking reflex" will soon fade, however.

UNDERSTANDING YOUR CHILD'S BEHAVIOR

My newborn sleeps almost all day. Is this normal?

In the beginning, most babies sleep most of the time. Although some babies sleep only ten hours a day, and some as many as 23, the average is about 17 hours, equally divided between day and night. What's more, periods of wakefulness and alertness are very brief and irregular at first. They usually last no more than a few minutes at a time. By three months of age, babies typically sleep 15 hours—ten at night and five during the day. By six months of age, the average is about 14 hours—11 during the night and three during the day. However, it is important to remember that there is great variability in sleep patterns among individual babies. So don't be alarmed if your baby is awake and alert more or less than these averages during the early months. Also, keep in mind that babies tire rather easily. Even if your baby is sleeping many hours each night, he still may not be able to go more than a few hours without a nap during the day.

When can I expect my baby to start sleeping through the night?

There is no set age at which all babies routinely begin sleeping through the night. At first, sleeping is tied closely to feeding; babies will tend to fall asleep when they're full and wake up as soon as they're hungry. It is not until about three or four months of age that being tired generally takes priority over being hungry. It is also at about three or four months that babies can stay awake for relatively long stretches. They become considerably more active during the day, so they are likely to remain asleep throughout the night. Therefore, although your baby may start sleeping through the night somewhat earlier or later, you can reasonably expect to see this beginning to happen somewhere between three and four months on average.

How can my baby be so totally calm one minute and so totally upset the next?

You have to realize that babies perceive things differently than we do. In the beginning, their senses are very sensitive. Bright lights, loud noises, sudden movements, etc. are likely to alarm them. Furthermore, they have little or no experience to help put

PATIENCE SOLVES A LOT OF PROBLEMS

Perhaps the best tool that parents can have for coping with their babies during the first months of life is patience. As delightful as babies can be, they also can do a lot of strange, inconvenient, annoying, and alarming things. Fortunately, because babies are developing at a rate that is faster than at any other time of life, many of the problems they pose require only that you wait a little while for them to go away. For instance, the tendency of newborns to startle violently at loud sounds, bright lights, or sometimes for no apparent reason at all is pretty scary. However, just when you reach the point where you think you can't stand it any more, their nervous systems become less sensitive and this frightening behavior simply disappears. Another good example is their emerging sociability. At first, the total helplessness of newborns almost forces their mothers and fathers to fall in love with them. Then, after a few weeks of constantly caring for a largely unresponsive newborn, the attraction starts to fade a little and some resentment begins to creep in. All of a sudden, the first smiles appear, and the baby quickly becomes dearly beloved again. A few weeks later, just when those smiles are becoming old hat and the parents begin wondering if they'll ever establish a real relationship with their baby, true social awareness kicks in, and giggling, tickling, and various other irresistible forms of interaction become possible. Therefore, if you find yourself anxious about something that your baby is doing or is not doing, be patient. Chances are that very soon he will grow out of or into whatever the behavior in question may be.

things into perspective. They also have no sense of relative intensity or duration. As a result, they have very few "moods." When they get upset, they are enraged, and when they are comfortable, they are as content as can be. And as far as they're concerned, whatever state they're in may last forever. It will be a few months before your baby's physical and mental capacities have developed to the point where he can better cope with the world and the way it works. Only then will his moods swing less widely and abruptly.

Sometimes, being picked up and held is exactly what he wants.

My newborn's cries vary widely in tone and intensity. Do different cries mean different things?

When a newborn cries, it is strictly a reflexive response to physical discomfort. So even if his cries vary in tone and intensity, it is not because he has any real control over what he is doing or is intentionally giving meaning to his vocalizations. Some researchers claim that by using sophisticated equipment to analyze pitch and decibel level, they can distinguish "hunger" cries from "pain" cries or whatever. The subtle differences they can detect, however, certainly are not apparent to the naked ear. It is not until about three or four months of age that babies realize they can use the cry intentionally as a true communication device. From that point on until they become capable of speech, they gradually develop cries of varying types in an attempt to express their needs and desires more effectively. Therefore, for most of this period, you are better off looking to see what's wrong with your baby rather than trying to tell by the nature of his cry.

Sometimes when my baby cries, I can't find anything wrong, but he stops soon after I pick him up. Why is that?

One of the maddening things about little babies is that they often experience discomfort of a sort that is not readily apparent to their parents. Most of the time, you will notice that your baby has not been fed for a while, that he is cold, that his diaper is soiled, etc., and as soon as you take care of the problem, his crying stops. But there inevitably will be times when you won't be able to find out what's wrong, and of course, your baby won't be able to tell you. However, one of the nice things about little babies is that they can be soothed easily on occasion simply by being picked up, rocked, and moved gently through space. By the way, as they get to the end of this period, babies begin to suffer new sorts of discomfort from time to time—namely loneliness and boredom. They will use the cry to alleviate these conditions as well. In such cases, being picked up and held by their parents is exactly what they are looking for.

Is it possible for my baby to calm himself?

Although he won't really know what he's doing at first, your baby may be capable of calming himself from time to time if he is fortunate enough to have one of his hands come in contact with his mouth. Sucking, even if it is not followed by nourishment, is a very soothing activity for babies. That is why pacifiers are so popular with babies and such a blessing to their parents. By three or four months of age, your baby will have developed sufficient control and coordination to bring his hand to his mouth purposefully and regularly. So when he is moderately distressed, he may attempt to calm himself by bringing his hand to his mouth and sucking on it. However, even at this point, he will be counting on you to take care of most of his needs—particularly the major ones.

What is meant by the term "temperament"?

Temperament is a term used to refer to a baby's personality. As is the case with adults, babies come in all different kinds. Some are jumpy, fussy, easily irritated, and difficult to comfort, while others tend to be relaxed, calm, slow to be bothered, and quick to be soothed. The term "temperament" is used rather than "personality" because while it is clear that babies come into the world with various character traits, there is little evidence to suggest that these traits are in any way permanent. In other words, at two days of age, your baby may very well display a distinctly difficult or easy type of temperament. However, he may or may not display an entirely different type at two weeks of age or two months of age. What's more, even if his temperament stays fairly consistent during this period, it's not a reliable guide to what his personality will be like when he gets older.

How will my behavior affect my baby's temperament?

For the most part, your baby's temperament is independent from your behavior. You should not feel that you did anything that caused him to be especially difficult or easy. However, how you cope with your baby's temperament is largely within your control. Pediatricians and psychologists can analyze your baby's behavior and come up with an objective reading of how difficult or easy he is. But "difficult" and "easy" are subjective terms. Parents who are naturally laid-back may find a certain type of baby easy to handle, whereas naturally high-strung parents may find the same baby impossible. Parents who had an extremely easy baby the first time around may feel that their second child is a terror, even though most other parents would consider him a piece of cake. Therefore, to the extent that you can remain patient and calm despite some trying displays of temperament, the more likely it is that the situation will remain within tolerable limits, and the quicker it will seem to pass.

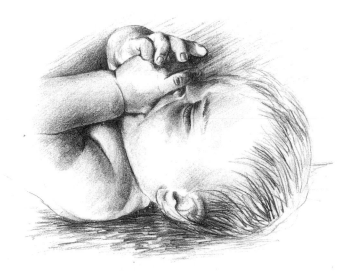

Sucking on his own hands may soothe him at times.

My newborn's movements are very abrupt and jerky. Is that normal?

It certainly is. In the beginning, a baby's behavior is very fragmented in nature. His innate reflexes allow him to "do" things, but the things he does are totally controlled by stimulation from outside his mind. What's more, they are all done independently from one another. For example, as mentioned before, if his random movements bring his hand in contact with his mouth, he will suck on his hand. But as yet, he is unable to bring his hand to his mouth on purpose. As the weeks go by, however, your baby will begin to realize that he can control his movements to a greater and greater extent, and he will gradually learn to start coordinating his various activities. Although he still will be a long way from smooth and graceful, by the end of this period you can expect your baby's movements to be much more deliberate and efficient.

Even when he is awake and alert, my newborn doesn't seem very interested in doing anything. Should I try to get him "involved"?

In making the transition from the womb to the outside world, babies require a two or three week "adjustment" period.

For the bulk of the first month, they are primarily concerned with their own comfort. They have no desire to interact to any great extent with their surroundings. Moreover, they have very few capacities with which to do much interacting. Therefore, attempts to stimulate your baby at this point will be largely futile. In addition, he is likely to find them intrusive and irritating. By the end of the first month, he will be ready to start exploring his environment, and at that point, you won't need to do any coaxing.

Since he can't get around on his own, how can my baby begin to explore his world?

Your baby's early explorations will consist of soaking up his immediate environment through his senses. Although he was born with an abundant amount of curiosity, and it would appear that he has few capacities with which to satisfy it, bear in mind that everything is brand new to your baby. For the first couple of months or so, he will be fascinated by everything from his bedclothes to his crib rails, and he will be totally entranced

As her senses improve, she will spend much time absorbing the details of nearby objects.

by your face and the sound of your voice. He also will spend hours just trying to figure out what various parts of his own body are and how they work. While he may appear to be a largely passive creature, in reality, your baby will be very busy. He will be getting familiar with the sights, sounds, smells, tastes, and textures to which he will be exposed simply by being in the world.

How will my baby's explorations change as the months go by?

After a while, your baby's senses—especially his vision—will improve considerably, so he will be widening his sensory horizons with each passing week. He also will be paying closer attention to small details of nearby objects. Once he starts putting together the activities of his eyes and hands, his explorations will become much more active in character. This will be especially true sometime after four months of age, when he develops the capacity for visually directed reaching. Anytime something comes within his range, he will attempt to get hold of it. Once he does, he will spend a lot of time investigating every aspect of it with his hands, eyes, ears, and mouth.

My baby often will be intensely interested in some object, but as soon as he drops it, he seems as if he could care less. Why is that?

Throughout this period, your baby will be interested only in things that are directly evident to his senses. He is not yet able to "picture" an object in his mind once it is removed from his hands or his line of vision. It will be a few months before your baby has developed this ability—referred to as "object permanence"—which signals the beginning of memory. For the time being, as far as your baby is concerned, anything that is out of sight is out of mind as well. Therefore, no matter how curious he may be about an object, once it is gone, he has nothing to which he can apply that interest.

Many times my baby moves his arms and legs around a lot, but without any apparent purpose. Does this mean he's bored?

On the contrary. What he is doing is simply exercising his body, and babies enjoy doing that almost as much as they enjoy exploring. Again, you have to realize that each ability your baby achieves is brand new, and using that ability is going to be very exciting for him. Remember when you first got your driver's license and couldn't get enough of driving around, even if you didn't really go anywhere in particular? It's a similar experience for your baby. Once he figures out how to thrust his legs, how to work his eyes and hands together, how to turn over by himself, etc., the mere act of doing so will thrill him to no end and he won't be able to get enough of repeating the processes over and over again.

Even when I talk to and play with my baby, he remains very quiet and unresponsive. Should I just leave him alone?

That would be inadvisable. It is difficult for some parents not to take the unresponsiveness of their babies personally. But the fact of the matter is that for the first two or three months, babies simply do not have the social awareness that is

He will be entranced by your face and the sound of your voice.

BEWARE OF "ADULTOMORPHISM"

One of the more common problems to which new parents fall prey is the tendency to lapse into what is called "adultomorphism"—ascribing adult motivations to the behavior of their little ones. This is a very natural thing to do. After all, we more-than-halfheartedly believe that the dog is "in misery" when we leave him at the kennel before going on vacation, and even more incredibly, that the vending machine is "out to get us" when it takes our money but won't give us any candy in return. So is it that unreasonable to give mature emotional and mental powers to a baby who is considerably more beloved and often more exasperating? Moreover, it is virtually impossible to think or talk about a baby's behavior without using some standard language for emotional states and mental activities. For instance, it would be awkward to say anything other than "he's so happy you came home early" or "he's determined to get out of eating his beets" when describing what's happening with your baby at certain times and in certain situations. However, it is important for mothers and fathers to remember that babies do not perceive, comprehend, or react in any way resembling the manner in which adults or even slightly older children do. When things are going well, indulging in a little adultomorphism is probably harmless. The real potential for trouble comes when your baby does something annoying or intolerable, or when you accidentally do something that causes him discomfort or harm. If you forget that what's happening does not have the same meaning or long-term significance to your baby that it has for you, the levels of anger or guilt that you feel will be inappropriate and may even become dangerous on occasion.

necessary for all the giggling, squealing, tickling, and other fun interactions that parents may be expecting. That doesn't mean that your baby is not interested in you. On the contrary, he will be entranced by your face and the sound of your voice. For a while, however, he will be interested in you in the same way that he is interested in inanimate objects. There-fore, you can expect him to exhibit the same quiet demeanor and sober expression that are elicited by these other things. However, once smiling and social awareness set in, interacting with your baby will not only be more enjoyable, it will become absolutely irresistible.

Lately my baby has been trying to suck his feet and toes like he sucks his hands and fingers. Is this unusual?

At first, your baby didn't even know he had feet, as they were outside the range in which his eyes could focus clearly. Even though his vision may have improved sufficiently to

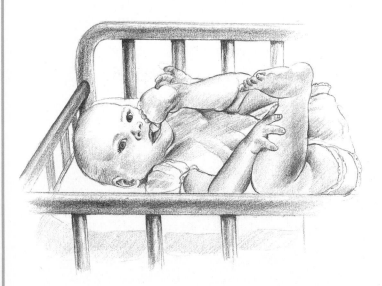

By the end of her third month, she will discover she has feet, too.

see them a while ago, he probably was preoccupied with his first major discovery—his hands. However, starting near the end of the third month, armed with better vision and ever-increasing curiosity, babies broaden their horizons. One of the first new things they discover are their feet. The feet make for fascinating visual targets. In addition, thanks to the flexibility of their bodies at this point, babies can also bring their feet and toes to their mouths for further exploration by other senses. Thus, your baby's fascination with his feet may seem bizarre on the surface, but it is a healthy sign that his interests and abilities are expanding.

Sometimes it seems as if my baby is talking to himself. What's going on?

Other than crying, your baby will be able to produce a variety of sounds right from the beginning. At first, he won't even realize that these delightful little "baby sounds" are coming from his own mouth, although he will enjoy listening to them. As the months go by, he will develop the awareness that he is producing these sounds, and he will learn how to control his vocal output to a certain extent. Once he has achieved these capacities, your baby will spend hours playing with his own saliva, making squeaking sounds, babbling, and otherwise entertaining himself with his own vocalizations. He will not as yet be at the point where true language learning can begin, and he therefore won't really be "talking" to himself. But this repeated practicing and appreciation of his own noise-making ability does set the stage for the emergence of genuine language skills a few months later.

When I'm watching television, my baby will look up at the screen from time to time. Is he interested in what's going on?

Not at all. Throughout this period, your baby simply will not have the capacity to understand the words and images that are being presented, so there is nothing on television that will be able to hold his attention. On the other hand, the television will be able to get his attention periodically. By the fourth month, your baby will be tuning in to sounds of all kinds, and he will be able to orient quickly and accurately to the source of any loud, sudden, unusual, or familiar sound. Therefore, what you are seeing in your baby's behavior is not an interest in what's going on, but rather a reaction to what's coming out of the television. You may notice that he looks up more often at the start of a commercial than at any other time. That's because commercials are designed to be slightly louder and have more abrupt sound changes than regular programming. It is precisely these characteristics that are most appealing to your baby at this point.

Occasionally my baby will simply stare at something for a very long period of time. Is this normal?

This is another case where an apparently bizarre behavior is actually a sign that your baby is developing normally. Throughout life, but especially during the first months, the eyes are the primary means of exploring and investigating the world. This fact, added to the notion that each day your baby is seeing many things for the very first time, results in a considerable amount of what is referred to as "steady staring." For an adult, such behavior often is an indication of limited awareness—steady staring usually means that a lot may be going on in the mind, but not much attention is being paid to the object of the fixed stare. However, for a baby, the opposite is true. Since the baby's mind works only with material that is being fed directly into the senses, a steady stare reveals that the baby has found a wealth of new information in what his eyes are perceiving, and he is actively taking in as much of it as he can. Once your baby's focusing ability becomes fully mature at about three

months of age, you can expect to see more and more of this behavior in the course of a day.

Lately, my baby has begun rolling over and pushing himself across the floor. Does this mean he's trying to crawl?

Not necessarily. Clearly, he is trying to get himself from one place to another, but that doesn't mean he is specifically attempting to perform a new ability. Quite often, a baby's interests will go a little further than what his abilities enable him to handle at the moment. Toward the end of this period, your baby will be able to see and hear many things that are some distance away from him. What's more, he may be starting to get bored with exploring and investigating the things that are in his immediate surroundings. Consequently, driven by his ever-increasing curiosity, he may try anything and everything he can do in an attempt to expand his environment. Unfortunately, at this point, his body probably won't be quite ready for crawling, so you may see a variety of strange strategies for self-propulsion. Of course, none of them will be as effective as crawling. So once his physical growth catches up with his intellectual interests, he will spend a lot of time perfecting the crawling process and will quickly abandon these less efficient forms of transporting himself.

Toward the end of this period, she'll be anxious to explore beyond her immediate area—and she may try a variety of methods to get there.

DAILY CARE BASICS

My newborn seems so fragile. How do I handle her safely?

When you handle your newborn, it will be natural for you to be gentle and careful. But there are a couple of specifics you should keep in mind. First, your newborn's head is rather large in comparison to the rest of her body, and her neck muscles are not yet strong enough to control it. So whenever you pick her up, hold her, or move her, you will have to support her head and neck (see "Handling Your Baby"). Second, your baby will not appreciate abrupt movements. She's likely to startle and cry if you scoop her up too quickly. The best way to help her feel secure is to pick her up slowly and gently and keep her close to your body whenever you hold her. You may want to try holding her cocoonlike in your arms, so she can look up at your face as she cuddles to the rhythm of your breathing. You might also try the burping position, with her head resting on your shoulder and your hand supporting her neck and back. You'll need to experiment a little to find the positions that are most comfortable. No matter which you choose, however, be sure to provide the physical support and sense of security that she needs.

What type of diapers should I use for my baby?

Today's parents have an assortment of diapers—from prefolded cloth to disposables—from which to choose. Which type you choose will depend on a variety of factors, including cost and convenience. Many parents opt to use both types—cloth at home and disposables when away from home. You may want to experiment before you settle on a favorite. See the following questions for more on the advantages and disadvantages of different types of diapers.

What are the pros and cons of using cloth diapers?

Many parents choose traditional cloth diapers, which come prefolded 14 x 20 inches or in the original 27 x 27 inch square shape. Most cloth diapers can be folded to fit both infant and toddler, with extra padding where your baby needs it. Cloth diapers are generally the least expensive option if you have easy access to a washer and dryer and can wash them yourself. A more expensive but often more convenient option is to use a diaper service, which will provide cloth diapers, pick them up, wash

and sterilize them, and deliver them back to your door. Cloth diapers are also "recyclable"; you can wash them and reuse them over and over again. On the other hand, using cloth diapers can be less convenient than using disposables. Even if you have a large stock of cloth diapers, you'll have to wash them frequently. They must be washed separately from your clothing, and they must be double rinsed. Another inconvenience concerns what to do with the diapers in between washings. If you are away from home, you'll have to find a way to rinse a soiled diaper and carry it back home. At home, you'll need to have a place to keep soiled diapers between washings. Cloth diapers are also not as airtight as disposables. This can be inconvenient for parents, but it may actually be better for baby's skin. Because they allow moisture to evaporate, cloth diapers may help to decrease diaper rash. On the other hand, because they do not hold in moisture as well, they may leak, which means you'll have to change bedding and clothing more often. Using disposable diaper liners or plastic pants can help, as can double diapering. But liners add to expense, and plastic pants trap moisture next to the skin. A better solution is to double diaper, especially at night or if the baby is older. And finally, unlike disposables, cloth diapers do not come with built-in fasteners. The traditional way to fasten them is to use diaper pins. If you use these, you'll need to be careful about pricking the baby. Another option is to

HANDLING YOUR BABY

1. When picking her up, slide one hand under her head and neck, and slide the other under her back and bottom.

enclose cloth diapers in the soft plastic "tie at the hip" covers. Velcro-fastened diaper holders are also available.

What are the pros and cons of using disposable diapers?

Disposable diapers are the first choice for many parents. They're available in sizes from premature to extra-large toddler. Some even come with extra padding in front for boys or in back for girls. Disposables do tend to be the most expensive option, but they are more convenient than cloth diapers, especially when you're away from home. They are easy to use, store, and carry. They come with sticky tabs that hold them in place, so you don't need diaper pins or special holders. They save time because there's no diaper laundering. And they tend to be less likely to leak. Unfortunately, some of the disposables with pleating and elastic around the tummy and thighs are too efficient; they keep urine in very well, but they don't allow air circulation. So while they protect clothing and bedding, they may also help promote diaper rash. Keeping the diaper fairly loose and checking it frequently for urine or feces can help. Another problem with disposable diapers is that while they're easy to throw away, they do not biodegrade easily.

How often should I change my baby's diaper?

Your baby's diaper should be changed whenever it is wet or soiled, which will be many times throughout the day and night. This is true no matter which type of diaper you use but is especially important if you use disposables or plastic pants over cloth, which can trap moisture against your baby's skin and cause irritation. At night, check your baby's diaper when you feed her, and change it if necessary. If you use cloth diapers during the day, you're likely to know right away if her diaper is wet or soiled. If she's wearing disposables or plastic pants, you may need to check frequently to see if her diaper is wet or dirty.

How do I diaper my baby?

Some parents use a waist-high changing table, some simply spread a clean towel on the floor, and others prefer to change their baby on a padded surface near the sink. Regardless of which surface you use, never take your hands off your baby or leave her during diapering. Even new babies can wriggle and fall off a raised surface. Diapering on the floor or using a changing table with a belt that fastens around your baby's tummy may help to

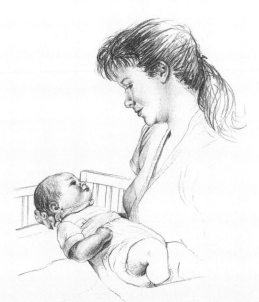

2. Continue to support her head, neck, and back as you lift her. Pick her up gently and slowly, and keep her close to your body.

3. When holding her, keep her close to your body. You can let her head rest on your shoulder, but continue to support her head and back from behind with your free hand.

PREVENTING DIAPER RASH

Careful skin care, frequent diaper changes, and proper diaper care all help to prevent diaper rash. Babies of the most conscientious parents can and do get diaper rashes, but the number and severity can be cut down by following some simple guidelines.

- Change the baby frequently. Urine and/or feces can have an irritating effect on her skin. The end result is diaper rash.
- Avoid letting her sleep in a soiled diaper.
- Dress her in loosely fitting diapers and let her go bare-bottomed whenever practical. Air helps to keep her skin dry.
- Whenever practical, avoid using plastic pants or diapers with gathers around the tummy and thighs. These can trap moisture close to her skin and keep air from circulating through.
- When cleaning her diaper area during changing, use water only or water with a small amount of soap added. If you use wipes, alternate their use with plain water.
- Wash gently in the folds of the genital area for girls and below the penis for boys. Also, make certain the anal area is thoroughly clean.
- After washing the diaper area, rinse thoroughly with a clean, wet cloth or plain water. Some moms do this by placing the baby next to or in the sink. If you do, be sure the water is not too warm and that the faucets are covered so that they won't burn her skin. Never leave her unattended in or near the sink for even a second.
- Pat her bottom dry before putting on a clean diaper. If you use powder or lotion, remember that less is better and that neither is necessary.
- Store soiled diapers between washings in a diaper pail containing half a cup of vinegar and enough water to cover the diapers.
- When laundering diapers, use a mild soap, and run the diapers through the rinse cycle twice. Avoid fabric softeners, which may leave a residue that can irritate your baby's skin.

prevent such accidents. Still, you should be sure that everything you need is within reach before you begin. If you discover that you've forgotten something, take the baby with you to get it. Never leave your baby unattended for even a second unless she's in her crib or strapped into her carrier. Once you've gathered your equipment, lay the baby on her back and unfasten the wet or soiled diaper. Gently grasp your baby's ankles, lift her legs and bottom, and take the diaper off. Wipe off as much feces as possible with the dirty diaper. Next, gently but thoroughly clean the baby's diaper area using a washcloth and warm, slightly soapy water (use only mild soap made especially for babies). See "Preventing Diaper Rash" for more on how to clean the diaper area. Once you've rinsed the diaper area thoroughly, pat it dry. Then raise the baby's bottom as before, and slip the clean diaper underneath. Once you have arranged the diaper, lay the baby's bottom on it. Bring the diaper up between the baby's legs. If you are using disposables, lay the baby on the end with the tapes, and tape the back edges over the front. If you are using cloth diapers, pin the back edges over the front ones. When fastening with a pin, slide your hand between the pin and the baby's skin so she won't get pricked. Also, be sure the pins are tightly fastened with the heads pointing away from the baby. If you use diaper

HOW TO PUT THE DIAPER ON

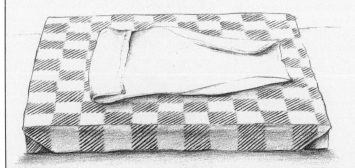

1. Spread the diaper on a clean, flat surface. If it's a disposable diaper, do not smooth out the center pleats; leave them gathered to fit between your baby's legs. If it's a cloth diaper, fold the diaper in at the sides and in back so that it fits your baby.

pins or any type of ointment, lotion, or powder, be sure to keep them out of your baby's reach as you are diapering. If you use powder, pour a small amount into your hand first, keeping it away from your baby's face; inhaling powder can irritate her respiratory tract.

How should I store and wash soiled cloth diapers?

To store soiled or wet cloth diapers before washing, you'll need a diaper pail containing half a cup of vinegar and enough water to cover the diapers. Diapers that are merely wet can be tossed directly into the pail. Soiled diapers, however, should be rinsed before being placed in the pail. When you're ready to wash the diapers, drain the pail and place the diapers into the machine. Wash the diapers separately from other clothing. Use hot water with a minimum amount of soap (not detergent), then double rinse the diapers. Do not use fabric softener, since it may irritate your baby's sensitive skin. Be sure the diapers are dried thoroughly, either in the dryer or on the line, before being folded.

When and how often should I bathe my baby?

Babies don't require a daily bath. In the first two or three weeks of life, before the umbilical cord heals, your baby shouldn't have a tub bath. A sponge bath (in which she's not actually sitting in water) given three to four times a week is usually adequate at this stage (see page 29 for directions). Her diaper area, face, and neck should be washed whenever necessary. Once the umbilical cord has healed, your baby will be ready for a tub bath (see page 30 for directions). Even then, however, two to three times a week should be adequate. More frequent bathing can dry your baby's skin. Choose a convenient time for your baby's bath. You'll need to give her your undivided attention during the whole process, so aim for a time when you won't be disturbed. If the phone rings or someone comes to the door, have someone else answer it, or just ignore it. You will not be able to leave the baby, and taking her with you could cause her to get chilled. You'll also want to pick a time that's convenient for your baby. You don't want to bathe her immediately after a feeding, nor do you want to bathe her if she's screaming to be fed. Try for an awake time between feedings when you both are relaxed and comfortable.

2. Gently place the baby on the diaper. If it's a disposable diaper, place the baby's bottom on the side with the tabs. Lift her legs in one hand, and use the other hand to adjust the diaper.

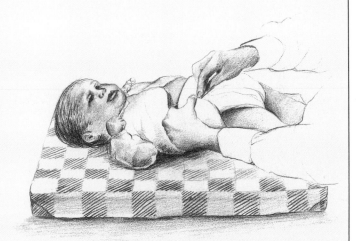

3. Bring the front of the diaper up between the baby's legs. If it's a disposable diaper, tape the back edges of the diaper over the front, and fold the plastic top in at the baby's waist to prevent leakage. If it's a cloth diaper, pin the back edges over the front, using your hand to shield the baby's skin and making sure the head of the pin is facing away from the baby.

CARE OF THE GENITALS

Careful skin care in the genital area can help prevent diaper rash and infections.

- When cleaning the genital area, use a soft washcloth.
- Use warm water or warm water with a small amount of gentle soap, and be sure to rinse thoroughly with clear water.
- For newborn girls, wash gently in the folds of the genital area; be sure to gently wipe (not rub) from front to back.
- For newborn boys who have been circumcised, be sure to follow your pediatrician's recommendations for caring for the penis. If you notice bleeding or any sign of infection (pus, redness, or swelling), notify your pediatrician.
- For newborn boys who have not been circumcised, external washing and rinsing is recommended. Since the natural separation of the foreskin from the glans may not be complete for several years, do not attempt to forcibly retract the foreskin. If you can partially retract the foreskin without using pressure or causing pain, you can clean the part of the glans that is exposed. Otherwise, leave it alone until the foreskin has separated from the glans.
- If you have any questions about the care of your newborn's genitals, contact your pediatrician.

Where should I give my baby a sponge bath?

Sponge baths during the first two to three weeks of life can be given wherever you and the baby can be comfortable. Be sure the room is comfortably warm and that you keep her partially wrapped as you wash her. If you have a wide enough counter next to your kitchen sink, you can pad it with fluffy towels and hold the baby there as you wash her; the sink can be used to hold the bathwater. Changing tables can be convenient for sponge baths. Some parents, however, prefer to hold the baby on their lap with one hand and wash her using the free hand. This can be a little tricky, so if you're unsure of yourself, use one of the other methods.

When my baby is ready for a tub bath, should I bathe her in the bathtub?

The bathtub is probably too large a space for you to comfortably support and wash your baby. You'll need to hold her throughout the process, so you'll want to choose a smaller space. You can purchase a baby bathtub or a changing table with a built-in baby tub for this purpose (many of these are designed to support your baby's head as you bathe her, although you'll still need to keep a hand on her at all times). You need not go to this expense, however. You can bathe her in a dishpan in the sink or you can simply line the sink with rubber mats or towels and bathe her there. You'll need to be sure, however, that you cover all faucets and that you turn the cold water off last, so that the faucets are not scalding hot should your baby get near them. You'll also have to support her head and back with one hand as you wash her with the other. No matter where you choose to bathe your baby, however, be sure the room is warm and that all slippery surfaces are lined with rubber mats or towels.

How do I avoid touching my newborn's soft spots when I wash her hair?

You don't want to avoid touching your baby's soft spots. The soft spots, like the rest of your baby's head, should be washed gently to keep them clean and prevent cradle cap. The soft spots, or fontanels, are small areas on the baby's head where the skull bones have not yet fused. They are covered with a tough protective membrane, as well as with skin, so normal handling can't possibly hurt the baby. The purpose of the

(Continued on page 31)

HOW DO I GIVE MY NEWBORN A SPONGE BATH?

Before you begin, gather your supplies. You'll need a soft towel; a washcloth; and a mild, pure baby soap. Partially fill a container or sink with water that feels gently warm, not hot, to your elbow. Turn the cold water off last, and be sure the faucets are pushed out of the way or covered. Have all water heaters turned down to 120 degrees Fahrenheit.

1. Keep your baby wrapped or partially clothed as you wash her face and ears with the washcloth dipped in plain warm water.

2. Hold her under your arm using the "football carry": Your arm supporting her neck and back, and your hand supporting her head. Gently wash her head using your fingertips and a small amount of baby soap (or baby shampoo). Keep her head tilted downward slightly, so the soap does not run into her eyes. Rinse thoroughly with plain warm water, and pat her head dry.

3. Hold her on your lap or on the bathing surface, and remove her shirt. Gently wash her chest, arms, and legs using your fingers or the washcloth and a small amount of soap. Dip the washcloth in plain water, rinse the areas, and pat them dry.

4. Support her neck and head as you gently turn her on her side. Wash her back, rinse with the washcloth dipped in plain water, and pat her back dry.

5. Remove her diaper. Using the washcloth and a small amount of soap, gently clean the diaper area, especially between the folds for girls and around the penis for boys. Dip the washcloth in plain water, rinse the area, and pat dry.

6. Diaper and dress your baby quickly to avoid chilling her.

HOW DO I GIVE MY BABY A TUB BATH?

Before you begin, gather together everything you will need, including a couple of soft towels, a washcloth, and a mild baby soap. Fill the baby tub with a few inches of water. The water should feel pleasantly warm, not hot, to your elbow. Turn the cold water off last and push the faucets out of the way or cover them. Have all water heaters turned down to 120 degrees Fahrenheit.

1. Undress your baby and wrap her in a towel. Dip the washcloth in plain warm water, and gently clean the baby's face and ears.

2. Using the "football carry" described for the sponge bath, hold her over the tub. Tilt her head downward slightly so that soap does not run into her eyes. Gently wash her head using your fingertips or the washcloth and a small amount of soap. Rinse with plain water, and pat dry.

3. Gently lower her, bottom first, into the tub, keeping one hand under her bottom and the other under her head and neck.

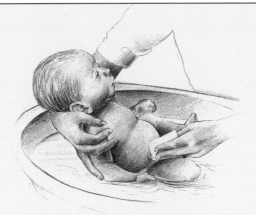

4. Grasp her firmly under her armpit or around her shoulder so that her head and back are resting on your arm. Using the other hand, wash her chest, abdomen, arms, legs. Gently wash the genital area, especially between the folds for girls and around the penis for boys. Be sure to clean in skin creases. Rinse with bathwater.

5. Gently sit her up, use your free hand to grasp her under the armpit from the front, then lean her forward so that her head and torso are supported by your arm. Once you have a secure hold on her, use the other hand to wash and rinse her back.

6. Slip your hands under her armpits, carefully lift her out of the tub, and cradle her to you. Wrap her in a dry towel, and pat her dry carefully.

fontanels is to allow the skull bones to slide over each other slightly during birth so the baby's head can pass through the birth canal. They also allow for the tremendous growth in the baby's brain during the first year of life. The small fontanel at the back of the head closes up within one and a half to three months of birth. The larger fontanel on the top of the baby's head completely closes by 12 to 18 months.

How should I take care of my newborn's belly button?

After birth, a clamp is placed on the umbilical cord, and the cord is cut. By the time you take your newborn home from the hospital, the clamp will have been removed. The stump that remains usually falls off during the second or third week after birth. Until the stump has separated and the area has healed, you'll probably be advised to clean the area with isopropyl (rubbing) alcohol. This should be done three to four times a day (or with every diaper change if that's easier to remember). To clean the area, pour a small amount of the alcohol onto a clean cotton ball and wipe the area where the cord stump meets the skin. If the stump falls off but the belly button remains moist or there is a little oozing of fluid or blood, continue to clean the area regularly with alcohol and cotton until it is clean and dry. If there remains a shiny, gray lump where the cord stump separated, an umbilical granuloma may have formed. This is another way the cord sometimes heals. If you notice such a lump, discuss it with your pediatrician. He may want to apply a medication called silver nitrate to help speed healing. Infections of this area are very rare. However, if you notice increasing redness around the cord, especially if the area is tender, notify your pediatrician at once.

How should I clean my baby's ears?

You can clean your baby's outer ears at bath time using a soft, wet cloth (do not use soap). Gently wipe the outer ear and ear folds. Be sure to wipe behind the ears, since this is a good hiding place for cradle cap (basically, cradle cap is baby dandruff). The baby's inner ears, or ear canals, are self cleaning. Never use cotton swabs, tissues, your finger, or anything else in the baby's ear canals. Not only is it unnecessary, it can be harmful. The rule of thumb for cleaning your baby's ears—as well as your own—is to never put anything smaller then your elbow into the ear. If you ever suspect that there is a problem with your baby's ears or with her hearing, consult your pediatrician.

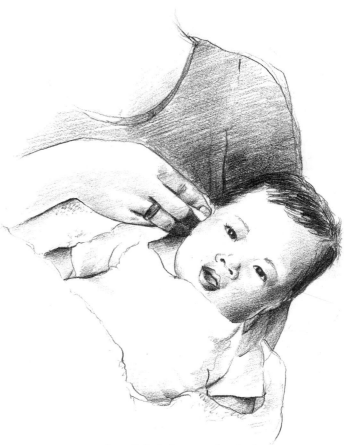

You can use a soft washcloth dampened with plain water to gently wipe your baby's outer ear and ear folds. Do not, however, put anything into your baby's ears.

My baby scratches herself with her fingernails. What's the best way to trim her fingernails and toenails, and how often should I do it?

Although you can put your newborn in a nightie with sleeves that cover her hands, you'll still need to keep her fingernails short and smooth. There are baby nail scissors and baby nail clippers with rounded edges available, but these are still very sharp. Inexperienced, and even some experienced, parents can sometimes trim too closely and injure the finger, especially when the baby pulls away unexpectedly. Using a soft emery board to file the fingernails down is usually the best method. It may take two of you to get the job done at first. One of you can hold the baby while the other grasps one of the baby's fingers at a time and carefully files. File the fingernails as often as necessary to keep them short and smooth; this may mean once a week or once every other week, depending upon how quickly your baby's fingernails grow. Your baby's toenails grow more slowly than her fingernails, but they require attention, too. File or trim them as you do the fingernails, just not as often. Don't be surprised if you have trouble even seeing the toenails on the smallest toes. A newborn's toenails are not well developed, and they may grow crooked or look rather odd for a while; just keep them smooth, and avoid trimming them too short.

Is it okay to have the baby sleep in our room? When is the best time to move her to her own room?

This is basically a matter of preference. If it is more convenient or reassuring for you to have her sleep in your room, then that's what you should do. Since you may be feeding your newborn every three, four, or five hours throughout the night, you may find it helpful to have her bassinet or cradle in your bedroom. This is especially true if you prefer to nurse her from a reclining position. On the other hand, some parents find that listening to their baby's noises disturbs their sleep. In that case, you'd be better off to put her in her own room. If you do decide to have the baby sleep in your room, you'd probably want to move her to her own room when she is down to one nightly feeding or when she has started sleeping six to eight hours straight each night.

When I put my newborn down for the night, is one position preferable to another?

Babies often have or develop a favorite sleep position, and they'll let you know if they're uncomfortable. For now, however, when you put your newborn down, you may want to rotate the

SWADDLING YOUR BABY

Newborns often seem to like being swaddled, or wrapped snugly, in a blanket. Swaddling helps keep her warm and protects her from drafts. In addition, because your newborn's movements in the early weeks of life are generally abrupt and jerky, swaddling her before you put her down to sleep may help keep her own movements from waking her up. Being wrapped cocoonlike in a blanket can also help her feel more secure when you pick her up. To swaddle your newborn:
1. Spread a receiving blanket on a flat surface; fold the top corner down a few inches.
2. Lay the baby on the blanket, with her head on the folded corner.

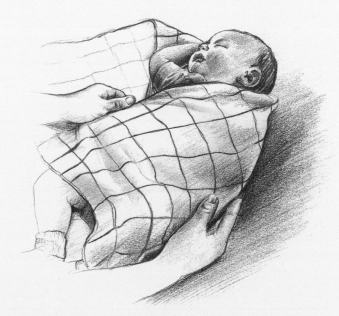

3. Take the corner near her left arm, and wrap it over her left arm and across her body. Tuck it under her right side.

position. Putting her down in only one position may cause her head to flatten a bit, because the bones in her skull are still pliable. If she seems to be comfortable in only one position, though, don't worry; her head will regain its normal shape in a short time.

How can I be sure my baby is comfortably warm when she's indoors?

Your baby's temperature control mechanism will not be fully mature until she is nearly a year old. Especially in the first few weeks of life, she will be extremely sensitive to cold and heat, and she can become chilled easily. Until her body can better regulate its own temperature, you'll need to keep her comfortably warm. The most comfortable room temperature for a baby is between 68 and 72 degrees Fahrenheit. You'll need to avoid placing her in the draft from an open window or air conditioner vent, however. And you'll need to position her crib away from heat registers; although the warm air won't hurt her, dust particles blown up by the furnace may irritate her nose and throat. Be sure to dress and undress her quickly, and avoid chilling by drying and dressing her quickly after a bath. New parents have a tendency to overdress newborns, so

you'll need to use a little common sense in terms of clothing and blankets. A good rule of thumb is to dress the baby in one more layer of clothing than is comfortable for you in the same environment. If you're comfortable in a shirt and sweater, the baby will probably be comfortable in an undershirt, a nightie or sleeper, and a receiving blanket. When you put her down to sleep, you may need to add another light blanket. If the temperature in the house is warmer, however, you may need to remove a layer or two. The color of your baby's hands and feet and whether they feel warm or cold to the touch can give you an indication of whether she's comfortable or not; remember, though, that a newborn's hands and feet are usually somewhat cooler than the rest of her body.

Should I worry about exposing my baby to the elements?

Since your baby's temperature control mechanism is not fully mature during this period, you'll need to avoid exposing her to extreme heat, extreme cold, and direct sunlight whenever possible. As a general rule, if the weather outside is uncomfortable for you, it will be uncomfortable for your baby, too. Outings are nice, but not necessary on a daily basis. On the (Continued on page 35)

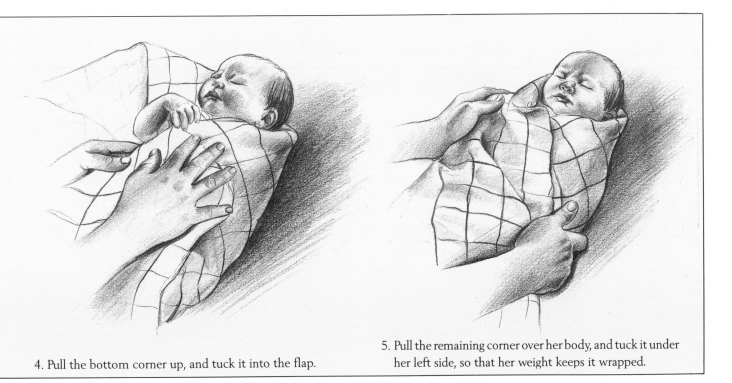

4. Pull the bottom corner up, and tuck it into the flap.

5. Pull the remaining corner over her body, and tuck it under her left side, so that her weight keeps it wrapped.

DRESSING YOUR BABY

To make dressing (and undressing) your baby easier, try to choose clothing that is fairly simple to put on and take off. Look for undershirts that have snaps down the front or side so you don't have to pull them over the baby's head. For pull-over shirts, look for those with snaps at the neck that can be undone to make the neck opening larger. No matter which types of clothing you choose, be sure to hold the baby during the entire dressing process; gather everything you need before you start. Also, be sure to support her head, neck, and back whenever you pick her up.

Open-Front Shirt or Sleeper
 1. Lay the shirt or sleeper out, and lay the baby on top of it.

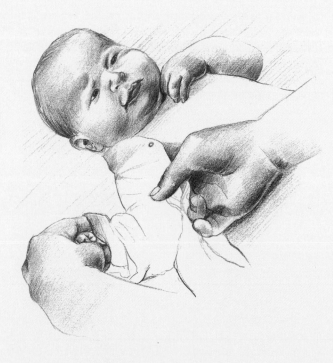

 2. Gather the sleeve with one hand, and use your other hand to guide her arm through. Do the same for the other sleeve.
 3. If you are using a sleeper, slide her legs into it. Then, fasten the snaps.

Open-Neck Undershirt
 1. Gather the shirt in your hands, and stretch the neck as wide as possible.

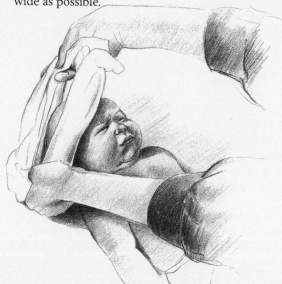

 2. Slip the back part of the shirt halfway under your baby's head.
 3. Quickly and gently lift the front over her face, and slide it down.

 4. Hold the sleeve open with one hand, and gently guide her hand through with the other. Do the same for the other sleeve.
 5. Pick her up, and support her head and back with one hand as you pull the shirt down with the other.

other hand, if it's pleasant outside and she is dressed appropriately, the fresh air and stroll can be good for both of you. If you need to take her out in cold or inclement weather, dress her in bunting or other clothing that covers her head, ears, hands, and feet, and then wrap her in a blanket. For a quick trip, you can loosely drape part of the blanket over her face for protection from wind or cold. If you have to take her out in hot or sunny weather, dress her in light clothing that covers her arms and legs and a bonnet that shades her face. Be sure to keep her in the shade; remember that sunlight reflected off water, sand, or concrete can cause sunburn even in what appears to be shade. Be aware, too, that the metal parts of car seats and carriages can become hot quickly.

Is there anything special I should look for when selecting my baby's clothing?

Besides comfort, convenience, and ease of cleaning, there are a couple of safety factors of which you should be aware. The first is the desirability of clothing made from flame-retardant fabric. Many manufacturers now are using such materials exclusively, but it is wise to read all labels carefully. The second factor concerns buttons, ribbons, and other decorative features. Make sure that any small item attached to your baby's clothing is fastened securely. If a button or whatever is pulled off or falls off, it can immediately become a choking hazard. Also, check to see that anything like zippers or elastics are stitched strongly into place. If the thread around such features begins to unravel, the article should be fixed or removed before accidental ingestion or strangulation becomes a possibility.

I am trying to be reasonable about clothing for the baby. Please give me an idea about what kind of clothing is necessary or desirable.

Layettes (a term used to describe the clothing/wardrobe for a newborn) are generally a matter of choice. You'll probably have, buy, or be given more articles of clothing for your baby than you need. The items most likely to be in short supply are diapers. Your baby will need a change of diaper whenever she is wet or soiled, which will be often. And no matter which type of diaper you use, you'd be wise to have plenty on hand. Your baby will also need a couple of changes of clothing daily.

Generally, at this age, your baby's daily (and nightly) wear will consist of a diaper; an undershirt; a nightgown, kimono, sleeper, or pajamas; and a receiving blanket. She may also need another blanket or quilt for sleeping. Other items she may need include a bonnet for warm-weather outings or a knitted cap for cold-weather outings; socks or booties if her sleepwear doesn't cover her feet; and sweaters, bunting, or similar clothing for outings in cooler weather. If you use cloth diapers, you may want to have a couple pairs of plastic pants, but use them sparingly.

What special care, if any, should be given to the baby's clothing and bedding?

Your newborn's skin is especially susceptible to irritation. So before coming into contact with your baby's skin, all new and old clothing, diapers, bedding, towels, etc. should be washed in soap or mild detergent and double rinsed (for flame-retardant clothing, check the manufacturer's label for any special washing instructions). Do not wash them with the rest of your laundry, and do not use fabric softeners, since many of them contain chemicals that may irritate your baby's skin. It's best to continue washing your baby's things separately for the first few months, until her skin becomes less sensitive. Cloth diapers should be washed separately in hot water and double rinsed.

Should I worry about keeping my baby's toys, teething rings, pacifiers, and other things she puts in her mouth squeaky clean?

You can worry about it, but it is highly doubtful that you'll be able to keep all such items completely sterile all of the time. Fortunately, although they obviously should not be exposed to constant filth, babies are able to tolerate considerably more dirt and grime in their systems than most new—and naturally anxious—parents can tolerate them having. Therefore, when purchasing or procuring such items, you should make sure that they can be easily cleaned, and you should give them all a good cleaning on a regular basis. But if your baby drops her pacifier on the floor and later picks it up and puts it in her mouth before you've had a chance to wash it off, don't panic. The act probably will cause you a lot more suffering than it will cause her.

NUTRITION AND FEEDING

Is it better to breast-feed my baby than to feed him formula?

The decision to breast-feed or bottle-feed is a highly personal one. Since you will be taking care of the baby, you need to feel comfortable with whichever method you choose. There are, however, some factors you should consider when making the decision. Breast-feeding has always been and remains the preferred method of feeding newborns for several reasons. First, breast-feeding gives your baby the best possible nutrition. Breast milk is the perfect food for babies, with a perfect balance of all the nutrients your baby needs (except, perhaps, for fluoride). And while manufacturers have brought formulas closer in composition to breast milk, they have not been able to duplicate it exactly. Second, breast-feeding can transfer some of your immunities against disease to your newborn. Many studies have shown that breast-fed newborns tend to have fewer and milder illnesses than those who are not breast-fed. These immunities are something that formulas just cannot provide. Third, when the baby nurses, it causes your

uterus to contract, which can help it return more quickly to its prepregnancy size. Fourth, breast milk is free, readily available, and at the perfect temperature for your baby. In addition, breast-feeding can be a wonderful and satisfying experience for both you and your baby. Having taken all of these factors into account, you may still feel that you'll be more comfortable bottle-feeding. In that case, you are better off using formula. Remember that, on the whole, babies do well whichever way you decide to feed them. And if bottle-feeding makes you more comfortable, you'll be better prepared to give him the loving attention that he really needs.

Do I need to start my baby out on formula if I intend to go back to work within a couple months of the birth or can I breast-feed him?

You do not have to forego breast-feeding just because you need to return to work soon after the birth. You can breast-feed your baby whenever you are at home. When you are at work, you can use a breast pump to express milk into bottles

NURSING POSITIONS

When breast-feeding your baby, you need to be comfortable and relaxed. So before you and your newborn leave the hospital, practice various nursing positions with the assistance of a maternity nurse or lactation specialist. This way, you'll be more confident and at ease nursing at home, and your baby will be assured of getting plenty of milk. You will probably use different positions depending on where and when you are nursing, how large your baby is, and what feels comfortable to you at the time; you can try the three positions illustrated here for starters. Be sure to see the sidebar on pages 38 and 39 for advice on offering the breast, and review the question regarding breast care (page 39). Also, check the question on proper diet for nursing mothers (page 37) to help ensure that you are getting the nourishment you need.

From a side-lying position, with pillows propped under your arm and behind your back, lay the baby on her side in front of you, and gently support her back with your hand. Roll forward slightly so that your nipple is level with your baby's mouth.

(as long as you have a way to refrigerate the bottles of breast milk at work). Then the bottled breast milk can be given to your baby the following workday by whomever takes care of him. If expressing milk while at work is uncomfortable or impossible for you, you can leave formula for the baby during your work hours and then nurse him when you are at home. If you don't express milk during the day, however, your milk supply will gradually decrease.

My husband and I both have allergies, so is it wise for me to breast-feed my baby?

Although there are special formulas available on the market for babies from allergic families, it can make a significant difference to your baby if you can nurse him for even a few months after birth. This way, you'll be passing on some of your immunities to your newborn through your breast milk. In addition, while very few babies are allergic to breast milk, a significant number of babies from allergic families develop allergic reactions to formula.

I'm breast-feeding, and I'd like to know if I should be on a special kind of diet. What about taking medications if I get sick?

Nursing moms do not need a special diet, just a nutritious, well-balanced one. You should be eating a variety of foods from the four major food groups (meat, dairy, grains, and fruits and vegetables) each day. Some obstetricians like to keep new moms on a multiple vitamin plus iron as added insurance. Now is not the time to seriously limit calories or reduce weight. While you can be careful, especially regarding desserts and fats, remember that you are using more than 500 calories each day for milk production alone. You also need to drink two to three quarts of liquid each day. Any woman who has nursed a baby can tell you how thirst becomes overwhelming the minute you start to breast-feed. So, whenever you nurse, keep a glass of water, milk, or juice within reach. Be sure to get plenty of fluids throughout the day as well. If you are not taking a calcium supplement, you'll need to be sure you're getting enough from your diet. Since milk products are a major dietary source of calcium, contact your doctor if you can't or don't drink milk. While some nursing mothers can eat

From a sitting position, with a pillow on your lap to help support the baby, cradle her head and shoulders in your arm as you offer her the breast.

From a sitting position, use the "football carry," with the baby's torso tucked under your arm. Your forearm should support her back and torso while your hand supports her head.

almost anything without getting indigestion or upsetting their baby's tummy, other nursing mothers can't. It's recommended that you avoid highly spiced foods while nursing, since they can give your baby gas. Some doctors suggest avoiding chocolate, because it may bother your baby's digestion and may contribute to the development of seborrhea (an abnormal increase in skin-oil production). Foods that are high in fat may also be a factor in seborrhea and cradle cap. Fortunately, as breast-feeding babies get older, they tend to become more tolerant of their mother's diet. Whenever you are ill, you should check with your doctor or your baby's pediatrician before taking any medication. Remember, anything you eat or drink is likely to be found in some increment in your breast milk. Caffeine and alcohol both filter into breast milk, although very small amounts probably have little effect on the baby. On occasion, however, caffeine (from coffee, tea, and colas) in mom's diet can cause the baby to be especially jittery. Also, any kind of narcotic substance, in addition to being harmful to you, is damaging to your baby. If you are using any drug or addicted to any drug or narcotic, give your baby a better deal and get some help. Meanwhile, don't breast-feed; give your baby

formula instead. In addition to getting adequate nutrition and fluids and avoiding drugs, there are other factors that affect the health and well-being of a nursing mother. Appropriate exercise is important for your overall well-being. You also need adequate rest to maintain your milk supply. How to get it? Rest when your baby is resting, and enlist help with baby care and daily chores so you can have some time each week to take care of your own emotional and physical needs.

Since I'm breast-feeding, how will I know if my baby is getting enough milk?

Babies who are not getting enough to eat are usually easy to spot. They let you know by demanding feedings too frequently and by not sleeping for any reasonable length of time; they're unhappy babies. On the other hand, babies who are getting enough breast milk act satisfied; they look full and content (at least for a while). As a nursing mother, there are clues you can look for to determine if your milk supply is

OFFERING THE BREAST

Before beginning, be sure that you and your baby are in a comfortable position. To avoid cracked or sore nipples, the baby needs to latch on to the entire nipple and as much of the areola (dark area) as possible. Babies sometimes thrust their tongues on the underside of the nipple, which can cause breast soreness. If your baby thrusts her tongue on the underside of the nipple, or if she has not taken enough of the areola in her mouth, gently remove her from the breast (using the method shown in step three), and try again. Likewise, when you remove her from the breast, do not allow her to tug on the nipple, as this can cause breast soreness and cracking as well. For more tips on preventing breast soreness, see the question on the next page regarding breast care.

1. With your forefinger above the areola and your middle finger below, compress the breast; this will make it easier for her to get all of the nipple and most of the areola into her mouth.

sufficient. Your breasts should feel heavy and full before nursing, and softer after nursing. You should be able to hear the slurpy, sucking noises of the baby and see and hear him swallow. You'll also probably observe milk dribble from his mouth when you stop to burp him. Most nursing moms also leak milk from time to time; this is a clue to supply, too. As a test, you might try expressing breast milk into a bottle after a feeding if you can. This can be offered to the baby after a feeding; if he seems to need it, you may need to continue expressing milk after feedings in order to stimulate greater milk production. Another test you can use is to offer formula after breast-feeding him; if he drinks a few ounces or more, he probably isn't being satisfied at his usual feedings. Offering formula regularly as a supplement, however, is likely to decrease your milk production; better to try expressing milk between feedings to help stimulate production. Anytime you are truly concerned about not having an adequate supply of milk, however, you should contact your pediatrician or breast-feeding consultant. Your pediatrician will be keeping track of your baby's growth and development through regular checkups and can advise you as to whether the baby is gaining weight as

expected. If he isn't, you will be advised regarding ways to increase your milk supply.

I'm breast-feeding my baby. Can you give me some tips on breast care during this time?

The single most important factor for maintaining healthy nipples is to make certain that your baby is taking all of the nipple and as much of the areola into his mouth whenever he nurses. If he latches onto only a small amount of nipple and is allowed to suck for some length of time, you're likely to wind up with sore, cracked nipples that can easily become infected. This is also true if you allow him to tug at the nipple when you remove him from the breast. So, be sure to follow the instructions for proper nursing technique (see sidebar entitled "Offering the Breast"). Start a feeding on one breast, and finish on the other. At the next feeding, start with the breast that you finished with the last time. Soon, you'll be able to tell which you started with at the last feeding by the amount of

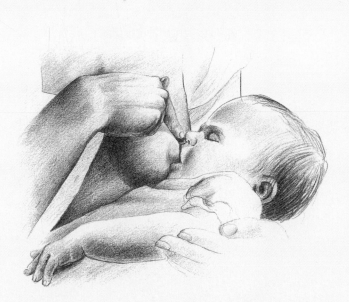

2. When your breast is full, you may need to use one finger to press down slightly on the breast so the baby can breathe through her nose.

3. When her sucking slows, or when it's time to switch to the other breast, gently break the sucking seal. Do this by sliding one finger between the inside of her cheek and your breast.

fullness in each breast. (The less full being the one you started with last time.) To keep track in the beginning, put a safety pin or ribbon on the bra strap on the side that you started with, and move it at each feeding. Gradually increase the nursing time on each breast from five minutes, to seven, to ten. Once your milk is in, 15 to 20 minutes should be the maximum on each breast. You'll need to use your judgment about when the baby has finished feeding and wants to suck only. When his sucking slows and he shows signs of being content, gently remove him from the breast. After your milk supply is totally established, there will be times when your baby is satisfied with one breast only. When this occurs, try to stop sooner the next time, and use the other breast to finish the feeding. This way, you'll be continually stimulating the milk production of both breasts at each feeding. If your breasts become uncomfortably engorged, you may need to express milk in between frequent feedings. Some moms require ice packs for a while to reduce discomfort. Avoid allowing the nipples to remain moist, which can promote cracking and bacterial growth. Try not to use nursing pads, since these tend to trap moisture against the breast. Instead, take frequent showers to allow leakage from overfull breasts to be washed away (avoid using soap on the nipples, however, since this may increase irritation). Change nursing bras as often as necessary to ensure dryness. Some professionals also advise nursing mothers to keep the nipples clean by wetting a cotton swab, cotton ball, or soft washcloth with clean water and swabbing around the nipples before each feeding. If your nipples start to feel sore or you see the beginning of a crack, applying a small amount of lubricating ointment or cream may clear it up. Anything more severe should be checked by your doctor. Do not ignore breast soreness or cracking. If an infection has developed, your doctor can treat it while you continue to nurse.

I'm bottle-feeding instead of breast-feeding. Will this affect my emotional bond with my baby?

Only if you worry about it too much. Emotional concerns about breast-feeding should be considered in the same way as nutritional concerns. Clearly, breast-feeding has certain advantages in providing your baby with key nutrients and immunities, but proper formula preparation can compensate for most of these if bottle-feeding is chosen or required. Furthermore, there are instances when breast-feeding may supply insufficient or inappropriate nutrition, so bottle-feeding is preferred. The same is true when it comes to establishing emotional bonds. Most

(Continued on page 42)

STERILIZING BOTTLES AND FORMULA

To prepare formula for your baby, you must sterilize the bottles and formula. To mix the formula, read the instructions on the formula container carefully. Most liquid concentrates are mixed by combining an equal amount of water and formula (for example, two ounces of formula to two ounces of water). Most powdered formulas are mixed by adding one loose, level scoop (contained in can) of powder to every two ounces of water. To sterilize, you can use either of these methods:

Terminal Heating Method
This technique is safest since it sterilizes bottles, nipples, caps, formula, and water all at the same time.

1. Clean bottles and nipples in warm, sudsy water; rinse well.

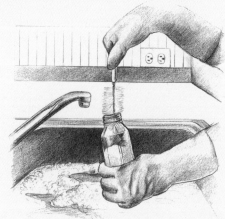

2. Prepare formula according to directions in a clean measuring cup or mixing bowl.

3. Pour prepared formula into bottles.

4. Place nipples (upside down), collars, and caps loosely on bottles.

5. Using a bottle rack, place bottles into sterilizer or large pot containing three inches of water.
6. Boil water for ten to 15 minutes.

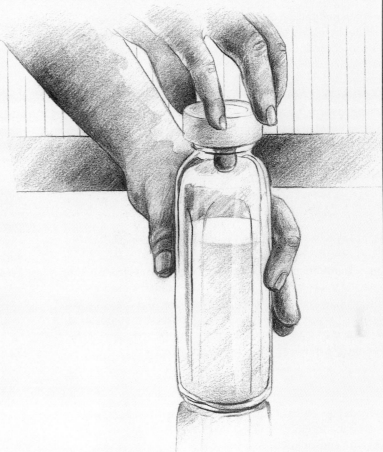

7. Remove from heat, and cool to room temperature.
8. Tighten collars and caps, and refrigerate until needed; use within 48 hours.

Single Bottle Method

This method is useful when preparing single bottles with powdered formula.

1. Place desired amount of water in each clean bottle.
2. Loosely cover with nipple (upside-down), collar, and cap.
3. Place bottles on bottle rack in sterilizer or pot containing three inches of water.
4. Boil water for ten to 15 minutes.
5. Remove from heat, and cool to room temperature.
6. Tighten caps, and store at room temperature or in refrigerator; use within 48 hours.
7. To use, remove cap and nipple from one bottle, and add powdered formula as directed; tighten cap; and shake well to mix. (Note: Powdered formula mixes better in warm water, so slight reheating makes mixing easier.)

women find the act of breast-feeding to be tremendously helpful in this regard, but it certainly is not the only way in which a solid, loving relationship can be formed between parent and child. In fact, most fathers manage to establish emotional bonds of enormous strength despite their inability to breast-feed. Moreover, if breast-feeding presents a problem, trying to force it is very likely to be counterproductive. Therefore, as long as you provide prompt, nurturing care to your baby in the best way you can, you may rest assured that you and your baby will develop emotional bonds that are as strong as they can possibly be.

Is it okay to warm the baby's bottle in the microwave?

Sorry, but nothing that you intend to feed your baby should be warmed in a microwave. Microwave ovens may warm foods unevenly, leaving "hot spots" that can burn your baby's mouth or lips. It is really not possible to test for these local hot areas, so it's best to use the tried-and-true, warm-water methods for warming bottles and food (see "Giving the Bottle").

Why did my pediatrician tell me to give my baby an iron-containing formula? Will the iron upset my baby's stomach or cause constipation?

Because of their rapid growth rate, many babies outgrow their natural iron supply in the first months of life and may become anemic from iron deficiency. Breast-fed babies generally receive enough usable iron in the breast milk, but many formulas, especially those made from cow's milk, lack this important mineral. Therefore, most pediatricians recommend iron-fortified formulas for bottle-fed babies. Careful studies indicate that the amount of iron in these formulas does not cause constipation or stomach upset.

My three month old is getting a commercial formula, and he loves his bottle. He's very plump, and I'm wondering if I'm feeding him too much.

Although babies can be overfed, it's generally not necessary to worry about a plump three month old. Thirty to thirty five ounces a day is the maximum amount of formula babies should receive. Few three month olds need more than this. If

your baby takes this amount or less, then he's probably doing fine. If you think your baby may be taking formula when he's no longer hungry but still needs to suck, you might introduce a pacifier. Pacifiers can satisfy a baby's sucking needs. However, if your baby is truly hungry, a pacifier won't satisfy him. Keep in mind that sometimes we can be too quick to offer feedings or pacifiers when our babies really are asking for other kinds of fulfillment or stimulation. Although at three months of age babies spend most of their time eating and sleeping, when they are awake, they need lots of one-to-one eye contact, cuddling, and interaction with you. If you are providing prompt feedings and plenty of attention, and your baby still consistently cries for more formula, discuss it with your pediatrician. On occasion, your doctor may advise you to begin offering a small amount of rice cereal. Three month olds are usually not ready for cereals (or any other solid foods), although cereals are occasionally used in especially large and demanding babies.

I like to give my baby his nighttime bottle in his crib. Is that okay?

Professionals agree that bottles should not be propped. You should hold your baby when you give him his bottle; then, put

GIVING THE BOTTLE

Before giving your baby a bottle, you'll need to warm it and test the temperature.

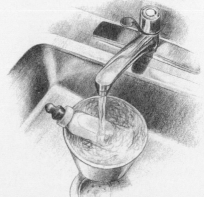

1. To warm a bottle of prepared formula or milk, take the bottle out of the refrigerator, shake it, and run it under hot water.

him to bed without it. If you put him to bed with the bottle and he is allowed to suck at will, milk may pool in his mouth, promoting tooth decay. Also, because of the proximity of the eustachian tubes, babies who go to bed with their bottles have a greater tendency to develop ear infections.

Although I'm a nursing mother, I'm trying to introduce my six week old to a bottle so I can leave feedings for him when I return to work. He's refusing to take a bottle and screams until I nurse him. Any suggestions?

Although a six-week-old baby may be more easily introduced to a bottle than an older baby, you're likely to have greater success if you have someone else give him the bottle. He would naturally prefer his mother's soft, warm breast to the foreign baby-bottle nipple. So enlist someone else to give your baby the bottle. Try to do this when the baby is truly hungry but before he's in a rage because of it. Another option is to try giving him a bottle a little earlier than you would usually breast-feed him; this not-so-hungry time will allow him to experiment with the nipple and get used to it. Another option is to express milk into a bottle from which he can be fed while you are at work. While the nipple may still seem odd, the liquid inside will be the breast milk that he is accustomed to drinking. This option also allows you to maintain your milk supply by stimulating milk production the way sucking does.

Should I keep my baby on a rigid feeding schedule?

All families develop parenting skills and philosophies tailored to their individual personalities, preferences, and lifestyles. What will work well for one family doesn't necessarily work well for another. When it comes to nurturing your baby, you may want to lean towards flexibility. Especially for young babies, feeding on demand, within reason, is preferred. By promptly answering his cries for food, warmth, and other physical needs during these first few months, you will be teaching your baby one of the most fundamental lessons of his life—that there are people who love him and will take care of him. If a baby appears to want hourly feedings, then something is wrong. On the other hand, a baby can be on a rigid four-hour feeding schedule and do well, but there will be days when he'll be hungry every three hours or every five hours. Your goal is to satisfy your baby's needs, so you'd want to feed him when he is hungry. The answer, therefore, is that healthy scheduling for babies should be neither entirely flexible nor inflexible.

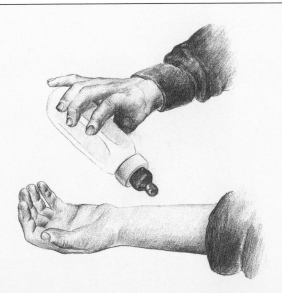

2. Test the temperature by squeezing a few drops onto the inside of your wrist. It should feel lukewarm, not hot.

3. Prop the baby in a semireclining position in the crook of your arm, and tilt the nipple end slightly downward to keep the nipple full of formula.

When should I burp my baby?

If you're breast-feeding, stop to burp your baby when his sucking slows down. If you're bottle-feeding, about midway through the feeding is a good time to stop and burp him. No matter which method you use, if your baby starts to fuss during the feeding, he probably feels an air bubble and needs to be burped. Hungry babies who are fed after they've been crying will have swallowed air already and may need to be burped sooner. If the baby starts to doze and you think he hasn't had enough, stop to burp, and he may begin again and finish his feeding. It's not necessary, however, for the baby to empty his bottle at each feeding. He may require different amounts at different feeding times, depending on his appetite and on how long it's been since the last feeding. When the baby turns away, stops sucking, or otherwise lets you know he's full, try for another burp. If he's sleeping and doesn't burp, put him down on his tummy or prop him up in an infant seat, and the bubble may come up by itself.

I can't always get the baby to burp. Should he burp after each feeding?

When nursing babies are sucking well and getting most of the areola plus the nipple in their mouths, they may not be swallowing much air and may not have to burp every time. The same is true for bottle-fed babies who are sucking well from nipples kept full of formula. If he really does need to burp, he'll let you know. When babies feel air bubbles, they get cranky. They make funny faces or grunt and cry to let you know they are uncomfortable.

My baby seems to spit up whenever he's been fed. How can I prevent this?

If your baby is eating well and developing as expected, it's nothing to be concerned about. There are, however, some helpful hints to employ with babies who are "spitters," or who burp up milk after feeding. First, keep plenty of cloth diapers handy; lay one on your shoulder or lap when you burp your baby, and hand one to guests who want to hold him. There are some other strategies, too. You might try burping him more frequently during feedings. Check the nipple flow from the bottle to make certain he isn't getting the formula too quickly. After feeding, gently lift him, in an upright position, to your shoulder, and burp him; then, lay him in a carrier or infant chair that keeps his head higher than the rest of his body. In addition, try not to change his diaper or bathe him immediately after feeding. If you are worried about his spitting up, discuss it with your pediatrician.

My newborn always has diarrhea. Will this stop when he starts eating solid foods?

The normal bowel movement of a newborn is loose and has a large fluid content. It is normal for a newborn to pass as many as one stool per feeding. The definition of diarrhea, therefore, is more than one loose stool per feeding. If you notice this occurring or if your baby is acting ill, consult your pediatrician. Since the first solid food that most babies receive is cereal, which is a stool-firming food, the loose, soft stools will become firmer. After that, the new foods added to your baby's diet may make the stools firmer or looser or have no effect at all, depending on the food.

BURPING POSITIONS

You can use any of these burping positions.

With her bottom resting on your forearm and her head resting on your shoulder, use your free hand to gently pat or rub her back.

How long should I give my baby supplemental vitamins and fluoride?

Most babies are given supplemental vitamins beginning in the first month of life. These may be contained in the formula or given as drops to the breast-fed baby. Many say that if a nursing mother is healthy, her baby will get adequate vitamins in the breast milk. Often, however, a pediatrician will prescribe a supplement of vitamins A, D, and C for the first year or so of life, just to be sure. Your pediatrician will let you know when it is no longer necessary to give these supplements, but it is generally agreed that no child over 18 to 24 months of age who is eating a varied, nutritious diet needs supplemental vitamins. In areas where there is no fluoride in the water, it is recommended that infants, children, and young adolescents receive fluoride daily. This is usually given as a vitamin/fluoride combination in children under two, and later as a single daily chewable fluoride tablet. The fluoride promotes improved dental health by decreasing the rate of cavities. In areas where there is fluoride in the drinking water, it is not necessary to provide fluoride supplements.

Is it necessary for babies to drink water?

Both formula and breast milk have a high water content. Many babies, therefore, do just fine without water until they are old enough to use a cup. If your baby takes the maximum amount of formula and wants more, you might try offering water. If you're nursing your baby, it's more difficult to know when he's had enough, so you might try offering water from time to time. All babies should be offered extra water in hot weather. If your baby is wetting several diapers a day, he's most likely getting enough fluids.

We work hard at keeping our weight down and want to be certain that our baby is slim. How do we go about this?

You are to be congratulated on your weight-conscious lifestyle. It will be of great benefit to your child, but not for a year or two. Babies are not little adults; they should not be on restrictive diets. Indeed, in recent years, experts have seen an

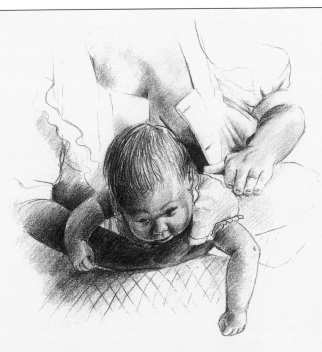

Lay the baby on her stomach across your lap. Use one hand to support her head; use the other to gently rub or pat her back. This is an especially useful position for larger babies.

Sit the baby crosswise on your lap. Grasp her under the armpit and lean her forward slightly so her torso rests on your arm. For a very young baby, cup her chin in your hand to support her head. Use your other hand to gently pat or rub her back.

increasing number of children who are failing to thrive because well-meaning parents have overly restricted their babies' diets. Babies require a much greater number of calories per pound of body weight and a greater percentage of calories from fat compared to adults if they are to grow and develop normally. Many pediatricians prefer to keep a baby on breast milk or formula until he is ready to take a cup (at about nine to 16 months of age). If your baby drinks from a cup before his first birthday, you can offer him two-percent milk unless advised differently by your pediatrician. Skim milk is lacking in sufficient fat to maintain adequate growth.

Is there a difference of opinion regarding when to introduce solid foods?

Most pediatricians believe that six months is an optimum time to introduce solid foods. If your baby is very large and is still hungry after getting the maximum amount of formula, you might start as early as four months. Still, at this stage, the important calories and nutrition should be supplied by breast milk or formula, and the solid food should be looked upon as a supplement. Parents who have allergies or allergic family histories will probably want to start later and be more cautious when introducing solids. Even if there are no allergies in the family, early exposure to some foods may produce a reaction that wouldn't occur if the food was introduced at a later age. In terms of which foods to introduce, it's probably best to begin with cereals and less tasty foods like vegetables, and progress gradually to tastier foods, like fruit and desserts. Avoid sweetening cereal or mixing it with fruit; babies naturally have a sweet tooth and have no need to acquire a taste for sweets. Never mix cereal in the bottle either. Although the cereal will be fairly watery, it should be offered with a spoon. It's messy at first, but one of the important goals of introducing solids is to gradually teach the baby how to eat them. Foods that are not naturally soft and watery should be pureed with a small amount of water before being served to the baby. Introduce no more than one new food a week. This allows time for you to see if the baby has an unfavorable reaction to a particular food. Many times, the same food can be introduced again later, when the child's digestive system is more mature. Avoid foods that have pieces that can break off and cause choking. Honey should never be given to babies less than a year old because of the risk of botulism (food poisoning). Egg yolks shouldn't be offered until the baby is at least six months old; egg whites shouldn't be offered until the baby is a year old because of the likelihood of allergic reaction.

SUGGESTED INTRODUCTION OF SOLID FOODS

You can start introducing solid foods when your baby is four to six months old. Begin with cereals unless directed otherwise by your pediatrician. Be sure to refer first to the question regarding when to introduce solid foods.

1. Cereal: Rice, then barley, then oatmeal
2. Yellow vegetables: Carrots, then squash, then sweet potatoes
3. Green vegetables: Peas, then beans, then spinach
4. Meats: Lamb, beef, veal, poultry, pork, fish (order not important); then egg yolk
5. Noncitrus fruits
6. Noncitrus juices (only after nine months of age)
7. Citrus fruits (orange, tomato, grapefruit, etc.)
8. Citrus juices
9. NO EGG WHITE OR HONEY UNTIL AFTER 12 MONTHS OF AGE

Chocolate and nuts should be avoided because they are both highly allergenic; nuts are also dangerous because of the risk of choking, and therefore should not be given to children under four to five years of age. For more information on introducing solids, see the next age group.

My six month old won't take a pacifier, but lately he's been sucking his thumb constantly—even between bites when I'm feeding him. What can I do about this?

Your six month old will eventually become more skilled at eating. One of the things he'll learn is to keep his thumb out of his mouth between spoonfuls. For now, gently remove his thumb from his mouth when you offer a bite. Your baby may have more time to stick his thumb in his mouth if you're feeding him too slowly. On the other hand, you may be feeding him too quickly, and he may be putting his thumb in his mouth to give himself a break. Experiment with the pace and see what happens. Most of the time, babies just stick their thumb in their mouth because they want to, regardless of what else is going on. Don't make a big deal of it, or he'll enjoy your reaction and have an added reason to do it. Summon your patience and sense of humor. You'll need more of both before he's eating nicely.

When I feed my baby, he often seems more interested in playing with his food than eating it. Should I stop him from doing this?

Unless it gets totally out of hand and starts to interfere with his getting proper nutrition, you might consider giving your baby a little slack here. As far as he's concerned, his food is just like anything else in his environment—brand new and very exciting. As a result, his initial inclination may be to explore it rather than eat it. At first, the different colors of the foods you serve him and the different sounds that are made by the spoon will intrigue him. Once he learns to move his hands under the direction of his eyes and becomes adept at using his fingers, he will become fascinated by the varying temperatures and textures of the food as well. Although it may make feeding your baby a bit more inconvenient and time-consuming, you may want to acknowledge his educational needs as well as his nutritional needs. Permit mealtime to be a learning session at least to a certain extent as well as a way to give him the nutrition he needs.

Lately, my baby appears to be trying to feed himself, but he's not very good at it. Should I stop him until he gets older?

Toward the end of this period, your baby will be attempting to do more things for himself, and of course, he will be having a tough time in the beginning. When it comes to something like feeding, you certainly will have to step in at some point to make sure that he gets sufficient nutrition. However, if you don't allow him to try it himself for a little while, he'll never have a chance to get better. While this can seem obvious, it often is overshadowed by the need to get things done, particularly if parents are busy. This can become a real problem, especially at later stages of development. Therefore, now is a good time to start allotting more time for things like feeding, dressing, bathing, etc. so you can begin to include your baby's efforts without creating stress for yourself.

Your baby will use his mouth not only to get nourishment but also to explore his world.

IMPORTANT PHONE NUMBERS TO KEEP READILY ACCESSIBLE

It is obvious that obtaining outside assistance immediately is very important in an emergency, but parents sometimes fail to realize how foggy their thought processes can become in a crisis situation. Therefore, in order to ensure your baby's safety, it is critical to keep a list of appropriate phone numbers posted clearly next to every phone in your house. When a serious accident happens, you don't want to be rummaging through drawers or flipping through notebooks in a desperate attempt to find the information you need. The list should contain phone numbers for the fire department, the police, the poison control center, the paramedics or an ambulance service, and the nearest hospital emergency room. There should also be explicit instructions regarding the fastest route to that hospital. The phone number of your personal pediatrician should be included as well, and if you may not have access to a car, the number of the local taxi service should be written in, too. Less critical, but often convenient, are phone numbers for a local pharmacy, your dentist, nearby friends or relatives who might be able to lend a helping hand, plus the gas company, the electric company, a locksmith, etc. By the way, it is also advisable to post the information that emergency service providers are likely to ask for, such as the exact birth date of your baby, any allergies she may have, the inoculations she has received, etc. You may be unpleasantly surprised by how much basic information you simply can't recall under stress. Finally, in preparing your list, always leave room for additional numbers that may become important later on. It is a rare list of more than a few months old that doesn't include the numbers for a baby-sitter who is usually available on short notice and a pizza place that delivers, too.

SAFETY AND HEALTH

Since she won't be able to get around much on her own, how much trouble can my baby get into during this period?

It's easy to get lulled into a false sense of security by your baby's relative lack of mobility during this period. However, it is important to realize that even a newborn is not a totally stationary creature. When upset, a baby only a few days old can propel herself a short distance by repeatedly digging her heels into a soft surface and thrusting her legs. As she gains more control over her body in the next few months and can sit up, roll over, etc., a baby becomes increasingly capable of moving herself at least a short distance from where she was left. Therefore, right from the start, it is never a good idea to leave your baby unattended for more than a moment unless she is in her crib; and never do so when she is on a high surface, in the bath, or near something hazardous. And, of course, you always have to be careful about the things that are in your baby's immediate environment, especially once she has learned to use her hands under the guidance of her eyes and starts reaching for objects regularly. This includes items you use in caring for her, such as diaper pins and baby powder. Don't assume she is safe in her crib unless you've first read the crib-safety question on page 78 and checked to make sure the crib you use meets or beats the requirements.

I can't be with my baby all of the time, especially during the night. How do you suggest I "keep an eye on her" when she is in her crib?

This is one area where today's mothers and fathers have a big advantage over parents from previous generations. Babies have always been able to summon help with a loud cry. However, various problems that affected their breathing, and thus prevented them from vocalizing loudly, often went unnoticed in the past, sometimes with tragic results. And many naturally nervous parents used to spend the first several weeks of their child's life getting up every couple of hours and going into the nursery just to make sure everything was okay. Now, however, it is possible to purchase relatively inexpensive walkie-talkie or intercom-type devices that allow you to monitor what's going on in the nursery from any other room in the house. Making an investment in these new electronic devices will give your baby added security and increase your peace of mind enormously.

My baby's two-year-old brother loves to play with her, but sometimes he doesn't seem to know his own strength. Should I keep him away from her?

It is very normal and natural for a two-year-old child to feel fairly intense jealousy and hostility toward a new sibling, and you can expect those harsh feelings to get worse as the months go by and the baby begins to demand more and more immediate attention. Many parents have difficulty accepting the fact that their older child is upset over the presence of their younger child, and they interpret acts of violence as situations where the older child "doesn't know his own strength" or some other comparatively benign circumstance. The fact of the matter is that you have to be very careful about your baby's safety whenever she is in the presence of a closely spaced older sibling. Because their feelings are so strong, and because they really don't understand the extent of their own capacities and the potential consequences of their actions, slightly older siblings have been known to cause very serious damage to small babies. Even if a two-year-old sibling is relatively accepting of the baby, his curiosity may get out of hand and significant harm may result. Therefore, while you should not keep her brother from getting to know his sister, you should make sure that he is well supervised whenever they are together.

Do pets present a problem?

It is difficult to say because dogs and cats, like people, have unique "personalities" and react differently to various situations and circumstances. Some pets, particularly if they were around a long time before the baby arrived, display almost siblinglike jealousy toward the new object of their owner's attention. Others are quick to warm up to the new arrival and can even become very protective toward the baby. Therefore, it is wise to wait several weeks before you leave your baby alone near a pet so that you can get a clear sense of how they will get along. In general, it also is a good idea to be on the lookout for inadvertent accidents triggered by pets. For example, a friendly but overly eager dog may jump up on a stroller or high chair, causing it to topple over. And an otherwise harmless cat may decide that the baby's crib is a warm and cozy place to sleep, possibly in a position that can cause serious problems for the occupant.

When your baby is in the presence of a closely spaced older sibling, it's wise to supervise the situation closely. Also, be sure to set aside some special time each day when you can give undivided attention to your older child.

Getting my baby into and out of her car seat is time-consuming and tiresome. Won't she be safe if I just hold her?

Holding your baby in your arms when she's in the car may seem like a safe thing to do, but in the event of a collision—even at very low speed—it provides virtually no protection for her at all; her momentum will tear her free and send her flying toward the dashboard or windshield. Car seats can be a tremendous inconvenience at times, but the statistical evidence is overwhelming that they do save lives. The substantial increase in the chances that your baby will survive even a major accident certainly make the investment of a little extra time and effort well worth it. Furthermore, the use of child restraints for children in this age group is now required by law in every state, so not strapping your baby in can get you into trouble as well! (See the question on page 79 for advice on purchasing a suitable, safe car seat.)

Is it safe to take my baby on an airplane?

It certainly is, even more so now that most airlines will permit parents to place their babies in suitable car seats during takeoff and landing. Perhaps the only thing to be particularly concerned about is ear discomfort as a result of sharp increases or decreases in cabin pressure during landing and takeoff. Because the eustachian tubes in their ears are narrower and more prone to collapse with altitude changes, little babies are especially susceptible to such problems. Therefore, avoid taking your baby on a plane if she is congested or has an ear infection; if she must fly, make sure your pediatrician has examined her and okayed the flight. Also, have your baby nurse or suck on a pacifier during ascent and descent to promote swallowing and reduce pressure on the ear canals. Since a hungry baby will suck more vigorously, make sure that she has not been fed shortly before takeoff or landing.

Is there anything I should be concerned about when taking my baby to the supermarket or shopping mall?

Unfortunately, in this day and age, parents must be aware of the possibility of child-snatching in such situations. The chances of your baby being taken are not nearly as great as the impression you may have received from the sensational news coverage that this phenomenon receives. Still, the fact of the matter is that it can happen and that parents need to be

A backpack or sling can help you keep your baby safe when you take her out in public.

careful. Particularly during this period, if convenient, it is a good idea to carry your baby in a backpack or sling so that she is in contact with you at all times. If you put her in a carriage or stroller, make sure she is securely harnessed, and never leave her unattended. Also, to the extent possible, try to plan your trips for times of the day when the stores are likely to be relatively uncrowded. Even if you keep your baby close to you, the pushing, shoving, and jostling that takes place during peak periods can cause problems which it may be just as well to avoid completely.

When strangers admire my baby, they sometimes ask if they can hold her. Is it safe to let them?

This is a personal decision that has to be made on a case-by-case basis. While caution is always appropriate whenever your baby is in the presence of people you don't know, you can make yourself crazy by assuming that every stranger is getting ready to run off with your child. Therefore, if you feel comfortable with the circumstances and have a good feeling about the person, you shouldn't feel as if you have to abide by a policy of never allowing anyone other than family members to enjoy your baby. However, particularly during this period, you have to make sure that whoever picks up and holds your baby—stranger, friend, family member, or whatever—knows what he or she is doing. Not everyone may be aware that your baby needs proper neck and head support when held at this age, so a well-meaning but uninformed person may be unintentionally but distinctly hazardous. In addition, avoid allowing anyone who has symptoms of a contagious illness to hold the baby.

What can I do to protect my baby from fire and other household emergencies?

The best way to protect your baby from such things is to prevent them from happening. Especially during this period, when she has absolutely no capacity to remove herself from harm's way, and when her ability to ask for help is severely limited, your baby is very much at risk in such situations. Therefore, this is a good time to purchase and install smoke detectors, a fire extinguisher, and other such equipment; and if you already own these devices, double-check to see that they are in good working order. In addition, you should obtain a special window decal for the nursery so that fire fighters and other emergency personnel will be able to find your baby quickly. Finally, always remember to remove your baby from the house before you try to deal with any emergency yourself. If you fail and the situation gets out of hand, it may be too late to redirect your efforts toward finding your baby and getting her to safety.

How will I know if my baby is getting sick? When should I call my pediatrician?

Parents rapidly become expert and accurate assessors of how their baby feels. When does cranky or out-of-sorts become a sign of illness? If your baby is crying more for no apparent reason, and the cry sounds like she's in pain, investigate. If her diaper is dry, there are no pins sticking her, and you can find no reason for her distress, consider how she's been feeding, sleeping, and acting. Any sudden or distinct change in your baby's personality or demeanor can be a sign of illness. Has she been wetting a larger or smaller number of diapers than usual? Have her stools been unusually loose and more frequent? Has she vomited? Does her skin feel warm or moist? Does she look pale or flushed? Is she acting lethargic or withdrawn? Does she have a fever? (CALL YOUR PEDIA-

WHAT YOU NEED TO KNOW IN CASE AN ACCIDENT HAPPENS

Although it is not necessary for you to become an expert on all health and medical procedures pertaining to babies—that is what pediatricians are for—it is advisable for you to take the time to become familiar with certain basics so that you can help your baby before expert help arrives in times of emergency. Your local chapter of the Red Cross, the Heart Association, or other such organization, or your local hospital, health clinic, day-care center, or other such agency probably can help you to acquire essential training in first aid and CPR (cardiopulmonary resuscitation) for babies. Even if you have had similar training before, taking an update or refresher course certainly wouldn't hurt. And you should note that providing first aid and CPR for a baby involves many considerations and techniques that are significantly different from those that are applicable to older children and adults. Choking, poisoning, head injuries, cuts, burns, etc. all need to be handled at least slightly differently with babies. By the way, if at all possible, responsibility for learning these first aid and CPR procedures should not be relegated to just one parent. The more people who have this information—including close friends, relatives, and baby-sitters, as well as both parents—the more likely your baby is to receive proper treatment when an unfortunate incident occurs.

SUDDEN INFANT DEATH SYNDROME

Sudden Infant Death Syndrome (SIDS) refers to the sudden, unexpected, and unexplained death during sleep of a seemingly normal and healthy baby. The victim is usually between the ages of one month and one year, with the peak incidence at two to three months of age. SIDS is very rare prior to two weeks of age or after six months of age. The incidence of SIDS is highest in black and American Indian babies; in babies of young, single mothers; in babies whose mothers have abused drugs during pregnancy; and in babies who were born prematurely. If you fall into one of these high-risk groups or if there is a history of SIDS in your family, discuss this with your pediatrician. It is important to remember that SIDS can occur without any warning or any past history. In these cases, the parents must be advised that nothing that they did or did not do caused the loss or could have prevented it. Often, the emotional scars that these parents carry because of guilt can be as severe as the loss of the baby. Most cases of SIDS cannot be prevented.

TRICIAN RIGHT AWAY IF YOUR BABY IS LESS THAN SIX MONTHS OLD AND HER TEMPERATURE IS ABOVE 100 DEGREES FAHRENHEIT.) Is she coughing? Does she have a stuffy or runny nose? Does she seem to have trouble breathing? Do her eyes look clouded, glassy, or red rather than clear? If you answered yes to two or three of these questions or even to one that concerns you, call the pediatrician. Your pediatrician may suggest that you wait and see or may feel confident after consulting with you that it's not necessary to see the baby at this point. On the other hand, your pediatrician may advise you to have the child seen immediately. There are times when you may feel that your questions sound stupid. Ask them anyway. An important part of the pediatrician's job is to be a resource for parents. A parent's concern is a very important reason for calling the pediatrician.

My doctor believes in taking the baby's temperature rectally, but I'm afraid I'll hurt her. Can I use a thermometer strip or just feel her forehead instead?

If and when you think it's necessary to assess your baby's temperature, the method of choice is still by the old-fashioned rectal thermometer. Moms have been feeling foreheads for generations, and it's a lovely Mom thing to do, but it's not accurate. And while the strips are much easier to use, they do not have the accuracy of a rectal thermometer. Taking your baby's temperature rectally does not hurt her. If you've never taken a child's temperature rectally before, ask for guidance when you are at your pediatrician's office. Be sure you know how to find and read the mercury level as well. You can also refer to the illustrated directions on page 53. With proper instruction and practice, you'll be an expert in no time. Remember, too, that it's not necessary to take the baby's temperature unless you think she's ill. A fever is only one symptom of illness, so be sure to pay attention to how your child is feeding and acting as well. However, if your baby is less than six months old and has a temperature above 100 degrees Fahrenheit, call your pediatrician immediately.

What medications and equipment should I have in the house in case my baby gets sick?

At this age, the most important piece of equipment to use in case your baby gets sick is the telephone. It is essential to consult
(Continued on page 54)

TAKING A RECTAL TEMPERATURE

Select a rectal thermometer that has a short, round mercury bulb. (It's often helpful to have a spare on hand in case of breakage.) Learn to read it before you need it. To read the thermometer, roll it back and forth between your thumb and index finger until you can see the top of the mercury column. Practice this until you can read it quickly.

1. Clean the bulb end of the thermometer with rubbing alcohol or soap and water, and rinse with clear, cool water.
2. Shake the mercury column down so that it reads below 96 degrees Fahrenheit. Do this by tightly gripping the end opposite to the bulb and snapping your wrist so that the mercury moves down toward the bulb.
3. Place a small amount of lubricant on the bulb end of the thermometer. Vaseline, baby lotion, lubricating jelly, etc. are all acceptable.

You can also lay the baby on her back and use one hand to hold her legs up in the air; this position will not work, however, with a squirming baby or uncooperative older child.

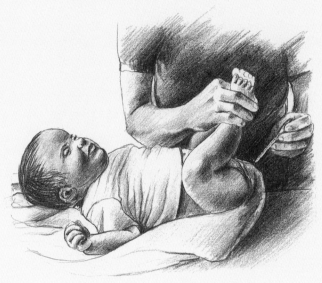

5. With your free hand, insert the lubricated end of the thermometer one to one-and-a-half inches into the anal opening. Hold the thermometer between your second and third fingers and keep that hand cupped over the baby's bottom. Hold in place for two minutes.
6. Remove and read.

This technique will work for children of all ages. By the age of four or five, however, an oral temperature can usually be taken by placing an oral thermometer in your child's mouth and having her hold it under her tongue for two minutes. Digital thermometers are also available. They are much more expensive than mercury thermometers and may not be as accurate. For routine use, stick with the traditional mercury-filled glass thermometer.

4. Place the baby in a facedown position on a firm surface. With tiny babies, you can lay the baby facedown across your lap. Using the palm of your hand closest to the baby's head, apply firm pressure to the baby's back just above the buttocks. If the baby tries to roll over, increase the pressure.

with your pediatrician whenever you think your baby is sick. In addition, you'll need a rectal thermometer, and you'll need to know how to use it properly (see previous page). You may also want to keep some acetaminophen drops on hand in case your pediatrician advises you to give them to your baby to relieve discomfort or bring down a fever (if your baby develops a rectal temperature over 100 degrees Fahrenheit during the first few months of life, immediately call your pediatrician for instructions). Another very useful item to have on hand is a cool-mist humidifier to help make your baby more comfortable during respiratory illnesses. Finally, a bottle and dropper filled with saltwater nose drops (see recipe on this page) is useful to help clear your baby's nasal passages when she has a cold.

RECIPE FOR SALTWATER NOSE DROPS

Mix half a measured teaspoonful of salt with one-and-a-quarter cups (ten ounces) of water. Pour the solution in a dropper bottle, and use as a nasal flush to loosen thick mucus and to help clear your baby's clogged nasal passages.

I have a cold, and I'm afraid my baby is going to get it. Is there any way to prevent this?

Unfortunately, among the many things a family shares are cold viruses. As far as prevention goes, if you wash your hands frequently, throw used tissue in the garbage, and try not to sneeze on the baby, there's little else you can do to protect her from your cold. Some parents use surgical masks (which most likely frighten the baby), but by the time your cold symptoms are "full blown," you've already exposed the baby. You're far better off trying to stay in optimum health yourself and to avoid exposing yourself to people who have contagious illnesses. Unfortunately, as yet, we do not have a vaccine that can prevent you or your baby from catching a cold.

A cool-mist vaporizer can help your baby breathe easier when she has a cold. Be careful not to let the mist drench your baby or blow directly at her face. Also, be sure to keep it clean and to put fresh water in for each use.

What do I do if my newborn gets a cold?

Treatment of a cold in an infant varies a little from the way it's treated in an older child or an adult. Most babies (especially those that are breast-fed) handle colds well. Still, your baby's smaller nasal passages can more easily become blocked, and this can be troublesome since she must be able to breath through her nose to feed successfully. If the stuffiness interferes with her appetite, it may be helpful to use a humidifier (cool-mist type) in her room and to apply a homemade saltwater solution as a nasal flush (see recipe on this page). Do not give your infant any prescription or nonprescription medication without first checking with your pediatrician. Likewise, if your baby develops a fever over 100 degrees Fahrenheit or stops eating, contact your pediatrician.

My husband is worried about the possibility of our infant developing a serious reaction to childhood vaccinations. How can I convince him that our infant should be immunized?

Congratulate your husband upon becoming a parent at a time in the history of mankind when you can prevent your baby from getting most of the life threatening, crippling, and debilitating communicable diseases of childhood. Proper immunization will protect your child from diphtheria, tetanus, whooping cough, polio, mumps, measles, and rubella. The latest vaccine in the arsenal against disease is HiB. Hemophilus influenza type B was once the major cause of meningitis in young children. Many of those afflicted died; others suffered significant hearing loss. A chicken pox vaccine is also currently being developed. Although chicken pox is usually not a severe disease, there are occasionally complications that can be life threatening, especially to a child with a compromised immune system. The side effects or reactions from these immunizations usually include minimal discomfort, a slight fever, and, sometimes, irritability for up to 48 hours. The severe or unusual reaction you hear about may happen once in 300,000 children, and many of these are not documented sufficiently. In other words, the child in question was likely developing or exhibiting a pre-existing condition. Parents of today are indeed fortunate to be able to promise their children a healthier future free from all these diseases. What's more, while you're convincing your husband about the necessity and privilege of immunizing your child, inform him of the necessity for all adults to get a tetanus/diphtheria booster every ten years. Ninety-seven percent of recent cases of tetanus occurred in adults. MMR (measles, mumps, and rubella) reimmunizations are recommended for adults born after 1956 unless they have a record of having received a second immunization or have had a case of measles that was documented by a physician. If you had the immunization before your first birthday, it should be repeated.

My husband smokes cigarettes. I've told him it's harmful to the baby, but he thinks that if he smokes in the adjoining room, it's okay. Is it?

Your baby can be inhaling smoke from her environment even if it's not directly in her face. Many studies provide us with statistical proof that secondhand smoke definitely does affect the number of upper-respiratory infections and middle-ear infections in children. Children of smokers have more colds,

RECOMMENDED IMMUNIZATION SCHEDULE FOR CHILDREN

Age	Immunization
Two months	DTP and oral polio
Four months	DTP and oral polio
Six months	DTP
Nine to 12 months	Tuberculin test (may be repeated at one to two year intervals; consult pediatrician)
15 months	MMR
15 to 18 months	HiB
18 months	DTP and oral polio
Four to six years	DTP and oral polio

DTP = Diphtheria, tetanus, and pertussis (whooping cough) vaccines given as single injection
MMR = Measles, mumps, and rubella vaccines given as single injection
HiB = Hemophilus influenza type B (meningitis) immunization

COPING WITH COLIC

If you have determined that your baby has colic (see question), the following tips may help you cope. Remember that colic is a self-limiting set of symptoms that's usually tougher on the parents than on the baby.

- Try to console the baby with some kind of movement, such as rocking, walking, or a ride in an automobile.
- Do not overfeed a colicky baby, because an over-filled tummy can increase her discomfort.
- Talk calmly to her, if possible, to let her know that you are concerned and available.
- If you feel you are losing your patience or per-spective, get someone else to take care of the baby for a while until you feel better.
- If you are having trouble coping with the crying or it seems really excessive, consult your pedia-trician and have the baby examined to make sure that everything is normal.

ear infections, bronchitis, and pneumonia, and they show reduced pulmonary (lung) function. More recent research has indicated that the occurrence and severity of colic and coliclike conditions in babies can be related to secondary smoke. For many years, secondhand smoke has been a known factor in the severity of asthma in children. Studies investigating croup show tobacco smoke to be a contributing factor here, too. We could go on, but these reasons should be more than enough to convince responsible parents that they need to provide their children with a smoke-free environment. If your hus-band can't quit, have him do his smoking outside.

What is colic? Do all babies get it?

Colic means different things to different people, even to pediatricians. In general, colic refers to repeated episodes of inconsolable crying in a baby who previously was not espe-cially fussy. The episodes of crying usually begin a few weeks after birth and occur during the day and at night. Nothing the parents do makes any difference. After what seems like for-ever (but is usually less than two hours), the baby calms down or sleeps and is back to her usual self. This pattern may be repeated several times daily. Most babies do not get colic, but those who do can try the patience of even the best parents. There have been many theories about what causes colic, but we still really don't know. The important thing to remember is that no matter how bad it seems, colic disappears as quickly as it appears, usually when the baby is about three to four months old. To determine whether your baby has colic, think about other factors that may be making her fuss. Is she hungry, thirsty, or uncomfortable? If she is breast-fed, did her mother eat anything unusual that might be causing the baby abdominal discomfort? Does the baby have any other signs of illness, such as vomiting, loss of appetite, fever, or diarrhea? If the answers to these questions are negative, then you're probably dealing with colic (see the sidebar on this page for tips on coping with colic).

What is infant acne? What can be done about it?

There are two times in life when children develop acne. We all know about the teen years, but many are not aware that the same type of rash can occur in the newborn. In response to withdrawal from maternal hormones, some babies develop a mini version of acne on the face, neck, upper chest, and back. The lesions look just like a small version of teenage acne and appear in the same places because they involve the same oil-producing glands. The good news is that in a few weeks these "baby zits" will gradually go away without any kind of treatment. Although they can be upsetting to parents, they don't bother the baby at all, so it's best to leave them alone.

How will I know when my baby is teething? Will it make her sick?

Babies get their teeth at different ages and at different rates. On the average, babies begin to teethe at about six to eight months of age and erupt about one tooth per month until they have 20, which is the total number of deciduous or "baby" teeth. Many babies begin to drool at about three months of age and fool their parents into thinking that they are teething. Actually, the drooling is from the salivary glands, which are just becoming active. Babies have no symptoms from teething until a tooth is about to erupt (break through the surface) and the area of the gum around the tooth begins to swell or bulge. Although many babies erupt teeth without any symptoms, teething may cause fussiness, soreness of the gums, drooling, runny nose with clear mucus, slightly elevated temperature (rarely over 100.4 degrees Fahrenheit), and slightly loose bowel movements. You can help make your teething baby more comfortable by letting him chew on cool, firm teething objects and by using an appropriate dose of acetaminophen drops (not aspirin). Check with your pediatrician, however, before giving your baby any medications.

My two month old always has tears coming from her left eye. Sometimes the discharge is yellow and thick. Is something wrong?

Tears (the natural lubricant of the eye) are produced by a gland on the outside of the upper eyelid; from there, they flow across the eye. They are picked up by a tiny duct on the medial (nose side) of the lower lid, and drain into the nose. If you look carefully in the inner part of your lower lid, you will see a tiny opening through which the tears drain. Occasionally, this duct is blocked at birth, so the tears well up and spill out of the eye and onto the face. This is by far the most frequent cause of tearing from one eye only in a young baby. In most cases, the tear duct will open by itself, and the unusual tearing will stop. Sometimes, however, a mild infection occurs

On average, babies begin to teethe at about six to eight months of age.

because of the obstruction. This can result in the tears becoming yellow and thick. Applying warm, wet packs to the closed eye may help get rid of the infection; if it does not, contact your pediatrician. You may be instructed to use some antibiotic eye drops or ointment and/or to use a massage technique to help encourage the duct to open. In a very small number of infants, the duct does not open by itself and must be surgically opened, usually during the end of the first year of life.

My baby was born with pink-red birthmarks on her forehead, her eyelid, and the back of her neck. Will they go away?

The type of birthmark you describe usually fades with time, often several years. Unless there is a family history of similar marks on the face and head that are permanent, these "stork bites" are of only minor significance. They are most often found on the back of the neck, on the hairline above the neck, on the eyelids, between the eyebrows, or on other parts of the face. They require no treatment.

What is cradle cap? How should it be treated?

Cradle cap is best thought of as infant dandruff. It consists of oily, yellow scales, which can be thick or thin and may be patchy or involve most of the scalp. It often starts after the first few weeks of life and may last for months if not treated. The scales can even become so thick that hair can't grow through them, resulting in temporary bald spots. Cradle cap is not contagious, but it can be a real nuisance. The best treatment is to lather your baby's scalp with a mild baby shampoo, and gently scrub the scales off with a soft brush or your fingernails. Don't worry about touching the fontanels (soft spots). While it may feel like the skull is open beneath them, there is actually a tough, protective membrane under the skin. If the cradle cap persists after several days of daily shampooing, switch to a dandruff shampoo and use the same technique. The scales will loosen and come off. It may be necessary to continue the vigorous shampoos throughout the first few months of life, after which the cradle cap will become less of a problem.

My breast-fed newborn girl has been having drainage from her vagina. Is this normal?

Whitish vaginal drainage and even a small amount of bloody mucus is normal in female infants, especially those who are breast-fed. It is a response to maternal hormones. It causes no symptoms and is self limiting, usually lasting only a few weeks. It requires no treatment and is definitely not a reason to discontinue breast-feeding.

My breast-fed newborn son has noticeable swelling under both nipples that seems to be increasing. It doesn't seem to bother him, but it looks and feels like he has little breasts. Is this normal?

What you are describing is a normal variant that occurs in some infant boys and girls. It seems to occur more often in breast-fed babies, but may occur in those on formula also. It appears to be a response to maternal hormones in the baby's very sensitive breast tissue. It will resolve itself without treatment and without a change in feeding method. Occasionally, there is even a tiny amount of whitish fluid that comes from the enlarged breasts. This is also a variant of normal and should not cause concern.

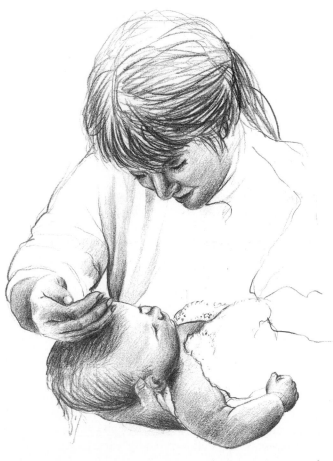

To treat cradle cap, lather your baby's scalp with a mild shampoo, use a soft brush or your fingernails to gently rub the scales off, then rinse thoroughly.

Is it dangerous to take my newborn into a room that's crowded with people?

Whenever possible, you should avoid exposing your newborn to crowds of people because of the possibility of her catching a contagious illness. If it is necessary to take her into this kind of situation, you'll want to take a few precautions. Ask anyone who has any symptoms of illness to please refrain from coming near the baby. Limit the number of people who hold her, or better yet, show her off while you're holding her. If necessary, use some excuse for not passing her around, such as "She's very fussy," or "She's been spitting up a lot today." Tell people that your pediatrician doesn't want her to be handled too much and that kissing spreads germs. On the other hand, you can put her down in a room away from everyone else and have a sitter or close relative watch her for a while.

Should I have my newborn boy circumcised?

Circumcision (a partial removal of the foreskin of the penis) is a procedure that may be done in the first few days of life. In certain cultures, it is done routinely as a religious ritual. Most parents of newborn boys have to make the decision about whether or not to circumcise as soon as they know their newborn is male. We recommend that parents-to-be take the time to decide this issue prior to the birth and that they take the following information into consideration.

1. Most pediatricians will support whatever decision the parents make, so it is up to the parents to make an informed decision.
2. The American Academy of Pediatrics has recently issued a revision of their previous policy statement regarding circumcision. In it, the Academy points out that infant males who are not circumcised have a very small chance of developing a urinary tract infection in the first year of life. Aside from this issue, there is no true "medical" reason to have a baby circumcised.
3. Most mothers agree that it is easier to clean and care for a circumcised penis.
4. There is some pain involved during the circumcision. The baby, however, quickly recovers from it. Some physicians who perform circumcisions prefer to use local anesthesia, while others feel that it is not necessary.
5. There is an extremely low incidence of complications from the local anesthesia and from the circumcision itself.
6. It is important to some parents that their son look like his father, brother(s), and other boys his age, whether circumcised or not. Therefore, you may want to take the circumcision rate in the community into account.

Remember that as long as you inform yourself about the options, there is no wrong answer in this matter. Whatever is decided, discuss the care of your son's penis (circumcised or not) with your pediatrician. If your newborn son has not been circumcised, do not attempt to retract the foreskin and clean beneath it. The foreskin separates gradually during the first few years of life. Forcibly retracting it at this age may cause pain and bleeding and may harm the penis.

Why does my baby have hiccups all the time?

Hiccups are brief spasms of the diaphragm (the structure which separates the chest cavity from the abdominal cavity); they occur frequently in young babies. Many moms who frequently felt their babies hiccupping in the womb often note the same tendency during the first few months after birth. Many babies hiccup when they are hungry, perhaps as a result of the empty stomach pulling down on the diaphragm. Hiccups are also common at the end of a feeding; burping may help to relieve these. Perhaps the most important aspect to note here, however, is that hiccups are normal and self limiting. In most babies, they cause no distress or other behavioral changes. If hiccups do not bother your baby, don't let them bother you.

How can I be sure that my baby is seeing normally?

At birth, a baby's vision is not fully mature, but it does improve rapidly in the early months of life. By about four months of age, your baby's color vision will be almost fully mature, and she will be able to focus on distant objects as well as those that are nearby. To get an idea of whether your baby is seeing normally, check to see that she follows the movements of your hand or face or a brightly colored object with her eyes. Make sure her eyes move together as she does so. Also check to see that when she is facing a light source—such as a sunny window or a lamp—the reflection from the light falls at exactly the same spot on the colored portion of both eyes. After the second or third month of life, if you feel that your baby is not following this developmental pattern or you notice that one or both of her eyes seem to wander when she looks at an object, discuss it with your pediatrician. Since your child learns more through her eyes than through any of her other senses, it is important to try to make sure that her visual abilities are normal for her age.

How can I tell if my baby is hearing properly?

From the moment of birth, you can tell if your baby is deaf by noticing whether or not she startles when exposed to loud sounds. Fortunately, complete deafness is mercifully rare. On the other hand, mild to moderate hearing loss—due to congenital defects or infections—is difficult to detect and can have serious consequences in terms of understanding and learning how to use language. Starting at about four months of age, you can—and should—screen your baby regularly for possible problems in this area. Because she should be able to orient accurately to the source of sound at this point, you can test her hearing ability by standing a few feet behind her and quietly calling her name. Even if she is occupied with something, she should turn, look at you, and smile. Repeat this process from several different vantage points, gradually decreasing the loudness

of your voice until you're nearly whispering. She should still turn, look, and smile in response. If your baby repeatedly fails this "whisper" test over the course of several days, don't hesitate to get her to your pediatrician and insist that the problem be investigated and taken care of as soon as possible.

My baby likes to stiffen her legs when I hold her in a standing position. Can it hurt her legs to stand this way?

Most babies, starting at about four to five months of age, like to bear weight on their feet and even bounce while being held in an upright position. Many babies are also noted to have bowed legs at about fifteen to eighteen months of age. These two facts are probably responsible for the myth that this early weight bearing causes bowed legs later in life. This just isn't the case. The desire to bear weight on the legs in early life as well as the usually temporary appearance of bowed legs in the second year of life are normal and expected. They are in no way related. If your baby enjoys bearing weight on her legs and bouncing on her feet, indulge her.

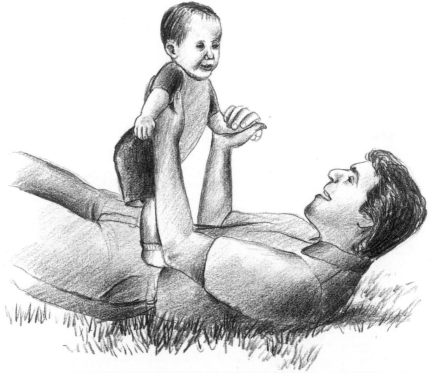

If he enjoys bearing weight on his legs and even bouncing up and down, go ahead and indulge him. Such exercises aren't harmful as long as you keep him from falling.

ON BEING A PARENT

Now that the initial excitement of having my first baby is over, I find myself feeling down—almost depressed—from time to time. Is this normal?

While severe postpartum depression—often induced by hormonal imbalances—is mercifully rare, a strong dose of the "baby blues" is quite common. After the excitement and anticipation that fills a first pregnancy, the day-after-day drudgery of actually caring for a newborn tends to be a real letdown. Furthermore, although becoming a parent presents many new opportunities, it clearly signals the end of a relatively carefree period in life and the onset of some rather daunting responsibilities. The realization of this fact can be overwhelming at times. Therefore, you shouldn't worry too much about feeling down on occasion during the first weeks. And you can be assured that a lot of these feelings probably will melt away as soon as your baby starts giving you those first smiles.

I've never been so exhausted in my life. Will I ever get a decent night's sleep again?

Don't count on getting one for a while. It may take several weeks or even months before your baby manages to sleep through the night. What's more, it's likely to take somewhat longer than that before you really believe he's going to sleep through the night and can allow yourself to relax enough to get a full night's sleep. Therefore, you may have to adjust your own habits to a certain extent. Once your baby starts settling into a reasonably regular sleeping and eating schedule, you need to take advantage of every opportunity to get some rest while he is quiet and content. Also, you might want to abandon any claims you may have had to being an immaculate housekeeper and gracious host. Taking care of yourself is more important than seeing to it that your home is spotless at this point; and until you get your strength back, you should feel free to tell well-meaning but intrusive friends, relatives, and neighbors who want to visit the baby that you're simply not up to receiving a steady stream of guests right now.

It's quite common to feel down or even depressed from time to time as you adjust to life with your new baby.

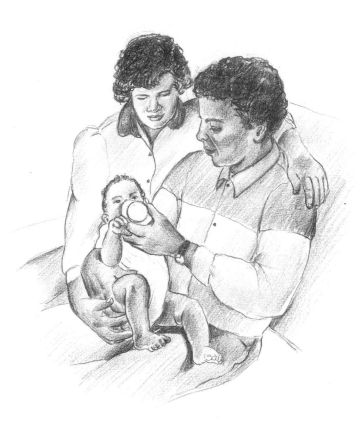

Both parents can play a special role in their child's development and care.

Having a baby has brought us closer together in a spiritual sense, but our sex life has virtually disappeared. Does this happen to everyone?

Just about, although it is typically a very temporary phenomenon. Obviously, the wear and tear on a woman's body during childbirth makes having sex rather uncomfortable for a while. Furthermore, the fatigue induced by middle-of-the-night feedings and diaper changes does a lot to diminish the sex drive. After the first several weeks, however, a lack of sexual activity may be a sign that some serious underlying psychological problems are beginning to develop. For example, a woman may resent the fact that she is doing all of the hard work and dirty chores connected with taking care of the baby while her husband gets to waltz in and play Daddy after all the drudgery is done. Conversely, a man may resent the fact that his wife and child seem to be developing a very special and close relationship while he is being left out. Therefore, if your sex life doesn't start to make a reappearance after a reasonable amount of time, the two of you should sit down and discuss the situation. If problems persist, you might consider seeking counseling.

Does the father play a special role in raising a child?

We all have certain images of what a father does as opposed to what a mother does, but it is important to realize that those images are culturally induced. The fact of the matter is that with the singular exception of breast-feeding, there is nothing that women are inherently more qualified to do than men when it comes to taking care of babies. Some studies have found distinct differences between the ways in which fathers interact with their children as compared to the ways mothers do. As it turns out, however, when the traditional positions are reversed—that is, when the fathers take over primary responsibility for child rearing while the mothers work outside the home—so do the interaction styles. Therefore, the father does indeed play a special role, but that role does not necessarily have to be any more or less special, nor does it have to be essentially different, from the role of the mother.

How can we both take an equal part in parenting?

The best way to form a true parenting partnership is to plan it in advance. Modern mothers and fathers simply can't make assumptions about who will do what according to traditional standards; these standards are becoming more irrelevant every day. In this day and age, there is no reason why a mother-to-be and father-to-be can't sit down before the birth and fully discuss what will need to be done and who will do it so that everyone involved will be content. In general, it is recommended that both parents share all child-rearing chores and responsibilities equally to the extent possible. This allows both parents to get a full understanding and appreciation of all the difficulties involved, as well as to receive a full share of all the rewards that are available. As opposed to a strict and mutually exclusive division of labor, this sort of system helps to promote cooperation and reduce resentment; both parents will have pretty much the same perspective on whatever problems arise and will have pretty much the same set of experiences to either endure or enjoy.

Will a baby suffer if he has a single parent?

Despite what you may have read or heard about sex-role development and other such issues, there is no evidence to suggest that a child who has a single parent is destined to encounter specific problems of any kind. On the other hand, there is ample evidence to suggest that enjoying and being effective at the process of parenting is a lot tougher when you're flying solo. Taking care of a baby involves a lot of hard work, and it also provides some of life's sweetest pleasures. As is the case with anything else, if you can share the experience with someone else, the bad times are easier to deal with and the good times feel even better. Of course, this does not mean that a single parent should run out and find the first available mate, but it does suggest that a single parent should consider enlisting a support system—friends, relatives, other single parents—so that he or she doesn't have to go through everything alone all the time.

Forming a parenting partnership means sharing child-raising chores and responsibilities equally to the extent possible. This allows both parents to experience both the joys and the difficulties of raising a child.

My newborn doesn't do much except sleep, eat, and soil his diaper. Is there anything I can really teach him at this time?

Believe it or not, during these first weeks, you will be teaching your baby the most fundamental lesson of his life. No matter how good-natured your baby is, and no matter how adept you are at tending to his needs, there inevitably will be many times every day when he is hungry, cold, or otherwise suffering some physical discomfort. When this happens, he will cry; and when he does, you will probably show up and do whatever you can to reduce his discomfort. This constantly repeated cycle of discomfort, followed by crying, followed by your presence, followed by the reduction of discomfort teaches your baby—on a very basic level—that there are people who love him and will take care of him. The resulting capacity to trust in his world will help him to feel secure and to engage in healthy relationships for the rest of his life.

During the first months, responding promptly to your baby's cries will not spoil him. It will teach him that he is loved and that there are people who will take care of him.

Won't I "spoil" my baby if I respond immediately to all of his demands?

During the first months, it is really impossible to "spoil" a baby. In order for that process to take place, there has to be a capacity for intentionality and manipulation on the part of the baby, and that simply doesn't exist in the beginning. When your baby cries at this point, he is doing so reflexively in response to physical discomfort. He has a genuine need that requires reasonably immediate attention, and there is nothing he can do to alleviate it himself. Therefore, by "giving in" to his "demands," you are merely teaching him that he is loved and will be taken care of. You are not, in any way, giving him the impression that he can "boss you around."

Lately, my baby has started crying when he's bored and lonely as well as when he's in physical discomfort. Should I respond immediately to these cries too?

Starting at about four months of age, armed with a growing social awareness, your baby will begin using the cry deliberately to get your attention, not only as a reflexive response to physical discomfort. Once this happens, the possibility of "spoiling" enters the picture. It is important to keep teaching your baby that every effort will be made to meet his needs—and being rescued from boredom or loneliness certainly is a valid need—but you also can start teaching him that his needs are not the only things that matter in life. Therefore, if you hear a cry that sounds like a call for attention rather than a reaction to physical distress, your first response can be something like "I hear you, but you'll have to wait a minute—I'm busy right now." Your baby won't understand a single word of what you say, but through your actions, you will be teaching him that although he is still loved and his needs will still be taken care of, he won't always be able to get whatever he wants whenever he wants it.

My baby is thrilled when I give him lots of attention, but is it necessary for me to "entertain" him all the time?

Certainly not. Although you will always be a special target of his interests, your baby also will be increasingly interested in the world around him. If your baby appears to be content only when you are interacting with him, he probably is not getting enough opportunities to explore and investigate the nonpeople parts of his environment. You might consider providing him with access to a greater number of objects to play with, and you certainly should consider putting him in an infant seat and moving him to different parts of the house so he has new and different scenes to look at and listen to. Pleasant interchanges with his parents should be a major part of your baby's early experience, but it should not be such a large part that it prevents him from learning about other things as well.

If my baby doesn't understand what I'm saying and can't speak himself, what's the point in talking to him?

No one is sure exactly how language learning gets put into motion. However, extensive research has repeatedly shown that babies who are talked to often during the first months of life eventually develop superior language skills to those who are exposed to a lot of silence from the people around them. This sometimes is not an easy thing for parents to do. After all, we don't talk regularly to chairs, fire hydrants, and other things that don't talk back, so it's hard to get into the habit of talking to a little baby. Therefore, if talking a lot to your baby is not something that comes naturally to you, you should consider making a concerted effort to do so. It doesn't matter too much what you say, as your tone and inflection will communicate much more than the actual words at this point. Hearing a lot of words spoken by human voices, however, will help trigger one of the most important processes in your baby's early development.

While you don't have to entertain your infant all the time, he certainly will enjoy being near you whenever possible as you take care of other tasks that need to be done.

Is it important to read books to my baby?

As in the case with talking to your baby, reading to your baby seems to be important as well. Even though he won't be able to understand the words, much less recognize characters or follow plots, he will appreciate the tone, inflection, and rhythm of your voice as you read. Although the evidence is neither direct nor conclusive, research does seem to indicate that this in some way instills an appreciation of books on a basic level. What's more, children who are exposed to books right from the beginning tend to do better with reading skills later on. At this point, what you read to your baby is not important, but you certainly should consider getting into the habit of regular sessions as soon as possible. In fact, you may find that reading to him as you rock him is a very effective way of getting your baby to fall asleep at certain times.

I don't know any lullabies and have a lousy voice anyway. Am I depriving my baby of something special if I don't sing to him?

There is no evidence to suggest that babies are destined to suffer in any way if they are not sung to by their parents. However, it is clear that listening to their parents sing is something that babies do enjoy a great deal. The critical factor is that the singing has to be something that the parents enjoy doing as well. If the people who are singing aren't having fun, the experience—at best—will be meaningless for the one being sung to. Therefore, it is a good idea to stop worrying about knowing lullabies or having a wonderful singing voice. If you feel like singing, just sing—whatever you want to sing in whatever way you can. As long as singing to your baby makes you feel good, you can be assured that your baby will get the same— if not more—benefits as he would if he were being serenaded with classics by Caruso.

I've heard that babies should be stroked and massaged a lot. Is that true?

It is undeniably true that babies need a lot of tactile stimulation during the early months; but it also is undeniably true that most parents provide more than enough stimulation simply by doing what comes naturally in the course of caring for their babies. Problems are more likely to occur if parents start feeling that there is something special they should be doing and become self-conscious about touching their babies. Therefore, if you feel inclined to take a course in infant massage, as long as it's something you're comfortable with, there certainly will be no harm in it and you'll probably find it enjoyable. But if it's something that makes you feel awkward or strange, you and your baby will be better off if you just go on doing what you've been doing all along.

Whether or not you can carry a tune, your baby will enjoy listening to you sing to him—as long as you enjoy it, too.

How can I help my baby develop his physical skills?

There is nothing you can do to prod your baby into developing his physical skills—holding his head up, rolling over, sitting up by himself—before he is ready. However, once he is ready, he can be prevented from developing these skills if he is not given enough opportunities to attempt them and practice them. You probably won't have to make any special efforts in this regard, but from time to time, make sure that you are periodically placing him on his stomach so he can try lifting his head, that you are not keeping him harnessed or restricted in some other way that would prevent him from moving freely much of the time, and that you are not being too eager to help him "finish it off" when he makes an effort to roll over, sit up, or whatever by himself.

How can I help my baby learn how to use his eyes and his hands together?

Acquiring sensorimotor skills—such as being able to find one's hands, and then being able to use the eyes and hands together to reach for and grasp an object—is the first phase of intellectual development. Since most parents are eager to have their child become as bright as possible, attempts to speed up the process of acquiring these skills are very common. Researchers have studied an enormous variety of methods for many years. However, the evidence indicates that during the first months, sensorimotor development ordinarily cannot be accelerated to any significant extent. Babies who have no "stimulation" beyond their crib rails and bedclothes seem to acquire these skills at roughly the same pace as babies who are exposed to high-tech mobiles, elaborate crib gyms, and other forms of "educational" toys and equipment. Again, if they are overly restricted and/or deprived of the kind of stimulation that is contained in an ordinary environment, babies can be prevented from developing these skills; but most parents, simply by doing what comes naturally and without going overboard in terms of effort and expense, end up doing the very best that can be done for their babies in this regard.

How old should my baby be before I leave him with a baby-sitter for an evening?

There is no set answer to this question. It probably is a good idea to wait a few weeks until your baby's sleeping and

WHAT'S IN A NAME?

What you name your baby is entirely up to you, but it is important to realize that your choice in this matter will have tremendous consequences for your child. While this ordinarily is not a major problem, some parents choose a name for personal reasons that eventually wreaks havoc on their child's day-to-day experiences throughout his life. Because of this, some countries—such as Sweden—actually have enacted laws that prevent parents from giving their children bizarre, unwieldy, or otherwise inappropriate names; it is considered a form of child abuse. Of course, no matter how careful you are in this regard, current events and nicknames can make even the most conservative choices problematical at some point in the future. For example, parents who named their boys Adolf in the 1920's had no idea that Hitler was coming along, and many parents named their boys Roosevelt without realizing that their pals would call them Rosie later on. However, in general, a little common sense and sensitivity can go a long way. Although unusual spellings—such as Jahn rather than John or Mairee instead of Mary—are distinctive, they also can be disruptive. Diminutive names—such as Willie or Cissy—may be fine for family use, but they can be embarrassing when an air of formality is appropriate. Names which typically are given to members of the opposite sex—such as Carroll or Joyce for boys and Toni or Bobbi for girls—certainly haven't prevented some people from becoming happy and successful, but they typically produce a lot of unnecessary suffering during the school years. Taking names from famous historical figures or popular cultural heroes may give you some pleasure, but it also may imbue your child with an identity that is not his in interactions with other people. Therefore, before bestowing a name upon your unsuspecting baby, take a little time to make sure that it will be primarily a source of pride and not a constant source of pain for him.

eating patterns become somewhat predictable before you leave him with a sitter for several hours. If an emergency arises or something important comes up, however, there really is no reason to believe that your absence is going to cause serious problems for your baby, even if he is only a few days old. The major consideration usually isn't when the baby is ready to be left with a sitter, but rather when the parents are ready to leave him with a sitter. It is natural for new parents to be overly anxious about the possibility of something going wrong, as well as for them to believe that no one but them will be able to do what needs to be done for their baby. After a while, it probably will be a very good idea to give yourself a break and go out for an evening alone. However, in the very beginning, leaving him with a sitter should be avoided if it's a big deal to you and makes you uncomfortable.

I have to leave my baby with a baby-sitter for the evening. What can I do to feel more at ease about it?

Do your "sitter homework" and you'll be able to leave your baby and most of your anxiety at home. Ask friends, neighbors, and relatives for the names of sitters that they use regularly. Then, do your own interview with the prospective sitter. Ask her to come and stay with the baby while you take a bath or do other things at home. This allows you to see for yourself how comfortable and competent she is with your baby. Walk her through all the routines she will have to perform, making sure to point out any and all special requirements, idiosyncrasies, medical problems, dietary restrictions, temperamental pieces of equipment, favorite toys, etc. Point out safety measures and discuss them in detail. Make sure she is familiar with all emergency procedures and equipment for the building in which you live. Go through your written list of rules and expectations. Is she allowed phone privileges? If so, put a limit on them; nothing makes a parent more uptight than not being able to get through to their home when they're checking in. If she passes the "at home" test, plan an evening at a friend's home where the phone is readily available. Let the sitter know where you will be at all times, and see to it that she has ready access to your list of critical phone numbers, including the number where you can be reached, the number of your pediatrician, the numbers for emergency services such as fire and police, and one for a relative or friend to contact in case you can't be reached for some reason. Until you're comfortable with each other, explain to her that you want to be "bothered" by her slightest question or doubt. Tell her you will call during the outing. If you're still worried, try coming

Doing your baby-sitter homework can help you find a sitter you trust and can help you leave at least some of your worries behind when you need to spend some time away from your baby.

home early to see how the sitter and your baby are getting along. If all goes well, the next outing can be a movie, play, shopping, or whatever.

We both plan on continuing our careers. When will our baby be old enough for day care?

Most day-care centers will not accept babies younger than three weeks of age, and many will not accept babies younger than six weeks old. However, this is not really a matter of the baby being old enough. The key concern is whether or not the parents are prepared to separate themselves from their baby for a substantial part of the day. Some parents are comfortable doing so at the three-week mark, others won't be ready for it until much later; you will have to decide what feels right to you. The quality and accessibility of the day-care center also should be considered. Especially during the early months, it is critical that your baby receive a lot of prompt, nurturing care. You must also realize that no amount of care from competent day-care personnel can compensate completely for a severe lack of the special kind of care that only you as parents can provide. Your baby has fundamental emotional needs during this period, and finding outstanding day care can be difficult. So, in general, as long as there is an option, many child development specialists prefer to see parents wait until the six-month mark before they place their baby in a day-care center on a full-time basis.

We are planning on placing our baby in day care, but we feel guilty about it. Should we?

Guilt is the emotional equivalent of physical pain. It tells you that something is wrong. Rather than just suffering through it, you should attempt to identify the underlying problem so you can stop it. Perhaps you feel guilty because you really don't want to be away from your baby. In that case, stay home with him if you can. You may be feeling pressure to "get out of the house and do something important," but the fact is that nothing is more important than helping your child get the best possible start in life, and nothing makes a more significant contribution to society than a good job of parenting. Perhaps you feel guilty because you have to work outside the home for personal or financial reasons, but you're afraid that your baby will receive inadequate nurturing and attention in a day-care center. In that case, do everything you can to find the highest quality center possible. In addition, try to compensate for whatever shortcomings it has by remaining completely and actively involved in every aspect of your baby's day-to-day experience. Other options you might look into are working only part-time; seeking a job at a company with on-site day care, so that you can look in on the baby during your lunch hour and breaks; job-sharing, in which you and another parent work alternate days at the same job while splitting the salary; or working out of your home. Above all, remember that, as a parent, you inevitably will feel guilty about a lot of things from time to time, but it's only a "bad" thing if you don't respond to it constructively.

Is my baby more likely to be in danger in a day-care center than at home?

If the day-care center is of high quality, with a properly designed and maintained physical facility and a well-trained and experienced staff, your baby will not be in serious danger. Of course, babies in group situations are at greater risk for getting infections and contagious diseases, but proper health standards and practices keep this problem from getting out of hand. The key thing to be concerned about is determining whether or not a particular day-care center is indeed of high quality. Most states have fairly good licensing requirements for such operations, but even the best licensing requirements are no guarantee. In many areas, personnel are so overburdened that a day-care center may go many months and even years without an on-site inspection. Therefore, it is up to you to check out the day-care center yourself on a regular basis to be sure that all rooms, equipment, and procedures meet—and continue to meet—your standards.

How do I go about finding a high-quality day-care situation for my baby?

Begin by talking to relatives, friends, and coworkers about their day-care arrangements, and gather a list of possibilities. Next, start inspecting as many facilities as possible. Don't just talk to someone on the phone; go to the facility, more than once if possible, to see for yourself whether it is appropriate and safe for your baby. Among the questions you will want answers to are:
• Does the facility accept children your baby's age?
• Is there a waiting list?

If you need to put your baby in a day-care situation, finding a high-quality facility is only the first step. You'll also need to be actively involved to ensure that your presence is felt at all times.

- Is the facility licensed? While a license does not guarantee a safe environment, most licensed facilities are generally inspected once a year and are evaluated for important factors such as sanitation, fire alarms and extinguishers, and caregiver qualifications. They generally must also have liability insurance. To learn about state regulations in your area, contact your state's department of social services.
- Who will be taking care of your baby, and what are their qualifications? Babies need a steady, experienced, concerned caregiver who will be available for cuddling as well as for taking care of basic needs. Ask to speak with the caregivers, see their credentials, and watch them in action.
- How many caregivers are available? A facility should have a ratio of at least one adult for every three children to be able to provide the necessary care for your baby.
- Do all personnel practice good hygiene? Do they wash their hands before and after tending to each baby? Is the facility itself clean and neat? Are equipment and toys clean and well-maintained?
- Are there arrangements for sick children? Is a pediatrician on call to provide advice?
- Are all personnel trained in first aid and emergency procedures?
- Is it an open facility? In other words, are parents welcome to drop in unannounced and see all areas of the facility?
- Is there a parents' association or other arrangement that allows you frequent access to your child's caregiver? Is there a system for supplying caregivers with feedback about your baby's behavior at home and for receiving similar feedback from them?
- Is the facility easily accessible from your work/home? Are there fees or other penalties charged if you are late in picking up your child due to bad weather, traffic, or car trouble?

Finding a high-quality day-care facility may not be easy, but the more time, effort, and thought you put into the process, the more likely it is that your baby will be safe and that you will have some peace of mind.

How can we remain "completely involved" in our baby's care when we both work?

It's simple. Just remember that day-care personnel are neither your personal servants nor surrogate parents for your baby. Rather, they should be treated as partners in the child-rearing process. This means that you must discuss with them any and all issues having to do with child-rearing policies and practices that will be employed both at home and at the center. It means that you must provide the personnel with full, detailed accounts of what your child does at home and get from them full, detailed accounts of what your child does at the center. It means that you will have to become a part of your child's day-care environment. Most day-care centers have a parent-teacher association, and through that, you can see to it that your priorities and preferences are part of the overall atmosphere and flavor of the center. You also can volunteer your time and talent to your child's individual classroom as often as possible. Day care is not an "answer" but rather an "opportunity," and it's up to you to make the most of it. Too many parents make the mistake of thinking that once they've selected a high-quality facility, their job is done. If a high-quality facility is to do everything it can for your baby, your "presence" must be felt at all times.

Despite taking every precaution, I can't stop worrying about my baby's safety. Am I an overly anxious, overly protective parent?

You certainly are, but you are also a very typical parent. There is nothing more precious to you than your child, and particularly because he is so helpless at this point, it is natural and normal for you to be constantly concerned about his well-being and to be overwhelmed by feelings of complete responsibility. To a certain extent, this is healthy, in that it prods you to do the very best you can to provide a safe and appropriate environment for your baby. However, there will be times when it becomes uncomfortable, and you will gradually have to learn how to relax. As you gain experience and confidence, this will get easier, and although accidents will inevitably occur and set you back a few steps now and then, you'll eventually reach a point where your baby's safety will still remain strongly in the back of your mind at all times, but it will not consume the major part of your consciousness on a daily basis.

JOINING (OR FORMING) A PARENT SUPPORT GROUP

Most parents spend a lot of time reading books and magazine articles, listening to lectures, attending classes, and engaging in other activities in search of experts who will provide them with insightful information and will calm their fears about raising a child. However, many parents overlook some of the best experts available—other parents. Child rearing is not an exact science, and because they have to speak in generalities and talk about averages, the professional experts often present a distorted picture of the child-rearing experience. And, since these experts have a sometimes overwhelming air of authority about them, it is often difficult for parents to receive real comfort from them in certain situations. Therefore, it would be a good idea for you to consider joining a parent support group. Chances are, a few already exist in your community, and you can find them through listings in your local phone directory or newspaper. If there are none, you can start one yourself by posting notices at church or synagogue, the supermarket, or other suitable places. It is almost impossible to extol the benefits of these groups too much. Parents who participate report that they simply couldn't buy anything as valuable as the wealth of practical tidbits they pick up from other mothers and fathers, nor could they ever be made to feel better than they do when they hear that someone else is going through precisely the same emotions and dealing with precisely the same problems that they are. Especially if you can find a small group where the other parents have children who are approximately the same age as yours, you are guaranteed not only to get a lot of information and support, but you'll probably have an enormous amount of fun and form a number of strong and lasting friendships.

A SAMPLING OF SUPERB HOMEMADE TOYS

Particularly during this period, it is never necessary to buy toys for your baby. While stores contain many commercial items that are safe and suitable, none of these products have play value that cannot be duplicated through the application of a little time and talent in your own home. For example, instead of purchasing a mobile, you can simply get a piece of cardboard or white poster board, draw a basic sketch of a human face on it, and attach it securely with adhesive tape to the side of your baby's crib. It may not look like much to you, but as long as it is placed at the proper distance from her eyes, she will enjoy gazing at it just as much as something more complicated and expensive. Using a wooden dowel rod strung across the top of her crib and lashed securely with string on either side, you can provide your baby with a more than adequate crib gym. Simply use two or three pieces of string (to provide stability) to suspend some lightweight, brightly colored pie plates from the rod, and your baby will have a ball swiping and batting at them. By taking an egg-shaped candy or panty-hose container, filling it with discarded buttons or dried beans, gluing it together well, and then gluing on a wooden tongue depressor, you can make a rather ugly but completely effective rattle that your baby will appreciate just as much as any store-bought one. In fact, if you check out what is being offered in the stores, think about what makes them entertaining, then come up with just a bit of ingenuity and creativity, you'll be amazed at how many toys you can make yourself. Just be sure to abide by all the safety standards, such as using nontoxic materials and seeing to it that what you make is durable and can't be broken apart into small pieces by your baby.

SELECTING TOYS AND EQUIPMENT

What role do toys play during the first six months of life?

Play is the business of babies, and toys are the tools of their trade. The items that your baby encounters as she begins to explore her world will nurture her expanding curiosity. They will provide her with chances to collect information that she can use to build concepts of increasing complexity. They will challenge her to develop skills. And they can help her have some fun. However, remember that, during this period in particular, virtually everything in her environment will give her the opportunities and experiences she needs. While appropriate toys certainly can be a part of these processes, no individual item has a unique or tremendously powerful capacity to either teach or entertain your baby all by itself.

What are the important factors to keep in mind as I go about choosing toys for my baby?

First and foremost is safety. Remember, anything that is in your baby's hands is likely to end up in her mouth. Make sure that any item—or any removable part—is no less than an inch-and-a-quarter in any dimension so that it cannot be swallowed and gagged upon. Avoid anything with sharp corners, jagged edges, or pointy protrusions. And see to it that all materials and paints used in the production of any item are nontoxic. Next, check for durability. Don't be shy about removing a toy from its box and giving it a good going-over. If it can be broken into little pieces, if buttons or other decorations can be torn off without too much effort, etc., the toy is potentially dangerous. Also, if it cannot be washed easily and often, the toy can become a health hazard. And finally, look for play value—that is, the extent to which an item matches the current interests and abilities of your baby.

I understand that toy manufacturers have to abide by extensive federal regulations. Does this mean that all products on the market are guaranteed to be safe for my baby?

These regulations go a long way toward protecting your baby from unsafe playthings, but they are not an absolute guarantee. It is always possible that a slightly defective item will slip past the safety checks and end up in a store. Moreover, many toys from other countries that are not subject to such regulations, and many toys that were produced before the regulations went into effect, end up on the more informal markets, such as rummage sales, flea markets, etc. Therefore, before purchasing any plaything for your baby, you would be wise to give it a good going-over yourself to make sure that all safety factors are in order. Furthermore, it is a good idea to periodically check toys you have purchased to make sure they are in good repair. An item that passes all safety checks at the time of purchase can immediately become a serious hazard as soon as it is broken, chipped, or otherwise damaged.

Is the recommended age range that appears on the box a reliable guide when it comes to determining play value?

Unfortunately, no. Because toy manufacturers must comply with federal safety regulations to avoid lawsuits, you can be fairly confident that the age range on the box takes safety considerations into account. Play value, however, is another

matter. The interests and abilities of children change so rapidly during the early years that the truly appropriate age range for nearly all items is rarely greater than a few months. However, since the toy companies are trying to sell as many of their products as possible, it would be financially self-defeating for them to list meaningful but very limited age ranges. Therefore, they typically exaggerate the recommended age range in order to entice as many purchasers as possible. While these recommendations may make sense from a business standpoint, they are almost totally useless as reliable indications of play value. For example, notations such as "for children from birth to age two" are common; however, the interests and abilities of a newborn are likely to be much different from those of a two year old.

Since my baby's interests and abilities will be relatively limited during this period, do I need to buy her a lot of toys or just a few well-chosen items?

While it's true that your baby's interests and abilities will remain somewhat limited, they will advance fairly rapidly

With a little ingenuity, you can make a variety of entertaining—and inexpensive—toys for your infant.

during the first six months. As a result, you may need a large number of different items to keep her entertained and challenged as time goes by. However, this does not mean that you have to make a lot of purchases. Babies at this stage are entranced by and can learn from a wide variety of simple objects, and thus do not need to have a lot of "toys" per se. Moreover, since their interests and abilities change so quickly, it is unnecessary and unwise to invest too heavily in any single plaything during this period. It is helpful to note that there is no toy in any store that your baby must have in order to develop any important concept or skill. Likewise, there is no commercial product with a play value that cannot be easily equalled or even surpassed by collections and combinations of ordinary things you can find lying around your house.

What would be an appropriate first toy for my baby?

Remember that it will be at least two or three weeks before your baby is interested in anything except her own comfort, so, until then, she really won't have much use for toys. Toward the middle to end of the first month, she probably will be awake and alert a little more often, and she will begin to look around at her immediate surroundings. Thus, a well-designed mobile makes an excellent first toy. But be careful. Many commercial mobiles are designed to look most attractive to an adult walking into the nursery rather than to a very young baby lying in the crib. Make sure that the mobile you purchase (or make) has visual targets tilted toward your baby so she can get a good view. Also, keep in mind that during

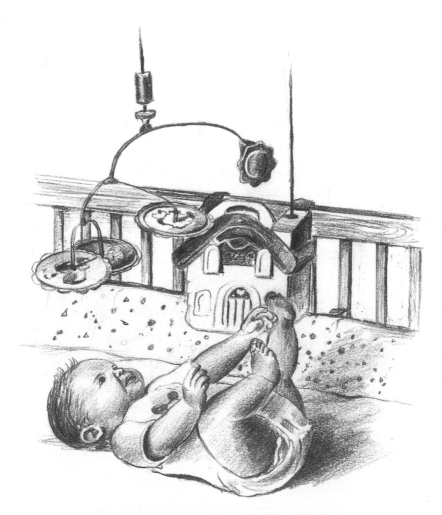

A boldly colored and properly positioned mobile makes an excellent first toy for your infant.

the early months she will be able to focus clearly only on objects that are approximately eight to 12 inches away from her eyes, and she will be in the "fencer pose" (looking off to the side) some of the time, so be sure that the mobile is placed in a proper position and at an appropriate distance. Babies at this stage find it easier to focus on bold colors and contrasts, and human faces are their favorite things to see, so choose (or make) targets accordingly. Don't worry about buying some expensive item that claims to present an especially effective color scheme or geometric pattern. Boldly colored shapes or pictures or even a simple drawing of a human face will do just as well. And finally, make a note to remove all mobiles in a couple of months when your baby will be able to reach for and grab them.

What can I put in and around by baby's crib for her to look at?

In addition to mobiles, babies are fascinated by mirrors. If you attach an unbreakable stainless-steel mirror to the side of her crib, your baby will have hours of enjoyment watching the constantly changing images. Keep in mind that reflected images appear to be twice as far away as the mirror itself, so affix the mirror closer to your baby than you would a mobile while her focusing ability is still limited. As her vision improves over the course of the next few months, you can start introducing colorful pictures on the walls of her room, changing them periodically to avoid boredom. A prism hanging in the window produces an artificial rainbow in the room that your baby may find intriguing. And don't forget to provide items for

An unbreakable mirror mounted on the side of his crib will provide him with hours of enjoyment as he watches the changing images.

her other senses. A music box will bring pleasure to her ears, a variety of textured blankets will interest her sense of touch, and a vase with different flowers or a container for assorted perfumes and scents will be pleasing to her sense of smell. Just remember to keep all of this "stimulation" fairly gentle, and take note that it is all nice, but none of it above and beyond what you would ordinarily find in the room should be considered absolutely necessary.

When she was born, my baby received a lot of rattles and stuffed animals as gifts, but she doesn't play with them. Is this unusual?

Not at all. Although these items typically are among the first playthings presented to babies, they constitute very poor choices for newborns. In the first place, newborns tend to keep their hands in a fisted position, so it is necessary for an adult to pry open their fingers before giving them an object to hold. Once the object is placed in their open hands, they will

grasp it reflexively. However, they will have no idea that they are grasping it, so they won't even look at it—much less shake it or hug it. And, after a few seconds, they will simply drop it, and will show no interest in retrieving it or even any awareness that it is gone. It will be several weeks before your baby can interact with these items effectively.

Once my baby starts using her hands and eyes together, what can I do to enhance her visual/motor activities?

At first, your baby's ability to coordinate her hands and eyes will be rather crude, and she will still be keeping her fingers clenched most of the time. Therefore, her visual/motor activities will consist largely of simply batting and swiping with a closed fist. At approximately two months of age, you can introduce a sturdy crib gym comprised of a strong bar with large target objects suspended well within the range of her arms. Starting at about three months of age, as her fingers unfold and her reaching ability begins to become refined, you

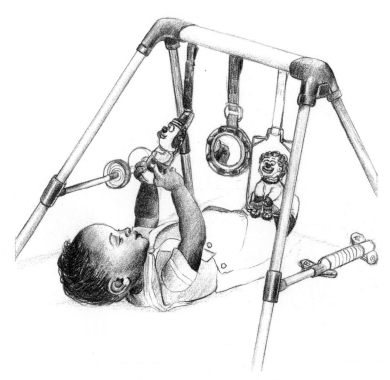

A crib gym should have targets that return fairly quickly to their original position so that your baby has a fair chance to grab them.

can replace this basic crib gym with a more complex device consisting of rings and knobs for your baby to grab or hit; this cause-and-effect feature will provide added enjoyment for your baby. However, do not invest a lot of money in any such item, because as soon as your baby can sit up by herself at approximately five and a half or six months, crib gyms become a safety hazard and should be removed.

Are most of the crib gyms sold in toy stores appropriately designed for babies?

A lot of them are, but many of them are not. The primary design problem found in commercial crib gyms is the use of a single piece of string to suspend the target objects. Remember, your baby is learning to use her hands under the guidance of her eyes for the first time, and getting the hang of it isn't easy. If she reaches out and is lucky enough to grab the target object on her initial attempt, fine. But if she misses and just grazes the target, it will start swinging back and forth wildly,

and she is likely to become extremely frustrated as she makes further attempts. Therefore, any crib gym you choose (or make) should be designed so that the target objects are suspended by plastic or some other semirigid material that allows them to return relatively quickly to their original position; this will give your baby a fair chance to try again. Another common problem is that the recommended age range printed on the box is exaggerated, and the purchase price is high. As enjoyable as these toys are for babies, they will be appropriate only for a brief and specific period of time, so it is suggested that you invest your money accordingly.

What can I provide to keep my baby entertained when she's not in her crib?

Whenever your baby is not in her crib, she will be entertained to a considerable extent simply by the new sights and sounds to which she is exposed, as well as by the people who pick her up, hold her, and play with her. For those times when

Even something as simple as newspaper can make an entertaining toy for your baby. He'll enjoy the sounds it makes as he tears it and crinkles it in his hands.

she is by herself for a while on a blanket on the floor, for instance, you can provide her with a collection of safe, suitable objects for her to explore with her senses. As she becomes more adept at using her fingers to pick up and manipulate things around her, she will enjoy various store-bought items, like rattles and teething rings, along with a wide variety of ordinary household items, such as coasters and key rings. Make sure all items are nontoxic and too large to be swallowed, and try to introduce new textures, colors, and sounds on a regular basis. Also, remember that when she drops, throws, or otherwise loses an object, she won't be able to retrieve it herself. So in order to avoid doing a lot of fetching, it is wise to supply her with a few items within easy reach; using suction cups or string to hold or tether items will limit her opportunities to investigate them and may constitute a safety hazard.

Are there any items that are especially effective in keeping a baby entertained during diapering or bathing?

Your baby's entertainment requirements will not change during such episodes, but your need to keep her entertained may increase substantially. Therefore, if you discover that some particular item seems to hold a special fascination for your baby (a shiny ring with a colorful collection of keys, for example), you may want to hold it "in reserve" and bring it out only when she's especially fussy and/or you're especially busy. Keeping a mirror suspended beside the changing table or bath area will help keep your baby distracted as well. In addition, don't forget that during this period you are easily your baby's favorite toy. Talking to, making faces at, singing to, and stroking your baby will give her a lot of pleasure and occupy a lot of her attention while you get things done.

Is there any toy that is particularly appropriate for a ride in the car?

Keeping your baby entertained while she's in the car may seem problematic on the surface. After all, it is difficult to provide a lot of safe, suitable objects for her to explore with her hands and mouth, and you certainly won't be able to retrieve any that she loses. You can affix a couple of items to her car seat, but she's likely to become bored with them in a hurry. Moreover, your ability to entertain her yourself will be severely limited. However, during this period, babies rarely

require any toys at all when they're in a car. The new and constantly changing sights and sounds usually keep them entranced. What's more, the motion of the car often induces sleep within a short period of time.

Are there any items that my baby and I can play with together?

Not really. For the first two or three months, your baby won't even have a clear sense that you and she are separate entities. For the balance of this period, even though she may have developed interpersonal awareness (awareness of herself as a separate person), her capacity for purposeful, intentional activity will remain limited. Therefore, truly "interactive" items and activities are largely inappropriate at this point. However, once your baby has developed interpersonal awareness, she certainly will be a "reactive" creature and will greatly enjoy simple games that place her at the center of your attention. Making faces, gently bicycling her legs and clapping her hands, and other such activities will entertain her endlessly. They will also set the stage for future games in which she will be able to initiate the action.

How can I make sure that my baby's crib is safe?

Your crib is a reasonably safe place for your baby as long as you've taken appropriate precautions in procuring it and setting it up. You should look for a crib that has a seal of approval from the Consumer Product Safety Commission. The slats of the crib should be less than two-and-three-eighths inches apart so your baby's head cannot get caught between them; you might consider using a set of soft bumpers as well. Naturally, all finishes should be smooth; all paints used should be nontoxic. All hinges and screws should be well set and out of reach, and there should be secure safety latches on the drop side that cannot be tripped, either by your baby or by any curious older children who may have access to the nursery. Also, check to see that the mattress fits snugly—if you can fit two fingers between the mattress and the side of the crib, your baby's head could become wedged there. Make sure the mattress is firm, and don't use any soft pillows or blankets that can become easily bunched; until your baby can lift her head up high for long periods of time by herself, suffocation when lying facedown in materials that are too soft or easily bunched is a real possibility.

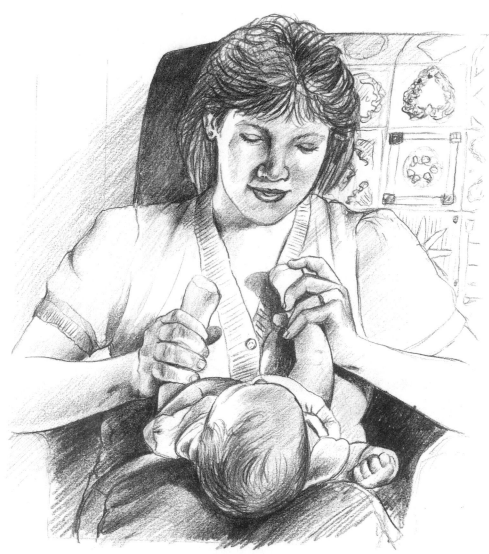

Later in this period, she'll get a kick out of it when you bicycle her legs, clap her hands, or softly poke her and make sounds.

There seem to be several different types of car seats. What should I look for when purchasing one?

For babies who cannot sit upright for long periods of time, or in general, for babies who are less than nine months old or weigh less than 17 to 20 pounds, you should use an infant seat that props the child in a rearward direction and is secured into the front seat of the car. For older and larger children, a seat that holds them upright in a forward-facing position and can be secured into the back seat is appropriate. The latter sort of car seat comes in two types. One is the child model, which has a protector that is lowered in front of the child and is padded to protect her in case of a crash. Since it is locked in place with only the standard seat belt, this model is very convenient, although it limits a curious child's visibility. The other type is the harness model that holds the child in place with shoulder, lap, and crotch straps. In recent years, the manufacturers of these devices have developed many excellent models that can be used in several different ways. In any case, make sure that whatever seat you buy has a label indicating that it meets all federal requirements, that it is comfortable for your baby, that it isn't overly complicated to use, that it fits your car, and that it isn't difficult to attach in case you want to use it in more than one car.

MAKING THE MOST OF YOUR EQUIPMENT PURCHASES

As already noted throughout the answers in this section, there are important safety factors to consider when selecting equipment for your baby. However, you also need to consider practicality. Certain items, such as a crib, a high chair, and a car seat, should be regarded as virtual necessities. But what about all those other items that are for sale? If you're not careful, you can spend a lot of money in a hurry. Therefore, before making a purchase, it is a good idea to review your reasons for obtaining a particular product and see if you can come up with an alternative that will do just as well. For instance, a carriage provides a comfortable ride for a newborn, but once she can sit up by herself, it becomes hazardous. Consequently, you might consider getting a stroller that can be adjusted into a reclining position for the younger baby and into an upright position as she gets older. Similarly, a bassinet and a cradle quickly lose their suitability, whereas many infant seats are designed to convert into either a reclining or upright position and will serve a similar purpose in the early months. A special changing table complete with storage shelves and drawers can make diapering more convenient, but any waterproof surface of sufficient size, placed at a comfortable height and within easy reach of needed supplies, will do the trick. Items such as rocking chairs and slings or backpacks (or frontpacks) can be very nice, but only if they are going to be used. Think about whether you're likely to really use them, and if you are, make sure that they are comfortable before you buy. In general, with a little sound judgment, you often can avoid putting a real strain on your budget in order to provide proper and sufficient equipment for your baby.

Are there any special hazards associated with larger pieces of equipment, such as infant seats, high chairs, and strollers?

There are several hazards, so again, when making purchases, look for the seal of approval from the Consumer Product Safety Commission. Key things to keep in mind are stability and security. Any such device should have a wide base that keeps the device steady and decreases the chance of tipping. It should also have a good harness that fastens firmly and prevents your baby from falling or climbing out. Good support also is important. Particularly during the early months when your baby's back, shoulder, and neck muscles are relatively weak, it is critical that such devices provide sufficient propping. Any minor shortcomings in this regard should be compensated for by folding and fitting in blankets or towels accordingly. Finally, make sure that all surfaces are smooth and nontoxic, and that all hinges, latches, and other such features are in good working order and inaccessible to your baby's hands and fingers.

I've noticed that babies seem to enjoy mechanical swings and jump seats, but I've heard that these products are dangerous. Is that true?

Possibly. It depends on how well-designed they are. Babies, especially during the first few months, need considerable support for the head, neck, and back whenever they are in an upright position. So you need to find a swing or jump seat that provides enough support. With jump seats, you also have to be careful about placing too much stress on delicate bones and joints. If you can find such a well-designed device, your baby probably will enjoy being strapped firmly into it—but only for brief periods of time. As is the case whenever she is kept in one place, with limited options for exploration and investigation, your baby is likely to become bored eventually. Also, as this period draws to a close, overusing any type of restrictive device may limit the number of chances she has to start learning how to get around by herself. Finally, using these devices more than occasionally is dangerous to the extent that they become substitutes for human contact. In other words, your baby may not object to being in her swing or jump seat from time to time, but she will always prefer to be rocked or bounced by you.

Restraining your infant in a suitable car seat is an absolute must whenever she rides in a car—no matter how short the trip.

What about walkers? I've heard that they interfere with proper development of motor skills.

The jury is still out on this one. A well-designed walker (one that provides adequate support and cannot be tipped over easily) will allow a baby to get around on her own before she learns to crawl and walk. For this reason, some child development experts feel that such devices can help to ease a lot of the boredom and frustration that inevitably occurs during the end of this period. While conceding that this may be true, other experts are convinced that using a walker deprives a baby of opportunities and reasons to begin learning how to get around on her own. In addition, the American Academy of Pediatrics points out that walkers are both unnecessary and potentially dangerous. Therefore, if you do decide to use a walker, it is wise to use it sparingly. Also, remember that although your baby may have a fair amount of fun while she's in her walker, the device will enable her to get into a lot of trouble as well, so constant supervision will be required whenever she's in it.

What do I do if, despite all my efforts to keep my baby entertained and happy, she still seems to get bored or frustrated every once in a while?

Be patient. Particularly as babies approach the end of this period, it is inevitable that they will become bored or frustrated from time to time. After all, they've had several months to soak up everything in their immediate environment, and although they now can see, hear, and otherwise sense all sorts of interesting and exciting things going on "out there," they are as yet unable to get to those things on their own. You can double and triple your efforts to bring your baby new and different items and carry her to different areas of your home in order to expose her to new and different scenes. However, no matter how hard you try, it's not likely to be enough. But just wait. Within a few weeks, your baby will achieve the capacity for getting around on her own. When she does, a whole new world of opportunities and experiences will open up for her, and educating and entertaining her will become a piece of cake.

6 MONTHS
TO
1 YEAR

The second half of the first year constitutes a very special period in the life span. Your baby will begin crawling, and she will start to understand some of the language that she hears. She may even take her first steps and say her first words. Her concepts of time and space will expand, and her capacity to interact with you will increase. As your baby acquires increasingly complex abilities and encounters more complicated objects and situations, she will have the opportunity to learn many critical lessons. How well she does will depend largely upon how skillfully you handle the job of shaping her environment and supplying her with appropriate experiences. Your baby will be venturing into a much wider world at this point. She will need you to provide enthusiastic support as well as responsible guidance. You may find the challenges involved to be somewhat imposing on occasion. Rest assured, however, that with adequate awareness of what to expect and sufficient energy to follow through on a few simple strategies, most of these challenges can be mastered easily. The consequences of coping with them successfully will be enormously pleasurable and rewarding for both you and your baby.

HOW YOUR CHILD DEVELOPS

How much physical growth can I expect to see in my baby during the second half of his first year?

Although your baby's rate of growth will start to slow down a little, you will continue to see rapid progress during this period. By the time he is a year old, your baby probably will weigh roughly three times as much as he did at birth and be one-and-a-third times as long. You will also notice that he has "grown into his body" to a major extent. A lot of development will have taken place in the lower portions of his body, so his head will no longer appear so disproportionately large. He is likely to have several teeth at this point, and he may have started to grow hair that will have fairly permanent color and characteristics. It is important to remember, however, that while babies come a long way in physical growth during the first year, the distance they travel is relative to where they started. Therefore, if your baby was at the lower end of the normal range in weight and/or length at birth, it is still too early to expect that he will have caught up to the averages.

When will my baby begin to crawl?

You can expect your baby to start crawling at almost any point during this period (and you should prepare for it by safety proofing your home). Some babies begin crawling at six months of age or even slightly earlier; others don't begin until they are a full year old. Typically, the onset of crawling can be expected at roughly eight months of age. However, during this period and increasingly as your baby gets older, you will be able to rely less and less on "typical" expectations. The normal age ranges for the onset of physical abilities get wider and wider. Therefore, it will become much more difficult to try and predict precisely when your baby will start doing various things by consulting a developmental chart or by comparing him to another child. As if to prove this point, some babies never crawl—they go directly to a more advanced activity. Many babies go from scooting (propelling themselves with their arms), to pulling themselves up, to cruising (see next page), and then to walking without spending any time crawling at all. If this happens with your baby, you should know that it doesn't seem to signify anything special about overall development, so it's nothing to get overly excited or concerned about. Of course, if you ever suspect that your child is not developing normally, consult your pediatrician.

Some babies spend time pushing themselves into a crawling position without actually going anywhere before they learn to crawl.

How will I know my baby is getting ready to crawl?

You probably won't. A lot of babies go through a "precrawling" stage in which they propel themselves short distances by rolling over or pushing themselves across the floor. Others spend a few days or even weeks pushing themselves into a crawling position without going forward before they actually begin to crawl. But these are by no means universal phenomena. There are many babies who seem to be just lying on the floor one day, then crawling like crazy the next. As is the case with any development that has serious implications for safety and educational opportunities, it is a good idea to be well prepared for crawling long before it happens. If you wait until your baby actually starts crawling or try to anticipate the onset of this skill too closely, you may be unpleasantly surprised by how much trouble he has already gotten into before you can safety proof his environment.

What is meant by the term "cruising"?

Cruising refers to a baby's ability to walk while holding on to something, such as the edge of a sofa. Sometime between

eight and 14 months of age, your baby will become capable of grabbing on to something and pulling himself up into a standing position. Shortly after that, it is likely he will begin cruising. Cruising constitutes an important stage between crawling (or scooting) and walking. It allows the baby to move about in a full upright position without subjecting himself to the difficulties and dangers of walking unaided (a skill for which he isn't quite ready). Some parents make the mistake of equating cruising with walking, and they move their baby away from any props because they fear he'll continue to use these things like crutches. Actually, the opposite is true. Cruising allows a baby to practice skills and build confidence so that the act of true walking will come along more easily and effectively.

When can I expect my baby to start walking on his own?

You can expect your baby to start true walking as soon as he is ready, which is as early as nine months of age for some babies and as late as 18 months for others. Typically, babies achieve this major milestone sometime around the first birthday. Unfortunately, parents often tend to place more emphasis on the onset of walking than it deserves from an overall devel-

Cruising allows your baby to practice walking skills and gain confidence so that true walking will come along more easily.

Your baby will start walking when he is ready—which may be as early as nine months of age or as late as 18 months.

opmental perspective. They may "brag" about how soon their baby started walking or "bemoan" the fact that their baby is over a year old and still hasn't started. The fact is that the age at which a baby starts to walk, as long as it is within the very wide "normal range" noted above, is no indication of lasting physical prowess, intelligence, or anything else. So while it is traditional for parents to do so, you should try not to compare your baby's progress in this area to the progress of other children.

Will my baby be able to walk up and down steps before his first birthday?

Actually, it will be quite some time before your baby becomes adept at "walking" up and down steps. However, sometime between seven and 11 months of age, typically at about nine months, you can expect your baby to begin "climbing" up the stairs. Unfortunately, it probably will be about two or three months later before he becomes equally adept at climbing down the stairs. Although stairs probably will be the favorite subject of his climbing activities, once your baby has demonstrated this ability, he will be capable of and interested in climbing anything up to about six inches in height. In other words, his climbing interests may include a few pieces of furniture in your home as well as several of the barriers that you may have put up to keep him out of danger when he first learned to crawl.

How adept at climbing furniture and other things will my baby become during this period?

Sometime between eight and 14 months of age, typically at about ten months, your baby will become capable of climbing things up to roughly 12 inches high. It may not be obvious, but this means he probably will be able to climb up onto most pieces of furniture in your home. For instance, it may be three full feet from the top edge of the sofa to the floor, which would seem, therefore, to be out of his reach. However, at this point, he may be able to climb from the floor to the seat of the sofa, then from the seat to the arm, and finally from the arm to the top ledge. Consequently, when you go about figuring out precisely what your baby will be capable of conquering with his increasing climbing skills, make sure you divide the large pieces of furniture into any smaller increments that he may be able to conquer.

Don't be fooled by her small size. By ten months of age, she may be able to climb things up to 12 inches in height and conquer several pieces of furniture by climbing in increments.

Will my baby's small muscle skills develop rapidly during this period as well?

They certainly will. In fact, you probably will be amazed at how adept your baby becomes at manipulating things with his hands and fingers with each passing month. Of course, his dexterity still will be somewhat limited. For instance, anything that requires him to turn a knob, twist off a cap, or wind up a ratchet-type device is likely to remain outside his skills during this period. However, he will be quite able to pick up very small objects, such as raisins and bits of cold cereal, and to operate simple mechanisms, such as push buttons, levers, and hinges. He also will become very deliberate and accurate when it comes to moving small objects and fairly coordinated with regard to throwing or banging them around.

Since he will be so physically active, will my baby have a chance to learn a lot during this period?

Once your baby starts to crawl, he will have embarked on the greatest period of learning in his entire life. He is still within the "sensorimotor" period of intellectual development, which means he depends on his senses and physical movements to learn. Consequently, with each new physical skill he acquires, he will become that much more able to expand his horizons, add to his experiences, and increase the amount of information entering his mind. In the space of just a few short months, he will have gone from being familiar with little more than his own body and the items in his immediate surroundings to having knowledge of innumerable objects and areas throughout your home.

You'll be amazed at how adept he becomes at picking up small objects—and putting them in his mouth. So you'll need to do your best to keep potentially dangerous items out of his reach.

How will my baby's senses and physical abilities help him to learn?

During the first months of life, your baby spent a lot of time just acquainting himself with what his body could do and with the basic qualities of objects he encountered. Now, as he goes about his more complex and numerous activities, he will discover that he can do a lot more interesting things and that objects have a lot more fascinating qualities. As a result, he will be able to gain enough information to begin building a basic classification system in his mind. Early on, your baby will merely apply his new skills at random. For instance, he will first suck on something he finds, then shake it, then throw it. Eventually, as his various actions produce different results or different degrees of the same result, he will start to develop a simple sense of how to sort out his world. By hearing a toy make a rattling sound, watching a ball roll, and feeling the soothing effect of a teething ring, he will learn that some objects are "things to be shaken," others are "things to be thrown," and still others are "things to be sucked." He also will learn some essential principles about the relationship between actions and things, such as harder, faster, louder, etc.

As he explores his surroundings, he'll use whatever "tools" he has to begin sorting out his world.

Will my baby only understand "what" happens, or will he understand "how" it happens as well?

At first, your baby will not have a true understanding of cause and effect. All he will realize is that his behavior has some "magical" power. Thus, for example, he may notice that banging on his crib rails results in the crib bumpers flapping; and, enjoying that event, he will repeat his banging to make it happen again. Later, he may notice the window curtains fluttering in the breeze, and he may very well bang on his crib rails in the expectation that this will cause the curtains to move again. By the end of this period, however, your baby probably will have a much better sense of cause and effect. As a result of using his simple strategies over and over again in different situations, he will have learned a great deal. He will be able to start coordinating his strategies to cope with more complex challenges. For example, earlier on, if he saw a toy on a table but couldn't reach it, he might have been stuck. He might have waved his arms or kicked his feet, but all to no avail. Now, there is a good chance he will crawl over and pull the tablecloth, causing the toy and everything else to tumble down to where he can reach it.

Is my baby now capable of "intentional" action?

In the most basic sense of the word, your baby is now indeed capable of "intentional" action. By using one object to reach another, he is demonstrating that he is capable of simple problem solving and is engaging in truly purposeful, goal-directed behavior. However, it is important to remember that your baby still is a long way from what could be called "premeditation." In other words, when presented with a given set of simple circumstances, he will be able to "figure out" what to do and "plan" a course of action accordingly. However, his ability to do so will be limited to things that are immediately available to his senses and movements, and only his needs and desires of that moment will be factored in. Therefore, although your baby may display some strong and distinct intentions, be careful not to read too much into what he is doing at this stage.

What is meant by the term "object permanence"?

Object permanence refers to a baby's capacity to hold an image of something in his mind after it has been removed from direct contact with his senses. During the first months of life, if your baby dropped, threw, or otherwise lost something with which he was playing, that was it—out of sight was out of mind. Starting at about seven or eight months of age, you will notice that your baby will look around a bit for items he has just lost. This indicates that he can now retain a picture of the item in mental form. Interestingly, however, the manner in which he uses this new capacity will remain closely tied to his physical experiences for a while. For instance, if you hide a toy under a pillow, your baby will look for it and may eventually find it there. Then, if you put the toy under a different pillow, even though he sees you doing it, he may immediately look for the toy under the first pillow instead. To him, the act of "finding" is still limited to the initial experience. In other words, although your baby will be developing some major mental abilities, it will take him some time to learn how to use them effectively in various situations.

Does this mean my baby will remember everything from now on?

This does mean that your baby probably will "remember" most of what he encounters, but he won't "remember" any of it for very long. The capacity to retain a mental image in the mind does indicate that the function of memory is now in place. At first, however, that memory is extremely short-term. Consequently, if your baby loses something, he will look for it. If he doesn't find it within a few seconds, however, he will forget about it. With each passing week, his memory will become a little longer. Even by the end of this period, though, the mental images that he forms probably won't hang around for more than a minute or two. Keep in mind that this doesn't mean your baby won't be able to "recognize" things. He definitely will react in an appropriate manner to many things with which he is familiar. However, for the time being, those things will still have to be directly available to his senses for the most part in order for his "knowledge" of them to be activated.

Even though he isn't talking yet, my baby seems to understand some of what I'm saying to him. Is this possible, or am I imagining things?

One of the more common misconceptions about babies is that they don't start language learning until they start to talk.

WHAT ABOUT BABIES WHO ARE BORN PREMATURE?

During the past decade or so, medical science has made tremendous strides in the areas of prenatal and perinatal medicine. Many premature babies who previously would not have survived more than a few hours or days are now being saved. Unfortunately, it will take a while before psychologists and educators have enough experience with such children to be equally expert at predicting their rates and patterns of development during the early years. Clearly, if the extent of the prematurity is severe and there are serious physical deficiencies or complications at birth, there will be directly related developmental problems. However, for those children who are essentially healthy, the picture is a little cloudy. The research simply is not extensive enough at this point to make any broad, declarative statements. The general consensus among child development specialists, however, is that parents of premature babies should use their baby's original due date—as opposed to his actual birth date—as a standard for measuring his progress against the usual standards and norms. In other words, if the average age of onset for a particular ability is eight months of age, and your baby was born two months premature, you can expect him to achieve that ability somewhere around ten months of age instead. Again, this is simply a general rule of thumb. In addition, it appears that the older the child gets, the less likely there are to be any substantial differences between what can be expected of him and what can be expected of a full-term child, so this rule of thumb may be applicable for only two or three years.

The fact of the matter is that "receptive" language develop-ment (understanding spoken words) usually begins well before "expressive" language development (saying words). Although he may not speak for several months yet, sometime between six and eight months of age your baby will start to understand the meaning of his first words. By the time he is a year old, you can expect him to understand up to a couple dozen words. These first understood words will relate to things with which he is very familiar—"bottle," "spoon," "diaper," and his own name are typical examples. He also is likely to under-stand a few simple instructions at this point, such as "wave bye-bye," "give a kiss," and "stop."

My baby has started to do a lot of babbling, but he hasn't really said anything intelligible yet. Is something wrong?

Not at all. Babies are fascinated with sound, whether or not it is connected to language. Earlier on, you may have noticed your baby gurgling and otherwise entertaining himself in his crib. Now that his ability to make sounds is getting more refined, he will enjoy producing speechlike vocalizations, even though he really isn't trying to "say" anything. Since he is developing the capacity for imitation as well, you may notice that he's starting to mimic your voice tones and inflections. Listening to him "talking" like this without hearing him say anything intelligible may be disconcerting. Keep in mind, how-ever, that at this point he is producing sounds largely for the purpose of "play" rather than specifically for communication.

When can I expect my baby to actually say his first words?

The normal range for the onset of speech is incredibly large. Some babies say their first words at almost the same time that they begin understanding words (between six and eight months of age). Others hardly say anything until they are almost two years old. As is the case with walking, parents have a tendency to put more emphasis on this milestone than it really deserves. As long as your baby displays an ever-progressing understanding of words during this period, you should not worry about whether or not he is speaking. There is no evi-dence whatsoever that ultimate levels of language skill, intelli-gence, or anything else are tied to the age at which a baby begins to talk, so try to avoid making inappropriate compari-sons between your baby's performance and that of other children in this regard.

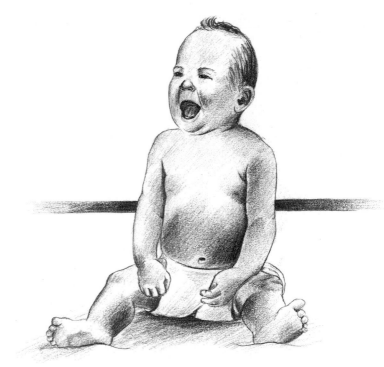

Although he probably won't be able to "say" anything, he'll enjoy making all sorts of speechlike sounds.

Since he's now getting around on his own, is my baby becom-ing less dependent upon me for emotional support?

On the contrary. Your baby is now capable of getting around on his own—or at least capable of doing so comfortably—because he has you for emotional support. Although it may seem like a contradiction on the surface, the fact is that your baby can begin to move away from you only when he is confi-dent that you will still "be there" for him when he needs you. Babies who are insecurely attached to their parents have a lot of trouble moving out to explore the world because they lack such trust; instead, they must keep trying to establish an emo-tional bond with the key people in their lives. The fact that your baby is eagerly venturing out on his own means his bond with you is strong enough to sustain brief but significant sepa-rations. However, at this point, the formation of that special bond is still some distance from being complete. So while he's certainly going out on his own a lot, you'll notice that he is rarely going very far for very long. And while he's certainly interested in exploring new things, you are still his favorite target of interaction.

All of a sudden, our baby has started getting upset when he is approached by anyone other than us—even by his grandparents. Is this normal?

Episodes of this "stranger anxiety" during the second half of the first year are quite normal, although they are by no means universal. When babies first develop social awareness, they tend to be extremely gregarious and will accept approaches from just about anyone. Now, however, as they strengthen key emotional bonds and develop a greater sense of social interactions, they tend to focus on the key people in their lives—typically, their parents. With many—but not all—babies, this focusing of affection results in a strong exclusion of almost everyone else. This produces alarming rejections which can be quite disturbing to people—such as grandparents—who were readily accepted just a couple of months earlier. Whether or not a child experiences these episodes of stranger anxiety doesn't seem to make a significant difference in overall development. In any event, they usually diminish a great deal and may even disappear completely by the first birthday.

I've heard that the roots of self-esteem are formed before the first birthday. Is this true?

It certainly is. What your baby thinks about himself comes primarily from two sources—what he can do, and what other people think about what he does. During this period, your child will be spending a lot of time and effort struggling to crawl, pull to stand, climb, walk, etc. Whenever he finally accomplishes one of these tasks, he will actually feel a sense of physical relief. The good feeling that comes with eventually achieving what he has set out to do is the earliest form of "self-satisfaction." Furthermore, whenever he achieves one of these new skills, he usually witnesses an outpouring of enthusiastic applause and genuine excitement from his parents. These parental responses gradually become internalized, and they serve as the foundation for your baby's "pride" in his own achievements.

THE DAWNING OF DEVELOPMENTAL DIVERGENCE

The abilities that emerge during the first six months of life apparently are so essential to survival that they hold up remarkably well to changes in environmental conditions. In other words, as long as a baby is exposed to anything resembling a "standard" environment during the first half year, his developmental progress is not likely to be in jeopardy. However, during the second half of the first year, this picture starts to change dramatically. The optimal development of many skills is clearly sensitive to outside factors from this point on. As a result, it is during this period that noticeable differences in rates and patterns of progress begin to surface fairly regularly among different groups of children according to gender, race, ethnicity, etc. Of course, the debate about whether or not these differences are largely due to genetic heritage and chromosomal makeup has raged for decades, and probably will never cease completely. But research overwhelmingly indicates that nearly all of these differences can be explained by such changeable factors as socioeconomic status, cultural traditions, and child-rearing styles. For example, perhaps the most consistent gender difference that has appeared over the years is the fact that the language development of girls proceeds more quickly than that of boys. However, extensive studies have shown that parents routinely talk a lot more to their female babies than they do to their male babies. Research also shows that baby boys tend to suffer more ear infections than do baby girls. Both of these factors could have an effect on language development. Therefore, even though child-development specialists admit that there are gender, race, and ethnic differences in development, this does not mean that they accept them as unalterable.

UNDERSTANDING YOUR CHILD'S BEHAVIOR

Will my baby now be awake and alert for virtually the entire day?

Maybe she will and maybe she won't. During the second half of the first year, the sleeping needs and patterns of babies become even more variable. On average, babies tend to sleep about 13 hours a day during this period. The normal range, however, can be anywhere from as few as nine hours to as many as 18. Typically, babies will sleep approximately ten to 12 hours during the night and will supplement that with two naps during the day. The naps may last as little as 20 minutes or as long as two to three hours. If your baby's sleep requirements were on the high end of the range during the first six months, you probably can expect her to remain on the high end, and vice versa. Beyond that, you will just have to wait and see what your baby's own individual sleep requirements will be as time goes by.

Once my baby starts to crawl, will I have to entice her to begin exploring beyond her immediate environment?

On the contrary—you may find it impossible to stop her. The innate curiosity that all babies have is a powerful force. For the couple of months prior to the onset of crawling, it builds up to almost uncomfortable levels. Babies can see and hear all sorts of things that are some distance away, but they can't get to them on their own, so frustration tends to set in. Consequently, as soon as they achieve the capacity for loco-motion, they're off and running—or crawling, as the case may be. And you certainly don't have to worry about your baby being afraid at this point. While curiosity is inherent, fear is something that has to be learned. As long as your baby has been made to feel safe and secure so far, there is no reason why she won't venture out into her wider world eagerly.

Will my baby's curiosity be limited to "places," or will she still be interested in "things," too?

Your baby will be interested in everything. Of course, she will spend a lot of time scooting around to every area of the house to

She will now spend a lot of time investigating and exploring the details of everything she encounters.

which she has access. However, she also will spend a great deal of time investigating anything and everything she finds in those areas. First of all, with her new capacity for locomotion, she is likely to encounter an enormous number of items that she never came across before. Each one will be totally fascinating to her. Furthermore, now that she is more adept at using her body—and particularly her hands and fingers—she will be investigating all items she encounters much more thoroughly than before, even those with which she previously had a fair amount of experience. By the way, your baby also will begin to develop a strong interest in how things work, so simple gadgets will be a favorite target of her curiosity.

My baby is fascinated by a flushing toilet. Is this strange?

This is perfectly normal and quite common. We tend to take the toilet for granted. To a baby who is being exposed to it for the very first time, however, it is an irresistibly intriguing and exciting thing. The seat, the base, the water, and all the other parts present a variety of textures and temperatures to the touch. The flush creates a flurry of sights and sounds that are extraordinarily rich and varied. And the flush handle is so simple to use that even the baby herself may be able to operate it, yet it produces results that are spectacular. Consequently, it really is no surprise that almost all babies fall in love with the toilet, especially if they are given opportunities to flush it themselves. But keep in mind that toilets are dangerous—a baby is capable of crawling in and could drown—so these activities must always be closely supervised at this point.

Will my baby's curiosity also include people to a great extent?

Yes and no. During this period, your baby will become intensely curious about the key people in her life—her parents. Virtually everything you do will be of interest to her. She also will be interested in your physical features (a fascination with earlobes, for instance, is common). On the other hand, this intense interest in the primary caregivers often comes at the expense of everyone else. You may discover that your baby is no longer as "friendly" toward outsiders as she used to be. However, although you will continue to be a favorite object of her curiosity for a long time to come, this reluctance to include other people will diminish gradually. It may even disappear entirely by the end of the first year.

My baby ordinarily is very happy when she's exploring around the house, but when I take her out, she usually gets anxious and clingy. What's she afraid of?

She really isn't afraid of anything; she's probably just a little insecure—and that's perfectly normal. What you are seeing is generally referred to as "attachment behavior." As noted earlier, in order to explore and investigate her world, your baby needs to know that you are there for her in case she needs you. Since she is reasonably familiar with and therefore very comfortable in her own home, she probably will exhibit such behavior only occasionally in the house. However, going out involves the introduction of a whole new set of items and experiences. Before she can go about absorbing them, she may feel the need to double-check her emotional base. Despite its often unpleasant nature, this sort of behavior actually is a healthy sign at this point. And although it may get fairly

DOES BIRTH ORDER AFFECT BEHAVIOR?

Over the years, research has consistently shown that birth order is routinely related to various behavioral traits. For instance, firstborns tend to be more verbal than their siblings, but their siblings tend to be more independent. Also, firstborns tend to be more "successful" in the conventional sense, but their siblings tend to suffer less stress and be generally more content. Of course, these traits are by no means universal—there are always numerous exceptions. It is clear, however, that one's position in the family is usually a fairly influential factor. Again, it appears that these phenomena are not inevitable, but rather that they are the result of distinctly different child-rearing styles. Most parents will swear that they treated all their children exactly the same, but studies have revealed that this usually is not the case. Parents typically spend almost three times as many minutes each day in direct interaction with their first baby as they do with later babies. This could account for the greater verbal skills of firstborns and the greater independence of the younger siblings. Also, parents tend to be extremely anxious about the achievements of their firstborn, whereas by the time subsequent children come along, they've learned to be a lot more relaxed. This could account for the striving for success by firstborns and the relatively laid-back attitude of subsequent children. Therefore, if you see your child developing a trait of which you are not particularly fond, and someone attributes it to the fact that she is the firstborn, the middle child, or the baby of the family, keep in mind that it may be the result of something in your own behavior that may be easily altered.

intense on occasion, you can expect it to start diminishing by the end of this period.

Would my baby rather explore than spend time with me?

As far as she's concerned, your baby is spending time with you as she explores. Your general presence constitutes a significant part of her experience at all times. She will rarely venture very far away from you for very long. In addition, when she goes off to explore and investigate her wider environment, she will repeatedly return to you in the course of her activities and try to initiate a more direct kind of interaction. Therefore, you should not interpret her increasing independence as a sign that she's losing interest in you. In fact, there still will be plenty of times when your baby will prefer to interact with you exclusively. A good balance between social and nonsocial interests, with a lot of easy flow between the two, is a sign of healthy progress during this period.

If my baby loves to explore, why will she sometimes stop her explorations and seek me out?

Occasionally, your baby will simply tire of her explorations and will seek you out for a change of pace. However, her approaches to you more often will be for one of three major reasons. The first is that she is hurt and needs comforting; for example, she may get her finger caught in a doorjamb and want you to kiss it and make it better. The second is that she is stuck and requires adult assistance; for example, she may be pushing together and pulling apart a panty-hose container, and the sixth time she pushes it together she can't get it apart again. And the third is that she has made a new discovery and would like to share her joy and excitement with someone; for example, she may find an old piece of chewing gum covered with dust balls under the sofa, and she may simply be overwhelmed with the wonder of it all. By the way, once she gets whatever it was she needed or wanted from you, you can expect your baby to go on her merry way. As a result, most of these exchanges will be relatively brief.

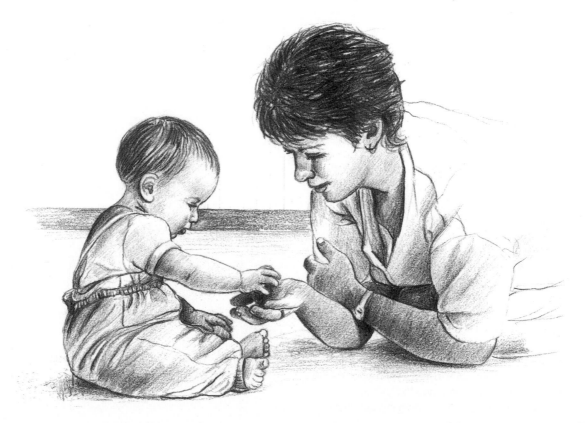

During her explorations, she may sometimes seek you out simply to share her excitement over something she's discovered.

My baby goes off on her own without problem, but when I leave her, she tends to get very upset. Does this mean she's insecure?

Yes, but probably only a little. Remember, although your baby's sense of attachment to you is very strong during this period, it is not totally complete. Whenever she's feeling confident about that attachment, she will not hesitate to initiate a separation. However, when you initiate a separation, there's a chance that you will catch her off guard and cause her some concern. Despite the fact that her concern may be expressed as something resembling minor panic, you can be assured that this is probably only a temporary reaction. Day-care personnel and baby-sitters routinely report that within a few minutes after a separation that has left both the parents and the baby severely distraught, the child usually recovers quite nicely. The parents, on the other hand, generally continue to suffer until everyone is reunited later. Therefore, this is not something about which you should worry a great deal. As time goes by and your baby repeatedly sees that while you may leave her on occasion you will always return to her, this will become less and less of a problem.

My baby usually approaches her three-year-old brother easily, but when he approaches her, she often cries. Why is that?

Although your baby's intense interest in people will be largely restricted to her parents during this period, it will include other members of the household to a significant extent. You can expect her, therefore, to be curious about her brother's activities and to approach him fairly often. However, because a slightly older sibling is likely to feel a lot of jealousy and hostility toward a baby and has probably expressed his resentment in somewhat violent fashion for several months, your baby has learned to be wary when she is approached by her brother. She also has learned that her cries will bring you to rescue her in case of trouble. Consequently, what you are seeing now is a sign of her increasing intelligence. On a simple level, she has figured out that it is better to cry before her older brother gets close enough to do any harm than to wait until the damage has been done. By the way, while this self-protection mechanism is usually very effective, it can cause problems sometimes. If you're not aware of it and don't keep a close eye on the situation when they are together, there is a good chance that your son will be unjustly accused of harming his little sister on occasion.

She'll put nearly everything she finds into her mouth so she can "investigate" it further.

My baby still puts almost everything into her mouth. Is this normal?

It certainly is. Although your baby is becoming more adept at using her hands and fingers every day, her mouth will still be her primary tool for sensory exploration during this period. You may notice that she will first manipulate an item and then suck on it, gum it, and perhaps even try to eat it. On occasion, you also may see her put something into her mouth directly, almost as if by force of habit. Furthermore, you should be aware that when your baby is hungry or thirsty, she will eat or drink almost anything she comes across—no matter how horrible it smells or tastes. Babies simply are not very discriminating at this point, so you have to be careful about what they have access to. This tendency to put everything in the mouth may diminish somewhat as the months go by, but it probably will linger at least a little for quite some time.

My baby spends almost as much time throwing and banging objects as she does studying them. Is something wrong with her?

Not at all. When your baby throws and bangs objects, she is studying them just as much as when she is looking at them or feeling them. Previously, her interest in various items was limited to their basic sensory characteristics; but now, her inter-

THE SURPRISING STRENGTH AND SPEED OF BABIES

Just when parents finally feel that they have recovered from the exhaustion that comes from staying up with their newly arrived infant, they find that they are beginning to suffer from a new kind of exhaustion—that which comes from trying to keep up with their newly crawling baby. Most first-time parents are absolutely amazed by the speed and strength displayed by their little babies during the second half of the first year. There's a story about Jim Thorpe—Olympic champion, professional football player, and one of the greatest athletes in American history. It seems that one day he volunteered to baby-sit for his neighbors who had a newly crawling baby. Thorpe decided that the easiest thing to do would be to get down on the floor and just follow the baby wherever she went and do whatever she did. Several hours later, when they returned home, the neighbors found Thorpe fast asleep on the floor and their baby still going about her explorations with full vigor and enthusiasm. This story may fall into the "legend" category, but it probably contains more fact than fiction. Don't be fooled by your baby's tiny stature and innocuous appearance—she's going to be a real tiger during this period. So now that she probably will be sleeping through the night for the most part, make sure you take advantage of that fact and get a good night's sleep yourself—you're really going to need it the next day.

ests have expanded to include both what these items can do and what she can do with them. For instance, before, she may have been content to investigate the look and feel of a key ring. Now, however, she is compelled to find out what happens to a key ring when it is dropped, what kind of sound it makes when it is shaken, and how you will react when she throws it. In other words, your baby is every bit as studious as she was previously, only now her studies have taken on a far more active quality in many cases.

When she's in her high chair, my baby likes to drop a lot of her food on the floor. Is she trying to make me crazy or what?

She may very well make you crazy with such activities, but that certainly is not her intention at this point. She simply

To your baby, his food is like many other things in his world— new, exciting, and full of opportunities to play and learn.

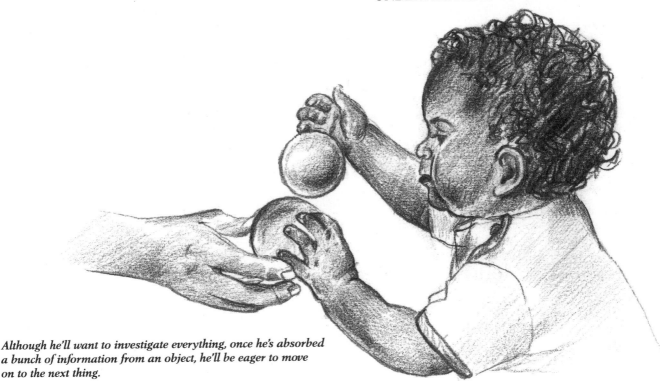

Although he'll want to investigate everything, once he's absorbed a bunch of information from an object, he'll be eager to move on to the next thing.

doesn't yet have the mental capacity to be malicious, so don't take it personally when she makes a mess at mealtime. This is just another instance of her healthy curiosity exploding all over the place. The food in front of her not only has nutritional value, it provides a number of opportunities for learning experiences. For example, she will be fascinated by the way a piece of gelatin wobbles when she touches it, she will be thrilled by the sensation she gets when she squishes it through her fingers, and she will be delighted by what she sees and hears when it goes "splat" on the floor. Consequently, this is a time when parents have to exercise a little patience and understanding. You may be in a hurry to get through the feeding, but your baby won't be able to resist studying her food in all sorts of ways before she eats it.

Although she can become intensely interested in an object or an activity, my baby rarely stays interested in it for very long. Is she hyperactive?

Only to the extent that all babies could be characterized as hyperactive at this point. Although babies are intensely curious, their attention spans are not very long. Remember, all of their thinking is still sensorimotor—that is, they are processing everything through their physical movements and senses. They

have yet to develop the ability to really work with mental images. Consequently, once they have absorbed a bunch of information from one object or activity, they quickly will move on to the next. Furthermore, you have to keep in mind that so many things around your baby are brand new and irresistibly intriguing to her. As captivating as any single item may be, it is constantly surrounded by high-powered competition, so your baby will be easily distracted from even the most fascinating ones.

Every once in a while, my baby will stop her explorations and appear to be just staring into space. What's happening?

This is just a continuation of the "steady staring" she has been doing for several months. Because she tends to be so active so much of the time, it may be a lot more noticeable and somewhat more alarming at this point, but it still is perfectly normal. While your baby is going places, doing things, and otherwise exploring and investigating her environment, there will be times when she is inclined to just sit and soak up the sights, sounds, and sensations that surround her. It may not be as impressive as her other activities, but this steady staring remains an important part of the way in which your baby learns about and comes to understand her world.

Once my baby achieves a new physical ability, like pulling herself to a standing position, she tends to do it over and over. Why is that?

Once your baby achieves a new physical ability, it takes time for her to achieve confidence in that ability, so she will do it several times just to make sure she's got it down pat. From that point on, she will continue to repeat the process for the pure pleasure she gets from exercising her body. In other words, these new skills are not only useful to your baby, they are exciting and enjoyable for her as well. Consequently, as part of and in addition to her explorations and investigations, you can expect your baby to spend a lot of time simply "working out." Naturally, she will continually be seeking out and conquering new physical challenges as the months go by, but she will constantly be taking opportunities to practice those physical skills that she's already mastered.

Since my baby still can't communicate by talking, why is it that she's doing a lot less crying now?

Although she may as yet be unable to put a lot of things into words, your baby is becoming increasingly effective in her nonverbal forms of communication. She is realizing that she is more likely to get what she wants through specific sounds and actions than through a general wail. Since you probably are anxiously awaiting her first words, it is easy to overlook how far your baby has come in this regard. If you think about it, however, the two of you have had some fairly full "conversations" recently. For example, when your baby came to you holding her empty cup, then gave it to you and uttered "uh, uh" or something similar, the result was pretty much the same as if she had come right out and said, "Pardon me, but I seem to be running low on this stuff, and I understand that you are someone who can get more of it for me."

Once she learns how to do something like pulling to stand, she'll practice it over and over again.

Lately, even though she isn't saying anything intelligible, my baby seems to be mimicking my voice tones and inflections. Is this possible?

It certainly is. It is during this period that your baby will first become capable of truly imitative behavior. Given her strong interest in you and her strong interest in sounds, one of her favorite things to imitate will be your voice. This activity not only is very entertaining for her, it is also an important part of language learning. By the way, you probably will notice that your baby is mimicking a lot more than just your voice. Because her body movements are not yet perfectly coordinated and graceful all the time, it may be difficult to pick up on occasion. However, if you watch her while she is watching you do something, you'll be able to see her attempting to do something similar herself. Toward the end of this period, you may even see a complete combination of voice and action imitation as your baby picks up a toy telephone and mimics the way you hold and dial it as well as the way you speak into it.

Obviously, my baby sometimes does things I wish she wouldn't, but is she truly capable of "misbehaving" at this point?

Although she has developed some capacity for intentional action, your baby's mental processes are still pretty much limited to dealing with the here and now. What's more, her own wants and needs are pretty much the only things that influence her behavior to a significant extent. This means that she is not really capable of either "premeditation" or "self-control." Therefore, she cannot be considered to be deliberately "misbehaving" in the standard sense of the word. However, her tremendous curiosity combined with her increasing physical skills certainly give her the ability to get herself into a lot of trouble and otherwise do things that can be considered "wrong" or "bad." Since she will not be able to comprehend such concepts on anything but an extremely fundamental level for several months, it is incumbent upon you to channel and set limits upon her behavior. In other words, at this point, your baby should not be condemned for misbehaving, but that doesn't mean you should ignore or tolerate the things she does that you wish she wouldn't do.

During this period, your baby will become capable of imitative behavior—and his favorite subject will be you. Toy telephone in hand, he'll mimick not only your mannerisms but your voice tones and inflections as well.

DAILY CARE BASICS

My baby kicks and squirms whenever I try to change his diaper. It's annoying as well as messy. What can I do to make it less of a hassle?

Babies love to squirm and can often make diaper changing a tussle or battle of wills. So whenever you change him, try to be firm and matter-of-fact. Have everything close at hand and be as quick and efficient as you can. While changing him, calmly and firmly restrain him and talk or sing to him to distract him; afterwards, give him big hugs and/or free him as soon as possible. You may be able to divert his attention during diapering by giving him a special toy to play with, one that you keep on the side for just such occasions. On the other hand, he may toss the toy and work on getting a reaction from you. If you're firm, however, he'll get the idea. Gather up your sense of humor and be assured this stage will pass.

Although I change my baby's diaper frequently, he still gets diaper rashes. Why? What else can I do to help prevent diaper rash?

Almost all babies get diaper rashes. Many factors contribute to these rashes, including skin color and sensitivity, amount of contact with moisture, amount of contact with air, and diaper type. Many disposable diapers fit so snugly that no air circulates to the baby's skin, so the natural skin moisture and urine stays on the skin and causes the irritating rash. To help minimize diaper rashes, use cloth diapers loosely fastened with diaper pins or diaper holders whenever possible. In the presence of a rash, remove the diaper as soon as possible after it becomes wet or soiled, cleanse the area thoroughly, and, if the rash is moist, apply a small amount of drying powder. Allow the baby's diaper area to air dry whenever practical, and use tight-fitting diapers or plastic pants as little as possible. Nothing prevents all diaper rashes, but these hints can help minimize them.

Allowing your baby's sensitive bottom to air dry whenever possible will help keep diaper rash to a minimum.

When time allows, making a game of dressing can help make the process more enjoyable for you and your baby.

My nine month old hates me to dress him. How can I make it easier for both of us?

Babies hate to hold still and they dislike having clothing pulled over their heads. So one of the best ways to make dressing easier is to use the simplest on-off clothing. Try to provide as many open-neck and open-front shirts (shirts with buttons or snaps) as possible. Pull-on pants with snaps in the diaper area are the simplest, but you'll still require a minute or two of the baby holding still to accomplish the task. Try not to use clothing with tight sleeves, since sticking little wiggly arms in them is cumbersome. Soon the baby will learn to help you by raising his arms, but not just yet. Remember, babies have no patience, and often their goals have nothing to do with yours. They will cooperate at times, but never when they sense that you're in a hurry or stressed. Try talking or singing to the baby throughout the process, even if you are in a hurry. If you have more time, play peek-a-boo with the clothing as you dress him; sometimes making a pleasant game out of it will distract and please him. If not, try not to display a major reaction when he fusses, since doing so will likely encourage a similar response from him. Be gently firm and brisk, and get the job done. When you're finished, offer him

big hugs and send him on his way. Always praise him when he displays preferred behavior. When he's older and able to help choose his clothing, offer him simple choices to give him some control over the dressing process.

Sometimes my baby takes long naps, then he doesn't want to go to bed on time at night. Can I influence his schedule?

You can try to influence your baby's schedule by determining the length of naps and the timing of meals, but usually the baby will sleep when he's sleepy and eat when he's hungry. Babies require different amounts of sleep and food at different times, just like their parents. With babies, the need for longer naps will often be associated with a rapid growth spurt. Although appetite can change from day to day, the need for an increased amount of food can also accompany a growth spurt. Depending upon your child-raising philosophy, you can remain flexible or you can try to alter the baby's schedule to better fit in with the family's schedule. If he's going to sleep at night only an hour or so later than you'd like him to, you can probably try to work around his schedule. However, if he's going to sleep two to three hours later than you'd like, you'll probably want to try nipping one of his daily naps. If the baby is sleeping too long at one nap time, you might shorten the next one. He may or may not be cranky the rest of the day. Likewise, he may fall asleep more easily at the preferred bedtime, or he may be overly tired and cry and fuss at you longer. You'll probably have to do a little experimenting. You might also try to stimulate and play with him more during awake periods; this may help him use up enough energy so that he's tired enough to fall asleep when you want him to. You don't, however, want to overstimulate or excite the baby just before bedtime, since this defeats your purpose. Your baby will need a little quiet time before he can relax and fall asleep.

My nine month old wakes me up at night because he is wet. But once I change him, he wants to play rather than go back to sleep. How can I handle this?

Try changing the baby just before you go to bed, and maybe that will get him through the night. You might also try double diapering, using plastic pants, or using a disposable diaper with extra absorbency to help him feel more comfortable and

allow you both to sleep through the night. Although the baby's skin needs to have some exposure to air to stay healthy, using the heavier diapering or plastic pants only at night may be okay. You might also try adding a blanket or using a sleeper to keep him warmer; it could be the cold more than the dampness that wakes him. Your baby expects you to take care of his needs. You have needs, too, but allowing him to just cry it out may not be the way to handle this. When you change him, be as brief as possible. Let him know it's time for sleeping. If he cries once his diaper has been changed, it's okay. If you allow him to keep you awake just to play, you reinforce his awake time, and he'll expect the same treatment in the future.

My nine month old has started to pull himself up in his crib. Is there anything I can do to prevent him from climbing out?

Pulling up in the crib is the first step in learning to climb out. Lower the crib mattress as a temporary measure. As soon as he comes close to climbing out, lower the rail to make sure he can get out without injury. You can also move the crib to a corner and pad the floor with extra carpeting. If you are still worried about him hurting himself, you might want to

If your baby has started to pull herself up in her crib, you can lower the crib mattress to keep her from climbing out.

put the mattress on the floor as his new sleeping arrangement until he is ready to try a youth bed. Once he can get out of his crib, however, you have to make sure that his room is safety proofed and that there is a gate at the door of his room to prevent him from wandering around and getting into trouble if he wakes up before you do. Do whatever is most comfortable for you and your baby while keeping him safe.

My baby fusses whenever I put him in his playpen, but when I need to get something done, it's the only safe place for him to be. How can I make him happier in his playpen?

Some babies never like their playpens. They feel thwarted and restricted—and they are. Still, it's much better to infuriate the baby than to allow him the freedom to hurt himself. Whether he likes it or not, the playpen is the safest place for him when you need to do something that takes you into another room or focuses your attention away from the baby. If the baby has his own room, you might try safety proofing the entire room and placing a gate at the door so that it can be used as a larger "play yard." This is satisfying to some babies, but not all. You might also try keeping the playpen from getting too cluttered; having a few toys rather than many and having more room to move around may make him happier in his playpen. Try rotating the toys used in the playpen. Remove some of the toys and keep them on the side; then, introduce them as surprises on different days. This may help to pacify him and keep him happy for a while longer. Finally, you might try putting him in the playpen on occasion even when you don't need to get something done. Talk to him from a distance and give him encouragement. Let him know he's really having a good time. After a short while, lift him out and tell him how terrific he is. This may help get across the idea that the playpen can be for play as well as for times when you can't be with him. Remember, you don't want to use the playpen as punishment or as a substitute for safety proofing your home, and you don't want it to become a substitute for your loving attention. On the other hand, it is a safe and helpful option for those occasions when you need to get things done and can't be with him.

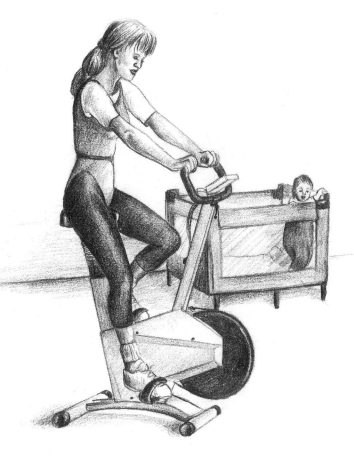

While you don't want to restrict your baby frequently or for long periods, putting him in a playpen can keep him safe when you need to get something done and can't focus your attention on him.

How often should I take my baby outside? Daily outings are almost impossible to arrange.

Fresh air outings and diversions provide a healthy change for little ones and their parents, but they're certainly not a daily necessity. When you do go on an outing with the baby, it should be a pleasant experience for you both. If it's a burden and scheduling is difficult, it's not worth it. Try to plan your outings for nice days, and be flexible if the weather lets you down. Many parents who stay home with their babies feel imprisoned and cut off from the outside world from time to time, so an outing can be an uplifting change. If that's the case, try to plan at least a couple every week or whenever it suits you. Keep in mind, too, that your outings can include meetings with friends or a destination with a purpose.

You'll need to clean her teeth, but if she wants to join in, you can let her chew on a small, soft toothbrush with your supervision.

My eleven month old has six teeth, and I want to take good care of them. How should I start?

You've already provided the most important care by supplying your baby with fluoride. You've also not allowed him to go to bed with his bottle. In addition, pediatric dentists recommend that you wrap some gauze around your finger and gently wipe the baby's teeth and gum line using a circular motion once or twice a day. Once the teeth are touching each other, you can also use dental floss. To do this, briefly and gently slide the floss along the side of each tooth, massaging slightly down and a little bit under the tooth. Afterwards, give your baby a drink of water to rinse. Be sure to let him watch you as you brush your teeth so that he can get comfortable with the process. As soon as he is willing, you can start to brush his teeth using a small, soft toothbrush with or without a tiny amount of toothpaste. You might even give him a chance to start "using" the toothbrush with your supervision, although he'll do more chewing than brushing and you'll need to do the actual cleaning. Most dentists recommend an initial dental appointment at about age two or when all 20 of the baby teeth have erupted. If you have any questions or concerns earlier, consult with your pediatrician and/or a pediatric dentist. In addition to these steps, it's important to keep sugary foods and drinks off the menu. If the baby is offered an occasional sweet treat, brush his teeth or at least have him drink some water when he's finished.

While daily outings are not necessary, an occasional trip to the park or stroll to the store can be a pleasant change for both of you.

How do I keep my 11 month old from putting everything—including rug fuzz—into his mouth?

There's no way to keep your 11 month old from putting everything into his mouth. Part of his job is learning about his environment, and tasting is one way he can do this. Your job is to remove all items that are potentially dangerous or harmful. You can also try vacuuming more frequently and keeping an interesting rotation of toys and safe household items available to distract him from rug fuzz. Remember, the more areas of your home you can make safe for your baby, the more opportunities he'll have to explore and learn. You'll want to save "no" for extremely harmful or life-threatening situations. If you find yourself saying "no" to him too often, you'll want to extend your baby proofing so that your curious baby can have a "no-no" free area. When a parent uses "no" for many things in the baby's environment, it becomes commonplace and frustrating to the baby. Although you can begin a form of discipline at this age, you'll want to use encouragement and positive reinforcement to accomplish this. When he does put an unappealing (to you) object into his mouth, don't overreact. Just remove it, and tell him it's not for eating. You'll want to divert his attention at the same time to something else. Try hugging and placing him somewhere else; handing him a more suitable object; or saying, "Let's do this now!" These ploys work and will continue to be effective for quite a while.

How frequently should I wash my baby's toys and pacifier?

Crawling babies and their favorite things spend a lot of time on the floor. Your baby's hands, toys, and pacifiers will get rubbed on the floor, furniture, carpet, etc. and then end up in his mouth. Once your baby is mobile, it's impossible to keep things truly clean. While your floors should be kept clean, they shouldn't be your first priority. Your rugs should be vacuumed more frequently since crawling babies like to pick at them, and anything they pick up will go into their mouths. Wash rubber toys whenever they're yucky or, if it's more convenient, give all washable toys a bath once a week. Be sure to wash them in warm, soapy water and rinse them well. Pacifiers should be washed and rinsed more frequently, depending upon where they've been. You'll want to have a few spares to rotate. When a pacifier hits the floor in a well-travelled place like the supermarket, theater, or shopping mall, you'll want to pocket it and offer the baby a clean one. If he tosses the pacifier frequently, you might consider tossing it for good. Keep in mind that most of the germs that cause illness come

No matter how hard you try, you won't be able to keep all of your crawling baby's playthings squeaky clean all the time. When his pacifiers, toys, or teething rings get "yucky," wash them in warm, soapy water and rinse them well.

from sneezing, coughing, or kissing. Some are passed from hand to hand. Although you want to protect the baby from as much germ exposure as possible, there's no way to make his environment germ free. Be reasonably cautious about his cleanliness and the cleanliness of his environment, and then, don't worry about it.

What kind of shoes should I buy for my baby to help him walk?

Babies do not need shoes to walk. Walking is a part of the developmental process and will occur when your baby has been cruising long enough to attain proper balance and confidence. First shoes (prior to when your baby actually bears weight on his feet) serve to keep his feet warm. When he starts to cruise, shoes also protect his feet. Look for the lightest, softest shoe you can find—usually, it's a canvas-topped, rubber-soled "tennis shoe." These are relatively inexpensive and entirely adequate for babies with normal feet. Babies with normal feet do not need high-topped or stiff-soled shoes. Remember, your baby will begin to walk when he's ready, regardless of whether he wears shoes or not.

I know they make sunglasses for babies, but should I get a pair for my baby?

Manufacturers have made baby sunglasses supposedly to protect a baby's eyes from bright sunshine. Babies don't like sunshine in their eyes. They don't like wearing sunglasses either, no matter how cute or silly they may look to you. While you do want to protect your baby's eyes in bright sunshine, this can be done by dressing him in a cap or bonnet. You'll also want to protect his skin by applying sunscreen and dressing him in lightweight clothing that covers his skin. If you're on an outing and plan to sit or picnic, find a shady spot for your baby. Always try to avoid exposing him directly to midday sunshine. When you put him in the shade, be aware that shade moves and that the baby may need to be moved often as well. Sun rays also reflect off of water and sand and may reach the baby when it appears he's shaded, so keep him in protective clothing even when he's in the shade.

Your baby doesn't need shoes to help him walk. When he starts to cruise, however, a pair of canvas-topped, rubber-soled shoes can help protect his feet.

NUTRITION AND FEEDING

Do I still need to sterilize my baby's bottles?

The answer to this question varies from area to area and from pediatrician to pediatrician, but for this age group, you probably don't. Most city water supplies are safe and clean and could probably be used at any age, but many pediatricians prefer that bottles, water, and formula be sterilized for the first two to four months (see page 40 for instructions on sterilizing bottles). For households that use well water, it is generally recommended that the water be boiled for ten to 15 minutes or that distilled water be used instead for the first six months. If you have any doubts about your water supply, check with your pediatrician to find out whether you should still be sterilizing.

What's the safest way to carry formula when I'm away from home with my ten month old?

When you're away from home, you can carry the formula in one of two ways. If you'll be able to use the formula within a couple of hours or if you have a way to refrigerate the bottle, you can pour ready-to-feed formula directly from the can to the bottle before you leave. The remainder should then be refrigerated until the can is empty. An equally good alternative, and one especially suited for extended trips away from home, is to use the powdered form of the formula. The powder can be mixed with water on the spot in the exact amount needed for one feeding. If there is a question about the local water supply, you should use distilled water, which is safer and is generally available in any drug store in inexpensive gallon containers.

How long should I give my baby supplemental vitamins? What kind is best?

Breast-fed babies are usually started on supplemental vitamins A, C, and D in the first month of life (along with fluoride, if it is not already in the drinking water). Babies receiving formula don't need added vitamins since the vitamins are already added to the formula. Most pediatricians stop the extra vitamins during the second year of life. After that time, a nutritious diet should provide the necessary vitamins.

Do I still need to give my baby fluoride drops?

Pediatricians and dentists recommend supplemental fluoride for all children who do not live in areas where the drinking water is fluoridated. The fluoride supplement is usually started in drop form at the first pediatric checkup and is continued into the teen years or until all of the permanent teeth are formed. The additional fluoride strengthens the teeth and makes them more resistant to caries (cavities). In appropriate doses, there are no negative side effects to the supplemental fluoride.

How and when should I try to get my baby to drink from a cup?

Like many other steps in development, the time to introduce a cup varies according to your baby's size and motor development. Some babies are ready to start "playing" with a cup as early as six months of age, while others are not ready until ten to 12 months of age. Most breast-fed babies who nurse until the age of nine months can be weaned directly to a cup

A plastic, no-spill baby cup with a lid and spout can help make his first attempts at drinking from a cup easier.

without using a bottle in between. Most formula-fed babies wean from bottle to cup between ten and 15 months. As mentioned above, at first your baby will probably spend most of the time playing with the cup. Then you can give her a few sips from a mostly empty cup (to avoid major spills) while you hold it for her. Once she realizes that she can get nourishment in some way other than sucking, she will experiment by taking more and more liquid from the cup. Soon she will try to hold the cup herself and eventually will be able to get more of the liquid into her mouth than on herself. Allowing her to use a plastic, no-spill baby cup with a lid and small spout may help make the transition easier and less messy. After that, it will only be a matter of time (and much parental tolerance) before your little one is handling her own cup or glass efficiently. This may occur as early as nine to ten months of age or as late as 15 to 18 months of age.

A good way to help her make the transition from bottle to cup is to offer her a cup of two-percent milk along with finger foods at mealtime.

If my baby drinks from a cup at mealtimes, should I still offer her a bottle?

This is another good way to start the transition from bottle to cup; you can try it at about nine to 12 months of age. At mealtime, along with baby food or finger foods, offer the baby a cup with two-percent milk in it, rather than the bottle. After the meal, you can offer her a bottle containing the amount of formula that she needs to complete her caloric intake for that meal. Gradually, she'll take increasing amounts from the cup while decreasing the amount she takes from the bottle.

When I begin the weaning process, should I put formula in my baby's cup?

There's a very good trick to use in this situation that really helps wean a baby from bottle to cup. Never put formula in the cup or milk in the bottle. When you think your baby is ready to begin weaning from bottle to cup, offer her small quantities of two-percent milk in a cup. The two-percent milk tastes better to most babies than the formula does so it helps make the transition even easier. Offer the cup first and the bottle containing formula after. Make sure that the total daily amount of milk and formula doesn't exceed 30 to 35 ounces. Gradually increase cup use and decrease bottle use. When you feel that your baby is ready to totally give up the bottle, don't just take it away. Give her a bottle filled only with water, and she will give it up on her own when she no longer needs to suck (usually between 12 and 18 months of age).

My ten month old still wakes me up for a bottle at night. Isn't she too old for this?

Assuming your baby is developing and growing normally and is taking an adequate amount of formula during the day, yes she is too old to be waking you for a bottle at night. Babies, like adults, generally wake up a few times every night. They check on their surroundings, shift positions, and usually go back to sleep. Sometimes, babies wake up because they are wet and need to be changed. Sometimes, they wake up if they are hungry. At other times, however, they may just want the comfort of a bottle or a cuddle with Mom or Dad. If your baby is taking 30 to 35 ounces of formula daily, that should be sufficient. If she still seems to get hungry at night, you might try giving the last bottle later in the evening and perhaps even moving her bedtime back a bit. You might also need to add a little cereal to her diet as a filler (ask your pediatrician if this would be appropriate). If she continues to wake you up at night, hunger probably has little to do with it; it's comforting and attention that she wants. In that case, when she wakes you up at night, minimize the time you spend with her by changing her diaper and putting her back to bed immediately. If she won't settle for this, give her water to drink, preferably from a cup, before you put her back down. It's also a good idea to leave a low-watt night-light on in her room so that she can see that everything is alright when she awakens at night. If, over the course of several nights, you gradually diminish the attention she gets at these night-time wakings, she'll probably give up on them. A little crying or anger won't hurt her; just let her know you love her but that it's time for sleeping.

My eleven month old is still taking a bottle, eats everything, and is chubby. Should she be getting skim milk?

You should not give your baby skim milk in place of formula because a diet containing skim milk may not provide enough fat to promote adequate growth. If your baby is getting 30 to 35 ounces of formula a day and is chubby, offer her water to quench her thirst or satisfy her need to suck. If you are in the process of weaning her from bottle to cup, be sure to use the bottle for formula and the cup for two-percent milk. This way, she will gradually wean from bottle to cup and from formula to two-percent milk at the same time. During this transition, the total amount of milk plus formula should remain the same—a maximum of 30 to 35 ounces daily.

My baby loves juice and drinks it all the time. Could this be harmful to her?

Almost all juices consist of about ten percent sugar, water, and little else except flavoring. Therefore, they should not be an important part of any child's diet. Often they are substituted, for the sake of convenience, for more nutritious foods. In addition, allowing the baby to go to bed with a bottle of any sweetened liquid (even milk) can cause decay of newly erupting teeth. The juice tends to pool in the baby's mouth as she sleeps; as it does, it is converted to a weak acid that can damage the teeth. For these reasons, it is recommended that juice be given sparingly or reserved as a special treat.

What foods, and in what amounts, are important for babies in this age group?

Between six and 12 months of age, your baby should be introduced to a large variety of foods in the form of store-bought baby food and/or food processed at home (see "Preparing Homemade Baby Food" on page 110 for instructions). In fact, by the time she's a year old, she should have tried most of the foods that she will be eating the rest of her life. You can discuss with your pediatrician the order in which you should introduce foods, or you can check the sidebar below for suggestions. Since even at one year of age she will still be getting more than 80 percent of her calories from milk, the amount of various foods should be determined by her appetite. In an average day, she should receive between 16 and 32 ounces of milk, two servings of cereal, two of vegetables, and two of meats, with fruits and juices used as snacks and desserts. Most children at this age eat three main meals each day plus snacks or smaller feedings. Snacks are usually offered at midafternoon, bedtime, and sometimes, midmorning. Her

SUGGESTED INTRODUCTION OF SOLID FOODS

You can start introducing soft or pureed solid foods when your baby is four to six months old. Begin with cereals unless directed otherwise by your pediatrician.
1. Cereal: Rice, then barley, then oatmeal
2. Yellow vegetables: Carrots, then squash, then sweet potatoes
3. Green vegetables: Peas, then beans, then spinach
4. Meats: Lamb, beef, veal, poultry, pork, fish (order not important); then egg yolk
5. Noncitrus fruits
6. Noncitrus juices (only after nine months of age)
7. Citrus fruits (orange, tomato, grapefruit, etc.)
8. Citrus juices
9. NO EGG WHITE OR HONEY UNTIL AFTER 12 MONTHS OF AGE

appetite will be determined by her rate of growth and physical activity so it can vary a great deal, even day to day. Let her appetite and desires be your guide. If you limit anything, limit the milk to the amounts mentioned above.

Can I make baby food for my baby instead of buying it?

You can make homemade baby food whenever your baby is ready for solids. It's preferable, however, to process your own foods only after you've introduced the baby to most baby foods. Using store-bought jars of baby food in the beginning can make it easier to introduce a variety of pure foods without much waste. When you do begin making your own baby food, you'll want to be discriminating about content and amount. Don't make more than enough for one or two meals unless you plan to freeze individual servings for later. Both store-bought baby food and homemade baby food require careful handling and refrigeration; opened jars of the store-bought variety as well as freshly processed homemade baby foods should be kept refrigerated, and neither should be kept for more than two days. Spoon only small amounts into your baby's dish and keep the rest in the refrigerator. If the baby requires more, retrieve the jar, put a small amount in the dish, and immediately refrigerate the remainder. In terms of content, any cooked vegetable or cooked, soft meat, poultry, or fish (carefully deboned) can be processed and offered to your baby. If the food isn't liquid enough for the processor, add a small amount of water or broth. Cooked potatoes, squash, beets, carrots, and peas can all be mashed or pureed in small amounts for your baby. Applesauce, pear sauce, mashed bananas, and cooked, mashed peaches are good choices as well. Babies like a variety of tastes and eventually can be offered many foods from your menu. Do not, however, add salt, sugar, seasonings, or any other ingredients (other than water or broth) to your baby's food. If you intend to process food for the baby using a food that you'll be serving to the rest of the family, separate the baby's portion before adding seasonings for the rest of the family's meal.

What are the first table foods I should offer to my baby?

After you have cautiously introduced most baby foods to your baby, you can offer many of the foods you eat. Mashed potatoes; mashed sweet potatoes; soft or pureed cooked vegetables; and cooked pureed fruits are all fine fare. Many parents take small portions from what they're serving that day and put it into the food processor to soften it for the baby. You can even offer pureed chicken, meat, and fish. Babies can have

---

PREPARING HOMEMADE BABY FOOD

It is often wise to introduce a new food to your baby using pure, commercially prepared baby food. Then, you can prepare the same food at home using cooked foods from the family's menu (see below). When you process baby food at home, be sure to prepare, cook, and serve it without any added ingredients; do not add salt, sugar, or seasonings to the baby's portion. Vegetables and fruits can be processed for one meal using a portion of the family's serving. Chicken, beef, or fish can be prepared in a slightly larger amount. If you process enough for more than one meal, refrigerate the remaining portion immediately and serve it the next day. Otherwise, freeze the remainder in single serving portions. Do not keep refrigerated baby food for more than two days.

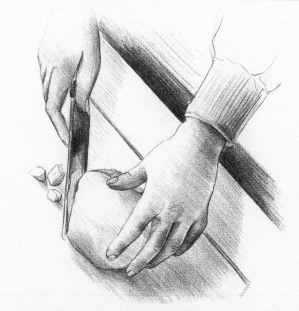

EXAMPLE:
1. Begin with chicken that was baked or broiled for the family. Do not add salt or other seasonings to the baby's portion.
2. Remove the skin, and cut the chicken into cubes.
3. Add broth (stock) or a small amount of water.

scrambled egg yolks or, when they're ready, pancakes made with the yolk only. Babies can also eat smooth, cooked cereal, but the baby cereal with added iron may still be the better choice at this age. Plain yogurt or yogurt with small pieces of soft fruit can be a favorite food for this age group as well. Be sure to read the following question for information on foods to avoid during this period.

My eleven month old is eating a variety of soft table foods. What foods should I avoid feeding to her?

It sounds like your baby is right on schedule and doing fine in the soft-food department. Even if you've followed the conservative program of introducing only one new food every five to seven days, and your baby has not had any food-reaction problems, you should still put off feeding her egg whites for another month because of the potential for allergic reaction. One other definite food to avoid prior to one year of age is honey, because of the danger of a disease called infantile botulism. Some professionals also advise against offering citrus fruits and orange juice until the baby is nine to 12 months old. Since your baby can't really chew as yet (molars come in after 12 months, and the ability to chew or grind with them comes much later), she won't be able to handle any foods that don't dissolve in her saliva. Table foods that need to be chewed should be pureed before being served to your baby. You should also avoid giving her any food that might chunk or break off in pieces of a size that might cause choking. Dangerous foods include nuts, popcorn, raisins, whole peas, raw vegetables, and chunks of apples, hard pears, or unripe melon. Chunks of meat or poultry can also cause choking. Indeed, hot dogs are the most common cause of choking accidents in young children and shouldn't be offered for a few years. You'll also want to try to educate your baby's taste away from sugary and salty foods, since she doesn't need them; doing so now may help her make healthier food choices as she grows.

Is it possible to educate a baby's taste for certain foods?

We certainly think it is. If you and your family eat a nutritious variety of foods every day, your baby will grow up eating them, too. Indeed, part of the reason for introducing fruits later and avoiding the addition of sugar and fruit to cereal is to let the baby get acquainted with less-sweet-tasting foods first. We're all born with a taste for sweets; it doesn't need to be encouraged. When you introduce table foods to your baby, your first choices should be nutritious ones. Although your

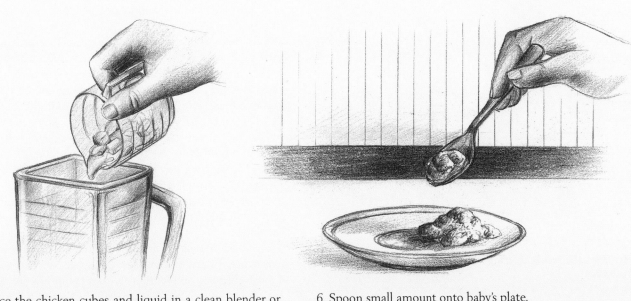

4. Place the chicken cubes and liquid in a clean blender or food processor.
5. Blend until smooth and free of chunks.

6. Spoon small amount onto baby's plate.
7. Immediately refrigerate unused portion for the next day or freeze in single servings to be used when needed.

baby needs more fat in her diet than you do and she needs to be offered a variety of foods, she definitely doesn't need foods that are deep fried, fried in butter, or highly seasoned. Like the rest of the family, your baby doesn't need very salty foods either. By introducing nutritious foods from the very start, you'll be educating your baby to make wise food choices in the future. You should also be cautious about using foods as a pacifier or reward. You want to impart a healthy attitude toward eating in general as well as toward specific food choices. Too many young children look first to food or sweets for comfort and consolation. Babies and children should eat when they are hungry, not when they're bored or in need of other kinds of nurturing. When you do offer her snacks, choose nutritious items, not junk food, sweets, or fried foods.

Her first table foods should be soft enough to dissolve in her saliva.

My nine month old eats baby food well, but she's having two loose stools a day. Could the baby food be causing the loose stools?

Two loose stools a day is an entirely normal pattern for a nine month old, as is one formed stool every other day or three to four loose stools daily. In other words, there is wide variation in the stooling pattern of normal babies. The number and consistency of stools is related to many factors, including illness, water intake, and, of course, diet. Some of the foods that cause bowel movements to be on the loose side are fruits, juices, and anything else that contains a lot of sugar. Foods that make stools firmer include cereals, milk (not formula), cheese, and many grain products. If your child is growing and developing normally and is having no symptoms other than the two loose stools, there is no cause for concern. If the problem increases or begins to bother your baby or you, discuss it with your pediatrician.

My 12 month old likes her high chair and eats pretty well, but she's a mess. When she's finished, she doesn't like to be wiped. Do you have any helpful hints?

At 12 months of age, your baby needs to be a mess. If she's getting some of the food into her mouth and enjoying it, then she's doing quite well, and so are you. Plan on a mess for quite some time. Mealtime needs to be enjoyable for her. She needs to be able to practice and enjoy feeding herself without being scolded for making a mess. To make things a little easier for yourself, put only a few to several bites of food on her tray at a time; this way, there's less to distribute elsewhere. Let her drink from a small plastic cup with a lid and spout, and put only a small amount of liquid in it at a time. When the baby is playing more than eating, take her out of her chair. Before she wanders off, use a damp cloth to gently but firmly wipe her face and fingers. Although you don't want to bathe her every day, you could consider taking her directly from high chair to bathtub on her usual bath days. Your baby also might enjoy going to the sink and washing her own hands and face with your help. Although it's bound to be a little messy, it's one way to help her feel more independent. Try to make wiping her hands and face a brief, pleasant experience. To make cleaning up the eating area easier, spread a sheet of plastic under her high chair before she sits down to eat; after the meal, fold it up, take it to the sink, and wipe it off. When it's necessary to scrub down the high chair, you might consider placing it in the shower and cleaning it there.

My 12 month old plays with her food and drops it on purpose. When I tell her "no," she cries and wants out of her high chair. Should I let her down?

Your 12 month old, as you know, has little patience for sitting still for any length of time. She's in the usual moving mode for this age. It's also normal for her to mush her food, examine it, eat some, and drop some. To make this phase easier on you, you can try to offer her only a few bites at a time and help her with her spoon. If she thinks dropping food on the floor is a game, try not to overreact. If your reaction is strong enough, you reinforce the game. Try to get the message across that food is for eating not throwing. Do it calmly and patiently. If she persists and is no longer eating, take her out of her chair. Then, feed her later when she's hungrier. At 12 months of age, she can let you know that she's hungry by gesturing or going to her high chair. Offer her small portions of a variety of foods, and change the menu daily to keep mealtime interesting.

My teething nine month old is constantly sucking on things. Her favorites are teething biscuits and graham crackers. Can these be harmful to her?

Teething biscuits and graham crackers are fine for snacks and for comfort during teething as long as the baby can handle them and as long as they liquify in her saliva. Graham crackers can sometimes break off and cause choking before they liquify, so you should try to break them up into smaller pieces. Allowing your baby to pick them up and put them in her mouth will also give her some practice with finger foods. You might try offering her a teething ring instead of snacks on occasion as well. Although gnawing on biscuits and/or toys throughout this teething stage will make your baby more comfortable, you should also try to provide her with other diversions, like some cuddling time with you.

Should my baby eat her meals at the same time as the rest of the family?

There's no hard and fast rule here. Whether or not you feed her at the same time that everyone else sits down to eat will depend in part on timing. If she has to wait for her dinner, she's likely to get cranky and impatient. Likewise, helping your baby to eat is hardly conducive to a relaxing meal and adult conversation. Babies are notoriously poor dinner companions. For family harmony, you might feed the baby first most of the time, and, if she wants to, allow her to sit in her high chair with small amounts of finger foods while the rest of the family eats. If you do decide to have the baby eat with the rest of the family, you might want to plan special dinners for you and your spouse on occasion, so that the two of you can have uninterrupted mealtime together. Although you want to remain flexible enough to accommodate the baby's needs, you'll need to take care of your own needs and the needs of other members of the family as well.

As long as he's getting some of the food in his mouth and enjoying it, he's doing fine.

SAFETY AND HEALTH

I can't imagine making my entire home safe for (and from) my newly crawling baby. Is it really necessary to childproof every room?

Accidents remain the leading cause of injury and death in children up to five years of age. Most of these accidents occur in and around the home. Since many (but not all) of these accidents are preventable, you need to be scrupulous about ridding your baby's environment of any potentially harmful objects and substances. The more rooms you can make safe and accessible for your baby, the better; however, this does not mean you have to completely rearrange your entire home. Some rooms simply may be impossible to make safe for your baby—such as a workshop or laundry room. You may want to keep other rooms—such as a home office—in their regular condition for purposes of your own convenience. In such cases, it is imperative that you find a way to close off the area so as

to effectively prevent unauthorized and/or unsupervised visits by your baby. Using a lock and key, installing a high hook latch, or placing a gate in the doorway will do the trick. It is still much too early to expect your baby to understand and follow verbal instructions concerning the concept of "off limits."

The kitchen seems like such a dangerous room for a baby. Won't I have to get rid of a lot of essential stuff to make it safe?

The kitchen can, indeed, be a very hazardous place for your baby. However, it also will be one of his favorite areas in which to play. Therefore, it is recommended that you make every effort to make this room safe for him—which does not necessarily mean getting rid of a lot of stuff. It does mean that you will have to install childproof latches on all drawers, closets, and cabinets containing poisonous materials and sharp or otherwise dangerous items. It also means that you will have

For rooms that you can't (or prefer not to) safety proof, you'll need to use a safety gate, securely latched door, or other device to keep your baby from entering.

to install similar devices on the garbage pail, dishwasher, and refrigerator. In addition, it will be a good idea to unplug all small electrical appliances when they are not in use; and when they are in use, be sure that the cords are not dangling down where your baby can reach them. When using the stove, remember to keep all pot and pan handles turned inward, be extra careful in handling hot liquids that could spill or splatter, and keep the baby away from the area when cooking is in progress. You might even consider removing the knobs that turn on the stove/range whenever you are not using them. When serving or consuming hot foods or liquids, be sure to set them down on the middle of the table, not near the edge. Since your baby may grab onto the edge of a tablecloth to steady himself or keep himself from falling, save yourself some work and worry by putting these away for the time being. Fold and put away all step stools. And, turn all water heaters down to 120 degrees Fahrenheit.

How can kitchen items be rearranged to make the room safe and more suitable for my baby?

Although there are many things in the kitchen that are hazardous to your baby, there also are many items with which he can have a lot of fun. Therefore, rather than simply locking up all the drawers and cabinets, you might consider rearranging things so that the dangerous materials are safely secured in the high cabinets and drawers out of reach of your baby, while those that are suitable for play are left unlocked in the lower ones. For example, knives, forks, graters, and other such utensils should be placed well out of reach. Your baby will appreciate it, however, if you keep the spoons and spatulas where he can get to them. The same is true for glassware as opposed to plastic cups. All small appliances must be inaccessible, but pots, pans, plastic containers, etc. can be kept at his level. One thing to watch out for is the possibility of avalanche. For instance, if you have moved canned goods and paper products into a lower cabinet, make sure that the heavier items are on the bottom and the lighter ones are on top so your baby won't be harmed by things that come tumbling down.

He'll enjoy playing with metal or plastic bowls, pots, spatulas, spoons, and other safe kitchen items. Be sure, however, that all potentially hazardous items, such as knives or glassware, are placed securely out of his reach.

My bedroom seems like a relatively safe place for my baby. Are there any special hazards I should be aware of in there?

Bedrooms seem to be made for babies at this stage of development. They usually contain soft carpeted surfaces to crawl across, soft furniture to climb upon, and lots of relatively harmless things like pillows and slippers to play with. However, there also are a few typical hazards that should be removed or locked up before your baby is given free access to the bedroom. Jewelry is fascinating to babies, but it can result in serious choking accidents. Similarly, perfumes, deodorants, makeup, and other such substances can lead to accidental poisonings. Belts, ties, shoelaces, and especially plastic bags (like those that are used to protect dry cleaning) can cause strangulation and suffocation. And, as in the living room, den, or family room, all unstable furniture or floor lamps should be removed, and all dangling cords should be taped down, unplugged, or moved up out of your baby's reach. Although it doesn't take much to make a bedroom safe, you do need to give this room a little time and attention before you allow your baby to enter it unsupervised.

Can the bathroom be made safe for unsupervised visits?

It is extremely difficult, and probably impossible, to make a typical bathroom safe for a baby at this stage of development. Even if you could manage to secure all the medicines, soaps, shampoos, nail clippers, hair dryers, scissors, tweezers, etc., the basic materials and equipment that constitute the bathroom would still represent an unacceptable level of danger. There simply are too many slippery surfaces, hard tiles, hot water faucets, water receptacles, etc. After all, more adults get injured from accidents taking place in the bathroom than any other area of the house every year, so it is unreasonable to expect that your baby will be able to manage it armed with his recently acquired physical skills. Unfortunately, babies do find bathrooms irresistibly fascinating, so making it completely inaccessible to curious little ones is a must. A highly placed hook latch probably will be more convenient but every bit as effective as a lock-and-key. To indulge his curiosity, however, don't forget to take him in the bathroom yourself on occasion and show him some of its more fascinating aspects under your close supervision.

Belts, ties, shoelaces, and plastic dry cleaning bags can cause strangulation or suffocation, so make sure they are placed well out of your curious baby's reach.

My baby spends a lot of time in the living room and den. What can I do to make those areas safe?

Living rooms and dens often contain a lot of furniture that can be hazardous to an eagerly exploring yet still relatively unstable baby. Sofas, coffee tables, desks, end tables, and the to rearrange your furniture accordingly. For example, make sure that he will not be able to climb onto the sofa seat, then onto the arm, then onto the back, then onto a bookcase, then up the shelves.

Besides the furniture, what kinds of things in the living room or den represent trouble for my baby?

In all rooms, you have to be careful about electrical outlets—which babies find irresistibly fascinating—and make sure they are sealed off with safety caps. Also, check all electrical cords to make sure that the insulation has not become frayed and that the wires are not exposed. The best way to spot hazards is to actually crawl around on your hands and knees in every room to get the baby's perspective of things. If you have any delicate and expensive video or audio equipment, make sure it is placed well out of reach of your curious but still clumsy baby. Go through all the knickknacks—such as cigarette lighters, remote control devices, paperweights—that are lying around on low shelves, and remove all those that are inappropriate for your baby's hands. Replace them with some suitable objects for his investigation. Keep in mind, too, that the floor or any other smooth and slippery surface will be hard enough for him to negotiate, but if there are small throw rugs on it, it becomes extremely hazardous.

The hard edges and sharp corners on furniture can be made safer for your crawling baby with soft bumpers or corner guards.

like usually have hard edges with sharp corners that can do damage to a newly crawling and climbing baby, so you might consider placing soft bumpers and round edge protectors on these trouble spots. Be sure to remove all unstable furniture (furniture that can be easily pulled or pushed over) to an area that is inaccessible to your baby. Also, watch out for rocking chairs and recliners. The little fingers of a crawling baby can get crushed underneath a rocking chair or caught in the folding mechanism of a recliner. In addition, table lamps and floor lamps can come tumbling down with a crash if your baby gets hold of the electrical cord, so see to it that the cords are either placed out of reach or taped down securely; if a floor lamp can be easily tipped over, remove it. Finally, particularly as your baby approaches the end of this period, keep in mind his growing ability to climb and his increasing tendency to reach very high places by climbing in increments, and be sure

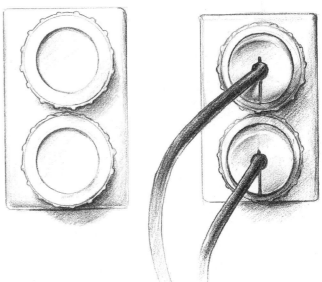

Babies are intrigued by electrical outlets, so you'll need to put safety caps on all those that your baby could possibly reach.

Should I close off all stairways with gates?

Climbing stairs will be one of your baby's favorite activities toward the end of this period, and it would be a shame to deprive him of all opportunities to attempt and practice stair climbing on his own. However, particularly since it will be a couple of months after he learns to climb up stairs that he will learn to climb down stairs, this activity obviously can be hazardous when unsupervised. Therefore, placing a gate at the top of all stairways definitely is recommended. As for the bottom, it is suggested that you place the gate at the third step up—especially if the stairs are carpeted. That way, your baby will have a chance to attempt and practice going up and down to his heart's content. Even if he takes a tumble from the third step, he is not likely to get more than a minor bump or bruise. Of course, even a minor bump or bruise is more than some parents are willing to risk, so this is a judgment call. Most mothers and fathers, however, find they are willing to trade a little bit of anxiety for the tremendous amount of pleasure this practice gives their baby.

I have a lot of plants around the house. Do they present a danger to my baby?

They certainly do. Many common household plants are poisonous, and you have to keep in mind that your baby is likely to put anything and everything he finds into his mouth. Get a reference list from your local poison control center, and make sure you get rid of all plants that are potentially lethal. As for those that are reasonably harmless if ingested, you still have to be careful about where they are placed. Dangling vines are particularly troublesome, as curious babies will routinely grab them and pull them down. And any flower pot, planter, or similar container fragments, etc. will eventually get into his hands and mouth. Make sure to keep up with your plant maintenance as well. A well-placed plant still can pose a choking hazard if its leaves are routinely falling off and fluttering to the floor.

I have a fireplace. Should I simply not use it until my baby is older?

A fireplace clearly represents some serious dangers for your baby, but it also has the potential to provide him (and you) with hours of entertainment and enjoyment. Therefore, as

Placing a secure safety gate at the top of every staircase is highly recommended. Placing the lower gate at the third step up from the bottom will give your baby two or three steps on which to practice climbing stairs without risk of serious injury.

long as you keep a close eye on your baby at all times when it is in use, there is no reason why the fireplace has to be retired completely. There are a few things to keep in mind, however. Whenever a fire is going, a screen should be secured or locked in place to keep sparks from flying out; a mesh screen is preferable to a glass screen in that it won't get as hot nor is it as likely to be touched accidentally by your baby. (If you have a wood-burning stove, it should not be used or it should be fenced in.) Also, take care with the pokers and other instruments—they typically are rather heavy and have some sharp points, so they should be kept well out of reach of your baby. Matches, lighters, and starter fluid likewise should be placed in inaccessible areas. And don't forget about the firewood. A neat pile of round logs next to the fireplace may look attractive, but they are an irresistible challenge to a newly crawling baby who will be in a lot of trouble when they come tumbling down.

Do I really have to worry about my baby crawling out an open window?

You certainly do, and you should make sure that all windows your baby might be able to get to are either locked or barred. It is not the case that babies are totally without self-protective senses, but those senses often are imperfect. For instance, researchers have conducted "visual cliff" experiments where babies at this age were allowed to crawl across a glass surface that extended out over the edge of a counter. When the babies reached the edge and looked down over the apparent "cliff," they usually seemed to sense danger and turned themselves around to go back. However, as they performed the turn-around maneuver, most of the babies managed to place their center of gravity over the edge, so if the glass hadn't been there, they would have fallen. Consequently, there is a good chance your baby may try to avoid falling out an open window, but the odds do not necessarily favor him succeeding.

Is it safe to let my baby play unsupervised in the yard at this stage?

That probably is not a good idea at this point. Given that everything he gets his hands on will likely end up in his mouth, there are simply too many things hidden in a typical yard that may present a problem. For example, a piece of broken glass that is easily noticed on the kitchen floor may be impossible

SAFETY-PROOFING PRODUCTS

Today's parents have a lot of help available to them when it comes to making their home safe for their newly crawling baby. Children's specialty shops and mail-order catalogs, as well as many hardware and department stores, now carry a complete line of items and gadgets that make safety proofing considerably easier than it used to be. You can purchase a variety of products such as door and cabinet latches, furniture bumpers, caps for electrical outlets, etc.; you can even get complete "kits" that come with extensive instructions and suggestions as well. If you are willing to spend just a little more money, you also can take advantage of some recent advances in battery-operated safety devices. These include not only walkie-talkie or intercom-type monitors, but things like door guards and water-level indicators as well. Door guards sound an alarm when the door is opened by an unauthorized little one, and water-level indicators sound an alarm when the water in the bathtub reaches an unsafe height. It certainly is recommended that you avail yourself of as many of these technological wonders as possible; however, you must be careful not to allow yourself to get lulled into a false sense of security. No such gadget is foolproof; and even those operating perfectly can't take into account every conceivable type of trouble. Going high-tech in safety proofing is a good idea, but it is in no way a total substitute for continued involvement and constant vigilance on your part. At best, these products should be regarded as capable backups rather than the primary guardians of your baby's safety.

to detect in the dirt. A small marble that is obvious on the carpet can get lost in the grass. Furthermore, insects, animal feces, and a variety of other items will be irresistible to your curious baby. Consequently, when you do take your baby outdoors, it is recommended that you spread out a large blanket for him to play upon with minimal supervision. When you cannot supervise his activities at all, place him in a playpen for the few minutes that you'll be away. And, of course, give him as many opportunities as possible to explore and investigate this special environment with your assistance as well.

My baby really likes it when I take him in the pool with me. Is that okay?

Taking your baby in the pool with you may not be a bad idea, but you must take proper precautions. First and foremost, you must realize that a baby cannot swim, nor can he really *learn* how to swim at this age. The American Academy of Pediat-

rics does *not* recommend group or organized swimming classes for children less than three years of age. One reason is that such instruction can give parents the feeling that their child is safe in the water—and this is not the case. No young child should ever be considered "water safe." Another major danger that is not well known nor always obvious is that when water enters a baby's mouth, he will swallow it. Because of his low body weight, it does not take much swallowing to create a chemical imbalance in his system, resulting in a condition called water intoxication. Water intoxication can lead to seizures and even death. The symptoms usually do not appear until an hour or more after the water is ingested, so it is difficult to detect when a baby is getting into trouble in this regard. Therefore, if you do take your baby into the pool with you, you *must* hold him and watch him carefully at all times, and you should not allow his head to be submerged. Both the water and air temperature should be warm enough so the baby does not experience a decrease in body temperature. At this age, the water should be warmer than 85 degrees Fahrenheit, and exposure should be brief.

If you do take your baby in the pool with you, hold him at all times, keep his head from being submerged, and make sure the water is warm enough for him.

Are there any new dangers associated with taking my baby for a trip in the car?

Your baby's increased physical skills are likely to cause many new problems during rides in the car. Using a car seat is still mandatory, but if he gets overly bored or overly excited, keeping him in the car seat may be difficult. Also, as he plays with various items, there now is the danger that those items can become dangerous projectiles if he starts throwing them around. In other words, you can no longer expect that your baby will simply fall asleep or in any way remain mostly stationary for long periods of time when he is in the car. Therefore, you must make sure that he is secured into his car seat as firmly as possible, and you should take care to provide him with suitable objects and activities that will keep him entertained and out of your hair as much as possible. And, if he does start to get out of control, you must resist the temptation to try and deal with him while you are still driving. As inconvenient as it may be, you should pull over to the side of the road and turn off the engine as soon as trouble starts, and don't try to get going again until you've got things back under control.

Can my baby get seriously hurt just playing with his three-year-old brother?

He certainly can, and you have to be very careful about the possibility at this point. After an initial unpleasant reaction to the new arrival, the older sibling very often goes through a period of acceptance, or at least tolerance of the little one. However, once the baby becomes mobile and demands a lot more immediate attention from the parents, the old feelings of jealousy and hostility usually return even more powerfully. To make matters worse, the baby may unwittingly intrude upon or interfere with his older sibling's activities on occasion or innocently take something that belongs to him; such actions can provoke some pretty intense reactions. Of course, some closely spaced older siblings don't express any physical aggression toward younger siblings. Some seem to adjust quite well and are even very protective of the baby; some show temporary signs of regression, such as wanting a bottle; and still others take out their frustrations on their toys. For safey's sake, however, it's important to be aware of the possibility and to keep an eye on them when they're together. Your baby is becoming increasingly capable of "taking care of himself," but his brother also is getting bigger and stronger every day, so your baby can be in danger if things get out of hand when the two of them are unsupervised.

ACCIDENTS WILL HAPPEN

This period is filled with many exciting opportunities for babies. Unfortunately, it also is filled with incredible anxieties for their parents. No matter how adept you are at safety proofing, and no matter how vigilant you are in supervising your baby's activities, accidents will inevitably happen. When they do, it is important for you not to overreact. Despite their small stature and delicate appearance, babies actually are rather hearty creatures, and they are capable of withstanding quite a bit at this point. Although they may scream and carry on a great deal when they first suffer a bump or scrape, within a few minutes, they probably will be on their way to resume whatever it was they were doing, with the unpleasant incident largely forgotten. On the other hand, no matter how slight the damage to their baby, the parents are likely to continue their suffering for quite some time. This is normal and natural, but you should make an effort to keep it from getting out of hand. If you go overboard in trying to make sure that another accident will never happen, you probably will do little more than make yourself crazy. More importantly, overprotectiveness usually results in overrestriction and/or oversupervision. The advantages that your baby will gain in physical safety as a result probably will pale in comparison to the disadvantages he'll suffer in terms of reduced opportunities to explore and investigate independently. While you must do everything in your power to see to it that major accidents are avoided, it is suggested that you try to relax and realize that a few bumps, scrapes, and bruises are a small price to pay for indulging your baby's curiosity and allowing his mind to expand to the fullest extent possible during this period.

How can his five-year-old brother be hazardous to my baby even when the older boy isn't around?

Keep in mind that the safety regulations concerning toys for older children are a lot more lenient than those for babies. Items that may be perfectly appropriate for your older child can be extremely hazardous in the hands of your baby. For example, a little toy truck may be a favorite toy of the older child, who will run it along the floor and go "rrumm, rrumm!" However, the baby is very likely to be interested in this toy in another way. There is a good chance he will pluck off the little wheels and put them into his mouth, saying "yumm, yumm!" Not only does this present a choking problem, but the sharp spoke that is now exposed may cause a lot of trouble as well. Therefore, it is a good idea to keep the toys of each child separate, and to do what you can to make the older child's room "off limits" to the baby unless you can be there to protect him from his brother's toys—and to protect his brother's toys from the baby.

How can I protect my baby when visiting other people's homes?

At this point, you probably won't have much choice but to place your baby in a portable playpen when visiting other people's homes. Even if they have small children themselves, you can't assume that their home has been safety proofed. And even if people who are eager to have you visit assure you that they will take appropriate precautions, you can't assume that they have done an adequate job of safety proofing. As long as your baby won't have to be restricted for several hours, keeping him in the playpen and/or under your supervision on such occasions probably won't present too many difficulties—especially if you keep a few favorite toys and some interesting new items in reserve and use them to keep him entertained at such times. Of course, if you are going to be spending a lot of time at someone's house and/or visiting regularly, you might consider asking them if at least one or two rooms can be safety proofed under your supervision so that your baby will have an opportunity to do some exploring and investigating on his own while he is there. Finally, whenever you take the baby to someone else's home or you have someone visiting you, be sure that all purses and/or luggage are put up and out of the way. Sometimes they contain medications, cigarettes, cosmetics, and small, sharp objects that can be very hazardous to your baby should he get his hands on them; if they do, your baby will find them given the chance.

My six month old had a cold and fever, and he couldn't receive his third DTP. Will a delay affect his immunity?

The series should be completed soon to ensure your baby's immunity to diphtheria, tetanus, and pertussis (DTP). The delay won't change or lessen the efficiency of the series. The reason for not immunizing a baby who has a cold and fever is to protect him from a possible reaction to the vaccine, which would add to his discomfort. Common side effects of the vaccine include fever, malaise, or irritability for 24 to 48 hours after the vaccine is given and some soreness and/or swelling at the injection site; these side effects, if they occur, are generally mild. Many times, parents are advised to give their baby acetaminophen drops at the time of the injection to help minimize fever and discomfort. Some pediatricians prefer a wait-and-see attitude. If your baby had no side effects previously, he'll most likely have none this time. Remember, giving your baby the proper immunizations is a very important part of preventive pediatric care.

My son will be going into day care soon, and I'm worried about his chance of catching meningitis. How can I protect him? Is he too young for the shot?

The "shot" that is available is to protect your baby from the most common cause of bacterial meningitis in children, Hemophilus influenza type B (HiB). At present, the recommendation is that this vaccine be given at 15 months of age, because this is the youngest age for which it has been proven effective. By the time you read this, a new vaccine may be available that can protect babies as young as two months of age. Your pediatrician is the best source of information about this vaccine, which is currently being tested. In the meantime, continue to avoid exposing your baby to ill children whenever possible (check into the policies regarding ill children at the day-care center, too), and be sure to have your son immunized at 15 months of age.

When should I take my baby's temperature?

An elevated temperature is only one sign of illness. If you suspect that your baby is coming down with something, you'll want to take his temperature. You may suspect that he's ill if he isn't drinking or eating well; if he is unusually cranky and irritable; if he vomits; if he acts like something is hurting him;

If you are ever worried about your baby's health, don't hesitate to call your pediatrician.

if he's perspiring or looks or feels flushed and warm; or if he seems lethargic. Any one or more of these observations may prompt you to take his temperature. Again, the baby's temperature is only one sign of illness; if you notice other signs that concern you, even if his temperature is in the normal range, you should consult your pediatrician. At this age, the most accurate way to take your baby's temperature is rectally. For instructions on how to take a rectal temperature, see page 53.

How high should a fever get before I call the doctor?

Fever is an ally, not an enemy. It is a method for the body to more efficiently fight an infection. At a temperature above 100 degrees Fahrenheit, the body more efficiently fights viruses and bacteria. In other words, the fever itself is just one sign that your baby is fighting an infection, so you want to look at other signs to try and determine the seriousness of the illness. How is the baby eating and drinking? Is he acting lethargic? Has the fever responded to acetaminophen, and does the

baby seem more comfortable when the temperature is down? Your pediatrician may be much more concerned about a baby who is acting very ill but only has a temperature of 101 degrees Fahrenheit than one who is acting normally but has a temperature of 104 degrees Fahrenheit. As stated before, one of the most important factors is how your baby is acting. If you are worried, call your pediatrician.

If my baby's fever is very high, should I give him a cold bath to bring his temperature down?

There is never any reason to give a baby a cold bath. If you are trying to bring down a fever, a warm (normal bath temperature) bath is much more effective. If you give him a cold bath, the blood vessels in his skin may constrict to prevent heat loss, thus driving up the temperature. Indeed, even a warm bath is rarely recommended to decrease the baby's temperature unless it is over 104 degrees Fahrenheit and does not respond within one to two hours to an appropriate dose of acetaminophen. If this is the case, you should consult your pediatrician before giving the baby a bath or taking any further measures.

How can I care for my baby when he has a cold?

Plan to provide as much comfort to your suffering little one as possible. Keep him warm and dry, and be prepared to rock and cuddle him to help prevent extra crying, which may increase stuffiness and swelling of the mucous membranes of the nose and throat. You can increase the humidity in his sleeping area by using a cool-mist vaporizer. You can use salt-water nose drops (see instructions for making these on page 54) to flush his nose (especially before feedings) and allow him to suck more comfortably. You can also gently insert a soft-tipped bulb syringe into his nostrils to remove mucus before feedings; this takes some skill and caution, however, because even the soft tip of the syringe can further irritate the nasal membranes. Depending upon the baby's comfort level, you can elevate the head of the crib; this may facilitate drainage of the nasal passages. Although your baby may not want solid foods while he is suffering from a cold, you do need to increase or maintain his intake of liquids. Colds in babies are rarely treated with any medication except acetaminophen and sometimes a decongestant. The symptoms may linger for two to three weeks. Colds are caused by viruses so there is no specific medication to shorten the course. Sometimes parents request an antibiotic, mostly because they feel they should do something, but an antibiotic won't cure a cold. You'll want to consult with your pediatrician about symptoms if your baby maintains a significant fever (over 100 degrees Fahrenheit measured rectally) for more than a few days, if he develops a fever after the first few days of a cold, if he refuses fluids for two or more feedings, or if he seems to be getting more ill than you think he should be with a simple cold. Babies can develop secondary infections (including ear infections, bronchitis, pneumonia, etc.) anytime during the course of a cold. If your baby develops a secondary infection caused by bacteria, then your doctor will prescribe the treatment of choice. Babies usually handle their colds well, although they will be uncomfortable for a few days. Parents, however, should never be shy about consulting with their pediatrician whenever they are worried about their baby's health.

How will I know when a cold becomes serious?

Most babies with colds at this age are not very ill. They may have a low-grade fever for a few days and be congested and cranky. If the baby develops a fever after the first few days of a cold or if he refuses all nourishment, including liquids, you should consult your pediatrician. More importantly, if you are really worried about your baby for any reason, discuss it with your pediatrician and, between you, decide if the baby should be seen.

When should I worry about a cough?

Any cough that concerns you should be reported to your pediatrician. You may be advised to have the baby examined. If you're sure the baby has just a cold, and that the cough is a "getting rid of mucus" kind of cough, it's probably okay to go a day or two and watch him. If he has a fever or other symptoms along with the cough, you may want to consult with your pediatrician. Babies can become ill quickly. If his cry ever sounds weak or if he acts lethargic or is having any difficulty breathing, you should consult your pediatrician. Sometimes babies (and young children) awaken with a cough that makes them sound like a barking seal. They sound and act like they're having trouble breathing. This condition is called croup and is usually caused by a virus that inflames the larynx and/or trachea. It's very frightening to parents as well as to the baby.

To treat it, go into the bathroom, close the door (and any windows), and steam up the bathroom by turning the hot-water taps on full force. Take the baby into the bathroom and, after a few minutes, his breathing should become easier. If his breathing doesn't improve quickly or if he also has a fever, call your pediatrician to determine if the baby needs to be seen. This is especially important since a very serious type of bacterial disease can start with similar symptoms. Fortunately, the disease, called epiglottitis, is much less common now that we have a vaccine (HiB) to prevent it.

Can a humidifier or vaporizer be harmful to my baby?

Humidifiers in the past have been harmful to children. The old hot-steam vaporizers were notorious for causing burns when tipped over or handled by little ones. Hopefully there are none around anymore. The theory of warm vapor sounded good, since warm air should feel better than cool air. In reality, by the time the mist reaches the throat or sinuses, the body has cooled or warmed it to body temperature anyway. The cool-mist vaporizers are safer as long as they are used and cared for properly. If you need to use an extension cord (which is unadvisable after the baby is mobile), make certain it's the right size and kind, and always avoid overloading electrical outlets. The vapor mustn't drench the baby, or it defeats the purpose. The mist stream should be a few feet from the crib and not pointed directly at the baby's face. The humidifier must also be kept scrupulously clean; otherwise, it may harbor mold and bacteria and spread them into the air. Follow the manufacturer's cleaning instructions, and always put clean water in for each use. Vaporizers can be a comfortable asset to cold sufferers (adults and children alike) when used properly. They're helpful to have around.

Is it okay to give my baby over-the-counter medications?

At this age, babies require very little medication of any kind. Acetaminophen to treat fever and perhaps some mild cough or cold preparations are often tried by parents prior to seeking medical advice. As previously mentioned, most colds go away spontaneously without any medication, and most fevers should be reported to your pediatrician if they persist or begin after the first few days of a cold, so there is very little reason to consider the use of over-the-counter medications (other than acetaminophen drops) without talking to your pediatrician.

Many medications that were formerly available by prescription only are now available over-the-counter. This does not always mean that they are safer or milder, so if you have any questions about a specific medication, call your pediatrician.

How do I give medications to my baby?

A soft plastic dropper can be used to give the baby any necessary liquid medicine. Some droppers have lines on them that indicate the correct dosage level of medications such as acetaminophen. If you're using an unmarked dropper to give liquid medicine, premeasure the medication with a measuring spoon, and pour it into a small container. Then, fill the dropper from the container by squeezing the rubber bulb. You may have to fill the dropper more than once for each dose, depending upon the amount required or prescribed for your baby. Slowly and gently squeeze the medication into the baby's mouth between his gums and the inside of his cheek. You don't have to hurry or give it all at once. He should swallow the medicine. If he is very upset, calm him before you give him the medicine; if you introduce the medicine when he is upset, he'll be more likely to resist, choke, sputter, or spit up. If you are patient and firm, he will learn that sometimes taking unpleasant medicine is necessary.

To give your baby liquid medication, use a soft plastic dropper. Fill the dropper with the appropriate dose, then slowly and gently squeeze the medication into the baby's mouth between his gums and the inside of his cheek.

I don't use swabs to clean my baby's ears. Will wax buildup affect his hearing?

Wax buildup will not impair the baby's hearing, but it may need to be removed in order for your pediatrician to view the tympanic membrane (eardrum). When this is the case, the canal can be irrigated and the wax washed away. Any wax that you see outside the canal can be gently removed using a damp washcloth. The ear canal has its own ability to push wax to the outside. Wax lubricates and protects the ear canal. Never use cotton swabs or anything else in the baby's ear. You can damage the thin layer of skin, cause infection, and push wax down against the eardrum. If you are concerned about your baby's hearing, consult your pediatrician.

How can I check my baby's hearing?

It is very important to diagnose a hearing loss as early as possible because of the importance of early hearing ability to normal speech development. Usually, the first people to become aware of impaired hearing in a baby are the parents. You notice how your baby responds to your voice when you know he is not looking at you. How does he respond to unexpected loud sounds? If you have any suspicions about your baby's hearing, discuss them with your pediatrician. There are very accurate methods to test hearing in children of this age, and your pediatrician can arrange for such testing to be done when it is indicated.

How can I tell if my baby has or is getting an ear infection?

Most babies who have ear infections are fussy and irritable, and many have rectal temperatures over 100 degrees Fahrenheit. The baby usually has had a cold or congestion for one to several days prior to developing the ear infection; ear infections are the most common complications of colds. If you suspect that your baby has an ear infection, discuss it with your pediatrician, who will probably want to see the baby if the symptoms persist. Many parents are concerned when their baby pulls on one or both ears. This is common among babies at this age, and if there is no accompanying fever, fussiness, or irritability, there is probably no ear infection.

If he pulls on his ear, but there are no accompanying symptoms of illness—such as fever, fussiness, or irritability—he probably doesn't have an ear infection. The twiddling may simply be a comfort habit.

How can I keep my baby from getting ear infections?

Allowing a baby to take a bottle to bed is recognized as a contributing factor in some ear infections. Formula or milk pooling in the mouth can be a good medium for the growth of viruses and bacteria (it's also known to be harmful to teeth). Because of the proximity of the openings of the eustachian tubes and the shortness of these tubes in babies, the ears can easily become infected. Therefore, you should never allow your baby to drink from his bottle while he is in his crib. Of course, you should avoid using anything to probe or clean the baby's ear canals, since some external ear infections are caused by damaging the thin skin covering of the canal. You should also try to avoid allowing water to enter the baby's ears as well; be sure to bathe him with his head well above the bathwater. If water does get in, it can be removed by gently tilting the baby's head from side to side. In addition, since most ear infections develop along with or after a cold, try to avoid exposing your baby to people who have upper respiratory infections (colds) whenever possible. Keep in mind, however, that no matter how cautious parents are, most babies, at some time or other, develop a congested or infected middle ear.

My baby has some scaling behind his ears. How should this be treated?

Scaliness behind the ears is often related to cradle cap or seborrheic dermatitis. If this is the case, first treat the scalp condition (see page 58), and the dry scales behind the ears may go away spontaneously. If the scales are dry and the skin is not cracked, lubricating the area with a baby lotion may speed healing. If the skin is cracked, moist, and red, there may be a low-grade infection, which usually responds to treatment with warm, wet packs followed by application of an antibiotic ointment. If these simple treatments don't seem to improve the situation, consult your pediatrician.

I know that some sun is healthy for my baby, but how much?

You won't be doing your baby any favors by exposing him to hot or strong sunlight for any extended period of time. There is no good reason for a baby to have a suntan and very good

When she's outdoors, protect her head with a cap or bonnet, cover all exposed skin with sunscreen, avoid midday sun, and keep exposure time short.

reasons for you to prevent him from getting a sunburn. Besides being a painful experience, sunburn can contribute to skin cancer later on. Babies also get prickly heat rashes from being too warm; they are most comfortable when temperatures are moderate. Therefore, if you want to take your baby on an outing in the sun, avoid doing so during midday, when the sun's rays are strongest. Schedule it for before 10 a.m. or after 3 p.m. instead. In addition, it's generally recommended that you protect your baby from the sun whenever you take him outside during the day (it is possible to get a sunburn even on a partly cloudy day, especially if you are near water or sand). Before the two of you step outside, be sure he's wearing a bonnet or cap that shades his face and neck and lightweight clothing that covers his arms, legs, and torso. It's also wise to apply sunscreen to all exposed areas of your baby's skin. There are many good sunscreens on the market, some made especially for babies. Choose a sunscreen with an SPF (Sun Protection Factor) of 15 or greater. A sun protection factor of 15 means that if your baby's skin would naturally start to burn after 20 minutes in the sun, with proper use of the sunscreen, he could be in the sun 15 times longer (300 minutes or five hours) before his skin would start to burn. That, of course, does not mean you should expose your baby for five hours; remember, babies do not like hot or bright sunshine or very warm temperatures. Many sunscreens are also waterproof for a certain period of time (after which they must be reapplied, so read the label to find out when you should reapply it). When applying a sunscreen to your baby's skin for the first time, it's preferable to cover a small test area first to make certain the sunscreen doesn't irritate his skin or cause a reaction. Most sunscreens work best if applied 30 minutes prior to sun exposure. Be sure to keep the sunscreen away from your baby's eyes and out of his reach. If your baby is under six months of age, keep him out of the sun.

A covered or shaded play area can help keep him cool and help protect him from the sun during warm-weather outings.

How do I know if my baby's rash is caused by a serious illness?

Most rashes in babies are not significant and go away on their own. Most serious rashes are accompanied by other symptoms that tell you that there is something wrong. Fever, vomiting, respiratory symptoms, lethargy, irritability, and pain along with a rash may mean that something more serious is going on and should be reported to your pediatrician. If the baby is well and the rash is not bothering him, don't let it bother you.

ON BEING A PARENT

Will it be necessary for me to teach my baby to crawl, pull to stand, walk, climb, etc.?

Not at all. Once her body is ready for it, your baby will begin to do these things without any prompting or instruction of any kind. However, she will need ample opportunities to develop and practice these skills, and she will appreciate your encouragement and praise as she achieves them. If she is kept too restricted or in any other way is prevented from attempting and practicing these things on a regular basis, she won't learn how to do them. And if she routinely senses disapproval or even just disinterest from you, she won't be inclined to do them. In other words, there really is nothing you can do to induce your baby to crawl, walk, climb, etc. before she is ready, but once she is ready, you certainly can obstruct and possibly even prevent her progress.

If my baby is struggling to achieve some new skill, like climbing onto the sofa, should I help her or just leave her alone?

This is somewhat of a judgment call. Clearly, if your baby's struggle has reached the point where frustration is setting in and she's becoming upset, it probably is a good idea to lend her a helping hand. However, stepping in before she's had ample opportunity to test the full extent of her own resources may impede her from making progress. After all, you can't learn to succeed if you never have opportunities to try. Unfortunately, first-time parents in particular tend to be overly anxious and often empathize inappropriately with what they too quickly perceive to be a distressing situation for their baby. As a result, they come to her aid too soon in many cases. Therefore, although it's never easy to watch your baby struggling with anything, try to err on the side of restraint and allow her to give it her best shot. By the way, when it comes to self-help skills, such as learning how to hold a spoon or drink from a cup, many parents step in too quickly not out of concern for the baby but rather for the purposes of their own convenience and busy schedule. Instead of allowing the baby to get food all over her clothing, her face, and her hair as she attempts to feed herself with a spoon, the harried parents take the spoon away from her and feed her themselves. Again, this is understandable, but the potential for problems demands that parents try to control themselves and give the baby a fair chance to learn how to fend for herself.

THE CONCEPT OF "LEARNING TO LEARN"

As they watch their babies go about their explorations, many parents worry that their children may be "wasting" a lot of time that could be better spent on more focused "educational" activities. They are concerned that instead of playing with pots and pans, their babies should be receiving direct instruction in specific subjects so they can learn shapes, colors, numbers, and all sorts of other things they will need to know later on. While these thoughts are understandable, they are badly misguided. The most important lessons that babies learn at this point are in the area of "learning how to learn." That is, through their explorations and investigations, they learn how to observe, analyze, adjust, and adapt to their environment. These skills will stand them in good stead no matter how their environment changes as time goes by. On the other hand, babies who are restricted and have their attention channeled into narrow avenues of experience may appear to make some impressive progress on the surface. When they are forced outside those avenues in the future, however, they may lack the ability to accommodate, much less take advantage of the new circumstances. Therefore, if you are tempted to step in and start introducing specific subjects into your baby's educational experiences at this point, keep in mind that the world you want to prepare her for is an ever-changing one. The particular pieces of knowledge she picks up may be beneficial things to have for quite some time. However, given the rate at which the world is changing these days, chances are that a lot of them will become obsolete before too long. If she never learns how to learn on her own, she'll have trouble picking up and adapting to the alterations, and as a result, may be at a serious disadvantage in the long run.

Won't I have to provide constant supervision for my baby's early attempts at potentially dangerous things like stair climbing?

In the beginning, it probably will be a good idea for you to be around as much as you can. First of all, babies learn to climb up things like stairs generally a couple of months before they learn to climb down, so your baby may need your help until she becomes adept at all aspects of a given activity. In addition, babies thrive on parental encouragement and praise as they pursue these things, so your baby may appreciate your providing her with a boost in the figurative sense as well as the literal sense. However, providing constant supervision on an ongoing basis is likely to be not only impossible, but inappropriate as well. As your baby becomes more active, it will be increasingly difficult to keep up with her. As she becomes capable of generating self-pride, it will be less necessary for you to applaud her every move. So plan on making sure that your baby's environment allows her ample opportunities to pursue and practice new skills in ways that won't put her in serious jeopardy, even when you can't be right there with her.

Once she can get around on her own, what is the best way to help my baby learn about her world?

The easiest and most effective way to "educate" your baby at this point is to make as much of your home as possible safe and accessible for her. Then, simply set her free to explore at will and on her own. Keep in mind that your baby will be both incredibly curious and incredibly naive. Consequently, making your home safe involves removing, replacing, or fixing anything and everything that she might damage or that might cause her harm (see the Safety and Health section in this age group for advice). By doing so, you will be providing your baby with an enormous environment containing countless items that she can use to gain experience. You will also be establishing an atmosphere that enables and encourages her to take maximum advantage of the opportunities made possible by her increasing skills.

Should I be sure to provide a lot of special items for my baby to explore and investigate?

By making a large portion of your home safe and accessible for your baby, you have already provided her with a wealth of

Now that he's on the move, he'll be coming across a variety of "everyday" items that he's never seen before.

"special" items for her explorations and investigations. Keep in mind that almost everything your baby encounters will be brand new and extremely exciting to her. We are thoroughly familiar with and take for granted things like wastepaper baskets, the knobs on the television set, stacks of folded laundry, flights of stairs, etc. However, these things are being experienced by your baby for the very first time. They present all sorts of interesting challenges to her growing abilities. In general, you may want to see to it that, whenever possible, safe and suitable items that ordinarily are out of your baby's reach get moved down to her level. Other than that, you really don't have to worry about making any special efforts in this regard.

Instead of trying to make my home safe for my baby, can't I keep her in a playpen and just give her a lot of stuff?

On the surface, it seems as if this strategy might work. But research has repeatedly demonstrated that it doesn't. No matter how many items you place in the playpen, sooner or later your baby will become bored. Without ample opportunities to actively pursue her interests and to exercise her abilities according to her own inclinations and schedules, her curiosity eventually will begin to dwindle. It has been shown repeatedly that from this point on, extensive use of playpens and other restrictive devices is routinely associated with poor physical and mental development. Even springing your baby for periodic supervised sessions won't make much of a difference. Evidently, no playpen in the world can hold anywhere near as many learning opportunities as a typical, safety-proofed household. And, no amount of supervised educational activities can compensate for the progress and pleasure a baby experiences when she does a lot of learning on her own.

Does this mean I should never put my baby in a playpen?

Of course not. There inevitably will be times when putting your baby in a playpen will be absolutely necessary, or at least appropriate. For example, if you are scrubbing the kitchen floor with a corrosive cleanser or fixing an appliance using an open tool box containing sharp instruments, you may be able to do so while your baby is exploring freely in another room. But if the phone or doorbell rings and you are going to be distracted for a while, it will be a good idea to restrict your baby until you can return to prevent her from wandering into the hazardous area. In addition, there may be times when you have something important to do for yourself, such as paying bills or even taking a nap, and you would prefer not to be disturbed by your baby for a while. In such cases, placing her in a playpen and providing some favorite or novel items probably will keep her entertained long enough for you to get the break you need. In other words, as long as it is not used to routinely restrict your baby for long periods day after day, a playpen is indeed a very important and appropriate piece of equipment to have around.

Other than setting up an appropriate environment, how can I play a role in my baby's education at this point?

In addition to designing a rich world for your baby to explore and investigate, you can add to her educational experiences in three important ways. First, you can help expand your baby's mind by occasionally alerting her to additional information and interesting associations that she may have missed as she

was exploring and investigating. Second, you can help her develop superb language skills by providing her with plentiful models of proper and appropriate speech. And third, you can start teaching her how to get along with other people by establishing and enforcing reasonable limits on her explorations and investigations (for specific examples of how to do these things, see the following questions). Keep in mind, though, that good teaching requires a highly motivated student. Therefore, your input—particularly in the first two cases—should be geared to the interests and abilities your baby is exhibiting at the moment; it should not be guided by some set of subjects that you think you should be teaching her. In other words, the easiest and most effective way to be an excellent teacher is to serve as a "consultant" rather than as an "instructor" to your baby.

How do I go about serving as a "consultant" to my baby?

In the course of her explorations and investigations, your baby will return to you routinely in the course of the day to obtain

As his "consultant," you can talk to him about what he's interested in at the moment, pointing out details and associations that he may have missed.

comfort, receive assistance, or share her excitement over some new discovery. When she does, her attention will be focused intensely. She will be highly motivated to learn as much as she can about whatever it is that has her attention at the moment. As you go about providing your baby with whatever she wants or needs, you can supply additional input into her experience. You can talk to her about whatever it is, stretching the subject just a little and throwing in a related idea or two. For example, if your baby comes to you thrilled about the candy wrapper she's just discovered behind the desk, you might say something like, "Oh, yes, that's a pretty candy wrapper! It's red and yellow, just like your shirt is red and this bowl is yellow. Do you hear the crinkly sound it makes? We can make that sound with this piece of paper, too." After a minute or so, your baby will be eager to get back to what she was doing, and you can let her go. Believe it or not, during the 25 to 50 such episodes that will occur each day, you will be supplying your baby with far more meaningful input than if you sat down with her for several hours of formal "lessons" each day.

How can I teach my baby to talk?

You can't. Probably since prehistoric times, parents have tried anything and everything to prod their babies to start speaking. No one has ever come up with an effective method. When your baby is ready, she will begin to talk. There is nothing you can do to coax her first words out of her. On the other hand, if you don't do a couple of important things, her progress in this area may be impeded. First, you need to talk to your baby a lot. Babies who do not listen much to language usually don't use much language. Second, you need to make sure she can hear clearly. As early as four months of age, you can use the whisper test (see page 60) to screen for hearing loss. Once she begins understanding words at about six to eight months of age, you can monitor her ability to understand words to ensure she's making steady progress. As long as your baby can hear properly and you have made a point to provide a lot of language for her to listen to, the best thing to do is relax and let nature take its course.

You won't be able to get her to start speaking before she's ready, but you do need to talk to her a lot.

I can see how making the whole house safe for (and from) my baby is a good idea, but shouldn't I leave out a few items so she can learn the meaning of "no"?

While this idea seems sensible in principle, it actually is quite unnecessary and rather ill-advised in reality. No matter how good you are at safety proofing your home, chances are that every day your baby will find another thing that you've missed—an open safety pin in a shag rug, a loose shirt button in the corner of a closet, a broken handle on a tool chest, the unraveling fringe of a floor-length drape. Such inevitable oversights will provide plenty of opportunities to teach your baby the meaning of the word "no." Of course, for your own convenience, you may wish to leave out a few items that you would prefer that your baby didn't touch, or even make a few whole areas "off limits" to your baby—and you are certainly entitled to do so. However, keep in mind that the more forbidden items and areas there are in her environment, the more danger there will be to your baby and the more aggravation you are likely to have in trying to keep her out of trouble. You will also run the risk of saying "no" so often that it becomes meaningless to your baby or begins to discourage her from indulging her curiosity by exploring and learning about her world. Save "no" for very hazardous or life-threatening situations whenever possible.

Once I'm sure that my baby understands the meaning of the word "no," can I ease up on some of the supervision and safety proofing?

This is something you may not want to do for a couple of years yet. First, at this point, your baby probably is still too young to have even such a strong concept stick in her mind reliably for a very long time. If you're not always there to reinforce prior admonitions, there could be trouble on occasion. More importantly, if you ease up on safety proofing and consequently have to say "no" over and over again throughout the course of the day, there is a good chance that the word will start to lose its impact because of overuse. A sharp "no" or "stop" uttered now and then will have a more lasting effect than a constant, nagging "no, no, no, no." And most important of all is the fact that if you have to use "no" too often, you run the risk of your baby associating the act of exploring with the displeasure and disapproval of the people who mean the most to her. Especially during this period, you want to be sure that the overwhelming message your baby receives in this regard is one of encouragement and praise.

No matter how much effort you put into safety proofing your home, your baby is bound to find some potentially dangerous item that you missed. Such occasions will provide enough opportunity to teach him the meaning of "no."

My baby is in full-time day care. As long as most of her waking hours are spent in that safety-proofed environment, wouldn't it be okay to keep her relatively restricted at home?

This is inadvisable for at least two major reasons. First, to the extent that you restrict your baby unnecessarily for any length of time, you are depriving her of learning opportunities. Babies do not keep schedules—studying in school and relaxing while at home. They are learning all the time, so it is inappropriate to set up a sharp distinction between what she can do during the day and what she can do in the evening. Second, keep in mind your greater emotional power as compared to that of your baby's teachers. No matter how much encouragement and praise they give to her explorations during the day, if she senses displeasure from you when she engages in such activities at home, there is a good chance your influence will win out. As a result, your baby may end up with diminished curiosity under all circumstances.

Is saying "no" or "stop" sufficient, or will I have to do more to "discipline" my baby at this point?

By the end of this period, it is almost certain that your baby will understand the words "no" and "stop." However, she is still very much within the sensorimotor stage, so messages are more likely to sink in if they are accompanied by physical action. Therefore, whenever your baby ventures into an off-limits area or engages in an undesirable activity, use a firm "no" or "stop," physically remove her from the offending situation, and channel her into a more appropriate direction. If she discovers a cigarette lighter and starts sucking on it, you can say "No, that's not a good thing to suck on," take it away from her, and give her something like a teething ring instead. Because her memory and attention span are short, she will soon forget about the lighter. And through your actions more than through your words, you will have taught her that there are limits to what she can do, and those limits will be enforced by you.

Lately, even though she's not hurt, hungry, or soiled, my baby has been waking up and crying in the middle of the night. How can I comfort her without spoiling her?

This is a very common phenomenon, especially at around eight to ten months of age. On any given night that your baby

cries, it is recommended that you go into her room the first time to make sure that there really isn't anything wrong. If her crying stops and a smile lights up her face as soon as you enter and the light goes on, that is a good indication that your baby has awakened to find herself a little lonely and bored, and she's crying simply in order to get some company. If that is indeed the case, it is recommended that you say to her, "I love you, but nighttime is for sleeping, and I'll see you in the morning." Then leave the room and don't return no matter how much she wails after that. Your baby probably won't understand anything you say, but through your actions, you will be teaching her that the major needs of the family (for a good night's sleep) will sometimes have to take precedence over her minor desires (for some nighttime company). In addition, you can use a low-wattage night-light in her room to

Simply saying "no" will probably not be enough to stop him from doing something that you don't want him to do…

help her feel more secure when she does wake up at night. Within a week to ten days, you can expect that she will once again be sleeping through the night.

My eight month old cries whenever I leave. What can I do to make these separations easier on both of us?

When you are out of sight and out of earshot, your baby may fear that she has been abandoned. She doesn't understand your being away. She also wants you when she wants you. So, she cries. At this point, you want the baby to be or become as flexible as possible. You will need time away from her, and you want her to get more accustomed to being without you

...you will also need to physically remove him from the offending situation and redirect his attention to something more appropriate.

for short periods of time. Some babies at this age develop a separation anxiety and/or a fear of strangers. A familiar loving sitter can help the situation. When you leave, the sitter can be holding the baby or playing with her. Before you go out the door, cheerfully and firmly say goodbye to the baby and leave promptly. If taking her to you for hugs and goodbyes starts her crying, then skip it and just wave bye-bye. Try to go about your business matter-of-factly and expect the baby to do fine. When you return, if she is awake, pick her up and give her hugs and kisses. Eventually, she will learn that while you may leave, you will come back to her again.

My baby spends more time in day care than at home. Does this mean she will be more attached to her teachers than she will to me?

It's possible, but it's not very likely. Keep in mind that day-care personnel are usually responsible for several babies at a time, so they don't have the same advantages you do when it comes to giving your baby undivided attention. Furthermore, no matter how competent, concerned, and loving these people may be, because she is not their child, it is almost impossible for them to convey the same sort of excitement, enthusiasm, and concern toward your baby that you can. Research has shown that although babies who spend a lot of time in day care do become attached to their teachers to a certain extent, the parents remain their primary targets in this regard. However, it is important to note that, during this period, your baby is still operating on very fundamental levels and in the here and now for the most part. Therefore, the quality of the time you spend with your baby won't completely compensate for a severe lack of quantity in interaction time. If your baby hardly ever gets to see you, she will have no choice but to try to form an attachment to someone who is a more significant part of her daily experience.

What can I do to make my baby feel good about herself at this point?

During this period, your baby will spend a lot of time struggling to achieve a variety of new physical skills—crawling, climbing, walking. When she finally manages to attain a new level, she will actually feel a sense of physical relief, which is the basis for a sense of self-satisfaction. Therefore, the first step in nurturing the roots of your baby's self-esteem is to

INDULGING IN HEALTHY SELFISHNESS

Parents of a baby in this age group, especially if it is their first child, often have a tendency to feel guilty if they do not respond immediately to every need of their child. They also have a tendency to feel like tyrants if they do not allow her to do whatever she wants. They typically are willing to make any sacrifice, endure any inconvenience, and in general do whatever it takes to ensure that their baby will never experience anything other than complete contentment. This is normal and natural, but it also can be dangerous for two major reasons. First, sooner or later, resentment will start to build in the parents. Second, the baby will receive the impression that the world revolves around her alone. Consequently, it is recommended that parents make an effort to practice "healthy selfishness," particularly at this point in their child's development. If you are tempted to rush to your baby the second she cries, even though you realize she's only asking for attention; to make excuses for your baby's behavior, even though you know that introducing some discipline would be appropriate; or to stay with your baby constantly, even though you are in desperate need of a break, you probably ought to make a serious attempt to restrain yourself. It is important that your baby learn that she is a dearly beloved, very special, and cherished member of your family, but also that everyone else in the family is dearly beloved, very special, and cherished, too. And it is critical that your baby learn that she has the right to explore and investigate her world freely, but also that her rights do not extend to the point where her activities unfairly interfere with the rights of other people. In other words, as paradoxical as it may seem, keep in mind that doing what's best for baby often means doing what's best for yourself.

make sure that she has plenty of opportunities to attempt and practice these skills. More importantly, your reaction to her accomplishments will become internalized and form the foundations for a healthy pride in achievement. Consequently, it is important for you to be around when she succeeds and to provide an appropriate emotional reaction. That's easy to do—just let out all the natural feelings of joy, excitement, and enthusiasm that arise whenever your baby shows signs of developmental progress. When she pulls to stand or walks for the first time, you can bet that it will be the most important event in your day—maybe even in that week or month. To the extent that you let your baby know how thrilled you are, she will learn to become thrilled with herself.

I've decided to stay home full-time with my baby, but lately I'm beginning to feel bored and trapped. Is something wrong with me?

Having primary responsibility for taking care of a baby 24 hours a day, seven days a week, is enough to make most normal people crazy after a while. Despite all the pleasures and rewards that come with helping your baby to achieve a great start in life, the inevitable stress, drudgery, and isolation are bound to get you down after a while. Consequently, it is recommended that, especially after your baby has passed the six-month mark, you consider some kind of part-time substitute care for your baby. This can be a formal day-care arrangement or something as simple as a twice-a-week play group or an every-once-in-a-while cooperative baby-sitting deal. The important thing is that you take a few hours a week to pamper yourself, relax, pursue some other interest, engage in adult conversations, and/or do anything else that will help you maintain your sanity and return to your child-rearing responsibilities feeling refreshed.

SELECTING TOYS AND EQUIPMENT

Now that my baby has become an active explorer and investigator, won't he need a lot of toys to keep him occupied?

At this point, your baby will need an abundance of items to feed his ever-growing curiosity, but he really will need very few "toys." As long as you've made your home as safe and accessible as possible for him, your baby will find a wealth of material to occupy himself in the course of his daily activities. It probably is a good idea to have several special items around when he has to be in a playpen or otherwise restricted for a short time. In general, however, making a lot of purchases won't be necessary. As far as your baby is concerned, few if any commercial toys will be able to compete with the common contents of a typical household in terms of entertainment and "educational" value. Substituting store-bought products for these everyday items is likely to result in disappointment for everyone involved in most cases.

Lately, my baby has started picking up books and turning the pages. Should I buy special books to encourage his "prereading" skills?

The first active interest that babies display toward books, typically at about one year of age, has nothing to do with reading. At this point, babies are fascinated by simple mechanisms. Hinged objects receive special attention—and the binding of a book is a perfect hinge. If you watch closely, you'll probably notice that your baby is not concerned with what's on the pages; rather, he's merely inclined to turn the pages back and forth. Therefore, the best "first books" for babies are those with stiff cardboard pages that their little fingers can manipulate easily. You really don't have to worry about content at all during this period. If you want to supplement his "book experience" at this point, it is suggested that you introduce him to cabinet doors, lunchbox lids, and various other devices that operate on a hinge, as this, as opposed to reading, is what your baby is focusing on for the time being. Of course, while your baby is not interested in reading, he will enjoy listening to your voice as you read to him, regardless of the content or subject of the reading material.

At this stage of development, his interest in books has more to do with the way the pages turn than with the content of the pages themselves.

What other common household items make particularly appropriate playthings?

The list is endless. As long as an item is nontoxic, too large to be swallowed, small enough to be manipulated easily, free from sharp edges or protrusions, and durable, your baby probably will have a lot of fun with it. Empty egg-shaped pantyhose containers, metal bandage boxes, and large thread spools should never be discarded, as they are among the favorite toys of babies at this point. Newspaper and even old slippers get a lot of playtime. Empty shoe boxes or large cardboard cartons, laundry baskets, and wastepaper baskets are a big thrill for babies once they start crawling and climbing. In addition, if you don't mind and if you take proper precautions, things like light switches, television and radio buttons, and telephone dials are totally fascinating to curious little ones.

With regard to my baby's toys, are the safety considerations pretty much the same as before?

To a large extent, they are. You still want to be sure that no removable piece of any item is less than an inch-and-a-quarter in any dimension, that there are no sharp edges or points, that only nontoxic paints and materials were used, etc. However, you have to keep in mind that your baby's play will be a lot more active at this point, and he will be doing a lot more with his toys than he did previously. Consequently, it is a good idea to check the durability of all products very carefully and to see to it that they can withstand all the hard banging, throwing, and dropping to which they now will be subjected. Also, remember that a toy that is reasonably harmless while being handled may very well become hazardous when it is thrown. In addition, it is suggested that you increase your schedule of periodic inspections to be sure that properly selected toys remain clean, unbroken, and in good working order.

How can I tell if a toy (or its removable parts) or household item is too small to be safe for my baby?

The general rule of thumb is that no item should be less than an inch-and-a-quarter in any dimension so that it cannot be swallowed or choked upon by your child. Of course, it is not easy for everyone to estimate an inch-and-a-quarter easily, and a ruler or tape measure is not always readily available. Several mail order catalogs and children's specialty shops now

Thread spools that are barren of thread and too large to be swallowed make fine playthings at this age.

offer "safety tubes"—plastic cylinders that can be used to test for appropriate size. It is recommended that you obtain one of these, but in the meantime—or even instead—you can use the cardboard cylinder from a roll of toilet paper or paper towels. If an object can pass through the tube, it is too small for your baby to play with. Of course, even the commercial tubes can't guarantee complete accuracy, so if it is a close call under any circumstances, it is better to play it conservatively and keep the item away from your baby.

Why is "toy storage" now a safety issue?

At this point, your baby will no longer be completely dependent upon you to procure playthings. He will become increasingly capable of getting things for himself. Consequently, it is a good idea to keep as many items as possible easily accessible to your baby during playtimes. However, when it is time to put toys away, be sure that they are not placed in areas that could cause problems for your curious baby. For example, if toys are placed on shelves, make sure that they are not only out of reach, but out of sight as well. When your baby sees a favorite toy, he will make every attempt to get to it, and he may end up taking a fall or perhaps causing an avalanche of items to come tumbling down. Another way to handle this is to store toys on low shelves that he can reach easily, with heavier items on the ground level and lighter toys on the shelves above; this way, if he does go for a toy, he won't put himself in serious danger. If you put his toys in a toy chest or box, see to it that it is latched securely; or, if you make the box or chest accessible, see to it that the lid stays up when open and won't close unexpectedly, thereby crushing little fingers or possibly even trapping your baby inside.

What about larger pieces of equipment, such as high chairs, strollers, and baby seats?

You have to remember that your baby is no longer likely to remain passive in a sitting or reclining position for long periods of time. At this point, when he is placed in one of these devices, he probably will attempt to stand up, climb out, etc. Consequently, it is a good idea to double-check the design and construction, making sure that the piece of equipment has a low center of gravity and strong joints and latches so that it won't tip over or collapse easily. Furthermore, it is suggested that you take extra time to be sure that your baby is harnessed in very securely. In general, plan on not keeping your baby restricted in such devices anywhere near as long as you did previously, and never leave him unattended in one.

My baby loves to chase balloons and soap bubbles. Are these things safe if he catches them?

Chasing soap bubbles and balloons is a lot of fun for babies once they can get around quite well. However, it probably is not a good idea to let your baby play unsupervised with balloons. If one should happen to break, your baby will likely need a little comforting as the sound will no doubt frighten him. Also, the pieces of rubber from the broken balloon (as well as balloons that have not been inflated) present a serious swallowing and choking hazard. It also is important to remember that when chasing either balloons or soap bubbles, your baby may be prone to accidents because his limited attention will be focused totally on the floating object. Therefore, make sure that there is plenty of room for him to crawl around without having to worry about bumping into something, falling down somewhere, etc.

Are all commercial toys for children in this age range a waste of money?

Certainly not, but you can end up wasting a lot of money if you are not careful with your selections and expenditures. Because babies now are a lot more active and can do so much more than they could just a few months ago, toy manufacturers tend to make products for them that are increasingly elaborate and expensive. However, a commercial toy has only a slim chance of breaking into a baby's consciousness to begin with. Even if it is a good one that manages to capture his attention, his interests and abilities are continuing to change very rapidly. In other words, even a great toy probably won't be good for very long at this point, so investing a lot of money in any one item is not likely to make sense.

Shouldn't I buy a "busy box" or "activity center" to keep my baby entertained when he's in his crib or car seat?

These products, which typically contain a button to push, a dial to spin, a lever to pull, etc., and which can be attached to

THE PROBLEM WITH PRESENTS

A child's first birthday is a major occasion, and many parents put in a lot of time and effort preparing a special celebration. Unfortunately, as part of the celebration, a lot of toys tend to be presented to the baby as gifts. Consequently, many parents suffer severe disappointment when their baby plays with these items for only a few minutes but spends several hours fooling around with the boxes, ribbons, and paper in which they were wrapped. The fact of the matter is that it is a rare toy that will hold a baby's attention for any length of time at this point. Therefore, spending large amounts of money to provide an abundance of elaborate playthings simply doesn't make much sense at this point. Moreover, although a baby will get an impression that he is the center of attention and probably will enjoy that immensely, he will not comprehend and thus not care about the concept of gifts. Therefore, when planning for your baby's first birthday, first Christmas, first Hanukkah, or whatever, try to avoid the temptation to show your love by showering him with toys. Alert friends and relatives that making expenditures for such items is not necessary as well. A few years from now you may incur your child's anger by giving him something as mundane as socks and underwear on these occasions, but for the time being, it will make little difference to your baby and may make a big difference in your budget.

the sides of various pieces of furniture and equipment, are very popular items—millions are purchased every year. However, it is apparent that their popularity is based upon the fact that they look like they will provide hours of entertainment, so parents are inclined to purchase them. In fact, the more elaborate (and thus, more expensive) a busy box or activity center is, the more likely that mothers and fathers will find it appealing. Once these products are presented to babies, they do get a lot of attention—but only for about ten or 15 minutes, until the novelty wears off. As soon as babies run through the various mechanisms a few times, they become bored and rarely return to these toys thereafter. Therefore, busy boxes and activity centers, despite their at-first-glance appeal, usually are a poor investment for children during this period.

Are "surprise boxes" any better than "busy boxes"?

They usually are. Surprise boxes typically contain a small row of jack-in-the-box type sections, with the trigger mechanisms being simple levers, dials, switches, and push buttons. In addition to being less expensive than busy boxes in most cases, these toys have two major advantages. First, the surprise aspect is far more motivating for babies than the simple ring, rattle, or whatever that is provided with standard busy box mechanisms. Second, each little section provides babies with an easily opened and closed door, and they love to simply move the hinge back and forth for long periods of time. Therefore, surprise boxes do constitute one of the better investments in the world of commercial toys. By the way, babies at this age are generally too young for the standard jack-in-the-box. They have a great deal of difficulty operating the winding mechanism, and they find it impossible to reset the pop-up part without a lot of adult assistance.

What kinds of kitchen items serve as especially enjoyable toys?

Your baby probably will be spending a lot of time in the kitchen, and fortunately, there are many items in a typical kitchen that make wonderful playthings at this point. In general, anything with soft, rounded edges, particularly if it is made of plastic, will be suitable for such purposes. Pots and pans, mixing bowls, measuring cups and measuring spoons, wooden spoons, spatulas, and plastic storage containers are perennial favorites. Paper products and canned goods also provide a lot of enjoyment—chasing a rolling can of tuna fish or a roll of paper towels can be a lot of fun. As your baby becomes more and more adept with his small muscle skills, you can even introduce items such as turkey basters and empty squeeze bottles (if the bottles formerly contained liquid soap or some other such substance, make sure they have been thoroughly rinsed out). Although empty cans constitute a hazard, empty plastic soda pop bottles will be a special treat for your baby (be sure to remove or firmly secure the plastic lid, however, since it may cause choking if swallowed).

A plastic storage container and a couple of wooden spoons make a safe and entertaining drum set.

Why are things like little picnic baskets and bandage boxes so popular with children in this age group?

During this period, babies become fascinated with simple mechanisms, especially devices that operate on hinges. Therefore, anything with a lid that they can open and close easily is likely to be a favorite plaything. Items such as little picnic baskets and bandage boxes have additional appeal because they allow babies to collect things and carry them around. Perhaps because of their growing ability to retain mental images, babies at this age seem to enjoy "hiding" various objects for short periods of time. Consequently, anything that provides them with opportunities to pick things up, put them in a closed container, and then take them out a while later will be very much appreciated. Unfortunately, indulging your baby's interest in such items may be a bit tricky. The "container" must be small enough for your baby to handle comfortably, but the

"things" that go inside must be too large for him to swallow, so making the appropriate match may take some extra effort.

My baby is becoming a real little tiger in the tub. What can I give him to keep him busy while I'm bathing him?

During this period, babies typically become quite active in the tub. Fortunately, they usually enjoy a variety of bath toys, ranging from many of the elaborate commercial models to the traditional rubber ducky and all the boats, sponge puppets, and floating soap bars in between. If you are purchasing bath toys for your baby, note that those which give him an opportunity to pour, splash, and squirt probably will be big favorites, and water wheels are a special added attraction. These toys will be appropriate and appreciated for many months, so they constitute one of the better investments in this area. On the other hand, your baby is likely to have just as much fun with a set of plastic measuring cups, a couple of sponges, and a turkey baster. In other words, there are probably many objects and devices already in your kitchen that will allow your baby to do just as much if not more pouring, splashing, and squirting as any commercial product.

Sponges and measuring cups, as well as traditional bath toys, can make his bath time more enjoyable for both of you.

You can give him a special treat by letting him crawl over you.

Is there any special equipment I should purchase to enhance the development of my baby's physical skills?

Although there are several excellent indoor gyms available commercially, your baby probably won't be able to make maximum use of these relatively elaborate devices for much of this period, so they probably are not a good investment at this point. Moreover, they really aren't necessary at all. Your baby will have plenty of opportunities to practice the physical skills he has acquired and attempt new challenges as long as he has access to a large portion of your home. Carpeted stairs (see next question), sofas, beds, and various other pieces of furniture will be more than adequate in this regard. You can make activities involving large muscle skills even easier to pursue by placing pillows, cushions, large cardboard cartons, and even yourself on the floor for him to crawl over.

I'm scared to death to let my baby climb stairs unsupervised. Is there a more risk-free activity I can substitute?

If allowing your baby to climb up to just the third step by placing a gate there instead of at the bottom (see illustration on page 118) is still more than you can stand, don't worry. Climbing babies are fascinated with "essence of step," and they really don't care too much about how many steps there are or how high the steps are. Therefore, as a substitute, you can use sturdy, stable boxes or padded boards to create a small set of steps in your living room, bedroom, or some other carpeted area. The steps need only be a couple of inches high, and there need not be more than three or four increments. Also, the platforms can be as long and wide as you want. Although you should make an effort to provide your baby with

supervised "real stair" experiences as often as possible, and you eventually will have to let him tackle them on his own, at this point, he will get ample practice and a lot of pleasure from these "substitute steps."

My local community center is offering a baby gymnastics program. Should I enroll my baby?

Most of these programs, particularly those operated by national franchises, are excellent. As babies develop new physical skills, they enjoy opportunities to practice and expand their capabilities. These programs typically offer safe equipment and appropriate activities for these purposes. Moreover, they generally are well supervised and fairly inexpensive. An added attraction is that they provide parents with a chance to get out of the house and mingle with other parents who have children at approximately the same age. However, you should know that no program of this kind has ever been able to prove that it provides lasting advantages for babies when it comes to large or small muscle skill development, coordination, self-confidence, or anything else—despite the fact that such benefits often are claimed in the promotional literature. If you and your baby are looking for some good fun outside the house, fine; but keep in mind that any special functions performed by the program can be easily duplicated in your own home with the furniture and fixtures already on hand.

Even a homemade set of three or four steps placed on a padded surface can allow her to practice her stair-climbing skills.

Are push and pull toys appropriate for children in this age range?

Push and pull toys are not particularly appropriate at this point for two major reasons. First, since babies are just starting to get around on their own and are focusing intensely on the basic skills involved, they ordinarily do not seem interested in bogging themselves down with such items. Second, even if they do show a little interest in these toys, using them can pose some serious hazards. If string is used for push-pull purposes, there is a chance that a baby could become entangled; the possibility of strangulation cannot be ruled out either. Even if the push-pull is based upon a pole or rod, there are potential problems. Remember, babies are still relatively clumsy during this period, and should they fall while pushing such a toy rapidly across the floor, they may become injured as a result of a poke. Therefore, it probably is a good idea to avoid push and pull toys, at least for the time being.

In addition to toys, are there any "games" that my baby will be able to play?

Not in the true sense of playing games. Your baby is still much too young to grasp such concepts as rules, taking turns, etc. However, he will greatly enjoy "reactive" games—activities that are initiated by you in which you really do all the work and he is simply required to respond enthusiastically. For example, once he has achieved object permanence and can retain a mental image in his mind for a short period of time, your baby will love to play "peek-a-boo." As he gets a little older, he will appreciate similar "hiding" games—such as "Where's Daddy?" or "Where's the toy?" Once your baby starts developing a receptive vocabulary and some imitative ability, simple pointing-and-naming games will be a lot of fun for him, too. He'll especially enjoy those centered around his own body parts, such as "Where's your nose?" and "Are those your feet?"

A simple game of "peek-a-boo" or "hide-and-seek" will have you both giggling.

BEWARE OF ADULT PERSPECTIVE

Babies do not buy toys for themselves. In fact, because of their limited communication skills, they can't even make their preferences clearly known. At this point, they are completely dependent upon their parents not only for the purchase of their playthings, but for the selection of their playthings as well. As a result, many manufacturers tend to design and market their products in ways that will appeal primarily to the adults who will purchase the toys, rather than to the babies who will eventually play with them. If you are not careful about avoiding adult perspective when shopping, you may encounter some problems. For instance, as noted earlier, busy boxes and activity centers are among the best selling toys year after year, even though babies hardly spend much time at all interacting with them. That's because many adults think they look interesting, and they often have a lot of fun fiddling with the little gadgets themselves in the toy store. Consequently, a good deal of money is wasted because parents erroneously assume that something which fascinates them will fascinate their baby as well. Another example involves the use of well known cartoon or television characters to decorate toys for babies—a practice that is quite common. Manufacturers spend a lot of money to procure the rights to use these characters, and their cost is passed along in the price of the toys. However, the pleasant associations we have with some of these characters are built up during later childhood; babies at this age don't know—or care about—the difference between these "stars" and generic animals, people, etc. Consequently, if you look at these toys through your own eyes rather than through the eyes of your baby, it is likely you will shell out extra dollars and get a little "status" but absolutely no additional enjoyment for your baby.

My baby is spending more and more time outdoors. Should I have anything special for him in the yard?

Not really. Your baby is still too young to enjoy an outdoor gym, swing set, or any other such major piece of equipment to its full extent. He will be endlessly fascinated by all the new things he is encountering during his explorations, so he probably won't need to be "entertained" by toys too often. When he does, simply transferring his usual playthings to a blanket laid out in the yard will most likely suffice. Perhaps the only special item that you might consider introducing is a small wading pool. There are documented cases of babies drowning in as little as two inches of water, so keep the level low and make sure you supervise at all times. However, as long as the proper precautions are taken, your baby will enjoy splashing around with a few cups, spoons, and other suitable items—especially on a hot summer's day.

Is it true that all babies develop a strong attachment to a stuffed animal, blanket, or some other "transitional object"?

A lot of babies do this, but certainly not all of them. The concept of a "transitional object"—something that provides security as a baby makes the transition from complete helplessness to early independence—fits nicely into various theories of development. In addition, many parents report that their baby will strongly resist going to sleep, taking a nap, or leaving the house unless he is given his special "fuzzy" or whatever. However, research has shown that although this phenomenon is certainly common, it is by no means universal. Quite a few babies never display an inclination toward such items; and furthermore, there is no evidence to suggest that there are any long-term differences in personality or emotional development between those who do and those who don't. Consequently, if your baby hasn't attached himself to something of this sort, don't worry. And definitely don't feel you need to go out and buy one of the "security toys" being marketed with claims based on erroneous and inappropriate assumptions.

Is it too soon to provide my baby with simple musical instruments?

It certainly is too soon to expect that your baby will have any real sense of music appreciation. It also is too soon to expect his increasing yet still rudimentary small muscle skills to be able to handle most musical instruments in the way they are designed to be used. However, that does not mean that musical toys are completely inappropriate at this point. Because your baby is very interested in both sounds and the concept of "cause and effect"—especially if he is the "cause" in some way—introducing him to a toy drum, keyboard, or xylophone may not be a bad idea. Avoid anything with strings or anything that requires your baby to blow in order to make a sound. Make sure that any such item you provide is very durable, as your baby will be doing a lot more "pounding" than "playing." In addition, be prepared for a lot of "noise" as opposed to "music" emanating from his efforts.

Is my baby ready for finger paints?

Not really. Your baby still does not have the mental capacity for true "creativity," nor does he have sufficient small muscle control to use these materials in anything more than a fairly crude manner. In addition, he probably will end up putting this stuff into his mouth. However, your baby will be very interested in colors and textures, and he may very well find things like clay or play dough to be fascinating and fun. Be very careful in checking to see that anything of this sort that you provide is nontoxic. Since your baby will do a lot more mushing, squishing, pounding, and throwing than "molding," be prepared for considerably more "mess" than "art."

If he has developed a strong attachment to a blanket or toy, don't worry. It's his way of feeling more secure as he makes the transition from helplessness to early independence.

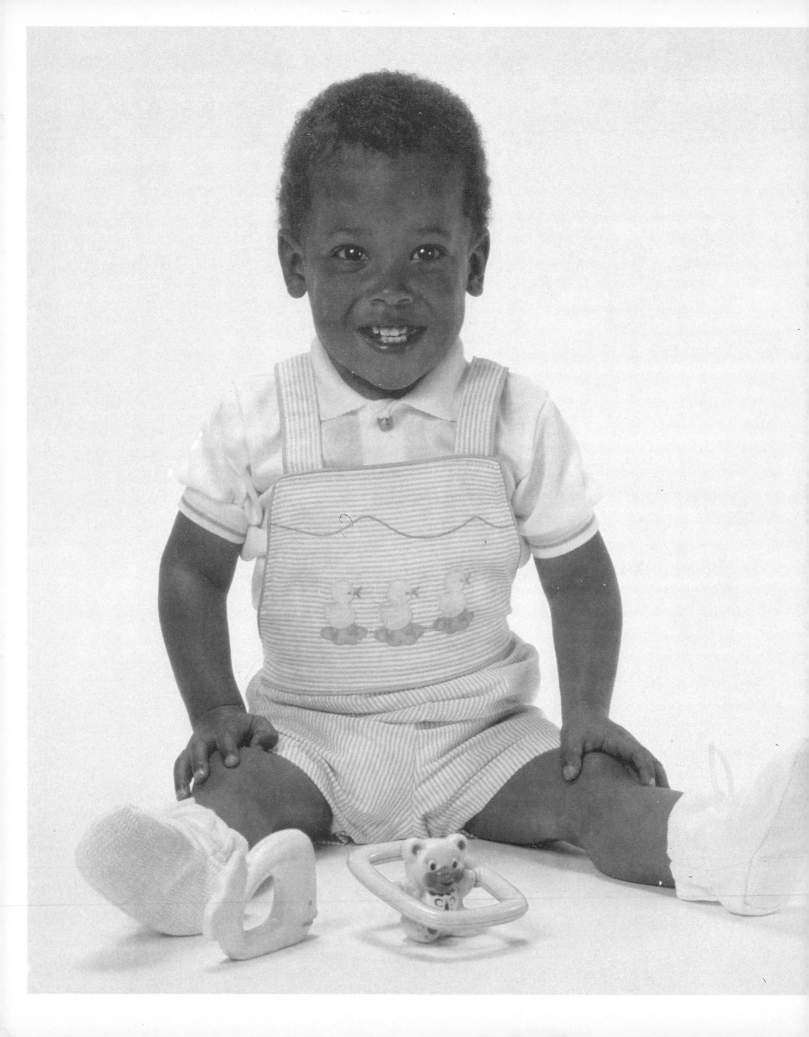

1 YEAR
TO
2½ YEARS

Between one year and two and a half years of age, your toddler will go through an amazing transformation. By the end of this period, your largely nonrational, nonverbal "baby" will have been replaced by a thinking, talking "child" full of determination and imagination. He will still be dependent upon you in important ways, but he also will be exhibiting a significant degree of independence. His world will expand enormously to include many out-of-home experiences. He will also show interest in interacting with people outside the family, especially children his own age. Furthermore, he will progress from a primarily reactive participant in social relationships to an active initiator and full partner with a strong and distinct personality. This transition will not always be smooth and easy. It is likely that you will find your patience and stamina tested by your toddler's ever-growing physical skills, his increasingly sophisticated mental abilities, and his more complex emotional states. However, as long as you appreciate the changes your toddler is going through and continue to encourage him as appropriate and control him as necessary, your payoff will be great. Your reward will be a competent and confident child who will be a source of pride and a challenging but delightful companion as well.

HOW YOUR CHILD DEVELOPS

How much growth in height and weight can I expect my toddler to experience during this period?

Quite a bit. Although her overall rate of growth will continue to slow down somewhat, your toddler will still make a lot of progress during this period. Typically, two-and-a-half-year-old children are between 33 and 38 inches tall, with the average somewhere around 36 inches. They weigh between 25 and 38 pounds, with the average somewhere around 32 pounds. Again, if your child was large or small in the beginning, you can expect that she will remain at the higher or lower end of these ranges at this point. It is possible, however, that you will begin to see her starting to approach the center of the norms. In any event, as long as your toddler is in good health, don't worry. Growth patterns are unique in every instance, and they are never smooth and regular.

All of a sudden, it seems as if my toddler is no longer a "baby" and is now a small "child" instead. Has her appearance really changed, or just my perception?

A little bit of both. During this period, toddlers mature a great deal both physically and mentally. By two and a half years of age, your toddler's physical proportions will have changed dramatically. Her head will no longer appear in any way oversized for her body; her lower limbs will no longer seem smaller than her upper limbs; and in many other ways she will have achieved "normal" human shape. These physical changes will be complemented and emphasized by the changes she experiences in other areas of development. It is during this period that your toddler will go from a nonverbal, nonrational creature to one who is capable of thinking and communicating in rather impressive ways. Although everything will take place gradually over many months, it is not at all unusual for parents to get a sudden sense of transformation as their "baby" disappears and their "child" emerges.

My toddler is walking and climbing, but she's very clumsy and unsteady. Is something wrong with her?

Nothing that won't be cured in a few months. When children first achieve these abilities, they don't possess them in full-

By the end of this period, you may be surprised to see that your little "baby" has matured into a small "child."

blown form. It takes a little time for them to become familiar with and refine their new forms of movement, so it is perfectly normal for them to be rather clumsy and unsteady for a while—which is why they are called "toddlers." However, as your toddler gains more and more experience, she will become increasingly coordinated and graceful. By the end of this period, you may be quite impressed by the control she has over her body and by the many things she can do. Whereas a one year old may only take one tentative step at a time, a two and a half year old will be running around at a mile a minute. While a one year old may take a few minutes to struggle her way up onto a sofa, a two and a half year old will scoot up a jungle gym in a flash. So be patient. Right now you may be alarmed by your toddler's clumsiness and unsteadiness, but very soon you may be alarmed by her skill and daring.

When will my toddler develop control over her bladder and bowel muscles?

This is a tricky subject. Typically, toddlers achieve the capacity to physically control their bladder and bowel muscles some-where between 18 and 24 months of age. However, simply having some physical control over these muscles does not mean that they are capable of complete control with regard to the functions of urination and defecation. It takes time and mental development for toddlers to learn how to recognize the sensations that immediately precede these functions, and even more time and mental development to learn how to respond appropriately. Furthermore, it will be several months before their control over their bladder and bowel muscles grows from momentary to significantly strong. Consequently, if someone claims to have a toddler who is toilet trained at 18 months, it probably means that the person has somehow managed to get her toddler to "hold it" for a few seconds while she whisks her off quickly to the bathroom. That's a long way from true toilet training.

Will I see much improvement in my toddler's small muscle skills during this period?

You certainly will. Although a one year old typically is rather adept at using her hands and fingers to manipulate various objects and operate simple mechanisms, a two and a half year old is incredibly more impressive in these areas. For example,

As he practices his new physical skills throughout this period, his movements will become increasingly coordinated and graceful.

a baby may be able to pick up a ball and throw it wildly, whereas a toddler will eventually be able not only to throw a ball with a fair amount of accuracy, but may be able to catch it quite reliably as well. A baby may be able to operate simple levers, such as light switches, whereas a toddler may be able to use something as complex as an old-fashioned nutcracker. In everyday routines, such as using cups and utensils when eating and drinking, and in special situations, such as using brushes and crayons when painting and drawing, you will see your toddler making tremendous progress in the strength and dexterity of her small muscles.

In the course of her play, my toddler now appears to be "figuring things out." Does this mean she's really starting to "think"?

During this period, your toddler will indeed progress from a "sensorimotor" style of thought to a truly rational mode. However, up until 18 to 24 months of age, her senses and physical movements will remain her primary tools for analyzing information and dealing with the world around her. It

won't be until after two years of age that she comes to rely heavily on the mental images in her mind. Even while she's still in the sensorimotor stage, however, your toddler will quite often be "figuring things out." You may notice that in addition to exploring and investigating, your toddler also will be doing a lot of "experimenting." No longer content simply to see what things are like and what happens to them as the result of some basic action, it will almost be like she is driven to find out "what if?" Even though everything must still be directly in front of her, she will start systematically applying different strategies and gauging their relative results through trial and error. Eventually, she will be able to carry out many plans and test various options in her mind before choosing one or two to be translated into direct action.

How can I tell when my toddler is beginning to use mental images and is engaging in true "rational" thought?

Somewhere between 18 and 24 months of age, your toddler will start to rely on her mental imagery to a noticeable extent. As she goes about her play and encounters some problem, she

No longer content to just investigate and explore, your toddler will be driven to find out "what if?"

likely will stop for a few seconds before proceeding with some plan of action. This is a sign that "the gears are turning," and she is running through several options in her mind. Of course, just like it took her many months to learn how to use her body effectively, it will take your toddler months and years to learn how to make the best use of her increasing mental capacities. Don't expect her to become fully rational overnight. At first, her thinking will be tentative, and she may very well support her mental analyses with occasional physical trials just to be sure. However, by the end of this period, you probably will see your toddler solving simple problems—such as how to get a toy out of a box, how to get your attention while you're occupied with something, or how to climb to the top of a high chest—quickly and easily.

Will my toddler now remember everything she sees, hears, and does and everything that happens to her?

As your toddler passes her second birthday, you can expect her to start retaining more and more of her experiences for longer and longer periods of time. Although she will be capable of creating mental images right from the beginning of this period, they will be rather weak and will not last more than a minute or two initially. However, by the end of this period, you can expect that your toddler will remember quite a bit from day to day, and she might remember particularly strong sensations and impressive experiences for months. Still, throughout this period, the major gains will be in the area of short-term memory, so don't expect too much from your toddler at this point. It will be more difficult to distract her from something in which she has a strong interest, and it will be easier to deal with her on a daily basis in terms of giving instructions, admonitions, etc. Overall and in the long run, however, it is likely she will forget considerably more than she retains.

Can my toddler comprehend concepts such as "later" and "tomorrow"?

Due to her expanding memory and increasing thinking skills, your toddler may have a pretty good understanding of these concepts—along with concepts such as "earlier" and "yesterday"—sometime around her second birthday or a little beyond. However, it will be a while before she can use these terms with any precision. Keep in mind that retaining mental

LAGS AND SPURTS

It is important for parents to realize that development tends to proceed in lags and spurts rather than in continuous, smooth transitions. When looking at a developmental chart, it is easy to get a false impression of the nature of "normal" or "average" development. Although the majority of toddlers may start at roughly the same spot and end up at roughly the same spot during this period, their individual rates and patterns of development will be very irregular and will rarely be identical. At various times, some toddlers will be increasing their physical skills in leaps and bounds while their language skills are just creeping forward; others will be making slow progress with physical skills and rapid advances in language skills. A couple of months later, everyone may very well have switched paces completely in all areas. Therefore, if parents expect their toddlers to progress in even increments at set times, they are likely to be alternately surprised and disappointed. They are also likely to be inappropriately talking about their toddler "falling behind" or "moving ahead." Perhaps it will help to think of your toddler's development as a leisurely cross-country drive from New York to Los Angeles. Even though she may get caught in some heavy traffic trying to get out of New York, she'll probably make up a lot of time zipping through the desert later on; if she rushes through the industrial states in the East, she may stop to soak up the scenery when she gets to the mountains in the West; and even though she may take an entirely different route than another toddler, chances are that they will both arrive in Los Angeles at approximately the same time.

images and moving them around in her mind is still new to your toddler. It will take many months and years before she has had sufficient experience to place a lot of things in all their proper relations with one another. Consequently, at first, "earlier" and "later" will have little meaning beyond "not now," and "yesterday" and "tomorrow" may mean nothing more than stronger versions of "earlier" and "later." It is therefore a good idea to help your toddler out by being precise and placing various events in relation to each other. For instance, "...after Mommy comes home and we eat dinner" will have considerably more impact on your toddler's mind than something vague like "...a little later this evening."

Even though she's fairly rational, my toddler can't seem to understand that her dreams aren't real. Is this unusual?

Not at all. Keep in mind that mental images are very new to your toddler. It will take quite a while before she fully understands how they work. The inability to distinguish dreams from reality is one sign of this immature thinking, and

It's not unusual for toddlers to talk to or be afraid of blowing leaves, rolling balls, and other inanimate objects in motion.

it is referred to as "realism." The sights, sounds, and sensations of her dreams are identical to those that your toddler experiences during the day, so at first, she has no way of distinguishing them. As adults, we often have trouble with particularly powerful dreams when we first wake up. Eventually, we can factor in certain pieces of information—like the fact that we're still in bed—and come up with a rational analysis of what we've just experienced. Toddlers, on the other hand, are operating on a very simple level and cannot handle a variety of factors all at once. Another example of this sort of thing is referred to as "animism." This is the toddler's conviction that anything that moves is alive. In her limited experience, that's the way the world works. Therefore, you may find your toddler talking to, becoming afraid of, or otherwise interacting "socially" with inanimate objects that she sees in motion.

When my toddler does something wrong and I ask her about it, her explanation sometimes strays far from the truth. Is she capable of lying at this point?

Not really. Your toddler's first forms of thought are extremely self-centered, or "egocentric." Her only frame of reference is her own personal experience, and at this point, she is completely incapable of seeing something from another person's perspective or taking into account factors that don't relate directly to her wants and needs of the moment. Consequently, when you question your toddler about something "bad" that she has done, she may be motivated primarily by a desire to avoid your displeasure; that desire will control the bulk of her thinking. The result may be an outlandish lie, but you can't really accuse your toddler of being "deceptive." For example, if you ask her, "Did you spill the milk?" she may think for a moment, then respond, "No, Joey (her older brother) did it." Her thinking ability at this stage allows her to come up with a previously successful strategy—blaming her brother for a mishap. It does not, however, allow her to take into account the fact that her brother is at school, that you were right there to see her do it, and that there's no way she's going to beat the rap.

Is my toddler still too young to have any sense of moral values?

As the months go by, your toddler will begin to get a fairly clear sense of "good" and "bad." But even by the end of this period, she still will not be able to comprehend the concepts of "right" and "wrong" in any meaningful way. Keep in mind that her thinking will be extremely egocentric at this stage, so what she chooses to do will be governed primarily by her own wants and desires of the moment. In other words, your toddler's "moral" reasoning will be based entirely on immediate rewards and punishments that she perceives for herself. She will not take into account the rights and feelings of others when making her decisions. As long as you monitor her behavior closely, you can serve as her "conscience" and help control any inappropriate tendencies. You can't, however, expect that she will be receiving reliable and valid guidance from within her own mind at this point.

My neighbor's toddler didn't talk until she was almost two and then seemed to start speaking in complete sentences. Is she unusual?

This phenomenon is certainly not typical, but it does happen fairly often. As discussed previously, the normal range for the onset of expressive language is anywhere between six months and two years of age. However, almost all children begin to understand words between six and eight months of age. Consequently, even though a toddler may not be saying anything, that does not mean she isn't developing language skills. Once she does start speaking, it should be no surprise that she starts speaking at a level that is considerably more complex than another child who began speaking many months earlier. This reinforces the fact that parents should not make too much out of the date at which their child starts talking. It is clear that the onset of the first spoken words has relatively little significance for overall language development in the long run. As long as your toddler is demonstrating normal hearing and an ever-progressing understanding of words, don't worry if her expressive language seems to be lagging behind.

Once my toddler starts talking a lot, can I assume that her ability to understand words and her ability to use them will progress at about the same pace from that point on?

Although both receptive and expressive language development will proceed rapidly from this point on, it is probably not a good idea to think of them as parallel processes yet. For the most part, even by the end of this period, toddlers will be able to understand many more things than they will be able

WHAT TO DO IF YOU'RE WORRIED

It is natural for parents—particularly first-timers—to be constantly worried about their toddler's development. In general, being just a little patient often goes a long way toward relieving many anxieties. However, it is an unfortunate fact that from time to time, genuine problems do arise that require active intervention. So, if your toddler repeatedly shows up at the lower end of the "normal" ranges and/or consistently deviates substantially from what is described as "standard" performance, it is not unreasonable at all for you to seek professional help. When you do seek such help, keep two major things in mind. First, pediatricians do not have all-encompassing expertise. Because they are the professionals with whom parents are likely to have routine contact, they tend to get asked about everything, even though their training and experience is not without limits. So if the problem is apparently physical in nature, such as abnormal growth pattern, apparent hearing loss, etc., then by all means consult a pediatrician; and be prepared to have the pediatrician refer you to a specialist for certain problems. On the other hand, if the problem has to do with a seemingly low level of language comprehension, an inability to operate simple mechanisms, or anything else that may be outside the clearly medical realm, it might be better to consult a developmental psychologist, developmental pediatrician, or early childhood educator. Second, because early development is so typically erratic and even bizarre on occasion, some professionals may occasionally lapse into the habit of automatically reassuring parents that there is nothing to worry about. However, as it turns out, the hardcore instincts of parents are fairly reliable. Therefore, if you find yourself chronically concerned about something, keep pursuing specialists until you get an answer that truly satisfies you.

to say. Learning how to produce all the sounds properly and put all the different parts of speech into their proper places will take many months and years. So you can assume that, in general, your toddler will be a considerably better listener than talker. On the other hand, due to their increasing imitative capacities, toddlers who are talking may often say extraordinary things. In most cases, they have no real idea of what it is they are saying. Consequently, if your toddler surprises you with a very impressive word or phrase, chances are she has merely mimicked something she has heard; it will be a while yet before she can pull the same thing out of her own mind.

Because of her increasing ability to imitate, you may hear your toddler say some pretty amazing things.

By the time she's two and a half, can I expect my toddler to understand just about everything I say?

By the end of this period, it is reasonable to expect that your toddler will understand somewhere between one half and three fourths of the everyday language she will use for the rest of her life. Consequently, for the most part, you probably will find it fairly easy to communicate with her. However, you have to be careful about expecting too much from your toddler at this point. She still will have a long way to go before she will be able to understand everything that pertains to her immediate experience, and it will be years before she will be able to handle complex concepts. So, for instance, you can give a toddler a complicated instruction, such as "Pick up your shoe, take it into the bedroom, put it in the blue box, and put the box under the bed," and you can expect her to comprehend all the nouns, verbs, and prepositions completely—even if she's never heard them put together in that particular way before. On the other hand, saying something like "You can't have that toy because we can't afford it and your Mommy would have a fit if I gave in to you again" is not likely to have full impact.

Sometimes my toddler says a phrase perfectly, but later she will say the same sort of thing all wrong. Why is that?

During the early stages of expressive language development, there are two distinct processes upon which toddlers are operating. One is imitation, and the other is mental reasoning. Consequently, your toddler will occasionally come out with something impressive simply because her ability to mimic is quite advanced at this point. However, later on she may attempt to put a similar phrase together in her own mind before she speaks, and because her mental capacities are still relatively limited, she is not likely to produce a perfect composition. Therefore, parents have to be careful about judging the quality of what their toddlers are saying. Even though it doesn't appear to be as good on the surface, a phrase that your toddler puts together herself is actually superior in some ways to a "perfect" phrase she produces simply by repeating something she's just heard.

Will my toddler continue to depend heavily on me for emotional support throughout this period?

In the beginning, it is likely that you will actually see an increase in your toddler's attachment behavior as her emotional dependency upon you reaches a peak. However, starting around 16 or 18 months of age, your toddler will begin to develop a strong sense of herself as "her own person" and will begin moving more and more toward emotional independence. Of course, this does not mean that you will no longer be important to her in an emotional sense. First of all, the confidence and trust in your support that she has built up

Although he's moving toward early independence, he will still look to you for the emotional strength he needs to see him through.

learns precisely what the limits are. It is only by repeated assertions and challenges that she comes to comprehend where her authority ends and the authority of her parents begins, and how strong each is when compared to the other. In other words, in order for her to become independent, a toddler often must fight against those upon whom she previously was completely dependent. She does so not out of anger or malice, but because she has few other ways in which to form a frame of reference. Therefore, as will be the case when this process is repeated on a much larger scale during adolescence, it helps if parents can avoid taking their toddler's "rebellion" phase personally at this point.

Will my toddler be developing permanent personality traits during this time?

Generally, it is somewhere around the second birthday that toddlers begin demonstrating personality traits that they are likely to maintain for years to come. Characteristics such as shyness, stubbornness, selfishness, and humor seem to start showing up routinely and consistently from this point on. Of course, it is possible that a child may have demonstrated any or all of these traits to a certain extent somewhat earlier. It is not until this point, however, that personality traits become reasonably reliable and stable. On the other hand, you should note that no characteristics of this kind should be considered completely permanent—human beings are capable of change throughout life. However, from now on, the longer a particular personality trait is entrenched, the more difficult it will be to turn it around or reshape it.

over many months is the bedrock for her personal security. Furthermore, in times of crises—and even in times of less traumatic but still significantly stressful circumstances—you can expect your toddler to count on you for the emotional strength she needs to make it through. But in terms of routine activities, by the end of this period, you can expect that your toddler will be comfortable playing alone for long periods of time. You can also expect her to become interested in establishing relationships with adults and peers outside the family.

Will my toddler make a smooth transition from dependency to independence?

Unfortunately, no. The process that a toddler goes through in establishing a strong sense of self can be extraordinarily unpleasant for her parents. Understanding and becoming comfortable with her own personal power is not something that a toddler achieves overnight. It involves a lot of pushing limits, testing wills, and other exercises through which she

UNDERSTANDING YOUR CHILD'S BEHAVIOR

How much will my toddler's sleeping and napping patterns change during this period?

Your toddler's overall sleep needs probably will decline very little and very gradually. By the end of this period, he may be sleeping only an hour or two less during any 24-hour period than he was sleeping at the beginning. Most toddlers manage to continue sleeping through for 11 to 12 hours a night, so the reduction in sleep time most likely will come at the expense of daytime naps. At one year of age, most toddlers still will require two naps a day, but by two and a half, many get by with only one. The transition is not always smooth, and your toddler may experience an awkward period at around 18 months of age. Two naps will be too much, yet one won't be enough. He may suffer from chronic crankiness, and your regular schedules may get thrown off for a while, but this should be a fairly temporary problem.

Now that he's been doing it for a few months, will my toddler's interest in exploring and investigating his surroundings start to decline?

On the contrary. As long as your toddler has not been subjected to long periods of restriction, you can expect his explorations and investigations to continually grow in scope and intensity throughout this period. Now that he has begun experimenting as well as exploring and investigating, he will find an infinite number of fascinating ways to learn about his world using his ever-expanding physical skills. One thing to keep in mind is that as his ability to explore and investigate becomes more efficient and effective, boredom becomes a greater danger. An infant needs several weeks to soak up his immediate surroundings, and a baby may require several days to take advantage of everything a single room has to offer. However, toddlers are incredibly active in this regard, so make sure your toddler's horizons are stretched at a pace that will keep up with his skills. Although this probably doesn't have to involve anything extraordinary or unusual, it may very well mean opening up his world to include places outside your home on occasion.

Giving her chances to explore outside your home will provide her with a variety of fascinating ways to learn about her world.

My toddler gets a real kick out of running around, stopping, then running around again without really going anywhere. Is this normal?

Believe it or not, it is. As toddlers gain greater control over their bodies, they often enjoy exercising their new skills simply for the sheer delight of doing so. Some parents become alarmed when their toddlers engage in an activity that doesn't have an immediately apparent purpose. Keep in mind the fact that this sort of behavior is very important to toddlers—it's one of the few ways that such young children have to feel good all by themselves. Many years from now, when your child gets his driver's license, it won't seem strange to you if he wants to just drive around some afternoon even though he has no particular place to go. So, at this point, understand that your toddler—who has just become able to walk and run comfortably and confidently—is getting a great deal of pleasure from "spreading his wings."

My toddler seems to be constantly underfoot. How can he learn anything on his own if he's always with me?

The key word in this question is "seems." Attachment behavior tends to increase in intensity at the beginning of this period. Due to a toddler's increasing physical abilities and communication skills, it also tends to increase in effectiveness. Consequently, many parents feel as if their toddler has become something like a second layer of skin. Fortunately, this should be only a temporary condition. Within a couple of months, your toddler will be spending much more time away from you. In fact, by the end of this period, you may be surprised to find that you miss having him around during much of the day. By the way, keep in mind that interactions with you are part of your toddler's learning "on his own." He will learn a great deal by watching and imitating you, and he will need you for periodic "consultations" in the course of his activities. So despite his capacity to be somewhat annoying at times, be careful not to make yourself unapproachable to your toddler.

My toddler will eat or drink anything—even stuff out of the dog's dish! Is this unusual?

It is a common misconception that a toddler's sense of smell and sense of taste serve as self-protection mechanisms, and that he will not eat or drink things that clearly are not fit for

---

DON'T TAKE IT PERSONALLY

The middle part of this period can be a really tough time for parents. After many months of enjoying a sweet, innocent, loving baby, they now find themselves saddled with an annoying, willful, unmanageable monster. Of course, not all parents have it perfectly easy in the beginning, and not all parents have it so rough at this point. However, this is the typical scenario. If you do find yourself in this situation, it is important to remember not to take your toddler's behavior personally. For the most part, he is not reacting directly to you or anything you've done, but rather to powerful forces created by his rapid progress in various areas of development. For example, when your negativistic toddler says "no" in response to one of your requests, he isn't doing so because he no longer likes you or because you have failed to anticipate and analyze the circumstances properly. Rather, he is simply responding to a strong need to assert himself and challenge any authority with which he is confronted. When your ritualistic toddler screams in response to some simple act you've unconsciously performed, again, he is not doing so because you are mean or incompetent, but rather because he has a strong need to maintain a rigid sense of order. This does not mean that you should tolerate your toddler's unacceptable activities, nor does it mean that you can't feel bad on occasion. It will be impossible to completely avoid the feeling that your toddler has rejected or turned against you. However, to the extent that you can understand what he's going through and respect his behavior for the developmental progress it represents, you will be able to prevent such feelings from overwhelming you and overshadowing the many accomplishments and positive behaviors your toddler also will be exhibiting during this period.

human consumption. As your toddler has demonstrated, this definitely is not so. As long as a toddler is hungry or thirsty, he will eat or drink just about anything. Therefore, it is up to you to make sure that your toddler is completely protected in this regard. Eating out of the dog's dish probably won't cause your toddler serious harm; but if you've been lax about something like a bottle of ammonia, a package of plant fertilizer, or anything else that is poisonous because you couldn't imagine your toddler getting close to it, much less ingesting it, he could be in serious danger.

How will I know my toddler is entering his "rebellion" phase, and how long will it last?

This phase will hit you like a brick between the eyes. Starting at about 16 or 18 months of age, you will discover that your toddler's favorite word has become "no." This signals the onset of "negativism," which is a key component of this phase. Every instruction you give to him and every request you make of your toddler from this point on is likely to be met with strong resistance and even downright refusal. Your toddler will constantly challenge your authority and pit his will against yours. Remember, this is a perfectly normal part of the developmental process, and you must try not to take your toddler's defiant and uncooperative behavior personally. It would be nice if this phase simply passed all by itself within a short space of time, but the fact of the matter is that personal power and control are at issue, and your toddler will not complete this phase until those issues are resolved. If you treat him with understanding, respect, and fairness, yet never let him get the impression that he is the boss, you can reasonably expect him to return to general civility sometime around his second birthday, or a little before that time if you're lucky.

As he tests the limits of his power (and yours) and struggles toward independence, nearly every request you make is likely to be met with resistance or downright refusal.

In what other ways will my toddler assert his independence?

One characteristic of toddlers going through this phase is extreme possessiveness. Next to "no," "mine" is their favorite word, and they actively seek to establish domain over anything and everything they can. In addition, once they have established something to be their private property, they tend to hold onto it and protect it at all costs. Toddlers in this phase also tend to develop very strong preferences. Previously, it probably didn't matter much to him whether vanilla or chocolate ice cream was being served. Now, all of a sudden, the particular flavor offered becomes a major issue. And, once he has made his choice, it will be very difficult to persuade him to change—even for very legitimate and logical reasons, such as the fact that you've just run out of that flavor. Again, as long as such behavior is understood and respected but is not allowed to get out of hand and become intolerable, you can expect your toddler to return to a less intense mode of existence within a few months.

Although he's been talking for only a short time, my toddler sometimes says incredible things. Where do these words and phrases come from?

Probably from you. A large portion of your toddler's early utterances will be direct imitations of things he hears. As a result, he often will come out with something that seems far beyond his capacity to comprehend—and, in many cases, it probably is. Toward the end of this period, your toddler also will be developing a rather active imagination, and some of the outlandish things he says may come from the strange and new ideas he is starting to put together in his own mind. By the way, your toddler will be imitating everyone and everything he hears, so if you don't remember saying something he is now repeating, chances are that he picked it up from a neighbor, the television, or some other source.

My toddler really enjoys carrying on a conversation with me, but he doesn't always seem to understand or remember much of it. Is this strange?

Not at all. Especially toward the end of this period, your toddler often will be delighted to engage in "conversation" with you, but there's a good chance that, in many instances, his agenda and yours will be distinctly different during the

Next to "no," "mine" will be one of her favorite words during the rebellion phase.

interaction. While you will be concerned with talking about something, your toddler probably will be focusing primarily on the words themselves. If you listen closely, you may notice that he is doing a lot of simple imitation, merely repeating what you have just said to him. You may also notice that he uses the same few words over and over again, either enjoying their sounds or practicing and perfecting his pronunciation of them. Consequently, a toddler's "conversation" usually appears to be a lot more sophisticated than it actually is. Keep in mind that your toddler is likely to be more interested in the form rather than the content of conversation and that his comprehension and memory skills are still some distance behind what his verbal skills may seem to indicate.

My toddler loves pointing-and-naming games with picture books, but he won't sit still for stories. Is he hyperactive?

Probably not—he's just too young for stories at this point. Somewhere between 14 and 18 months of age, toddlers typically do become very interested in pointing-and-naming games with picture books. Such activities fit in perfectly with your toddler's relatively short memory and attention span, as well as with his strong interest and growing ability in the use of language. However, to really appreciate a story, his memory and attention span needs to be longer and his ability to comprehend needs to be much greater. Therefore, it may not be until the end of this period that your toddler has the patience to sit still for the length of time needed to listen to a full story and the mental abilities needed to recognize characters, understand plots, and follow story lines. However, even at the beginning of this period, your toddler probably will enjoy listening to the gentle rhythm and tone of your voice as you read a story at bedtime or nap time, so don't give up this practice completely.

When can I expect my toddler to be content to play by himself for long periods of time?

Throughout this period, as your toddler adds experimentation to his explorations, you will notice that his activities are becoming more complex and time-consuming and his attention span is growing. As a result, especially once his attachment behavior becomes less intense, he will be approaching you to a somewhat lesser extent throughout the course of the day. However, his ability to be content playing by himself for

really significant stretches will increase dramatically after his second birthday. That's when his capacity for imaginative activities will kick in. Once he can create a variety of people, places, and things in his own mind, he'll be able to keep himself occupied for quite a while by "playing" with his thoughts and mental images.

How complex will my toddler's role-play and fantasy behavior become during this period?

In the beginning, your toddler will simply be imitating a few basic routines that he has witnessed often and with which he

She may start to use her own creative style in her pretend activities.

has a fair amount of experience. Typically, pretend telephone conversations, imitations of household chores, and pretend eating and drinking episodes are the first such activities to surface. However, by the end of this period, your toddler will be picking up raw materials for his imaginative activities from a wide variety of experiences both inside and outside your home. He probably will also be collecting "fuel" for his imagination from stories he hears and programs or movies he sees on television. Not only will he be repeating what he sees, he'll be attempting to put together his own combinations of characters and events. Consequently, while you probably will recognize the essence of his role-play and fantasy activities, you also will notice that your toddler is adding his own distinct flavor and flair at this point.

Lately, my toddler appears to be going through little "rituals" at bedtime, bathtime, mealtime, etc. He gets very upset if "standard procedure" isn't followed. Is this normal?

It certainly is. As toddlers progress through this period, they become increasingly capable of actively participating in and exercising some control over daily routines. However, you have to keep in mind that this sort of stuff is still new to them, and their capacity to handle everything involved is still somewhat limited. Therefore, toddlers have a need for these routines to be very familiar, stable, and consistent. If something is placed in a different spot, if something is done out of usual order, or if something new is introduced, it is no big deal to you, but it can throw your toddler significantly out of whack. Once your toddler has a chance to become thoroughly comfortable with and confident in his capacity to manage these affairs, he will become much more amenable to change and variations.

My toddler still has regular confrontations with his four-year-old sister, but lately, she often claims that he started it. Is this possible?

It certainly is. At the beginning of this period, your toddler probably was able only to protect himself from his sister's hostile advances by crying for help as soon as she approached him. However, as his physical capacities have increased, he has become able to return the abuse; and thanks to his growing imitative capacities, he knows precisely what to do. Since his sister is still bigger, stronger, and smarter, it is natural to

DO AS I DO—NOT AS I SAY

Especially toward the end of this period, many parents are occasionally alarmed by the things that their toddler says and does. Often, they find themselves spending a lot of time telling their toddler what to do and what not to do in certain situations. Unfortunately, they fail to realize that, at this point, a toddler's capacity to understand and follow instructions and explanations is extremely limited compared to his capacity to imitate the behavior he sees. Consequently, if your toddler is behaving in a manner that you feel is inappropriate, before you attempt to correct him directly, make sure that he isn't simply mimicking something he has seen you do. Some parents are shocked when they see their toddler hitting his dolls in the course of his role-play activities; they scold him rather than acknowledging that their toddler may have seen them spanking his older brothers and sisters on occasion. Some parents recoil in horror and reprimand their toddler severely when he turns to them and says, "You dummy!" or something similar rather than acknowledging that their toddler may have heard such epithets being hurled back and forth when his parents were arguing with each other. Of course, you can't be afraid to be human, and you can't premeditate every word and action you present to your toddler. At this stage, however, it is important to remember that telling your toddler to do one thing while you do the opposite will often be largely ineffective and may result in very unrealistic expectations.

assume that she is still in control of the situation. But keep in mind that prior to this point, whenever a confrontation took place between the siblings, the older one got chastised and the younger one got comforted. Consequently, at this point, it is very likely that his sister is trying to avoid such episodes. Your toddler, on the other hand, may be eagerly seeking to initiate them. Of course, that won't be the case at all times, so you'll have to keep a close eye on them to be sure who the troublemaker is in each instance.

I just had another baby, and my toddler seems to be intent on terrorizing her. Why doesn't he love his little sister?

Why should he? Remember, your toddler is still in the process of working out the fundamentals of his attachment relationship with you. As his "consultant," you are a very important component of his explorations and investigations. You are still a primary target of much of his interest, particularly when it comes to learning about social rules and language. Consequently, your attention is your toddler's most precious commodity, and his sister is taking it away from him. To make matters worse, your toddler simply does not have the mental capacity as yet to deal with complex explanations about the nature of love and family. As far as he is concerned, attention equals love, and his new sister is taking you away from him. To expect your toddler to love his baby sister at this point would be like your husband bringing home another woman, announcing that she is going to be "our second wife," and expecting you to love her just as much as he does.

Will my toddler eventually lighten up on his little sister as he gets used to her?

After the fuss and bother of the initial few weeks is over and you have settled down into a routine with the new baby, your toddler probably will lighten up a little. After all, his sister will

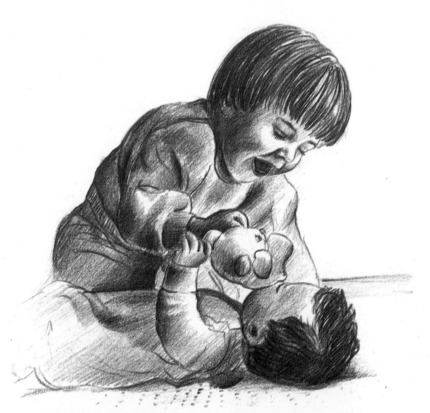

At times, he may be very protective of his new little sister. Keep in mind, however, that he is likely to be jealous of the attention she gets and may try to take it out on her on occasion.

be sleeping a lot in a crib in another room and won't require as much of your time in the course of the day. Therefore, she won't be as much of a threat to his relationship with you. However, be careful not to convince yourself that your troubles are over. A few months later, when the little one begins to crawl, she will once again require more of your attention, and she will require it immediately on many occasions. That attention is likely to come at the expense of your toddler. Therefore, after a brief period of peace, you can expect a renewal of hostilities, and the situation is likely to be more intense and stressful than it was before.

While my toddler appears to play nicely with my neighbor's toddler, up close it's clear they're each doing their own thing. Why is that?

What you are seeing is referred to as "parallel play." As they near the end of this period, toddlers begin to show an interest in being with peers. At first, however, their capacity to interact with other children is very limited. As long as your toddler is not overwhelmed by more than one or two playmates, and as long as his playmates do not attack him or take away his toys, he will enjoy their company. However, as you have noticed, at this point, his playmates are merely a prop for his own activities. He may involve another child in his play in the same way he would involve a doll or some other toy, but he won't be inclined to engage in truly mutual endeavors. He also is likely to do a lot of talking, but for the most part he will be talking *at* rather than *with* the other child. As he becomes increasingly comfortable with the presence of peers, and as his mental capacities increase, you will start to see more genuine peer interaction. By the end of this period, your toddler may begin to engage in true sharing, cooperating, taking turns, and other appropriate peer-oriented behavior.

I tried putting my toddler in a play group, but I saw more hitting and biting than sharing and getting along. Is this unusual?

Not at all. It isn't until the latter part of this period that toddlers begin to show an interest in peers, and not until the very end that they begin to become capable of understanding and putting into practice various concepts of cooperation that are necessary for pleasant peer interactions. Prior to this point, a toddler is likely to treat another child almost like an inani-

mate object rather than as another person, and he probably will treat her just as roughly as he treats his toys. During the second half of the second year, as a toddler goes through a phase of self-assertiveness and negativism, it is even more unlikely that he will be in the mood to treat other children with anything resembling civility. This does not mean that placing a toddler less than two years of age in any kind of group situation should be avoided completely. It does mean, however, that parents should not have unreasonable expectations about what will happen and that they must be sure that adequate supervision is available at all times.

"Parallel play" is common among toddlers. While he may enjoy having a playmate around, he's likely to treat her the same way he would a toy—as a prop for his own activities.

DAILY CARE BASICS

Is it too early to start toilet training my toddler?

Starting toilet training prior to the end of this period generally is not a good idea. Although the essential physiological requirement—that the toddler be able to control her bowel and bladder muscles—is usually fulfilled by two years of age, there are many other important parts to the process. A toddler must be able to recognize and communicate her needs effectively. She must also be able to handle unbuttoning, untying, or otherwise removing her clothing efficiently. In addition, she must be able to understand and carry out certain hygienic procedures like washing her hands. Even if a toddler is capable of all of the above by two years of age or so, there is a good chance that she still will be in her negativistic phase. Since toilet training requires that she comply with instructions and accede to requests, trying to start the process during this phase can cause nothing but trouble. Starting toilet training too soon can cause disappointment and frustration in parents, and fear and loss of self-esteem in toddlers. It may also delay the time at which a toddler actually starts using the toilet independently. Therefore, it is suggested that parents be as patient as possible and wait until later when their child will be considerably more cooperative, will have greater physical and mental capacities, and will be extremely interested in imitating grown-up behavior (see the "Daily Care Basics" section in the following age group for a list of signs that indicate when a child is ready to begin toilet training).

Although it may be easier or more efficient to wash her hands for her, she needs practice in order to learn how to do it herself.

My two and a half year old refuses to let me wash her hands. Although she gets them fairly clean herself, I worry about germs. Should I keep trying to wash them for her?

Of course she'd rather do it herself. It's normal for her to demand some autonomy and prefer to wash without you. There will be many such occasions when, as a parent, it will be easier, quicker, and more efficient to do something for your toddler rather than to encourage her to do it herself. You should try, however, to refrain from taking over the task yourself whenever possible. Your toddler won't learn how to wash her own hands unless she has opportunities to try it herself. She needs practice to develop skills in all areas. This is also how she practices independence and develops autonomy. Encourage her to do her best hand washing before meals, and then, don't worry about it. Praise her when she does a good job. If you're not thrilled with the job she's doing, suggest that you wash each others hands together so she can learn from you. You might also present her with her very own nail brush to see if this helps her to stay at the task longer and do a more thorough job. On occasion, you might even suggest that she give her dolls or toys a bath in the sink (under your supervision); this is likely to get both her toys and her hands clean.

Do I still need to hold my toddler when she's in the bathtub?

Toddlers always need to be watched while they're in the tub. While some still need a hand on them, others can manage well without. You definitely need to be close enough to grab her if she should stand up or slip so that you can prevent her from falling or having her face go under the water. No-slip rubber mats can make it easier for her to keep her balance, but you'll still need to wash her and supervise her in the bathtub for some time. You'll also need to continue to be careful about the temperature and the height of the water in the tub. A couple inches of water is enough. The water should feel pleasantly warm to the sensitive skin on the inner part of your elbow. All water heaters should be turned down to 120 degrees Fahrenheit. Cold water should be turned off last, and all faucets should be covered. For your own comfort, find a position that allows you to keep your eyes and a hand on your toddler without putting too much strain on your body. Kneeling next to the tub and having both hands free for washing and playing is ideal if the bathtub isn't too large or too tall. Some parents sit on a small stool or low chair to make it easier on their knees. Experiment to find the position that works best for you.

My toddler loves her bath and would play for hours if I let her. How frequently should I bathe her and how long is long enough?

Playing in the tub can be fun for a toddler, but it can also be very drying to her skin. Ten to 15 minutes is a nice long bath and, depending on how dry her skin is, less time is probably better. You'll want to limit baths to two or three times a week. On days when you don't bathe her, use a wet washcloth to clean her face, hands, diaper area, and any other areas that need it. When bathing her, avoid using bubble baths or similar products since they can be irritating to your toddler's skin

and can sometimes cause vaginal or urinary tract infections in little girls. Since soap left on the skin can cause irritation and additional drying, it's preferable to avoid letting children sit in soapy water for any length of time. For the same reason, showering instead of bathing children is preferable whenever practical because it helps to remove soap residue. Rubber shower heads that fit onto the tub faucet are especially helpful for rinsing off soap and for washing and rinsing hair.

My toddler used to love baths, but now all of a sudden she seems to be afraid of the water. What happened, and how can I get her to enjoy her bath again?

Sometimes getting soap or shampoo in the eyes or inhaling water can be traumatic enough to turn a toddler off to bathing. Likewise, slipping and getting her head under water can also make a toddler fearful of a bath. While you'd probably be aware if one of these unpleasant experiences occurred, your toddler may not have reacted very much at the time. Another possibility is that the bathwater was a little too warm or cool for her last time. To make bathing more pleasant, take special care when testing her bathwater. It should feel warm to your wrist or elbow, but probably cooler than you'd prefer for your own bath. Put just a couple of inches of water in the tub; less water may be more comforting. Give her a favorite toy and encourage some playtime before you wash her. Keep your hands on her if she's truly afraid, and talk to her throughout the process. You might try playing a naming game by pointing to her nose, ears, eyes, belly button, and tummy and allowing her to name them first if she can. Let her try doing some of the washing, too. You might also try bathing or showering with her. Be sure to get into the tub or shower first and then lift her in. When it's time to get out, either hand her to a helper for drying or lift her out onto a towel first and then get yourself out. If your toddler won't even go near the bathtub, she may still be small enough to fit into the sink. If so, you can try bathing her there until she gets over her fright.

My toddler always looks a mess. I give her a bath every evening, but how can I keep her clean during the day?

Being a toddler and learning new skills is a messy business. Toddlers have to run, fall, climb, roll, crawl, put everything into their mouths, and wipe their dirty or sticky hands on their clothes. Eating is messy too. A successful meal is one in which she gets at least some of the meal into her mouth while the rest goes on the floor, on her face, on her clothes, and in her hair. Therefore, you shouldn't be overly concerned about her looking squeaky clean all the time. You're very likely to drive yourself up the wall if you do. Of course, you'll want to wash her hands and face before and after meals and before bedtime for hygiene purposes and to prevent her from putting her sticky fingers everywhere. Giving her a daily bath is not recommended, however, since it can be very drying to her skin. If you feel you must bathe her daily, make it a brief bath and use as little soap as possible. Remember, it's her job to explore, touch, play, and learn—not to keep clean.

Should I still wash my toddler's clothing separately from the rest of the family's wash?

Baby clothing is washed separately and double rinsed to help prevent irritation of the baby's more sensitive skin. The detergent used for the family wash is generally stronger and, therefore, more likely to have an irritative effect than the pure mild soap used to wash baby clothing. Although your toddler's skin is still susceptible to irritation, it's no longer necessary to wash her clothes separately. There are some fabric softeners that may bother her, but even that's less likely now. However, you'll probably still want to continue washing her diapers separately for aesthetic reasons and because they still need to be washed in hot water and double rinsed.

How can I make my teething toddler more comfortable?

To make your teething toddler more comfortable, you can offer her cool liquids to drink and crackers or teething biscuits to gnaw on. Sucking on a pacifier, especially the one-piece variety that can be refrigerated or frozen, may also bring some relief. Some professionals recommend rubbing ice on the toddler's gums as a temporary pain reliever, but do this only if your toddler is willing. If your pediatrician agrees, you might also try to relieve teething pain by giving your toddler an appropriate amount of acetaminophen. While teething can make your toddler uncomfortable and cranky, it will not make her ill. She may develop a low-grade fever of up to 100.4 degrees Fahrenheit the day or two before a tooth erupts, but her temperature will return to normal after the tooth erupts.

DENTAL HYGIENE

Your toddler's teeth need to be cleaned at least twice a day, especially after meals. For a young toddler, you may continue to use gauze wrapped around your finger to wipe her teeth and gumline. Once she's willing, however, you should introduce a small, soft toothbrush (with or without a small amount of toothpaste). Gently brush her teeth using an up-and-down motion. After brushing, floss her teeth by gently sliding the dental floss along the side of each tooth, massaging slightly down and a little bit under the tooth. Let her watch you as you brush your teeth, and be sure to give her a chance to try brushing her own teeth, too. Increasingly during this period, she will want to imitate you and attempt to do some things herself. Although you'll still need to make sure you get her teeth clean, allowing her to try brushing can help her get into the habit of taking good care of her teeth. Most pediatric dentists suggest that children have their initial visit at age two or three. It is best to make the first appointment once all 20 of the deciduous (baby) teeth have erupted. Of course, if you have a concern or see a problem before then, consult your pediatrician and/or pediatric dentist.

Should I insist that my two year old take a nap?

Most two year olds still need a nap (or even two) every day. Some toddlers skip them from time to time or prefer to go without, but not many. Chances are, when your toddler is tired, she will take her blanket and head for her bed, tell you that she wants a nap, or simply stop what she's doing and fall asleep. In such cases, you should let her nap. If, on the other hand, she's happily and busily playing, you can probably let her skip the nap. If you find that she's unbearably cranky for the rest of the day, that she is so tired later on that she can't fall to sleep for the night, or that you simply need some quiet time for yourself, you could try to encourage her to take a nap the next time. If she's not sleepy, you could encourage some quiet playtime—with or without you—instead.

My toddler has been taking long naps, then I have trouble getting her to go to sleep at night. Is it okay to wake her from her naps or cut out one nap altogether?

It's definitely wise to experiment with shortening or skipping one or both nap times if you're having trouble getting her to sleep on time at night or getting her to sleep through the night. The problem is that, at this age, little ones will be cranky if they're not getting enough rest. What's more, if she's truly sleepy, she'll fall to sleep no matter how you try to keep her awake. If you find that shortening or dropping a nap makes her too cranky, there's another strategy you could try. When it's time for her to go to bed for the night, put her in her crib, bed, or room, and allow her to play quietly until she falls asleep. If you try this approach, however, you will have to emphasize to her that once you put her to bed at night, she's to stay there until morning, whether she spends the whole time sleeping or not.

How can I get my toddler to settle down before bedtime?

It's hard, and sometimes nearly impossible, to keep a toddler from running, jumping, giggling and otherwise expending energy. To help your toddler settle down for the night, however, you'll have to give it your best shot. Be sure to avoid any rough-and-tumble play for an hour or more before your toddler's usual bedtime. Instead, set up and follow a bedtime ritual. This ritual can include giving your toddler a snack, a cup of milk, or a bottle (for a young toddler); brushing her teeth; giving her a bath (two or three times a week, not every night); changing her diaper; and getting her into her pajamas. Do your best to keep any and all of these steps from becoming battles. To top off the nightly ritual, read her a book, tell her a story, sing her a lullaby, and/or say prayers together. When you're finished, tuck her in and kiss her goodnight. She may not fall asleep right away, but be sure she stays in her bed. To help her drift off to sleep once you have left the room, you might wind up a music box or musical toy that plays soothing music. Whatever the bedtime ritual, try to stick to it whenever possible.

A favorite toy, a cuddle with you, and a little bit of quiet time may help him settle down for the night.

My toddler has been climbing out of her crib at night. Now what do I do?

First, check to see if you are keeping anything in the crib that she has been using as a stepping stool to make climbing out

If she can climb out of her crib, you will have to take steps to keep her from harm.

easier. If she is clearly climbing out on her own, try adjusting the mattress to its lowest level. If it's already at its lowest level, there are a few choices. If it's clear that your toddler can get in and out of her crib without hurting herself, you may be able to let her sleep in it for now. Be sure to leave the crib rail down, however, and put padding or carpeting on the floor at the side of the crib where she gets out. If you think there's still a chance she could fall as she's climbing out, you can move the crib mattress to the floor and let her sleep there. Junior beds are nice but not really necessary. While a junior bed with a rail may help define the sleeping area and keep her from rolling off the bed, it won't be enough to actually keep her in the bed if she wants out. A regular mattress, with or without a frame, that is low to the floor will do just as well. Keep in mind that a toddler who is no longer confined in her crib is capable of getting up in the middle of the night and roaming about the house unsupervised. So if she no longer stays in her crib, make sure that she cannot expose herself to harm (see the following question), and make sure that her room is and continues to remain safe for her even when you're not in there with her. By the way, some parents move their toddler out of the crib and into a bed as soon as another baby comes along and needs the crib. Although this practice may be economical, it is not advisable—a toddler should not have to make this move before she's ready. Buy, rent, or borrow another crib for the new little one, instead.

I'm afraid my toddler will roam around the house while I'm sleeping. What can I do?

Safety remains the most important factor. A toddler is still too young to be roaming freely about the house while her parents are sleeping. If she can climb out of her crib, you will have to keep her from hurting herself. What you do will depend in part on the layout of your home and the abilities of your child. You can keep her in her room by putting a safety gate at her door or by using a piece of flexible material (like a stocking) to attach the doorknob to the doorjamb so she can't leave her room but can call out if she needs you. Another

If she wanders out to you before you go to bed, send her back to her room, or, if necessary, take her hand and lead her back.

possibility is to use a commercial safety net that attaches to the top of the crib and prevents her from getting out. Some professionals fear that such devices make the crib or room seem like a prison, however, and others worry that they can be hazardous in an emergency. (If you do use such a device, you might want to use a room monitor so you can hear her if she should become ill). Alternately, you could close off all areas that you don't want your toddler to enter at night. For rooms such as the bathroom, you can use high hook latches on the doors to keep your toddler out without inconveniencing the rest of the family. Hallway safety gates can prevent her from entering open areas. Safety gates should remain in place at stairways, and all doors leading outside should be securely locked. In addition, you need to teach her that nighttime is for sleeping and that her bed is where she sleeps. When you put her in her room for the night, tell her you expect her to stay there until morning—whether she sleeps or not. If she wanders out to you at night, send her back, or if you have to, take her hand and lead her back. Carrying her, making a big fuss, or allowing her to stay with you reinforces her determination to seek attention at night.

My toddler had been sleeping through the night for many months, but recently she has begun waking up and crying in the middle of the night. I can't find anything wrong, but it can take as long as an hour to get her back to sleep. How should I handle this?

Sometimes toddlers experience separation anxiety; they need to check and see if you're really there. They can also have nightmares or night terrors that cause them to be anxious and frightened when they wake up alone. These unhappy awakenings will eventually stop. In the meantime, however, for your own well-being as well as your toddler's, you need to shorten the amount of time you spend with her when she does wake up, especially if these awakenings occur every night. The next time she wakes up crying, comfort her and make certain that there's nothing bothering her physically (such as a wet or dirty diaper, a cold room, or an empty stomach). Be sure there's a night-light in her room and that any transitional object (such as a favorite toy or blanket) is within her reach. If she awakens again, go to her but don't pick her up; leave her in her crib as you pat her and tell her that everyone else is sleeping. If she continues to wake you up, comfort her from the doorway of her room; let her see you, and tell her that everything is fine but that it's time for sleeping. Finally, if it continues, just call to her from your room and reassure her that everything is

alright. Eventually she will learn that while you love her and care about her, it's time for sleeping. Don't give up, and by all means, don't bring her back to your bed with you; once you do, she'll demand such treatment in the future.

Playing with a ball or chasing each other around the yard can give you both a healthy workout.

How can I be sure that my toddler is getting enough exercise?

Toddlers usually wear themselves out with their running, jumping, exploring, probing, walking, and playing. They're busy all the time, and this constant activity almost always provides enough exercise. There are, of course, exercise classes that you can join with your toddler. Such classes can be a healthy and enjoyable diversion for both you and your toddler and can give you a chance to socialize with other parents. Still, these formal classes are by no means necessary for proper development or even for physical fitness. You and your toddler can get plenty of exercise by playing "hide-and-seek" or "follow-the-leader," by taking walks, and by chasing each other around the yard or park. As long as your child is growing and developing normally and sleeping well, she's probably getting enough exercise. If you are worried about her weight, stature, or development, however, consult your pediatrician.

He'll have fun helping you with simple chores like sorting laundry, and you'll be able to get your work done at the same time.

I try to take care of household chores when my toddler is napping, but sometimes I can't fit them all in. How can I involve her in my chores or otherwise keep her occupied while I get my work done?

First of all, if the remaining chores involve the use of hazardous materials, tools, or appliances, you should use a playpen or a play area closed off with a gate to keep your toddler out of harm's way. You can keep a couple of special toys on the side to be used in just such situations. Be sure to praise her for her cooperation and to give her some special one-to-one interaction time with you when you're done. If your chores do not pose a hazard to your toddler, then you should give her some choices of ways to keep herself occupied. She can either play nearby or she can help you. Toddlers like to feel helpful. Keep in mind, however, that while her skills and concentration will be increasing dramatically during this period, she still has a relatively short attention span and is still easily frustrated. So, offer her simple tasks. Ask her to bring the dirty cups from the table over to the sink so that you can wash them or

to bring her blanket over so that you can put it into the hamper. If you're going to vacuum, encourage her to get her toy vacuum and "help" you. If you'll be dusting, give her a small dust rag, too, so that she can join in. When you put dishes away, let her put the spoons away. If you need to set the table, let her put the napkins out. And, if you're baking, let her help put ingredients in the bowl or let her have her own piece of dough to make a miniature cookie, cake, or pie (be careful to keep her away from the oven, however).

I dread taking my two year old to her grandparents' home because I constantly have to hold her and keep her from touching things. What can I do in this situation?

One solution would be to invite her grandparents over to your home instead. If it's not always feasible, you might consider discussing your baby's needs and your parenting philosophy with your parents. Ask them if they'd mind removing some "untouchables" and safety proofing at least one room with your guidance. Remind them that toddlers need a play area or at least a small room where they can touch things without hurting themselves or anything else. Chances are, her grandparents will be more than willing to help make their granddaughter's visits enjoyable and safe. Another option is to plan very short visits and carry along a portable playpen or a bag of special toys. Some grandparents have special toys and things for their grandchild to play with. These are kept at the grandparents' house and brought out for her when she visits. When your little one becomes bored with her special toys or with her playpen and wants to explore, go for a family walk or take her out in her stroller. When you run out of comfortable time, take her home.

NUTRITION AND FEEDING

My 13 month old is still nursing. Do you have any tips for weaning him from the breast?

Some toddlers stop nursing on their own. Others stop when Mom weans them, and they never act like they miss it. A few stubborn toddlers don't want to give it up, especially if they are allowed to continue nursing much after 12 to 15 months of age. The easiest transition seems to be between ten and 15 months. The nursing should be diminished gradually for your sake and your toddler's. He should be drinking fairly well from a cup now and getting three meals and one or two snacks daily. His food and fluid requirements can be fulfilled without nursing. His sucking or comforting needs may not be so easily satisfied. If you haven't offered him a bottle previously, now is not the time to start. If you have been supplementing with a bottle, you should probably wait to take it away until he's totally weaned from the breast. First, reduce the nursing time at each feeding by two to three minutes for a couple of days, and then reduce it by a couple minutes more every few days. When you are ready, omit one feeding completely; the midday feeding will probably be the easiest to stop first. If stopping this feeding causes some soreness or breast engorgement, you can apply some ice for comfort and reduce your fluid intake. Keep reducing your nursing time during the other feedings, and offer your toddler a cup of two-percent milk after each reduced feeding. Within seven to ten days after you've eliminated one nursing period, eliminate another; a week later, one more. Soon, you should both be ready to stop the nursing completely; by that time, your breast milk production will probably have diminished or stopped completely. Throughout this weaning period, you'll probably need to offer a little extra support and comfort to your toddler. You may even find that your toddler substitutes a transitional item (like a blanket or stuffed toy) or starts sucking his thumb or a pacifier for comfort; either of these is fine if it helps make the transition easier for him. Congratulate yourself on providing the best start possible for your child and on helping him take this step toward independence.

I give my two year old a bottle at night because he doesn't seem to be drinking milk from the cup. Is this okay?

First of all, it's important to emphasize that your child should never be given his nighttime bottle in bed since taking a bottle to bed can promote tooth decay. Likewise, he should have his teeth brushed after the last meal (whether it's a bottle, a cup of milk, or a snack) before bedtime. What's more, at two years of age, your toddler doesn't need a bottle anymore. Your son will take more milk and other liquids from a cup if you remove the bottle. If you're worried about his intake of milk, you can offer milk in a cup more frequently. Two year olds should receive a minimum of 16 ounces of two-percent milk a day. To break the bottle habit, offer his nightly bottle with water only for a few nights or a week. Then offer only a cup of water after the bedtime ritual. To help make it easier for him, you can give him a new "big boy" plastic cup to take the place of the retired baby bottle. The cup can be a special nighttime cup and can be left at the bedside just for him.

Providing him with his own "big boy" cup may make it easier for him to give up his bottle.

PRUDENT DAILY DIET

Meat or meat substitute (2-3 servings daily)
Single serving suggestions:
1 oz cooked meat, fish, or poultry
1 whole egg (no more than 3 per week)
   or 2 egg whites
½ cup cooked beans or peas
2 tbsp peanut butter spread on bread
   or crackers
2 oz tofu
1 oz high-protein pasta

Dairy products (3-4 servings daily)
Single serving suggestions:
1 cup two-percent milk
1 cup yogurt
1½ oz cheese
½ cup cottage cheese
1 to 1½ cups ice cream (occasionally)

Grains (3-4 servings daily)
Single serving suggestions:
1 slice bread
½ hamburger bun or roll
½ bagel or English muffin
3-4 crackers (whole grain preferred)
½ cup cooked cereal
1 oz cold cereal (not sugary type)
½ cup pasta or rice

Fruits and vegetables (3-4 servings daily)
Single serving suggestions:
½ cup raw or cooked vegetables
   (appropriate for age)
1 cup leafy cooked vegetables
1 whole fruit—soft and/or cooked (apricot,
   banana, pear, apple, plum, peach, fig, etc.)
½ grapefruit or other citrus fruit
½ cup soft cubed melon

The lists above are only guidelines. What is offered and what is eaten is frequently very different. The most important way to evaluate a child's diet is by following his growth and development at routine health maintenance examinations.

I've heard of a "prudent diet" for adults. Is there a similar diet for two year olds?

A prudent or well balanced diet for a two year old should contain foods from the four basic food groups (dairy products, meats, grains, and vegetables and fruits). You should offer your toddler the appropriate number of servings (see sidebar) from each of these groups every day. Don't be alarmed, however, if everything you serve doesn't get eaten every day. Children (and adults) have different needs and preferences daily. In the long run, enough of each type of food will be eaten to provide an appropriate balance.

My 18 month old likes hot dogs and handles them well, but I've heard that they're dangerous for young children. Should I stop letting him eat them for now?

Hot dogs are the known culprit in many serious choking incidents in this age group. For safety's sake, you should avoid giving them to your toddler until he's much older. Even four to five year olds have a tendency to bite off big pieces and not chew sufficiently. Feed your son small pieces of soft cooked meats, fish, and poultry instead. Teach him to chew slowly and enjoy mealtime. And whenever he's eating, keep him in his high chair; chewing and swallowing needs his undivided attention at this point.

Are there other foods that I should not allow my toddler to have?

You'll want to avoid salty and sugary foods; toddlers don't need them. They usually don't like very spicy foods either, although some may enjoy them later on. As before, avoid foods that toddlers can choke on or inhale into their windpipes. Offenders include carrots, popcorn, nuts, hot dogs, uncooked peas, raw apples, raisins, and the like; at this age, all of the foods you serve him should become liquid in his mouth. Although he can probably handle soft fruits now, you'll still need to be careful about giving him big chunks of raw fruits or vegetables. To encourage him to make healthier food choices in the future, start him off with healthy choices now. For example, serve him whole grain breads and crackers rather than white commercial bread. Cooked whole-wheat or high-protein pasta is a good choice as well. Remember, too, that your toddler needs 30 percent of his daily calories from fat. So if your diet is very low in fat, you'll need to make sure he's getting enough fat in the foods you offer him. For instance, even if you're drinking skim milk, he'll still need two-percent milk to help him get enough fat for healthy growth and development.

Some days it seems like my two year old doesn't eat anything. He's no longer taking a bottle, and I'm worried he's not getting enough to eat and drink. What should I do?

Your concern is a common one among parents of children in the second and third years of life. It sometimes seems like a two year old's intake is almost nothing. It is important to remember, however, that during the first year of life a child triples his weight, while during the second year his weight increases only by a third. After that, the rate of gain slows even more, and so does the need for increased calories. Continue to offer your toddler the variety mentioned in the "prudent diet" on the previous page, and be sure to follow his growth in height and weight through regular medical checkups. If he is growing and gaining weight normally, don't worry about how much food he eats. If he's not growing as expected, consult your pediatrician.

How can I get my "picky" toddler to eat more?

Eating needs to be your toddler's job, not yours. Your toddler will not starve himself. As long as you offer him a variety of nutritious foods every day, he'll eat what he needs. Offer him small servings, and give him choices whenever possible. Since toddlers dislike having to sit still for any length of time, you might try offering him small meals five to six times a day rather than larger meals two or three times a day. Keep in mind that he'll eat more when he's going through a growth spurt than when he's not, so he won't always eat the same amount of food every day. Above all, try not to make mealtime into a battle of wills, and try not to put too much emphasis on eating. Don't praise him or reward him for eating, and don't use food as a comfort or reward. You want your toddler to learn that he should eat when he's hungry and that eating more or less is neither a good thing or a bad thing. Encourage him to choose healthy foods and allow him to eat as much as he needs, even if it's less than you think he should be eating. As long as he's growing and developing normally, he's getting the nourishment he needs.

FOODS NOT APPROPRIATE FOR TODDLERS

In addition to keeping foods that are high in sugar or salt off the menu, you should avoid serving your toddler foods which pose a choking hazard, including:

- Carrots
- Popcorn
- Nuts (including peanuts)
- Hot dogs
- Raw apples or potatoes
- Uncooked peas and beans
- Raisins
- Foods with seeds (sunflower, orange, melon, cherry, etc.) unless the seeds are removed
- Chewing gum
- Hard candy
- Grapes
- Caramels
- Celery
- Corn (on the cob or as kernels)

Allow her to eat as much as she needs from the variety of healthy foods you offer.

My two and a half year old doesn't like meat. What substitutes should I give him?

Good meat substitutes include poultry, fish, extra milk, yogurt, cottage cheese, hard cheeses, egg, tofu, peanut butter, high-protein pasta, and lentils. Eventually, your toddler may enjoy meat. Since we should all be reducing the amount of red meat we eat, however, he may be just as well off if he doesn't acquire a taste for it; just be sure he gets enough protein from these other sources.

My two year old loves eggs and has them for breakfast nearly every day. Can they hurt him?

Eggs are a good source of protein, although it's generally recommended that he eat no more than three a week. If you have a history of high cholesterol in your family, you may want to discuss this with your pediatrician. Try to serve him a variety of healthy foods to provide him with the nutrition he needs and to keep mealtime interesting. Try alternating the eggs with yogurt, fruit, pancakes, cereal, and bread. Remember, you want to get him into the habit of eating a variety of healthy foods.

My toddler loves soda pop and prefers it to milk or juice. How much soda would be bad for him?

Soda and other sweet beverages (including fruit juices) contain very little except sugar and water. Diet soda doesn't even contain sugar. There is very little food value in any of them. The ideal beverage for any child (or adult) who is thirsty is water. Water meets the thirst requirement but does not provide empty calories. It doesn't contain sugar, which can promote tooth decay, or artificial sweeteners, which your child doesn't need. If a child is given water as a thirst quencher starting in these early years, he will get used to choosing it as a primary beverage. Although milk is not an essential beverage, it is the most common liquid source of protein in the diet of most children. If your toddler is not allergic to dairy products, it's recommended that you give him 16 to 30 ounces daily of two-percent milk (including the milk that is added to foods). If your child does have an allergy to dairy products, consult your pediatrician about substitute sources of protein and other nutrients. Fruit juice is okay for occasional use. Soda can be given as a treat, but it should not be a part of his daily diet.

When it's time for a snack, offer her nutritious foods.

My two year old doesn't like citrus fruits, but he is getting a multivitamin supplement. Will the supplement take care of his needs?

Many children do not like citrus fruits when they are young but develop a taste for them later. In the meantime, the vitamin C contained in citrus fruits (including tomato) can also be found in many other foods, including berries, melons, leafy green vegetables, broccoli, peppers, cabbage, and potatoes. If you continue to offer your toddler a variety of foods, including citrus fruits and the other foods mentioned here, it is not necessary to supplement his diet with a multivitamin.

My two and a half year old likes whole milk and refuses to drink skim milk. Is the extra fat a problem for him?

Toddlers require more fat in their diet than adults in order for them to maintain normal growth and development. For that reason, serving skim milk to toddlers is not recommended. Two-percent milk is the better option. If you have a problem switching him to two percent milk, you can mix the whole

Your messages to her about choosing healthy foods will have more impact if you set a good example for her during these early years.

milk and the two-percent milk for a while, gradually reducing the amount of whole milk, until he's drinking two-percent only.

The baby-sitter flavored my toddler's milk with chocolate syrup, and now he prefers it that way. Should I let him continue to drink chocolate milk?

Some professionals would advise you to get rid of the chocolate now. Children and adults alike enjoy sweets, but sweet treats should be a limited part of the diet. What's more, you don't want your toddler to expect that everything he eats or drinks will taste sweet. Don't let him have the chocolate milk at mealtime. Offer him plain milk, and explain to him that he can have chocolate milk occasionally as a special treat or snack. You might even want to reserve it only for times when the baby-sitter is taking care of him. By the way, you'll probably also want to have a talk with your baby-sitter and explain the types of foods and beverages that you want your toddler to be offered in the future.

My family eats "fast foods" two to three times a week. My toddler really enjoys these meals. Can they be harmful to him?

Your child will learn his eating habits from you. Fast foods can't really harm your toddler, but by making them frequent items in your diet, you may be teaching him inappropriate eating habits for later. Although the calorie and fat content of fast foods may not be a problem for your growing toddler, they are taking the place of more nutritious foods. Still, eating fast food two or three times a week is probably okay for your toddler as long as you're serving him a variety of nutritious foods for the rest of his weekly meals and snacks. The "prudent diet" suggested on page 172, along with adequate fluids and any supplements prescribed by your pediatrician, should give him the calories, protein, and vitamins and minerals he needs. If you haven't been offering your toddler—and the rest of your family—a variety of nutritious foods at these other meals, now is the time to start. The whole family needs to start eating healthier.

My toddler wants to snack all the time, but rarely finishes anything I give him. Should I restrict the number of times he's allowed to eat?

Your toddler would probably snack all the time if you let him. Although his tummy doesn't hold very much at a time, *constant* snacking keeps him from ever being truly hungry. Cut him down to three meals and two snacks; depending on when he has his dinner, you might add a third snack before bedtime. Try to space snacking so it's far enough between meals for him to become hungry. When he is hungry, be sure to offer him nutritious meals and snacks.

My 18 month old doesn't like to sit in his high chair for any length of time. Do you have any suggestions?

Toddlers don't like to sit or remain still for any length of time. They like to move on to the next thing. Sitting and eating isn't particularly interesting to them. They'd prefer to eat on the run if they were allowed to. It's recommended, however, that your toddler be in his high chair whenever you offer him a meal or snack. He should be allowed to get down as soon as he's finished, within reason. You don't, however, want him to take a bite or two, get down out of his high chair, and then immediately ask to be put back in it. Before you let him down, ask him if he is finished and remind him that once he gets down, the meal is over. If he gets down, then comes running back for more, try not to get too upset. You can either give him one more chance or stand firm, depending on your parenting philosophy. If you try to act casually and not make a fuss, he'll eventually learn. While you can praise him for acting like a big boy when he's at the table, you don't want to put too much focus on what and how much he chooses to eat. While you want him to understand that eating is his job, you want him to learn that to sit and eat with the rest of the family, he'll need to behave appropriately. Discipline begins here, but only as positive reinforcement and praise for healthy choices, not as negative reactions from you. Let him know what's expected, but leave him room for autonomy. Whether he eats or not is his choice, but where he eats is yours. Don't worry; as long as you offer him a variety of nutritious foods, he won't starve himself.

Learning how to sit nicely at the table and feed herself will take some time and cause some mess. In the meantime, be patient, encourage her to do her best, and try to keep mealtimes pleasant.

I like to go out to dinner, and I often take my two year old with me. If there's a wait, however, he wants to run around and "entertain" the other diners. Any tips for making restaurant outings easier?

Have a little talk with your two year old about what is appropriate behavior for the restaurant. You'll probably need to repeat it over and over again for the next year or two. Keep in mind, however, that toddlers do not like to sit still or wait, and they shouldn't really be expected to. So when you go to the restaurant, bring along a book to read to him while waiting for seating or service. You might also try bringing along a snack or first course to satisfy him until the meal arrives. If these ploys don't help, seek restaurants that cater to little ones with immediate service and amusements. Save the more formal restaurants for times when he's not with you.

SAFETY AND HEALTH

I safety proofed my home as soon as my baby started crawling. Will it be necessary to make adjustments now that she's a toddler?

It probably will. Keep in mind that your toddler's physical abilities will be increasing enormously during this period. She will be capable of moving faster, farther, and higher with each passing week. Dangerous or delicate objects that were placed "out of reach" in high cabinets or on high shelves can no longer be considered inaccessible to your toddler. Some of the gates and latches that have been used to prevent her from entering various areas eventually will lose their effectiveness. Consequently, it would be a good idea to periodically re-evaluate your toddler's environment and make any necessary adjustments according to her recently emerging capabilities. By the way, it is important to do this not only from a safety standpoint, but to ensure that your toddler has full opportunity to use her newly acquired skills and continue to expand her horizons.

What kind of trouble can my toddler get into in the kitchen that she couldn't get into before?

For one thing, your toddler eventually will become adept at turning knobs, so there now is a greater danger that she will be able to turn on the burners on the stove. By the time she achieves this ability, it is possible that she will respond to strong instructions that the stove is absolutely off-limits, but it would be wise to keep a close eye on her anyway when she is in the kitchen. She should also continue to stay out of the area when cooking is in progress. As before, it may be a very good idea to remove the knobs that turn on the stove or oven when you're not using them. Your toddler also will soon have the strength to open heavy doors that were previously too much for her to handle. As a result, the refrigerator, the dishwasher, and the oven may become attractive—but extremely dangerous—places for her to hide. Although admonitions may be effective, again, it would be a good idea to put latches on these items (or move the latches higher if they're already there) if you anticipate your toddler entering the area unsupervised for more than a moment or two. And, in general, since her climbing ability will continue to increase during this period, any cleansers, knives, and other hazardous objects that simply had been placed on high shelves or in high drawers now must be more securely stored.

NEVER ASSUME

The people who staff hospital emergency rooms report that the most common phrases they hear from the parents of toddler accident victims are "I assumed she couldn't…" and "I never thought she could…" As they go about safety proofing their homes at the start, as well as when they go about making periodic improvements, many parents make the mistake of thinking in terms of their toddler's abilities of the moment. If she is climbing in six-inch increments, they assume that she can't climb 12-inch increments, and therefore consider something placed on a 48-inch high shelf to be far beyond her reach. If she is barely able to operate a simple lever mechanism, they assume that she can't cope with a twist-and-turn latch, and therefore consider something locked away in a cabinet with this kind of device to be safely secured. Unfortunately, such assumptions often lead to big trouble. Toddlers develop at rapid rates and in irregular patterns, and it is virtually impossible to predict exactly what your toddler will be capable of from day to day. Furthermore, many major abilities arrive with very little or no advanced warning, and your toddler's skill profile could change dramatically overnight. Therefore, as you go about designing a safe environment for your toddler's explorations and investigations, avoid making such simple assumptions; try to anticipate as much as possible. Giving your toddler current credit for any and all abilities that could possibly make an appearance during the next six months will give you a wide margin for error and go a long way toward ensuring the well-being of your toddler.

Lately, my toddler has become very adept at unscrewing the tops of bottles and jars. Will those childproof caps keep her out?

For the most part, childproof caps are very effective safety devices, but they can't guarantee inaccessibility with absolute certainty. In fact, some parents swear their toddler can get these caps off more easily than they can. Therefore, while you definitely should use childproof caps whenever possible and appropriate, don't count on them completely to keep your toddler out of things she shouldn't be getting into. Continue to keep all pills, potions, and other such items well secured in a locked or firmly latched medicine cabinet, and get rid of anything that you no longer need. Then, use childproof caps as a good backup. By the way, a childproof cap becomes worthless if the container itself is made of glass or any other breakable material, so be sure that anything hazardous to your toddler is kept in a sturdy plastic bottle or jar.

Now that my toddler is steadier on her feet and not quite so naive, is the bathroom less hazardous for her?

Not really. Although she certainly will be fairly steady on her feet and a fairly capable climber by the end of this period, she still may have a lot of trouble with the bathroom surfaces. Because they can get very slippery when wet, and because they are hard enough to cause serious damage in a fall, it just is not a good idea to let a toddler play on bathroom floors and fixtures. Furthermore, while your toddler is not as naive as she was previously, she is every bit as curious and a lot more capable. Turning on the hot water taps, opening up and manipulating the mechanisms in the toilet tank, and various other activities are no longer beyond her abilities. Since there is a strong potential for burns, drowning, and other major mishaps from such activities, it still is inadvisable to let a toddler spend unsupervised time in the bathroom.

Since his curiosity may still get the best of him and lead him into trouble, it's wise to continue supervising your toddler when he's in the bathroom.

My toddler now is able to reach and turn many of the doorknobs in my house. Should I put locks on those that I don't want her to open?

From a safety standpoint, that probably is a good idea. In terms of convenience, it may present a real problem. Consequently, as is the case with anything that becomes inconvenient, you may find yourself becoming lax about it and forgetting or simply not bothering to lock up all the time. Of course, that negates the whole notion of using locks. Fortunately, there is a more practical alternative, and that is the use of high latches. A simple hook-and-ring latch placed high enough so your toddler can't possibly get to it, yet still well within your reach, is inexpensive, easy to use, and solves the safety problem quite nicely. In addition, for certain doors, you may opt to buy one of those electronic alarms that sounds when the door is opened by an unauthorized person. These cost a little more money, but you may find their convenience worth it.

I have a sliding glass door leading to my patio. Is it a possible hazard to my toddler?

It certainly is. Believe it or not, many toddlers are injured every year by running through glass doors. Keep in mind that your toddler, particularly toward the end of this period, will be doing a lot of running around. What's more, she will be so caught up in her own excitement and enthusiasm that she may not always be concentrating on what is directly in front of her. Furthermore, although her vision skills are superb at this point, clear glass is not easily detected by anyone. Although adults have enough experience to be careful going through any doorway, you can't expect your toddler to assume or remember that there will be something blocking her path. This does not mean you have to get rid of your glass doors, however. A few brightly colored, easily visible decals placed on the glass at her eye level will provide sufficient visual targets to make your toddler alert and aware and help keep her out of serious trouble.

Lately, my toddler has become fascinated with garbage pails and trash receptacles. Should I only use those with latched lids?

Certainly, for any container that will hold organic matter or clearly hazardous materials like broken glass, tin can lids, etc., a strong latch for the cover is a necessity. Keep in mind that by the end of this period, your toddler will have impressive strength and dexterity, and she may be intensely curious about something she's seen you throw away. Therefore, you need to double-check the construction of both the container itself and the latch to make sure that it is inaccessible to her. On the other hand, as long as you are careful about what you put in them, it may not be necessary for you to seal off some of the simple trash receptacles in your home. Toddlers love to explore wastepaper baskets and investigate the different kinds of crumpled paper they find inside, so if you don't mind a little clutter, you may not want to deprive your toddler of all such opportunities for fun and learning.

My toddler loves to play dress-up with my clothes and accessories. Are there any special hazards associated with this kind of activity?

There certainly are. Providing your toddler with a collection of appropriate items is a wonderful idea, but allowing her to roam freely through your closets and drawers is not. Buttons, jewelry, and other such items can pose choking hazards; belts, suspenders, and any other elasticized material can cause strangulation; and many toddlers have had nasty spills while trying to walk around in a pair of high-heeled shoes. In addition, if makeup, deodorant, perfume, and other such things are kept in the area, they may very well enter into your toddler's play, and an accidental poisoning could result. Keep in mind that the bulk of the "raw material" that your toddler

Playing "dress up" can be fun for your toddler as long as you provide her with items that are free of potential hazards.

will be using for these activities comes from within her own head, so it is not necessary for her to have a huge amount of stuff available to her. By going through your things and selecting a few suitable hats, jackets, bracelets, etc., you will be providing your toddler with a sufficient amount of playthings and be keeping her safe as well.

My neighbor's dog is very friendly. Is it safe to let my toddler play with him?

Naturally, it is a good idea to steer your toddler clear of any animal with which you are not familiar. In cases where you know the animal and are confident that he will be friendly and gentle with your toddler, it is okay to let her play with the pet—but do not let her play unsupervised at this point. The danger here is not necessarily from the animal, but rather from your toddler. Toddlers are very curious, and they do not always realize the consequences of their exploratory and investigatory behavior on others—human or nonhuman. Consequently, it is very common for toddlers to pull tails, stick fingers in ears, attempt to climb upon and ride, hug too hard, and in other ways push even the mildest creature beyond his limits of endurance. When this happens, the animal's instinctual self-protection mechanisms may take over and put your toddler in serious jeopardy. Therefore, make sure that you are there to prevent the pet from harming your toddler by seeing to it that she doesn't harm the pet.

As long as she's prevented from running off, is it safe to let my toddler play alone outdoors?

Toward the end of this period, you may be able to feel more comfortable about letting your toddler play unsupervised in the yard for short periods. However, it is important that you not only prevent her from running off, but that you make sure there are no major hazards to her well-being within the confined area. A wading pool—even if it only has a couple of inches of water in it—can result in an accidental drowning; garden equipment left lying around can cause serious mishaps; and anything from plants to peeling house paint can result in a poisoning. Be sure that all unsafe areas, such as swimming pools, toolsheds, and garages are inaccessible to your toddler. Check, too, to make sure that any buckets, drums, birdbaths, and ponds are kept empty or inaccessible as well; your toddler can fall in headfirst and drown in a few

Even a friendly dog or cat can cause harm if pushed beyond endurance by a curious toddler's poking and pulling. It's wise, therefore, to keep him away from unfamiliar animals and to supervise closely when he's with the family pet.

minutes in as little as a couple inches of water. In general, it is a good idea to stay nearby even older toddlers.

Should I enroll my toddler in a special swimming class so she will be safer in the water?

As stated previously, the American Academy of Pediatrics does *not* recommend organized swimming lessons for children less than three years of age. According to the Academy, children of this age who participate in swimming programs are at increased risk of water intoxication—which can lead to seizures and death—as a result of swallowing too much water (see page 120). In addition, such instruction can lull parents into thinking that their child can swim and is therefore "water safe." A child of this age cannot truly learn how to swim, even with organized instruction. While she may develop the physical ability necessary, she does not yet have the appropriate judgment needed for safety. If she should fall into or otherwise enter a pool when no one is around, she won't know why and where to swim. She won't know that if she swims in circles rather than toward the side, she'll eventually tire. She won't know that if she swims toward the deep end rather than the shallow end where the steps are, she won't be able to get out. Therefore, a young child should *never* be considered "water safe." She should never be allowed in the swimming pool (or other body of water) unless you are holding her and watching her at all times, and she should never be totally submerged. In addition, all swimming pools should be completely fenced in, and the gate should have a secure latch that is out of her reach.

My toddler loves being in the water, but she can't swim. Is it okay to let her use flotation devices?

Experts on the subject are split on the issue. Everyone agrees that a toddler should never be allowed to be alone in the water even when she's wearing such a device; they are not one-hundred-percent reliable—the toddler could slip out, or the air could leak out. Some people feel that as long as an adult is with the toddler, these devices are harmless and allow her to have a lot of fun. However, the majority of experts are uncomfortable with flotation devices even under these circumstances, as they feel that using them gives a toddler a false sense of her own abilities. As a result, she may be tempted to go beyond those abilities if she somehow manages to get near deep

water when no one is around. By the way, if you ever take your toddler along in a boat, she and every other child should wear a life jacket—whether or not they are able to swim.

Whenever she's in a motor vehicle, your toddler should be secured in her car seat.

Lately, it has become a real struggle to get my toddler into her car seat. When can I stop using it?

Not until your child is over four years old and weighs more than 40 pounds. Until then, in order to ensure her safety, you must make sure that your toddler is secured in her car seat before you put the gearshift into drive. And, if your toddler should somehow manage to get out of her car seat at any point during the trip, you must pull over, stop the car, and resecure her. Many parents routinely have trouble getting their toddlers into their car seats and keeping them there, especially toward the end of this period. However, it is important that you make this a non-negotiable issue and never sacrifice your toddler's safety for the sake of convenience.

FREEDOM VERSUS SECURITY

During this period, toddlers are incredibly daring and adventuresome, which in turn often causes their parents to become extremely anxious and fearful. Armed with physical skills that are becoming more impressive every day, and motivated by ever-expanding curiosity, toddlers routinely take on new challenges to run faster and climb higher. Unfortunately, they occasionally bite off more than they can chew. Consequently, it is a rare toddler who doesn't crash or fall from time to time, and minor bumps and bruises are a regular part of a typical toddler's appearance. Some parents react to this by keeping their toddler severely restricted unless they can provide constant supervision for her activities. While this is understandable, it is also detrimental to the toddler's optimal development. Trading your toddler's freedom for your own psychological comfort is a bad bargain. As long as you have done a thorough job of safety proofing, it is also largely unnecessary. Simply learning to accept the fact that minor mishaps are an inevitable part of early childhood will be a considerably more productive strategy for everyone involved. This also applies to situations outside the home. Now that toddlers are capable of disappearing from sight or dashing toward heavy traffic in the blink of an eye, some parents react by confining their toddler almost exclusively to the home environment. While the peace of mind of the parents will be largely guaranteed by this strategy, there also is a good chance that the toddler's progress will be stifled. Again, although it is understandable, trading your toddler's opportunities to learn about her world for your own psychological comfort is a poor deal. In the long run, everyone will be better off if you merely recognize that having a toddler means that your nerves inevitably will be on edge from time to time.

Now that she's stronger and smarter, can I expect that my toddler will be able to "hold her own" in her confrontations with her four-year-old brother?

Although your toddler certainly will become stronger and smarter during this period, you have to keep in mind that her brother will be getting stronger and smarter too, so he'll still have the physical and mental advantage over his sister. Furthermore, while your toddler will be improving her capacity to take care of herself, she also will be increasing her capacity to get on her brother's nerves. Consequently, you can expect that confrontations during this period actually may become more frequent and more violent, and it is important for you to remain vigilant. By the way, especially toward the end of this period, you may notice many instances where your toddler and her brother start playing together quite nicely. If you remember to praise them both lavishly when they are getting along, you may be able to help minimize the number and intensity of their conflicts.

When I go out to the supermarket or mall, my toddler is no longer content to stay in a seat or stroller. Should I try using one of those "leash" devices?

It may be worth a try, but be careful. While the leash has to be long enough to give you and your toddler some potential for independent movement, it can't be so long that your toddler can get herself seriously entangled or that other people around you can get tripped, tangled, or otherwise endangered. If your toddler is going through her negativistic stage, you may also find that she strongly resists being hooked up to this kind of device. Therefore, it probably would be a good idea to avoid the need for a leash as much as possible. This can be done by planning your trips to the market or mall at times when the other parent (or a friend or relative) can come along so that while one does what needs to get done, the other can carefully supervise your toddler.

Is there anything I can do to help protect my toddler in case she somehow becomes separated from me?

There's not much. Toward the end of this period, your toddler undoubtedly will be able to tell someone her first name, but it is unreasonable to expect that she will be able to produce her last name reliably, much less remember things like her address, phone number, etc. Nor is she likely to be able to retain and follow instructions concerning approaching a policeman, staying away from strangers, etc. Some parents sew a little identification tag on the inside of their toddler's jackets and coats, and there currently are some movements directed toward having all young children fingerprinted. In general, however, the most effective protection you can provide for your toddler at this point is your careful supervision, which can largely prevent such events from occurring.

In fact, if a fire should break out in your home, chances are that your toddler will try to hide under a bed rather than run out of the house. Therefore, while it might be a good idea to start including your toddler in family fire drills, you certainly cannot count on her carrying out the procedures in a crisis. Her best protection will be your continued vigilance in checking smoke alarms and taking other preventive measures. Also, be sure to post a safety sticker on the window of her room so that, should a fire occur, emergency personnel will know where to look for her.

I am thinking about putting my toddler in the local day-care center. The classrooms and materials appear to be safe, but will she be in danger from the other children?

There are prices to be paid when you put your toddler in a group situation. First of all, it is well documented that children in day care are far more likely than stay-at-home children to develop a wide variety of contagious illnesses. High-quality centers take careful measures to prevent the spread of diseases, but you can expect your toddler to pick up anything that's "going around the neighborhood," from common colds, ear infections, and the flu to chicken pox. Until the end of this period, you can also expect that your toddler may come home with some minor bumps and bruises inflicted upon her by her classmates. Again, the personnel at high-quality centers provide adequate supervision so that a serious injury is very unlikely. However, keeping children at this age from occasionally engaging in small scuffles and tussles is nearly impossible. If you have a compelling reason to place your toddler in day care at this point, none of these noncritical hazards should really deter you, but you should at least be aware of them.

If you have to put your toddler in day care, keep in mind that while she probably won't be in any great danger, she will be more likely to pick up common colds and whatever else is "going around."

In case of fire, is my toddler still too young to understand and carry out simple emergency routines?

Toward the end of this period, it may be possible to get your toddler to participate in a family fire drill. Especially if she views it as a game of some sort, your toddler is likely to follow an escape-and-gather procedure fairly reliably. However, you simply cannot count on your toddler to respond appropriately in a real emergency. When frightened, toddlers quickly forget a lot of what they've learned. They are more likely to react in ways that have nothing to do with what they've been taught.

How can I tell if a bump on the head requires medical attention?

Almost all children suffer an accidental bump on the head sometime during their early years. Most of these bumps are not serious, but they frequently cause parents a lot of anxiety. Often, there is an almost immediate swelling at the point of impact, but this alone shouldn't worry you as long as there are no other signs of injury. The immediately formed lump usually means that a blood vessel has been broken just under the skin and there has been some local bleeding. Such bleeding would be under the skin but outside the skull so it is of less concern than bleeding that occurs within the skull. Signs of concussion or brain swelling in children usually include vomiting and/or unusual drowsiness. It is therefore recommended that a child who has sustained a blow to the head be observed closely for the next 24 hours. If the child begins to vomit or becomes difficult to rouse, call your pediatrician at once and follow his instructions. Don't try to keep your child awake after a head injury. If she falls asleep, observe her carefully and be sure that her level of consciousness is that of normal sleep. Check this every hour or two by giving her a gentle nudge or by rolling her over; make sure that her response is what you would expect during normal sleep. If it is not, or if your child begins to act abnormal in any way, call your pediatrician. This is another instance when you are better to be safe than sorry.

Minor scrapes, bumps, and bruises are an inevitable part of being a toddler.

What's the best treatment for cuts, scrapes, and bruises? How can I tell if a cut requires stitches?

A cut or scrape should be cleaned as soon as possible after it occurs. Often, the injury will look worse than it is until it is cleansed. Soak the area in warm, soapy water or wash it with a clean cloth that you've wet with warm, soapy water. Then rinse the area well with clear water. Try to stay calm throughout the procedure while calming and comforting your toddler. If the bleeding continues, apply pressure and a cold pack (ice cubes in a plastic bag wrapped in a towel) and elevate the area until the bleeding stops. If the amount of bleeding seems excessive or is difficult to stop, or if the wound is deep or uneven, call your pediatrician or seek medical attention. If the cut is not very deep and is not uneven, you can probably apply a butterfly bandage after cleaning; it will keep the edges of skin together and allow the injury to heal. In important cosmetic areas like the face and hands and across joints or bony areas, stitches may be more appropriate. If you have questions or concerns or are in doubt about proper treatment, seek medical advice.

My pediatrician told me to keep syrup of ipecac on hand in case of an emergency. Are there other medications I should have?

You are wise to follow your doctor's suggestion. Syrup of ipecac should be kept on hand to induce vomiting if an accidental poisoning should occur. (You will still have to call your pediatrician or the local poison control center before you use it, however, since vomiting should not be induced for certain ingested substances, such as hydrocarbons.) It is also advisable to have acetaminophen available at home to treat fever and/or pain. Some pediatricians advise parents to have a liquid form of antihistamine for allergic reactions, and some will recommend having a cough/cold preparation for treatment of respiratory infections. If your child has many painful ear infections, it is a good idea to have an analgesic ear drop available; this is a prescription item, however, so you will need to ask your pediatrician about it. This short list is as much medication as you will probably need, but consult with your pediatrician to be sure.

My toddler was ill several months ago, and the pediatrician prescribed an antibiotic. Now I think my child has come down with the same illness. Since I still have some of the antibiotic left, can I just go ahead and give it to her instead of bothering the pediatrician again?

It is not wise to give any medication, but especially prescription medication, for any illness other than the one for which it was prescribed. For most illnesses that require an antibiotic, the amount prescribed is just enough to treat that illness so that there should be none left over. Many antibiotics outdate in a few weeks and should be discarded after that date. Most important, it may be very difficult for a parent to determine if an illness in a toddler is really the same as the last one. A medication used for one illness may be contraindicated for another. Don't give your child any medication without consulting your pediatrician first, unless your pediatrician has told you that you may.

How can I tell the difference between a cold and the flu? How do I treat them?

Sometimes you won't be able to tell whether your child has contracted a cold or the flu. If you can't, it won't matter; and sometimes, if you can, it won't change the way you treat it. Colds and flu are both caused by viruses, and the flu that infects the nose and throat produces symptoms similar to colds. The type of flu that causes gastrointestinal symptoms is generally easy to identify. Either way, you'll want to treat the symptoms, since there is no medicine that will cure either condition. The symptoms are likely to include a stuffy or runny nose, fever, red and watery eyes, coughing, sore throat, loss of appetite, and malaise (generally feeling miserable). To relieve stuffiness, you can use saltwater nose drops (see page 54), a cool-mist humidifier in the toddler's bedroom, and perhaps a decongestant and/or cough medicine if your pediatrician suggests it. You'll want to pamper your toddler; give her plenty to drink; and offer her small, light meals. Encourage her to rest and engage in only quiet activities. Comfort her as well as you can, since crying will increase her stuffiness and discomfort. If your pediatrician approves, you can give her acetaminophen to help relieve fever and make her more comfortable; do not give her aspirin or ibuprofen. A cough that becomes severe or lasts more than a few days should be investigated. Any sudden worsening of her symptoms should also be reported to your pediatrician, since a secondary infection, such as bronchitis, pneumonia, or ear infections, can

---

THINGS TO DO AND NOT TO DO FOR A COLD

DO:
- Offer fluids frequently and provide small nourishing meals
- Pamper and offer sympathy
- Encourage adequate rest and sleep
- Treat fever (higher than 102 degrees Fahrenheit) and discomfort with acetaminophen
- Use disposable cups whenever possible to prevent spread of viruses
- Teach your child to wash her hands before and after meals and after using the bathroom
- Use a cool-mist humidifier in your child's room
- Watch for complications such as ear pain, severe cough, or a worsening of symptoms
- Call your pediatrician for advice if you think the illness is not following the expected course

DO NOT:
- Offer large, heavy meals
- Criticize or show impatience
- Allow a noisy or unpleasant environment in the child's room
- Give aspirin, aspirin products, or ibuprofen
- Share eating or drinking utensils
- Allow unwashed hands to handle food
- Use hot-water vaporizers
- Delay consulting with your pediatrician about significant changes in your child's condition

When she has a cold, comfort her as well as you can, since crying may increase her stuffiness and discomfort.

sometimes accompany a cold or the flu. Most of the time, however, the cold or flu will run its course, and your toddler will begin to feel better within three to five days and be well in a week or two.

How will I know when a cold is developing into something more serious?

If your toddler's symptoms worsen later in the course of a cold, a secondary infection or complication may be occurring. Coughing that deepens and becomes constant; fever that returns or shoots up; refusal of liquids; increased irritability; increasing fatigue or lethargy; crying or shrieking; or a red-streaked throat can all be symptoms of secondary infections or complications. Strep throat is one possible complication that should be screened for. An ear infection is also a possibility, since ear infections often follow a cold or upper respiratory infection. Remember, *anytime* your toddler's symptoms concern you, contact your pediatrician; this is especially true if her symptoms worsen after the first few days of a cold.

Will my doctor automatically put my toddler on an antibiotic if she has a severe cold or cough?

Children of any age are not put on antibiotics automatically for colds or for a cough. Colds are caused by viruses, and antibiotics are ineffective as a treatment for viruses. Antibiotics, however, may be prescribed to treat a bacterial infection that occurs or develops while the child is fighting a cold. Anytime you are concerned about your child's illness or the course it's taking, you should consult your pediatrician.

How high of a fever causes convulsions?

The height of a fever seems to be less important than how fast it rises in determining whether it will cause febrile (fever-related) convulsions. A rapid rise of two or three degrees is more likely to stimulate a seizure than a gradual elevation of four or five degrees. Another determining factor is the family history. Convulsions with fever tend to occur in certain families (up to five to ten percent of the population) and are very uncommon in others. For the comfort of your toddler, it is recommended that a fever over 102 degrees Fahrenheit be treated, usually with an appropriate dose of acetaminophen. In families with a history of febrile convulsions, the fever can be treated a bit more aggressively. If there is a history of febrile convulsions in your family, make certain your pediatrician is aware of it so that you can receive any necessary recommendations about treatment.

My 20 month old was excluded from day care because she had "pinkeye." How long will she need to stay at home?

Pinkeye (conjunctivitis) is a redness or pinkness of the white portion of the eye(s); it often accompanies a cold. It is usually caused by the same virus that causes the cold, although a secondary bacterial infection may also be present. A child with a cold and conjunctivitis is no more contagious than a child with a cold alone. There is really no more reason to exclude a child with conjunctivitis than a child with just a cold. This has been difficult for many caregivers to accept because of the long-standing feeling that conjunctivitis is more contagious than the cold itself. It just isn't. Treating the pinkeye with warm, wet packs placed on the closed eye(s) for five or ten minutes four times daily will often take care of it within a few days. If it does not, consult your pediatrician.

If you ever suspect a problem with your child's eyes, contact your pediatrician.

When should I take my child to the eye doctor?

This question is usually best answered by your pediatrician. As part of every well-child exam, the eyes will be examined. If any significant abnormality is found, further evaluation will be suggested. If you and your pediatrician both feel that the eyes are normal, an examination by an eye doctor is probably not necessary at this age. Some of the more common reasons to see an eye doctor include a tear duct that does not open by six to 12 months of age, persistent deviation of the eyes in or out, suspected cataracts, suspected vision problems, or any significant injury to the eye.

Do children outgrow ear infections?

The reasons that older children seem to get fewer ear infections than younger children are many. Most ear infections are preceded by an upper respiratory infection (a cold). Young children begin to get upper respiratory infections as soon as they are exposed to other people (especially other children) with colds. In our society, children are entering day-care and child-care situations at an earlier age, and such situations encourage the spread of cold viruses. As the child grows, however, she is exposed to more and more cold viruses, and her body begins to build up its defenses against them. So in the later childhood and adult years, she tends to get fewer colds.

In addition, during a cold, the eustachian tube (which equalizes pressure between the middle ear and the outside) becomes blocked and malfunctions, resulting in an infection in the middle ear. In younger children, the eustachian tube is shorter and more crooked and is therefore easier to block. In older children, the tube enlarges and straightens and is less likely to be obstructed when the child gets congested. Although ear infections can occur at any age, for these and other reasons, they are much less common after the age of five to seven.

My two year old has had three ear infections. Should I have "tubes" put in her ears?

Three ear infections in a two year old is not unusual and is probably not a reason to consider ear tubes. These tubes are small, hollow, plastic devices which are inserted through the eardrum to serve as a temporary back-up to the eustachian tube (the eustachian tube equalizes pressure between the middle ear and the outside). These tubes are usually inserted when there is evidence that the fluid in the middle ear space from an ear infection has not cleared after several months (or after several ear infections) and the child's hearing is impaired and/or his general health is affected. The decision to consider placement of ear tubes is one that should be made in consultation with your pediatrician and an ear specialist. The tubes are only temporary and can have some of their own side effects, including permanent scarring of the eardrum. For more specific information, you'll want to discuss this matter with your pediatrician.

How serious is chicken pox? Should I expose my toddler to it on purpose just to get it over with?

Chicken pox is usually a relatively mild disease in childhood, although a very small number of children who have a compromised immune system may experience serious complications. Chicken pox is marked by a rash that first appears on the torso and then spreads, over the course of a few days, to the rest of the body. It can involve the mouth and throat; in girls, it can even involve the vagina. Some of the lesions look like small drops of water on a red background. Overnight, the "drops of water" are usually replaced by scabs. Some children only get a few lesions while others may get hundreds. Chicken pox can be accompanied by runny nose, fever, and itching. The time from exposure to onset of symptoms is 14 to 21 days. The child is contagious until the scabs are dry and have begun to fall off; this can take a week to ten days. If the itching is severe, the pediatrician may prescribe an antihistamine to make the child more comfortable and help prevent excessive scratching, which may lead to scarring. There are different opinions regarding whether to expose your child deliberately or not. Since this is such a contagious disease, your child will usually be exposed at some point anyway. You probably should avoid exposing your toddler on purpose, at least until he's a little older and bigger. What's more, a chicken pox vaccine is currently being tested, so you may not want to purposely expose her to someone with chicken pox at all.

What is roseola? Do all children get it?

Roseola is a viral illness that most children will get sometime between six months and six years of age. It can be frightening to parents because it begins with a fever that is often very high (103 to 105 degrees Fahrenheit) but that is not accompanied by any other symptoms. Most of these children feel much better than you would expect them to with such a high fever. The fever lasts three to five days and then goes away. Within 12 to 24 hours, a rash develops all over the body. It is pink or red and rarely itches. The rash lasts less than two days, and the illness is over. Roseola is unique in that the fever and rash do not occur at the same time, and by the time the rash does appear, the child feels much better. Treatment with acetaminophen does not control the fever as readily as with other illnesses, but may bring it down enough to make the child more comfortable. Children recover very quickly from this illness despite the unusually high fever.

Is there any way to prevent my toddler from developing a reaction to the DTP booster?

The part of the DTP to which there are rare reactions is the pertussis (whooping cough) portion. If your child hasn't had a reaction previously, it would be very unlikely for her to have one this time. Serious reactions from the DTP occur about once in every 310,000 to 500,000 doses. However, the risk of serious complications from whooping cough in an *unimmunized* child is one in 10,000. In other words, the risk from the disease is many times greater than the risk of reaction from the immunization. Most children will have only a mild or

Keep in mind that your child's behavior can provide important clues for determining the seriousness of an illness.

minor reaction to the immunization; it may include temporary soreness at the injection site, a low-grade fever that lasts
only a short time, and crankiness for several hours after the
injection. If you would like to take a further step to modify
even these minor reactions, administer acetaminophen at the
time of the immunization. If you're still concerned, talk to
your pediatrician. Protecting your child from preventable
disease is vitally important to her health and well-being.

**I understand that between 12 and 18 months of age my
toddler will receive several immunizations—some that she
has never had before. Must she have them? Are any of them
dangerous?**

At 12 months of age, your daughter will receive a tuberculin
test. This simple skin test is very important because it is
necessary to diagnose and treat tuberculosis early in order to
get the best results. The test is repeated yearly in many
pediatric clinics, but the risk in your community may affect
the recommendation for how often your toddler should be
screened. At about 15 months of age, your toddler should
receive the MMR, which provides immunity to measles,
mumps, and rubella. The measles part of the vaccination may
cause a fever or a slight rash seven to ten days after the
injection. There's usually no reaction to the mumps or rubella
portions. If your toddler has a severe allergy to eggs, be sure to
tell your pediatrician before your toddler is vaccinated. Several
vaccines are grown on eggs and therefore may pose a greater
risk to your toddler. If your toddler does have such an allergy,
she will be given a skin test before getting the vaccine to
determine whether or not it is safe for her. There has been a
recent increase in the incidence of measles in this country, so
it's important to make sure that all family members, including
yourself and your spouse, have been properly immunized
against this disease. Check with your doctor to see if you need
a booster as well. In addition to the MMR, your daughter will
also receive the HiB vaccine to protect her from Hemophilus
influenza type B. This is not a flu but a bacterium that has
caused serious disease in many children five years of age and
younger. It is the most frequent cause of bacterial meningitis,
epiglottitis, and other serious diseases and complications. There
are no expected reactions to this vaccine. The DTP and oral
polio vaccinations will be repeated at 18 months of age and then
again at age five. If you have any concerns about the vaccines,
discuss them with your doctor. Keep in mind that you, as a
parent, are responsible for the health and well-being of your

---

RECOMMENDED IMMUNIZATION SCHEDULE FOR CHILDREN

Age	Immunization
Two months	DTP and oral polio
Four months	DTP and oral polio
Six months	DTP
Nine to 12 months	Tuberculin test (may be repeated at one to two year intervals; consult pediatrician)
15 months	MMR
15 to 18 months	HiB
18 months	DTP and oral polio
Four to six years	DTP and oral polio

DTP = Diphtheria, tetanus, and pertussis
(whooping cough) vaccines given as single
injection
MMR = Measles, mumps, and rubella vaccines
given as single injection
HiB = Hemophilus influenza type B (meningitis)
immunization

child. An important part of that responsibility is to protect her from getting diseases that can be prevented. Parents who do not immunize their children out of fear or ignorance are putting their children at great and unjustified risk. It's similar to expecting a toddler to cross a major highway by herself and not get hit by a car. *It would be a high risk gamble, and a senseless one for your child.*

My daughter has allergies. How can I make my home as nonallergenic as possible?

You'll want to try to identify the allergens (substances that produce an allergic response) in your child's environment. Sometimes they're easy to identify and remove. Other times, you'll want to consult with your pediatrician for help. If indicated, your child may need to have skin tests to help identify allergies and indicate specific treatment. Some allergic children will have allergies to house dust, mold, tobacco smoke, and bacteria; often, feathers, fur, and wool will cause reactions as well. You can try to remove or diminish these common allergens in her sleeping area by only having washable surfaces, curtains, and floors. Washing all the surfaces frequently and keeping dust to a minimum can be helpful in diminishing symptoms of some allergies. Remove stuffed animals from her crib or bed, and allow one or two toys that can be washed frequently. Make sure that the mattress is made of an allergen-free material or is completely enclosed in a safe and allergen-proof cover. Don't allow pets in the house, and keep her away from other people's pets. If she pets an animal to which you know she is allergic, bathe her, shampoo her hair, and launder her clothes as soon as possible. Air cleaners or electrostatic equipment for furnaces are said to be extremely helpful to allergic families. There are many of these on the market so you'll want to do some careful research before choosing one. If these steps do not make your daughter more comfortable, talk to your pediatrician.

If your toddler has an allergy to dust, washing her toys and bedding frequently may help diminish her symptoms.

My 15 month old always has a wet rash around her mouth. Is there an effective way to treat this?

What you are describing is probably a contact rash from the child's drooling. At this age, toddlers do a lot of salivating because they are teething. Measures to keep the area dry are the most effective in treating and preventing the rash. An absorbent, nontoxic powder dusted lightly on the chin is often helpful. Lubricating creams and lotions may also help since the skin frequently gets irritated and then becomes dry; as a result, the wet rash may become a dry, rough rash. Gently patting and blotting the area occasionally with a soft cloth may also help, but *wiping* too frequently can increase the irritation. Do the best you can for now. You will notice that the rash will gradually disappear as the drooling decreases.

Does a loose stool mean that something's wrong?

An occasional loose stool is nothing to worry about. Children have various patterns for bowel movements, and there's a wide range of what may be normal for your child. Loose and watery stool would usually be a sign that a food or beverage (or one of its ingredients) didn't agree with her or that she's getting an illness. Sometimes toddlers will have loose stools associated with colds or teething. Diarrhea is considered to be more than one loose stool per feeding; usually, it's accompanied by other symptoms of illness, such as a fever or abdominal cramping. If your toddler frequently has loose stools, but has no other symptoms of illness, you may want to decrease her intake of fruit and fruit juices to see if this helps. You might also want to investigate other aspects of her diet. Sometimes, identifying a certain food that doesn't agree with her and removing it from her diet will negate the problem. Anytime you are concerned about loose stools or diarrhea, contact your pediatrician.

Is my toddler constipated if she doesn't have a bowel movement for two to three days?

It can be entirely normal for a child to have a bowel movement every two to three days. If she isn't exhibiting signs of constipation (such as crying, severe grunting, or misery while having the bowel movement) and if she isn't excreting large, hard stools or many hard pellets, she isn't constipated. Some toddlers will grunt and fuss at the time they have a bowel movement because it's bothersome, and they have to stop and concentrate on something when they'd rather not. If the consistency of the stools seems normal and the pattern of bowel movements is fairly reasonable (every two to five days), don't worry. Of course, if you become concerned, discuss it with your pediatrician. Some toddlers can develop a habit of holding stools, and that can cause problems.

IMPORTANT REASONS FOR CONTACTING YOUR PEDIATRICIAN

- Routine well-child examinations and immunizations
- Drastic changes in your child's behavior
- Severe pain
- Severe or worrisome injury
- Prolonged high fever
- Persistent cough
- Foul-smelling drainage from the nose, eyes, ears, or anywhere else
- Persistent vomiting
- Unexplained, persistent rash
- Prolonged diarrhea
- Blood in urine or stool
- Anytime you are worried about your child's health or physical or emotional well-being

ON BEING A PARENT

Now that my toddler's interests and abilities are becoming more complex, should I be taking a more active role in "teaching" him?

Because of his longer attention span and greater language skills, it now will be possible for you to provide increasing input into your toddler's learning during daily interactions. However, it still would be a mistake to try to structure his activities to any great extent or to push him to focus on any specific subjects. Your toddler is still doing a great deal of "learning to learn," and his "education" still will proceed most efficiently and effectively if he is allowed to do the bulk of his learning on his own. Therefore, it would be a good idea to resist any temptation to become too instructive. Continue to make the job of "consultant" your primary role. In other words, when he approaches you during his explorations, point out related ideas that he may be missing, but concentrate on what he is interested in at the moment.

Given his increasing physical abilities, what can I do to make my toddler's environment more challenging and exciting for him?

A typical household contains more excitement and challenge than any toddler could hope for. What you need to do, therefore, is to continue making as much of your home as possible safe and accessible for him. As he gains greater skill, it might be a good idea to start widening his environment to include areas that were previously off-limits. For example, with your supervision, you might let him test his skills on a full flight of carpeted stairs. In addition, dangerous items that were previously placed "out of reach" on high shelves should be removed or locked up completely so your toddler will have an opportunity to now reach levels that used to be forbidden and beyond his capabilities. You might also consider expanding his horizons to include places outside your home. Finally, as your time and inclination allow, provide yourself as a playmate for your toddler. Using you as a running and chasing buddy, wrestling partner, or even just an object to climb upon or crawl over will give him plenty of excitement and challenge.

Being your child's playmate from time to time can provide him with opportunities for fun and learning.

When my toddler approaches me for assistance with something, should I help right away or give him a chance to work it out for himself?

This can be a little tricky. On one hand, it is important that your toddler know he can count on you for help. On the other hand, if help is provided too quickly too often, your toddler may get into the habit of depending on parental assistance entirely; he may not learn how to do a lot of things for himself. Therefore, when your toddler approaches you for assistance, as long as he is not clearly distressed, you might try exercising a little restraint. Assess the situation, and if you feel that the solution to the problem is within or near his capabilities, urge him to try solving it himself. As his language skills increase, you can even provide him with some suggestions if he appears to be stumped. But do not allow him to reach the point of frustration; be ready to step in as soon as your toddler shows signs that he is becoming upset.

Now that my toddler is talking, should I respond using the same level of language he uses?

Definitely not. Just as we often find ourselves unconsciously mimicking someone with a southern drawl or British accent, we sometimes end up responding to toddlers in the same manner in which they speak. This does not do a lot to improve a toddler's language skills. Of course, you can't talk to a toddler as you would talk to another adult. However, it is a good idea to use plain, simple language—clearly spoken with proper grammar—that is slightly above what you perceive to be your toddler's level of understanding. Remember that his understanding of words will be greater than his ability to say them. Keep in mind, too, that your toddler does a lot of language learning though imitation, and it is up to you to provide an appropriate model. It is believed that one reason younger siblings do not do as well in this area as firstborns is they often imitate their slightly older siblings, who provide relatively poor language models.

I am bilingual. Should I speak only one language in the home so as not to confuse my toddler?

The research on this issue is not very extensive, and therefore not really conclusive at this time. However, the general

---

THE SUPERBABY SYNDROME

In recent years, a lot of parents have been caught up in the "superbaby" syndrome—teaching their toddlers to do all sorts of impressive things. Most child development specialists are alarmed by this. They feel that most of these parents are well-meaning but seriously misguided and are putting their toddlers at risk for serious emotional problems. There is no doubt that if you expend enough time and effort, you can teach a toddler to do just about anything. But keep in mind that impressive performances do not necessarily reflect equal understanding. After all, Roy Rogers taught Trigger to count, but would you let that horse balance your checkbook? Similarly, many toddlers have been taught to use personal computers, to play Mozart, etc., but there is no evidence that these toddlers truly comprehend and appreciate what they are doing. They're simply doing tricks in most cases. Furthermore, research indicates that children who display precocity at early ages do not attain a lasting advantage over other children their age. For instance, many toddlers have been taught reading, writing, and math skills; but by the second year or so of elementary school, there are no differences in academic ability between these children and those who did not receive such training. Finally, clinicians are reporting that children who were subjected to the rigid instruction required to produce these skills, and whose parents constantly pushed them toward "success," are showing up with stress ulcers, nervous habits, low self-esteem, and other serious emotional disturbances. Remember, your toddler's development will proceed at its own natural pace, and it will grow horizontally as well as vertically. Therefore, rather than jerking him up to levels for which he is not ready, you are better off filling in around him as he moves along himself, thus providing a wide, solid foundation for whatever comes along in the future.

consensus among specialists on the subject is that a bilingual household is rarely a problem. In fact, it is often advantageous. As long as a child is exposed to two good language models—perhaps with one parent speaking one language exclusively—he may fall a little behind in language skills in the beginning, but will catch up quickly and become fluent in both languages. Children seem to have an enormous facility for absorbing language during the early years, and it appears as if the quality of language they are exposed to is of far greater concern than the quantity.

In addition to talking to my toddler, should I supplement our conversations with records, tapes, the radio, etc.?

Your toddler will be extremely interested in language throughout this period. Anything that produces appropriate sounds will probably fascinate him and provide him with a lot of enjoyment. Consequently, providing him with access to these things certainly wouldn't hurt. However, in terms of his actual progress in language development, they probably won't help too much either. Research has repeatedly shown that during the early years, there is simply no substitute for "live language," that is, words and sentences addressed directly to the child by real people. Furthermore, language concerning what your toddler is interested in at the moment will have the greatest impact, and these devices can't look and see what your toddler is up to. In other words, records, tapes, the radio, and the television can be used to supplement your conversations with your toddler, but they should never become a substitute for those conversations.

Early in this period, your toddler's attention span will still be very short, so don't be surprised if she doesn't stick around to hear the ending.

My toddler loves it when I read him a story, but sometimes he tries to get up and leave before I've finished. Should I stop him?

By trying to get up and leave, your toddler is telling you that this activity no longer interests him. To continue it is likely to cause nothing more than disappointment and frustration for everyone involved. Especially at the start of this period, when toddlers have a very short attention span, parents often feel their child isn't learning anything because he doesn't stick around long enough for something to have full effect. However, nothing will have an effect once it goes beyond the point where the child is interested. During a reading session, for instance, a younger toddler may enjoy listening to the sound of his parent's voice, he may be fascinated by some of the pictures in the book, and he may get a kick out of turning the pages. He does not, however, have the mental capacities needed to recognize characters and follow plots at this point. Consequently, as far as he's concerned, the session may be "all done" long before the story is finished. A few months later, things will change, but for the time being, it is suggested that you simply follow his lead rather than trying to force something upon him that he's not interested in.

What is the easiest way to encourage and enhance my toddler's role-play and fantasy activities?

The first thing to do is to understand what this kind of play is all about. Your toddler is collecting mental images from his ever-increasing experiences, and he is using his new mental capacities to retain them and move them around in his own mind. Therefore, providing the raw materials for his role-play and fantasy activities does not mean giving him a lot of toys; rather, it means making sure he has plenty of "real world" experiences to draw upon. A toddler who has never been to a zoo is not likely to know what to do with a pretend zoo set. A toddler who has never seen a construction site is not likely to know what to do with toy dump trucks and tractors. A toddler who has not been allowed to watch his parents work in the kitchen is not likely to know what to do with a make-believe stove and utensil set. On the other hand, a toddler who has had all of these experiences will eagerly create a multitude of scenarios using very few props and a lot of imagination.

Instead of "pretending," my toddler often attempts to do the real thing—which sometimes is troublesome or even dangerous. How do I handle this?

It is important to remember that encouraging and enhancing your toddler's role-play and fantasy activities does not mean excluding him from your activities. In fact, your activities are a primary source of his raw materials for pretend games. In addition, although your toddler is becoming increasingly content to play by himself, being with you is still among his favorite activities. Therefore, in these situations, you might consider working out a compromise. For example, if you are working in the kitchen, bring your toddler's pretend equipment and utensils in and encourage him to work alongside

Some chores that he would like to try doing "for real" are just too dangerous at this stage. For those activities, you might consider getting him a simple "play" set.

you. If he insists on getting involved specifically in what you're doing, see if you can find something safe and appropriate for him to do to assist you—mixing something in a bowl, for instance. To the extent that you can safely include him, you may get more "hindrance" than real help, but your toddler will get a lot of satisfaction and enjoyment while staying out of danger.

Every now and then, my toddler becomes extremely clingy and won't do anything unless I'm involved. Should I ignore him or push him away when this happens?

That probably would be inadvisable. During the early part of this period, attachment behavior typically becomes very intense as toddlers strive to firmly establish the emotional bond with their parents. While their behavior sometimes can become unpleasant and annoying, it is important to remember that there is a genuine need behind it. Therefore, it is suggested that you simply be patient and indulge your toddler in these periodic episodes. Within a few months, their number and intensity are likely to dwindle considerably. However, if you sense that the balance between your toddler's social behavior and exploratory/investigatory behavior is becoming unhealthy, you might want to check to see that he is being provided with a lot of access to his environment. Very often,

this clinging and demand for adult attention comes from boredom rather than from the normal emotional insecurity of this stage.

Some of my toddler's "rituals" are very time-consuming and inconvenient. Will it hurt if I occasionally try to eliminate or modify some of them?

Occasionally attempting to modify them probably is better than trying to eliminate them. Remember, there is a good reason why your toddler is engaging in such behavior. Consistent, stable routines help him cope with his new role as an active participant in the activities of his daily life. As he becomes more confident, you are likely to have some success making suggestions for alterations now and then. If you do too much too soon, however, you are likely to be met with strong resistance and considerable distress. Be patient, and praise your toddler for those parts of his rituals that are efficient, rather than simply scolding him for those parts you find inconvenient. By encouraging the positive and just waiting out the negative, you'll be doing what's necessary so as not to prolong this phase. As a result, you should see the major problems start to dissipate within a few months.

Lately, my toddler has been saying "no" to virtually every request or instruction. How can I avoid having confrontations with him all day long?

Keep in mind that your toddler's primary interest is in exercising his new sense of personal power. Defying you is merely a means toward this end. Therefore, the trick is to allow him to exercise his personal power as often as possible in ways that won't require a direct confrontation with you. This may take a little planning, but it can be done rather easily in the course of many daily routines. For example, when getting your toddler dressed in the morning, if you say "Please put on your shirt" or "Do you want to put your shirt on now?" it is almost inevitable that you will receive a "no" in response. However, if you say "Do you want to put your shirt or your pants on first?" you will be giving your toddler an opportunity to be "in charge" without having to challenge your overall authority. In other words, to the extent that you can offer your toddler choices instead of giving him instructions or making direct requests at this point, the unpleasantness between the two of you will be reduced to a minimum.

How can I tell if my toddler is actively resisting my authority or just introducing a new ritual?

This may be a little tricky to figure out at times, but in general, it should be clear what your toddler's intention is by the way he reacts to what you say to him. If your instruction or request is met by a cool "no," and your toddler looks at you for a reaction to his denial, you can be pretty sure that he is simply out to challenge your authority rather than trying to establish a new ritual. On the other hand, if it is met by signs of distress, fear, or even panic, and your toddler concentrates almost exclusively on maintaining what he was doing or reinstating some change you've made, then there is a good chance that you're dealing with ritualistic behavior. Again, it may not always be crystal clear, but don't worry. If what your toddler is doing is intolerable or dangerous, it is important that you assert your authority and retain control of the situation; altering one of his rituals now and then won't cause substantial, long-term problems. If what your toddler is doing is not such a big deal, however, it is important not to make it a big deal—as long as you win the "war," it won't hurt to let him win a small "battle" here and there.

If I tell my toddler to stop doing something and he doesn't stop, what can I do?

Discipline at this stage is not easy, but it is often extremely necessary. Keep in mind that, unlike before, you probably won't be able to simply distract your toddler and channel his attention into a more appropriate activity (although you could try). On the other hand, you also won't be able to make much of an impression with long-winded explanations, threats, or promises. You have to make your point succinctly and get your message across in language that your toddler understands. So, for example, if he is swinging on the drapes, you ask him to stop, and he doesn't, it won't help if you explain that he might tear the material and it will cost a lot of money to replace. It also won't help to tell him that if he doesn't cease, he won't get to go to Grandma's house next month. What you have to do is physically remove your toddler from the offending situation and hold him in a firm hug for a minute or two. You can talk to him about the situation and try to explain why you wanted him to stop doing what he was doing. However, it is the physical restriction—which he won't like because he would much prefer to be doing something else somewhere else—that will get the message across to him that this activity is unacceptable and that it won't be tolerated.

If she's doing something you don't want her to do, you'll probably still need to physically remove her from the offending situation in addition to asking her to stop.

After I discipline my toddler, he sometimes returns to the forbidden activity a few minutes later. Did I do it wrong?

You probably didn't do it wrong—you just didn't do it enough. Particularly while they're going through negativism, toddlers can be very resistant to discipline. In general, with their increased mental capacities, once they get hooked on something, it's often hard to get them away from it. Therefore, discipline for toddlers has to be not only firm, but persistent. If you remove and hold your toddler, then he returns to the forbidden activity, you'll simply have to repeat the process, this time holding for a little while longer than you did before. Sometimes, it's necessary to repeat the process several times before the message sinks in. Unfortunately, there really aren't any effective alternatives. As time-consuming and inconvenient as this continuous removing and holding may be, keep in mind that it will prevent your toddler from developing the notion that if he pushes hard enough and long enough he will eventually get his own way. Taking the time to do so now will save you a tremendous amount of grief and aggravation later on.

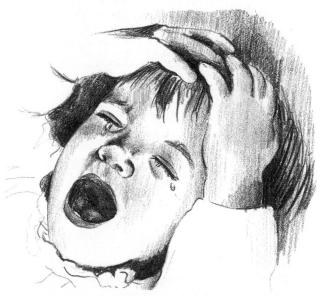

Generally, the best way to deal with a tantrum is to ignore it until your child calms down.

How do I deal with temper tantrums?

Temper tantrums are common among children in this age group. They are the result of frustration, because the toddler has not yet learned more appropriate strategies for attaining his goals and has not yet learned to accept that there are limits to

what he can get away with. During a tantrum, your child may cry, scream, pound his fists against the floor, and perhaps even hold his breath (although this is alarming, it is not dangerous; his natural reflexes will force him to take a breath before any damage is done). During a tantrum, you cannot reason with your toddler. Generally the most effective way to deal with it is to simply ignore it until your child calms down. Make sure he is not in danger of hurting himself, then just leave the room until the storm passes. When it does, you can give him a hug and try to reassure him that he is alright, but do not give in to his demands. For example, if he threw the tantrum because you refused to give him the cookie he wanted, don't break down and give it to him now. Doing so will only let him know that he can get what he wants through the tantrum, and he'll start having them all the time. If the tantrum occurs in public, whisk him off to a more private place until he calms down, or just take him home.

Can I help prevent temper tantrums?

It is a rare toddler who doesn't throw at least one tantrum during this period. While you may not be able to prevent all tantrums, you certainly can make them less likely to occur. Tantrums are the result of frustration, so the best way to help prevent them is to minimize the chance that your toddler will get frustrated in the first place. Indeed, much of the advice in this section is designed to do just that. For example, instead of telling your toddler to put on his shirt—a demand that is likely to provoke a "no" from him—offer him a choice. Ask him if he would like to put on his green shirt or his blue shirt. In this way, you leave him room for autonomy while getting him to do what you'd like him to do. In addition, continued efforts on your part to make your toddler's environment safe and accessible can help prevent the frustration that comes from hearing "no, no, no" from you all the time. And finally, be sure to praise your toddler when he does display appropriate strategies for dealing with frustration instead of only reacting to his inappropriate behavior.

Is my toddler old enough to be spanked?

Some people believe that if you spare the rod, you'll spoil the child. Others believe that hitting a child only teaches that violence is an acceptable way to deal with problems. This is a highly personal issue that must be decided by each family on an individual basis. Extensive studies of families who raised emotionally healthy, responsible, happy, decent children revealed that during the "rebellion" phase of toddlerhood, two out of three resorted to an occasional spanking. It was never brutal, it never became a regular occurrence, and it was not applied hours after the offending event. It usually consisted of a mild slap on the wrist or swat on the behind at the moment the toddler was engaging in something especially dangerous or overwhelmingly intolerable. And, it seemed to make a point without doing permanent damage. On the other hand, one out of three families managed to get through even this phase using just the removing and holding technique. So it is clear that spanking is not necessary to produce a well-behaved child. In general, child development specialists with lots of experience tend to agree you should try to avoid spanking, but you should not condemn yourself if on very rare occasions your toddler pushes you out of your idealism. In other words, if you plan on never spanking your child, you probably will end up doing it the proper number of times.

My toddler goes around biting people. How do I stop him from doing this?

Biting is very common among toddlers. During the early part of this period, it is possible that your toddler may be cutting several teeth and that he's actually biting only to soothe himself. Providing him with a more appropriate teething item may help. Later on, your toddler probably will be biting because this is one of the few ways that he can be effectively aggressive—particularly toward other children. In this case, you will have to treat his biting as you would any other unacceptable activity—with firm, persistent discipline that gives him the message that this simply will not be tolerated (do not, however, try "biting him back"). You can try introducing him to better ways in which he can solve his problems or vent anger, but it may be a few months before he fully understands and accepts these alternatives. In the meantime, you have to make it clear to him that he will not be allowed to hurt other people under any circumstances.

My toddler still sucks his thumb. Should I stop him from doing this?

That probably is not a good idea. Just like adults, toddlers experience a certain amount of stress as part of their daily lives. Consequently, it is not uncommon for them to develop self-comforting habits. Sucking their thumbs, carrying around or fondling a favorite blanket, and other such habits are very soothing for them. These activities are among the relatively limited options they have when it comes to coping with feelings of discomfort at this point. If you reprimand your toddler for sucking his thumb, or if you try to force him to stop doing it, you are likely to increase the amount of stress he suffers and thereby make things worse. On the other hand, if you understand and respect what he is going through and don't make an issue of it, your toddler probably will cease the habit on his own within a few months or years as he learns new and more socially acceptable ways of distracting himself and coping with unpleasant feelings.

Sucking her thumb, like other comfort habits, is one of the few ways she has to deal with stress.

My toddler seems terribly angry and depressed since the arrival of his baby brother. Is there anything I can do to help him feel better?

Keep in mind that your toddler's primary emotion is jealousy, and at this point, attention equals love in his mind. Therefore, the most important thing for you to do is to reassure him in language he understands that he is loved just as much as before. This means providing him with a special half hour or so of your undivided attention every day. Reading him a story while you're nursing the baby won't do the trick; it has to be time just for him with just the two of you alone. Also, don't make a big fuss over the baby right in front of him, and don't allow friends and relatives to do so either. After being the star attraction for many months, your toddler won't understand why everyone is virtually ignoring him and rushing to see his rival—he will resent it deeply. And don't force him to participate in the baby's care. If he shows some curiosity about the new arrival, it's okay to let him join in, but make sure that such activities are his idea and not yours. By the way, special sibling preparation books and programs usually don't work. Toddlers don't relate to future events very well, and they have a tough time comprehending concepts like fraternity and family at this point.

My toddler is in full-time day care. As long as his teachers are cracking down on his unacceptable activities, can I be more indulgent with him during our limited "quality time"?

This is a common attitude among parents, and it leads to a tremendous amount of trouble. Good discipline requires consistency. If a toddler is subject to one set of rules during the day and another set of rules in the evening, the result is likely to be considerable confusion. In addition, because of the greater emotional power that the parents possess, the more lenient arrangement is more than likely to be the one that determines how the toddler will behave under all circumstances. The biggest complaint that day-care personnel express about parents is the fact that they have a tendency not to follow through on discipline at home. And the biggest complaint that the parents have is that they can't control their preschool child who they overindulged as a toddler. Therefore, in order to be fair to everyone involved, it's best to drop this idea. Remember, discipline is the act of educating your child so that he will be able to get along comfortably and congenially with other people. As difficult and unpleasant as it can be at times, there is nothing more "quality" than that.

If he's willing, let him help you care for his little sister. If he's not, however, don't force him.

I'm thinking of putting my toddler in a day-care situation. Should I wait until he demonstrates a capacity to play well with other children his age?

This may be nice, but it certainly is not necessary. If you have no compelling personal reason to place your toddler in a day-care situation, and he seems to be quite content and busy at home, waiting until he shows an active interest in and some capacity for playing with other children his age may save everyone involved from a little anxiety. On the other hand, if you *need* to put your toddler into a day-care situation prior to this point, don't worry. High-quality day-care centers are set up so that toddlers have ample opportunities to pursue a variety of activities independently, so your toddler won't be forced into doing anything for which he is not ready. Also, well-trained, experienced day-care personnel are aware that toddlers often engage in aggressive behavior, so they are well prepared to provide adequate supervision to ensure that your toddler will not seriously hurt or be seriously hurt by other children at the center.

Will my toddler be slow to learn social skills if he doesn't go to a day-care center or participate in a regular play group of some kind?

The notion that toddlers need a lot of regular peer experiences in order to develop social skills is a common misconception. Some research has indicated that during the elementary school years, children who *did not* regularly attend day care, preschool, or play groups actually exhibited superior social skills as compared to those who did. The fact of the matter is that children learn a lot about how to get along with other people by watching and imitating the people around them. Stay-at-home children typically are exposed primarily to adults, who tend to be courteous, civilized, and polite when they interact with others. Children who spend a lot of time in group situations during the early years, on the other hand, often see a lot of hitting, biting, pushing and shoving, hair-pulling, etc. going on around them. Therefore, as long as you are providing your toddler with a good model of appropriate interpersonal behavior, you need not worry too much either way. Toddlers in day care don't necessarily learn social skills any faster than children who do not attend day care or preschool. Although they may pick up a few extra lessons in assertiveness, they may also pick up some less attractive lessons in aggressiveness. In other words, it all tends to come out pretty much even no matter how you slice it.

SPACING CHILDREN

Research has shown that the harsh feelings between closely spaced siblings is one of the single greatest sources of stress for many families. Although exceptions abound, in general, when children are spaced less than three years apart, the tone in the home tends to be chronically more unpleasant than when the children are spaced more than three years apart. Given the social dynamics involved, this is quite understandable. A child who is still a toddler when his new sibling arrives is still immersed in the attachment process and is still primarily home-oriented. Consequently, he has a lot to lose when a rival for the attention of his parents is introduced onto the scene. Furthermore, as a toddler, he does not have the patience, rationality, and other mental capacities to cope very effectively with the situation. A child who is over the age of three when his new sibling arrives already has established a firm attachment to his parents, and he has a growing interest in playing with peers and otherwise engaging in out-of-home activities. Moreover, he is quite capable of communicating his thoughts and feelings clearly and has the mental capacity to understand and appreciate concepts relating to his role as "big brother" and member of an expanded family. In other words, the baby is not as much of a threat to him, and to the extent that the baby does pose an occasional problem, he is far better equipped to deal with it. Of course, it is not always possible nor is it always desirable for parents to space their children three years or more apart for a wide variety of reasons. If they don't, they should not feel that they have condemned themselves and their children to unbearable conditions. However, it is important for them to realize that they have an inherently tougher road to take, and they should be prepared accordingly rather than expecting a Hollywood-type family where everyone gets along with everybody all the time.

Sometimes my toddler drives me crazy to the point that I want to abandon him. Am I a terrible parent?

No, you are a normal parent with a normal toddler. It is a rare parent and toddler who manage to get through this period, especially the middle months, without a lot of heartache and trouble. The developments that are taking place in the toddler almost inevitably will pit him against his parents on many occasions. Parenting can be extremely pleasurable and reward-ing, but it also has its hard parts, and this is one of the tougher times. Therefore, this is a good time to make maximal use of parent support groups, get-away weekends, day-care services, and anything else that will help to alleviate some of the pressure—many parents do. It also helps to remember that if you hold firm, your toddler soon will pass through this difficult phase—and also, that no matter how bad things get, they probably will be a lot worse when he goes through adolescence during his teen years!

It's natural to feel frustrated at times during this period. Keep in mind, however, that his rebelliousness will soon pass.

SELECTING TOYS AND EQUIPMENT

Are there any new considerations regarding toy safety at this point, and are all the old ones still in effect?

All the old ones certainly are still in effect. Toward the end of this period, your toddler may not be putting everything in her mouth all the time, but small pieces and toxic paints are still a threat. Of course, sharp edges and protrusions will remain hazardous for quite some time. And her older brother's toys still may cause a lot of trouble for your toddler—both from the items themselves and from her brother if he catches her using his stuff without permission. As for new considerations, keep in mind that your toddler's strength, dexterity, and curiosity will all grow steadily during this period, so durability becomes an even greater factor than before. Therefore, you have to be careful about things like access to compartments of battery-operated items. In general, keeping your toddler's playthings solid and simple is still a good idea.

Do toddlers need more toys during this period?

Ordinary household items still will go most of the way in meeting your toddler's interests and challenging her abilities throughout this period. However, as the months go by, it might be a good idea to start supplying her with a few more store-bought toys for several reasons. First, as your toddler's skills become more complex, it may not always be easy to find a suitable plaything lying around the house. Second, as your toddler becomes stronger, you may be less inclined to subject a lot of your household possessions to her growing capacity to abuse them in the course of her play. Finally, as your toddler goes through her rebellion phase and becomes very possessive, it is a good idea for her to have certain things that are hers and hers alone. Fortunately, a small collection of solid, simple products will suffice, so it is not necessary for you to make numerous purchases and spend a lot of money.

What is the favorite toy of toddlers?

It is a rare toddler who is not thoroughly enthralled by balls throughout this period. Your toddler probably will derive

---

THE ADVANTAGES OF USING A TOY LIBRARY

Choosing toys for toddlers isn't easy. Because their interests and abilities are still changing at a very rapid rate, an item that is appropriate one day may very well lose its appeal the next; and an item that is totally rejected one day may very well become a favorite within a week. Furthermore, as their activities become increasingly sophisticated, toddlers seem to become increasingly picky about their playthings. While almost all toddlers will enjoy a certain type of toy, each individual toddler will display peculiar preferences when it comes to shape, color, and other characteristics. Unfortunately, those preferences can change dramatically within a short period of time. Consequently, a lot of parents end up spending a lot of money for toys that spend a lot of time in the closet gathering dust. In order to avoid, or at least minimize this, it is suggested that you use a toy library. Many public libraries, parents' groups, and community organizations now are setting up collections of playthings from which parents can borrow a couple of items for a couple of weeks at a time. The process allows you to test the play value of any toy as it relates to your particular child before you buy it. If your toddler seems to really enjoy something, and if she sticks with it for more than a few days, then you can consider laying out the cash to get her one of her own. If your toddler shows little or no interest, you can simply return the item to the toy library and perhaps give it another try in a few weeks. Either way, you've managed to greatly enhance your chances of success in the hit-or-miss game of procuring playthings for your toddler.

She'll enjoy having a ball that she can carry around, throw, kick—and roll to you.

infinite pleasure from throwing, kicking, and otherwise exercising her physical skills with a ball and then watching it bounce, roll, and otherwise react to her actions. She also will enjoy the fact that she can carry a ball around easily. If the ball is very large yet very light, like a beach ball, the thrill she'll get will be tremendous. However, perhaps the most appealing thing about a ball as far as your toddler is concerned is that it allows her to effectively initiate social interactions with you. She will realize that if you roll or throw a ball to someone, that person has a tendency to roll or throw it back. So, for the first time, instead of patiently waiting for you to start a game with her, she now has something she can use to begin a game herself. The mechanical aspects of ball play are definitely alluring, but it is the potential for interacting with you that makes ball play totally irresistible to your toddler.

What other toys or games encourage play between toddler and parent?

Toy telephones are great for this purpose. Although your toddler will be content to conduct pretend conversations all by herself, the chance to sit down with you and carry on a two-way conversation will be a special thrill. Later on, as her role-play and fantasy activities become more complex, she will greatly enjoy having you participate in a pretend tea party

or other such event. Toward the end of this period, you also may be able to engage in a few very simple games with your toddler, such as hide-and-seek, tag, and follow-the-leader. At first, your toddler will be much better at being the seeker rather than the hider, the "tagee" rather than the tagger, and the follower rather than the leader, and it may be a while before she becomes comfortable switching roles. Nevertheless, she probably will be an eager and enthusiastic participant, and these games will provide a lot of fun for everyone involved.

What kinds of books would be appropriate for my toddler?

Your toddler's attitude toward books will change considerably over the course of this period. In the beginning, her primary interest still will be in just turning the pages back and forth, so books with stiff cardboard pages are most appropriate. As her memory, attention span, and language skills grow, your toddler will enjoy pointing-and-naming games with picture books. By the end of this period, those capacities will have grown to the point where story books will be appreciated. Therefore, it will be necessary for you to keep tabs on your toddler's ever-increasing abilities in order to select the type of book that would be suitable at any given time. As for which specific books would be best within each category, that too is dependent upon your toddler. There are no books that can guarantee universal appeal. If your toddler likes boats, get books about boats; if she likes animals, get books about animals; and so on. You might even consider using family photographs and personal experiences to make your own books, which undoubtedly will capture the fancy of your toddler.

Should I buy my toddler things like form boards and stacking rings so she can learn her shapes and colors?

Despite the apparent power of these items, they are entirely unnecessary. There is absolutely no evidence to suggest that children who are exposed to form boards, stacking rings, and other such toys learn their shapes and colors any faster or any better than children who are not. As long as your toddler has access to a wide variety of typical household items, there will be ample opportunities for her to learn these things. On the other hand, as long as these commercial items are durable and inexpensive, they may not be a bad investment. Toddlers do enjoy manipulating and carrying around the pieces as well as attempting to take them apart and put them back together. However, keep in mind that there is no "right" way to use these toys. Don't worry if your toddler isn't using them in the same manner that the child on the box or a child down the block is using them. She will learn just as much, if not more, by trying to put the square peg in the round hole, or by simply pushing it along the floor with her nose, as she will by doing what she is "supposed" to do with it.

Is it too early to introduce my toddler to puzzles?

At the beginning of this period, puzzles will probably be outside the interests and beyond the abilities of your toddler. However, as the months go by, it is likely she will start to find these items fascinating and enjoyable. Fortunately, manufacturers are now making a wide variety of one-, two-, and three-piece puzzles, so try to find some of these to give your toddler the best chance of success. Also, since manipulating the pieces in precise ways may be beyond your toddler's small muscle capacities for a while, look for puzzles that have small knobs or handles attached to the pieces. By the way, as with form boards and stacking rings, don't worry if your toddler doesn't use these toys in the manner for which they were designed right away. She will get quite a lot of enjoyment and learning from just fiddling around with the pieces.

What kinds of toys will enhance my toddler's large muscle skills?

Anything that allows your toddler to attempt and practice her emerging physical skills will be appropriate. A sturdy indoor gym with ramps to climb up and slide down, tunnels to crawl through, and other such features might be a good investment. Of course, you can probably create your own perfectly adequate gym using large cardboard boxes, cushions, stools, and other household items. Likewise, balls will give your toddler an opportunity not only to exercise the upper portions of her body as she throws them, but the lower portions as well when she chases them. Toward the end of this period, simple riding toys may become appropriate as well. As opposed to the standard tricycle, which is likely to remain beyond your toddler's capacities at this point, these toys should have a low center of gravity and seats that are not too high so they can be climbed upon safely and easily. They should also be powered by feet thrusting against the floor rather than by actual pedaling.

Whether it's store bought or made from boxes, cushions, and other household items, a sturdy indoor gym can help her practice her new physical skills.

I'm considering buying an outdoor swing set for my toddler. Will this be a good investment?

Your toddler certainly will enjoy a swing set, but it is probably not necessary for you to purchase one at this point. It still will be a while before your child will be able to use a piece of equipment like this unsupervised. For the time being, it probably would be a good idea to use the swing set at the local park or schoolyard during your regular outings. If for some reason you feel that having a set in your own yard is appropriate, make sure that you purchase one that is sturdy and can be anchored firmly so there is no danger of it tipping over. The seat should have a back support for your toddler, as well as some kind of harness that will hold her securely and prevent her from falling or slipping out. You should also double-check the locking mechanism to be sure that your toddler won't be able to intentionally or inadvertently open it by herself while in full swing.

Make sure that the harness is securely fastened before you give her a push.

What else can I provide to keep my toddler entertained outdoors?

Increasingly throughout this period, your toddler will enjoy playing in a simple sandbox. Armed with a few pails, shovels, and other suitable utensils, she will be able to keep herself entertained for hours. Before placing your toddler in an outdoor sandbox, it is a good idea to see if any local cats have used it as a litter box lately and remove the fecal matter. A shallow wading pool also will be a big hit, especially if it, too, is equipped with a variety of bath toys, beach balls, etc. Toward the end of this period, an opportunity to run through the lawn sprinkler may be appreciated by your toddler. If possible, you might consider setting up enclosed areas where your toddler can play with balls and use her riding toys. You have to make sure there is no chance your toddler will chase a ball or roll her riding toy into a hazardous area.

When can I expect my toddler to be ready to start riding a tricycle?

The age at which the strength, coordination, and savvy that are required to ride a tricycle all come together varies greatly among children. Most do not have the capacity to handle a tricycle by two years of age, but most do have the capacity by three years of age. Keep in mind that there is no reason to rush your toddler in this regard; she will have a lot of fun for many months using simpler riding toys. When you do think she's ready to start trying a standard tricycle, look for one that is sturdy, low to the ground, and easy to pedal and steer. Obtaining one that is brightly colored is a good idea as well; your toddler probably will prefer it, and it will make it easier for other people to see your toddler coming since she may not always watch where she's going. And remember that the mobility that a tricycle gives your toddler allows her to have a lot of fun, but it also enables her to get into a lot of trouble. Therefore, unless you can somehow restrict her riding to an enclosed, safe area, make sure that you are there to supervise her early riding activities.

My toddler seems very musically inclined. Is she too young to have a real instrument?

She probably is for two major reasons. First, although your toddler may enjoy listening to music and even producing it to a certain extent, she certainly does not yet have the ability to manipulate most instruments in anything more than a rudimentary manner. She also does not have the attention span and patience to sit still for the intensive lessons that would be required to improve her capacities significantly in that regard. Second, admonishing a toddler to "take care of her things" is simply unrealistic at this point. Although your toddler may do some appropriate things with an instrument, it also is likely that she will subject it to a fair amount of abuse. Since a real instrument generally costs a fair amount of money, and since you may want to have it available in good shape later on, providing one for your toddler probably is not a wise move at this point.

Will my toddler be interested in coloring books during this period?

She certainly will, especially toward the end of this period. However, at first, your toddler probably will have a lot of trouble holding a crayon, and she definitely will color outside the lines as much if not more than inside. Also, she may show an exclusive preference for one color and virtually ignore all the others. Therefore, rather than wasting coloring books, you might consider starting your toddler off with just plain paper and a few crayons. Later on, as her small muscle skills improve

Keep her "art" supplies simple at first.

and her interest in stories increases, using coloring books will become more appropriate. The same is true with paints, clay, and other art supplies. Keep them plain and simple at first, allowing your toddler to get the feel of the materials and utensils. You can gradually introduce more structure to these activities, but try not to push your toddler into any specific sort of procedure if she does not show an inclination to pursue it.

A small hammering toy can help him practice his hand-eye coordination.

What types of toys will enhance the development of my toddler's small muscle skills?

Your toddler probably will enjoy manipulating a wide variety of simple mechanical toys at this point. Anything that contains levers, push buttons, dials, hinges, etc. will get a lot of play time. Keep in mind that the play value of such items increases with the number of different things your toddler can do with them, rather than with the number of different things they do all by themselves. Therefore, complex battery-operated toys may entertain your toddler for a few minutes, but they will lose their fascination relatively quickly after that. Small hammering toys and peg boards also will be appropriate for small muscle skill practice, as will large interlocking beads that can be pulled apart and pushed back together easily. In addition, your toddler is likely to appreciate a set of small snap-together blocks that she can simply manipulate two or three at a time and, especially toward the end of this period, use to create some basic structures.

Will my toddler enjoy building with large blocks as well as manipulating small ones?

Toward the end of this period, your toddler may very well begin to show an interest in large-block projects. Most likely, her early efforts will center around other role-play and fantasy activities. For instance, she may use a few blocks to build a "house" for her dolls. Since her strength and dexterity still will be somewhat limited, it is a good idea to provide her with blocks that are fairly lightweight at this point; that is, made from cardboard, plastic, or some other such material as opposed to standard heavy wood. This will allow your toddler to construct things more easily. And, since she probably will enjoy knocking down her projects just as much as she enjoyed creating them, there is less likelihood that she may harm herself—or harm something or someone else in the house— in her enthusiasm.

My toddler really loves large, inflatable toys. Is this unusual?

Not at all. Toddlers love to just carry toys around, and the bigger the toy, the bigger the thrill for them. Particularly during their "rebellion" phase, the opportunity for them to latch onto something really large and keep it in their possession as they go about the house enables them to put on a display of personal power that is especially appealing to them at this point. Consequently, these inflatable items are big favorites, as they are big without being heavy and thus can be used to show off without straining a toddler's still limited physical capacities. A number of manufacturers are now coming out with lines of these toys. Most of them are very safe and sturdy; however, it is always a good idea to double-check to make sure that any inflatable toy won't burst easily and that the material can't be torn with minimal effort. Also, see to it that the air-intake nozzle can be plugged securely and that is it snugly recessed so that you are not constantly reinflating it.

What will be the most suitable toys for my toddler's early role-play and fantasy activities?

In the beginning, your toddler will appreciate a wide variety of plain, simple items ranging from a toy telephone to a collection of hats out of your closet. Basic dolls (simple stuffed dolls as opposed to more sophisticated dolls with lifelike

---

WHERE HAVE ALL THE PIECES GONE?

As your toddler moves around the house with greater ease, she is likely to be taking her playthings—and parts of her playthings—around with her as she goes. Unfortunately, she may or may not bring these items back. There is even a good chance that she will "hide" some of the smaller pieces in "interesting" places and then completely forget where those places and pieces are. Consequently, especially toward the end of this period, you may discover that pieces of your toddler's playthings are starting to disappear at an alarming rate—not to be seen again until some massive spring cleaning effort. Of course, you can avoid this by keeping your toddler's play restricted to a small specific area. The best option, however, is to simply realize that this is part of your toddler's play and it is bound to happen to a certain extent. To make it easier on yourself, your toddler, and your pocketbook, it is a good idea to avoid spending a lot of money on any particular item and to stay away from small toys with small parts that are "essential" rather than "easily interchangeable." In addition, it's wise to make periodic sweeps of potential hiding places around the house—such as under sofa cushions, behind the refrigerator, inside dresser drawers—to see if you can find those pieces that are among the missing. And remember, admonishing your toddler to "take care of her things" involves expectations that are inappropriate and unfair at this point, and it simply will not work.

features and movements) and stuffed animals as well as a couple of noncomplex cars and trucks will be enjoyed. In addition, any "pretend" implement that allows your toddler to "do what you are doing"—toy kitchen utensils, tools, garden equipment, and the like—will be a big thrill for her. Keep in mind that a very important part of your toddler's early role-play and fantasy activities often will be her audience. Consequently, since her parents are her favorite people and they are the ones who have the greatest emotional impact on her, it will mean a lot to your toddler if you make an effort to be around to supply appropriate applause and even enthusiastic participation on occasion.

Should I provide more complex role-play and fantasy toys as my toddler gets older?

Toward the end of this period, as her small muscle skills allow her to manipulate smaller items more easily and as her mental abilities enable her to retain and restructure her growing experiences, your toddler probably will begin to appreciate "play sets." These can be doll houses or little kitchens, farms, zoos, parking garages, fire or train stations, etc. The important thing to remember is that whenever your toddler engages in activity of this sort, most of her raw materials are taken from her own head. Therefore, it is not necessary to supply her with elaborate sets containing many pieces and rich details. In fact, past a certain minimal point, the more that is already in front of her, the less chance she will have to use her own imagination and creative capacities. Therefore, make sure whatever sets you supply her with at this point are relatively simple.

Do girls and boys begin to show preferences for different toys at this point?

When left on their own, toddlers rarely show distinct preferences for different toys according to gender at this point. Girls will choose trucks and hammering toys and boys will choose dolls and kitchen utensils just as often as the reverse. However, it typically is at around a toddler's second birthday that her parents begin to display strong preferences about the kinds of toys with which she plays. Interestingly, while girls routinely are applauded for playing with dolls and kitchen utensils, they usually are not criticized severely when they play with trucks and hammering toys. Boys, on the other hand, often experience strong reactions from their parents when they choose a toy that is not gender-appropriate in the traditional sense. Therefore, depending upon how you have consciously or unconsciously influenced your toddler's selection process, you may start to see some distinct gender-related preferences toward the end of this period. However, such inclinations certainly are not inherent.

Are there any items that are particularly appropriate for encouraging play between toddlers?

Truly cooperative and congenial peer play does not come overnight, so it is a good idea to be conservative in this area at first. Sand or water play, finger painting, building with blocks, and role-play and fantasy activities all lend themselves well to this purpose. However, it is a good idea to make sure that, whenever possible, there are "two of everything" in case the notion of "sharing" or "taking turns" either fails to show up or falls apart after a few minutes. Climbing apparatus, such as a couple of large cardboard boxes and a few cushions, or a collection of balls also encourage a lot of interactive play while allowing each toddler to "do her own thing" from time to time. If possible, you might consider introducing a piece of "sitting-and-spinning" equipment that requires toddlers to work together in order to make it go around, but don't expect them to get the hang of it immediately.

A simple "play set" can be fun for two.

2½ YEARS
TO
5 YEARS

From two and a half years to five years of age, your preschooler will make a tremendous amount of progress. She not only will continue to grow in stature and strength, but she will exhibit considerable coordination and grace as well. Her thinking abilities, although not yet fully mature, will become extremely sophisticated and impressive. There will be a virtual explosion in her imaginative and creative activities. She also will exhibit a significant capacity to interact cooperatively and congenially with her parents and with other people. In this and other ways, she will demonstrate that she is ready to be regarded as a full-fledged member of her family and a responsible citizen of her ever-widening community. This period will not be without occasional difficulties. For the most part, however, you will find that dealing with your preschooler is exciting and delightful. As you introduce her to and guide her through new and different experiences each day, you will have the opportunity to rediscover the world from her innocent yet interesting perspective. Indeed, you may very well learn as much from her as she does from you. There probably will be occasional challenges and a few pitfalls along the way, but as long as you remember to enjoy as well as educate your child, you are likely to have a wild and wonderful ride through the preschool period.

HOW YOUR CHILD DEVELOPS

How much growth in height and weight can I expect my preschooler to experience during this period?

Although his overall rate of growth will continue to slow somewhat during this period, you still will see impressive gains. By five years of age, preschoolers typically stand between 39 and 46 inches tall, with the average somewhere around 43 inches; and they typically weigh between 35 and 55 pounds, with the average somewhere just above 40 pounds. The normal ranges for height and weight steadily widen as children get older, so you have to expect more and more variability between your preschooler's height and weight and the averages for his age group. Also, keep in mind that pre-schoolers tend to grow in spurts and then may lag for a while. Therefore, don't expect your preschooler's position at the moment to be a permanent indication of his status. As long as he is not routinely hanging around one extreme of the chart, you probably have little to worry about.

What kind of advances will I see in my preschooler's large muscle skills during this period?

By the time your preschooler is five, he probably will have superb coordination and balance and be capable of moving his body quite effectively in relation to other things around him. Your preschooler will likely be able to walk up stairs one step at a time and, for the most part, be able to walk down stairs in the same manner. He may be able to balance himself on one foot for several seconds and may have developed excellent running, jumping, skipping, hopping, and climbing capacities. In ordinary, everyday activities—such as walking—you will notice that he is actually becoming rather graceful and adult-like. He may even be ready for activities such as skating or riding a bicycle.

He'll make impressive gains in coordination, balance, and grace throughout this period.

How much more adept at small muscle tasks will my preschooler become during this period?

Quite a bit. Throughout this period, your preschooler's fingers will become increasingly skilled and under control. He will be able to fasten and unfasten buttons and zippers and lace his shoes. He will be able to use paintbrushes and crayons with ease and probably will be capable of tasks like stringing small beads or cutting a fairly straight line with a pair of safe scissors. Your preschooler is likely to become very competent at using a cup without spilling and at manipulating his table utensils. He may be able to throw a ball with impressive accuracy, and he may be able to catch a ball using primarily his hands rather than his arms. He will be able to take apart and put together many of the everyday items in your home with ease. He'll also be able to use many small devices—such as pencil sharpeners and hole punchers—on his own.

When will my preschooler be fully ready for toilet training?

There is no set age at which preschoolers become physically and emotionally mature enough to understand and control what is happening during the toileting process. There are many facets involved, and the age at which each can be mastered varies greatly from child to child. Although voluntary control of bowel and bladder muscles may come in prior to the second birthday, and the end of "negativism" may occur at about the same time, it is a rare child who is successfully toilet trained before two and a half years of age. In order for things to go smoothly, your preschooler must be aware of the need to go and be able to communicate that need to you either verbally or by facial expressions. He must be able to understand—and preferably express as well—simple statements including terms such as "wet," "dry," "potty," "go," etc. He should be demonstrating an inclination for imitative behavior. He should be showing a dislike for wet or dirty diapers. He must be able to stay dry for at least a couple of hours. He must be able to pull his pants up and down. He should also be at a stage where he is anxious to please you and has a sense of social appropriateness. This is quite a lot, and if your preschooler hasn't mastered everything before four years of age, don't worry—he's still within the normal range. For more information on signs of readiness and advice on how to begin toilet training, see page 230.

Do the various parts of toilet-training readiness follow a predictable pattern?

Not at all. You may hear a variety of general "rules"—such as "first comes bowel control, then daytime bladder control, and

She'll learn how to button and unbutton her clothes, zipper her jacket, and lace her own shoes during this period.

finally nighttime bladder control" or "girls achieve bladder control before boys"—but the exceptions to these rules are so numerous as to make them virtually meaningless. Even children within the same family often display distinctly different patterns of readiness. Furthermore, given that there are so many factors involved in the total process, it is extremely difficult to predict precisely when certain combinations will come together in your preschooler. For example, your preschooler may achieve basic physical and emotional readiness relatively early, but if his small muscle skills are developing a bit slowly, he will have a hard time mastering daytime procedures which require him to handle more complicated articles of clothing. Therefore, it is a good idea to remain as patient as possible and to keep any and all expectations to a minimum.

Although he's clearly capable of rational thought, my preschooler is not always reasonable or logical. Is something wrong?

Your preschooler is perfectly normal. Keep in mind that the ability to use thoughts does not arrive in complete form. Your preschooler will have to learn how to process and manipulate ideas in the same way he had to learn how to employ and control his body early on. This requires a lot of experience over many years. Although he will have come a long way by the end of this period, your preschooler still will have some distance to go before you can count on him to "think" in the same way that you do. At this point, his thinking is still simple in form and limited in scope, and it is governed largely by his own peculiar view of the world. Consequently, whenever your preschooler displays a capacity for "logic" or "reason," what he says or does probably will make perfect "sense" to him, but it may not always make similar sense to anyone else.

Will my child continue to think of everything only in terms of how it affects him?

For the most part, your preschooler will be processing everything that happens strictly as it relates to his own experience. So, for example, if you ask him why it gets dark at night, his response is likely to be "Because I have to go to sleep." If he likes a certain flavor of ice cream or wants to participate in a particular activity, he will assume that everyone else feels the same way. If he gets hurt during an incident with another

He must be emotionally as well as physically ready in order for toilet training to proceed successfully. Starting before he is ready or pushing him too hard may delay the time at which he actually starts using the toilet himself.

child, he is not likely to accept the explanation that it was an "accident"—he got hurt, and as far as he's concerned, that's the bottom line. When he sees people on television, he may believe that they can see him, too. When sitting at a table, he may talk about something he's looking at as if you were looking at it, too, even though you may have an obstructed view from your side of the table. Keep in mind that your preschooler isn't acting "stupid" or "selfish" in such instances. He simply does not yet have sufficient experiences to interpret the way things work in any other manner.

Will my preschooler get better at distinguishing between what is real and what isn't during this period?

As he proceeds through this period, your preschooler will achieve a much better grasp of "reality." He will no longer believe that everything that moves is alive, and he will be able to tell the difference between a dream and a genuine experience. In fact, your preschooler probably will become somewhat obsessed with the notion of "real" and may repeatedly ask you if this, that, or the other thing is real or not. However, to a certain extent, your preschooler's judgment will be controlled by his own needs, fears, and desires; so if he has a particularly frightening nightmare or is especially fond of some television-induced fantasy, you may have a tough time convincing him that what is involved doesn't really exist. On the other hand, you may also become increasingly frustrated as he no longer is content with various make-believe items and starts insisting that he wants a "real horse" or wants to go on a "real picnic."

What are some examples of the "advanced-but-imperfect" reasoning my preschooler will use?

Your preschooler will begin to "figure things out" quite regularly during this period, and he will apply some fairly reliable rules in the process. However, these rules will be rather rudimentary and will not allow him to come up with the "correct" answer in every situation or under all circumstances. So, for example, if you present your preschooler with two rows of six evenly spaced pennies each, he will tell you that the two rows are equal; but if you spread out the pennies in one of the rows, he will tell you that there are now more pennies in that row because "longer is more." Similarly, if you present him and his brother with identical glasses of milk filled to the

---

THE NOTION OF "CRITICAL PERIODS"

In the course of absorbing information about early childhood, you may have come across books, articles, or professionals that refer to "critical periods" in development. The first month is supposedly a critical period for parent-child bonding, the second year is a critical period for language learning, etc. The implication is that if something doesn't happen at a specific time, it will never happen. This is a somewhat misleading notion. Clearly, certain developments typically take place at certain points, and when they don't, it usually causes problems. But child-development specialists with vast experience prefer to use the term "sensitive" periods rather than "critical" periods. Some things tend to go quite smoothly at certain times in the life span, and it is often rather difficult to introduce them or turn them around later on. For instance, a child who experiences routine hearing loss during the first two years definitely will have problems in language learning that will be very hard to overcome. However, it is important to remember that while development is very orderly in many ways, it is also very forgiving. We still don't understand all the processes involved as well as we would like to, and we can't always come up with quick and easy answers to every problem that arises. On the other hand, we do know enough to say that it is never "too late" for any child to learn anything. There are no circumstances under which parents should feel that they have no choice but to give up and stop trying. There will be times when opportunities are more open, but they are never completely closed.

same level, and your preschooler insists on having more, you can pour his milk into a narrower, taller glass, and he will be satisfied because "higher is more." Keep in mind that even though he may be "wrong," your preschooler is demonstrating good thinking skills. He just needs time to develop the capacity for taking multiple factors and exceptions into account.

What will some of the limits be on my preschooler's ability to "figure things out" at this point?

Perhaps the most noticeable limitations will be that he can only focus on one aspect of a situation at a time, and he can only think in one direction at a time. For instance, at the store, your preschooler probably will be adept at distinguishing amongst apples, oranges, and bananas. He may even comprehend the concept that all these items are pieces of fruit. However, if you purchase six apples, one orange, and one banana, and you ask him if you bought more apples or more pieces of fruit, he is likely to tell you that you bought more apples. For one thing, he can only view the red, shiny items as either apples or pieces of fruit at that moment—they can't be both apples and pieces of fruit in his mind. For another thing, he may be able to see that the apples are pieces of fruit, but that doesn't necessarily mean that he will see that some pieces of fruit can be apples. Again, this is not a sign of low intelligence. It simply shows that your preschooler needs time to become as quick, strong, and agile in applying his mental skills as he already has become in using his physical skills.

Will my preschooler be able to understand abstract concepts like "death" and "God" at this point?

Your preschooler will have a great deal of difficulty relating to anything on a purely abstract level. Consequently, even at the end of this period, he will have a tendency to translate anything having to do with such concepts into something with which he is familiar on a concrete level. For example, he may comprehend God as a sort of fatherly or grandfatherly figure or maybe even in terms of something like a lifeguard at the beach who watches over everybody. Similarly, death may be understood as a form of sleep—and it could be a while before your preschooler stops thinking of it as reversible. Keep in mind that his perception of such concepts may bring comfort to your preschooler at times, but they also may cause intense fear at others. For instance, he may be satisfied that

LIMITATIONS AND POTENTIALS

Many parents believe that, thanks to research in psychology and education, we now have the capacity to produce higher levels of achievement in young children than we ever could before. This is not quite true. It would be similar to claiming that, thanks to medical advances, we now can help people live longer than ever before. The fact of the matter is that two thousand years ago, the oldest humans lived a little past the age of one hundred—and the same is true today. What medical advances have meant is that more people are living longer lives. The same applies to early development. With recent insights obtained from research, more children are making more of their early potential. However, no one has learned to produce a preschooler who is any smarter than the smartest preschooler of a generation ago. Likewise, no one has figured out a way to make every preschooler as smart as the smartest preschooler. The danger of the popular misconception is that some parents feel that they should be pushing their child toward an ultimate standard of achievement. They further believe that anything short of that standard constitutes failure. It is important for parents to realize, however, that the best they can do is help their child make the most of whatever potential he has, and that all children have a different amount of potential in different areas. Encouraging and assisting your child to do his very best is fine. However, if you don't recognize, accept, and appreciate your child for exactly what he is, your efforts probably will never find fulfillment, and they are likely to be ultimately counterproductive.

By the end of this period, she probably will be able to remember her last birthday and may eagerly anticipate the next one as the "big day" draws near.

Grandma is going to sleep for a long time at one point, then later be afraid to go to sleep himself because he doesn't want to die. Also, be prepared to receive a lot of questions from your preschooler about the specifics of how God does this or that, what happens to you when you die, etc. as he continually strives to make sense out of these fascinating concepts.

How extensive will my preschooler's ability to remember and anticipate be at this point?

By the end of this period, your preschooler probably will have a very well-developed sense of time. His memory capacity will be quite strong, and he will be able to place various events in relation to each other fairly accurately. Consequently, your preschooler will remember last summer, last Christmas, his last birthday, and Grandma's last visit. He also will have a reasonably clear sense of what can be expected to happen the next time around. On an everyday level, he will have a clear sense of "lunchtime," "nap time," "dinnertime," "bedtime," and all sorts of other "times." He will be pretty adept at talking about "yesterday" and "tomorrow" or even "last week" and "this week." Although the subtle differences between "Tuesday" and "Wednesday" may still be beyond him, he will

probably be able to distinguish the weekend quite comfortably. Your preschooler will use phrases like "a while ago" or "in a few minutes" in a suitable fashion, but probably will be incapable of great precision. Time still will be sensed in relationship to important events in his own life, and it will be a couple of years yet before he has the abstract abilities necessary to tell time according to the clock.

Although his vocabulary is very impressive, my preschooler's grammar is horrible. Why the discrepancy?

While your preschooler will continue to pick up new words quickly and easily, learning how to put those words together will be comparatively difficult for him. At first, he simply mimicked whatever he heard, so his early grammar probably was pretty good. However, he is now at the point where he is no longer just imitating; he is actively retrieving words from his own mind and using his thought processes to put them together in a meaningful way. Unfortunately, he is at the stage where his rules for such procedures are very basic and straightforward. So, for example, a toddler might say "I have two feet" when mimicking his mother, but a preschooler will say "I have two foots" because he is applying the rule of adding an "s" to make a plural. Similarly, he might say "I goed to school yesterday" or "I wented to school yesterday." It will take time for your preschooler to learn and comprehend all the exceptions and special circumstances, so be patient. Give him credit for making real progress in language learning even if that progress results in his being "wrong" from time to time.

Sometimes my preschooler lisps or otherwise mispronounces words. Is this typical at this point?

It certainly is. Quite often, a preschooler will know the meaning of a word and how to use it properly but will as yet be unable to produce the sounds required to pronounce it with perfect accuracy. Since the "s" sound is typically one of the last to be mastered, it is not unusual at all for preschoolers to lisp. As a matter of fact, lisping remains common for many years. In addition, you may notice occasional "disfluency," similar to stuttering, in your preschooler's speech. While genuine stuttering may occur in response to stress with some

children, most preschoolers simply are quicker with their thoughts and feelings than they are with putting together and producing the words to express those thoughts and feelings. In other words, at this point, your preschooler's apparent "problem" in this area probably is due to a very normal condition—his mind is a little more agile than his tongue. As the months go by, you will hear less and less of this sort of thing.

My preschooler is very good at recognizing numbers and letters. Does this mean he's ready to learn math and reading?

Not necessarily. It is important to realize that activities such as recognizing numbers and letters, counting to ten, and reciting the alphabet are not always connected directly to doing math or reading. Your preschooler may enjoy these skills and activities strictly for their own sake. He may have no inclination whatsoever to do anything more than practice them and perform them over and over again. Math and reading require

He may enjoy recognizing numbers and letters, but that doesn't necessarily mean he's ready to move on to math and reading.

more abstract abilities, which your preschooler may very well not yet possess. If you push too hard and too fast, it is possible that you will destroy his pleasure in those that he has already acquired. Therefore, it is a good idea to wait until your preschooler shows more definite signs, such as asking "What does this spell?" or "How do you put those numbers together?" before you consider him truly ready to learn such things. And remember, early ability in these areas rarely makes much of a difference in the long run, so being patient probably won't be anywhere near as dangerous to your preschooler's progress as being impatient is likely to be.

My preschooler tends to "love" things or "hate" things, with very little in between. Is this a vocabulary problem or an emotional problem?

This is not really a "problem" at all, but rather a sign that your child is a typical preschooler. This is an age in which high degrees of exuberance and intensity can be expected. Compared to the average adult, your preschooler has very little experience with emotions, so he derives a certain amount of comfort in being at the extremes. Subtle shadings just are not his style at this point. Although his feelings are genuine and should be respected within reason, it is important to realize that they reflect a normal emotional immaturity rather than keen insight and judgment. As a result, when your preschooler announces that he loves going shopping, don't be surprised if he becomes bored and irritable moments after you arrive at the mall. Similarly, if your preschooler announces that he hates you, don't worry—he'll probably be climbing onto your lap a few minutes later.

The lessons she learns from you about talking, sharing, and being close will affect the way she interacts with others.

Lately, my preschooler has been handling separations from me easily, and he's quick to become close to new playmates, teachers, etc. Am I losing my importance to him?

On the contrary. How sociable a preschooler is typically reflects the social atmosphere in his home. If your child is quick to make friends and become close with other people, it probably indicates that he has learned that social relationships are pleasant and productive things. He is now eager to apply all the wonderful lessons he's received from you to a whole new world of people beyond his family. In other words, his interest in them is derived from his relationship with you and thus does not diminish that relationship in any way. If you ever need confirmation of this, just wait until a separation goes on a little too long or a crisis arises. You can bet that your preschooler will want you—and only you—in a really big way.

My preschooler seems to understand "good and bad" and "right and wrong," but he has some strange ideas about "crime and punishment." Why is this?

This is another case where a preschooler's lack of broad experience combined with his still basic logic abilities can cause him to come up with some seemingly strange ideas. When it comes to a concept such as punishment, most preschoolers have difficulty separating act from intention. Consequently, your preschooler may feel that someone who accidentally drops a tray of glasses is worthy of greater punishment than someone who breaks one glass in a fit of anger. Also, most preschoolers tend to be arbitrary about punishment since they have difficulty putting together a sophisticated system by which the punishment fits neatly with the crime. As a result, your preschooler may feel that a "time out" is a suitable punishment for everything from spilling milk to murder simply because this is the only punishment with which he has firsthand knowledge.

Will I still need to help build my preschooler's self-esteem during this period?

Nurturing the roots of self-esteem was a major consideration during infancy and toddlerhood when your child was exhibiting his first major physical accomplishments. It is equally—if not more—important now as he begins to demonstrate his increasing mental abilities. Your preschooler is putting together many thoughts and feelings, and he is eagerly expressing them at every opportunity. The extent to which he will learn to feel good about his mental abilities will depend heavily upon how key people in his life react to them. This is why an understanding of how your preschooler's mind works is so essential. Because his intellectual abilities have come a long way but are not yet fully mature, he often will come up with results that are "wrong" or "bad." Therefore, he may not receive the credit that his vastly improved reasoning processes deserve unless you realize and applaud the fact that he is, indeed, making great progress.

How good your child feels about her accomplishments will depend, in part, on how you react to the progress she is making. Your praise and encouragement still mean the world to her.

UNDERSTANDING YOUR CHILD'S BEHAVIOR

How much sleep and nap time will my preschooler require?

The rest needs of preschoolers vary enormously. How much sleep and nap time your preschooler will require probably will be more or less than the average, depending upon her needs up to this point. Typically, preschoolers sleep 11 hours straight through at night. Although they usually require a short nap at the beginning of this period, by the time they are five years of age, most have given up daytime napping completely. Nevertheless, setting up a special "quiet time" or "rest time" at midday is a good idea, even if your preschooler doesn't use it to sleep. The opportunity to simply take a little time out from the hustle and bustle of her daily routines and activities certainly is appropriate. It is likely to be appreciated by your preschooler—and it may be an absolute necessity for you!

Setting up a special "rest period" for her during the day—even if she doesn't sleep—can give you both a refreshing break.

Lately, my preschooler has been having terrible nightmares. Does this indicate that she has some kind of serious emotional problem?

Not at all. Nightmares are very common at this point, and they rarely amount to a significant problem—emotional or otherwise. In fact, you may be surprised on occasion when your preschooler recounts a nightmare with a certain amount of delight and excitement. Being afraid sometimes is fun for preschoolers. Once they have recovered from the initial shock of having a bad dream, they often treat the experience in the same way they would treat a scary story or movie that they've heard or seen—sharing it with anyone and everyone, and embellishing the particularly frightening events each time it is retold. By the way, some preschoolers experience what are referred to as "night terrors," in which they scream and move around furiously. As alarming as these are to parents, the preschoolers rarely remember them the next day. The occurrence of these especially intense episodes usually diminishes and then disappears within a few months.

Will my preschooler's eating habits become less peculiar during this period?

Typically, preschoolers are not as definite about their likes and dislikes at this point, although there still may be certain foods that are definitely favorites and others that simply cannot be tolerated. However, while their overall behavior in this regard may settle down, preschoolers are prone to going on "jags" from time to time. They'll all of a sudden insist on one sort of food over and over again or all of a sudden express a strong intolerance for another sort. These jags generally do not last very long, although they can be rather strong and persistent during the short time they are in effect. Therefore, in addition to offering your preschooler a variety of nutritious foods, it is a good idea to keep a few appropriate alternatives on hand in case you run into trouble in this regard on occasion.

My preschooler insists on dressing herself, but she makes some odd choices when picking out her clothes. Is this strange?

Certainly not. You have to keep two things in mind. First, your preschooler's primary thrill at this point is simply the act of dressing herself. The end result of her efforts is not nearly as important to her as the process itself. Second, your preschooler's egocentrism still controls her thinking, including the thinking she does in choosing her clothes. Consequently, her selections are based purely upon her particular likes and dislikes of the moment, and she could care less about how they will look to other people. If she really likes her purple polka-dot shirt because it's soft, and she really likes her lime green pants because they have shiny buttons, she will not hesitate to put them together despite the fact that the combination may produce horror in you and others. It is a good idea, therefore, to allow your preschooler to exercise personal power in selecting her clothes, but to give her somewhat limited choices so this doesn't get completely out of hand.

When someone else uses the toilet, my preschooler is intensely curious, yet she demands privacy for herself. Is this unusual?

Intense curiosity about toilets, bathrooms, and all the associated bodily functions is quite common during this period.

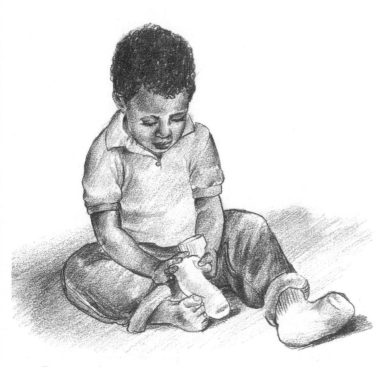

Encourage him to dress himself if he can. Let him choose what he'll wear for the day, keeping his choices somewhat limited to prevent any potentially outrageous combinations.

Similarly, a strong desire for privacy while toileting also is quite typical. Your preschooler's seemingly paradoxical behavior can probably be explained by her egocentrism. When she goes to the bathroom, she is thinking in terms of preserving her prerogative to be alone. On the other hand, when someone else goes, she is thinking in terms of indulging her need to know everything. Since she has a great deal of difficulty taking the perspective of another person, your preschooler simply doesn't perceive a conflict between these two attitudes. As long as you understand and respect her needs and desires in this regard and don't make a big deal about anything, you can expect your preschooler to eventually become more open about her own habits and more sensitive to other people's rights to a certain amount of privacy.

Although she was completely toilet trained for months, ever since her new baby brother arrived, my preschooler has had many accidents. Why?

This is a very common phenomenon when siblings are closely spaced. Keep in mind that your preschooler's baby brother is a formidable rival in her pursuit of your attention. She is likely to become extremely jealous when he is the primary target of your time and effort. Since you have no choice but to attend to her baby brother when he soils his diaper, your preschooler may perceive this as a "can't win" situation. She may therefore go along with the old adage that says, "If you can't beat 'em, join 'em." Of course, the attention that she is likely to receive will be negative attention, but as far as your preschooler is concerned, negative attention is better than no attention under the circumstances. As long as you treat these accidents matter-of-factly and thereby keep her "reward" to a minimum, and as long as you give her plenty of attention whenever she acts like a "big girl," she soon will realize that this is not the best strategy available to her and will soon drop it.

My preschooler is just a bundle of energy—always on the go. Are all children like that at this point?

Most preschoolers often seem to be in a state of perpetual motion. Given their greatly increased control over their bodies, they simply revel in the many things they now can do and they really enjoy pushing themselves to the limit. Unfortunately, while it is typical for preschoolers to behave in this manner, it is also typical for parents to fear that their

THE DOMINANCE OF INDIVIDUALITY

During their child's infancy and toddlerhood, many mothers and fathers—especially if they are first-time parents—spend a lot of time consulting books, articles, and charts to learn about the interests, abilities, preferences, and peculiarities that they can expect their offspring to exhibit. For the first two or three years, a lot of useful information can be gleaned from these sources. However, by the time children reach the preschool period, individual differences and variations become so numerous and so significant that "standard" descriptions and "average" expectations become very unreliable. Of course, a general characterization of three year olds or four year olds may help you put your preschooler's behavior in perspective and allow you to obtain some insight and understanding. In terms of day-to-day dealings, however, you will learn a lot more by focusing primarily on precisely what your preschooler is doing. Although all infants and toddlers are unique, they all do tend to do a lot of things in the same way at the same time. On the other hand, while all preschoolers have some similarities, lumping them all together very frequently is unfair and inappropriate. Therefore, now more than ever before, it is important that parents make decisions about their children based not upon what some book, article, or chart indicates they "should" be doing but rather upon the needs, aptitudes, and inclinations displayed by their preschooler. Proceeding exclusively "by the book" at this point only invites unnecessary anxieties and may very well lead to trouble.

preschooler is "hyperactive." True hyperactivity—where a child can never sit still, finds it impossible to finish anything, can't even quiet down for a few moments, and can't "turn off her motor" even if she wants to—is relatively rare. The more prevalent danger is that a preschooler will be saddled with this label not because she has an abnormally high energy level, but rather because her parents may have a very low level of tolerance. For more information on true hyperactivity, see page 255.

My preschooler loves to either shout or whisper and often does little in between. Is this normal?

This behavior is perfectly normal, and it probably is attributable to several factors. For one thing, your preschooler is most comfortable at the extremes of many things at this point. Just as she either "loves" or "hates" things, she tends to feel that occasions call for either really loud or really soft sounds. In addition, your preschooler is enamored by what she can do with her body, and her vocal chords fall into that category. The results of shouting or whispering are usually more dramatic than those that come from plain talking, so those activities naturally are going to be more attractive to her. Finally, most preschoolers become fascinated with the notion of "secrets," and your preschooler probably will enjoy turning anything and everything she can into a private, clandestine affair through whispering. As with most other symptoms of your preschooler's natural over-exuberance, you can expect this sort of behavior to diminish gradually as time goes by.

When she's climbing and exploring, my preschooler seems to be incredibly daring and adventuresome. Is this abnormal?

This sort of behavior is typical of most preschoolers. They have a strong sense of their power to do things now, and they are eager to take themselves as far as they can go. In general, this is not something about which you should worry a great deal. As long as your preschooler is in an essentially safe and suitable environment, it is not likely that her sense of adventure will overshadow her routinely good judgment with respect to the limits of her abilities. However, it is a good idea to keep a close eye on your preschooler in situations that are unfamiliar to her. For example, while waiting for someone at the airport, your preschooler may have an irresistible urge to climb upon and ride the luggage carousel. Or, while visiting a

He'll enjoy turning everything into a "secret" that he can whisper in your ear.

You may be surprised—and perhaps frightened at times—by his daring as he exercises his growing physical skills.

friend's house, she may become overwhelmed by her curiosity about where that large air duct leads to.

My preschooler sometimes sticks with a difficult task or puzzle for what seems to be an interminable length of time. Why doesn't she get bored or frustrated?

Your preschooler's natural exuberance generally will take her quickly from one activity to another. However, due to her vastly increased attention span, it is now possible for her to stick with a particular project that she finds especially fascinating for quite a long time. Consequently, boredom simply is not the ever-present problem it may have been before. As for frustration, that, too, tends to become less of a danger as your preschooler's activities become more complex. From your point of view, it may seem that she is unable to complete a task despite giving it hours of effort. However, as far as she's concerned, while she may not be able to do the whole thing, there may be a part or several parts that she *can* do. That partial success is more than enough to please and satisfy her.

It is also enough to keep her motivated toward figuring out the entire task.

Lately, my preschooler has been complaining a lot about boo-boos, stomachaches, and other assorted ailments. Is she a hypochondriac?

Not really, although it may seem that way at times. During this period, preschoolers not only develop considerable mastery over their external movements, they develop an increasingly strong awareness of their internal body functions as well. Consequently, "inside" sensations become fascinating, and there is an intense need to know what's going on in there. Since parents usually provide a lot of attention and do a lot of explaining whenever accidents or illnesses occur, preschoolers naturally are inclined to raise the possibility that they are in physical need of such services in order to satisfy their curiosity. As a result, many of their ailments can be cured with a quick kiss on the trouble spot and a long talk about what may be involved.

My preschooler finally stopped sucking her thumb, but now she won't let go of her favorite blanket. Will she always have an annoying habit of some kind?

Although these activities may be "annoying" to you, keep in mind that they are among the few ways in which your preschooler can cope with the stress that is an inevitable part of life. Fortunately, as they proceed through this period, most preschoolers manage to find an outlet for most of their tension through active, exuberant play. When they are especially stressed, they may simply run around real fast or talk real loud rather than suck their thumbs, bite their nails, rub their blankets, etc. Therefore, patience on your part is probably all that is necessary to solve this "problem." However, keep in mind that these activities may continue to surface on occasion for several years, and all preschoolers tend to continue using them for self-comfort at bedtime and other times when their options are relatively limited.

Although she frequently uses her imagination when painting or drawing, my preschooler often tries to copy a picture she sees. Does this mean she has limited creativity?

Your preschooler probably has as much if not more creativity as any other child her age. What you have to realize is that, like all other children her age, your preschooler is interested in a lot more than just being creative during painting and drawing sessions. At this point, preschoolers also are driven to explore the limits of their ability to control the brushes and crayons. One of the best ways to do this is to test their imitative skills. Furthermore, during this period, preschoolers become fascinated by tiny details; so while you may be concerned with "the big picture," your preschooler may be more interested in absorbing, analyzing, and trying to replicate little parts. In other words, parents should realize that, given their varied agenda during art sessions, preschoolers should be praised for being good "copiers" as well as clever "creators."

Even at this age, she may need her favorite doll or special blanket to help her relax and cope with stress.

Lately, my preschooler has begun asking "Why?" incessantly. Does she really want to know, or is she just trying to drive me crazy?

There are three major reasons why preschoolers ask "Why?" repeatedly. First, they are insatiably curious about anything and everything, and they genuinely want to know. Since an answer usually not only satisfies one question but often inspires another, an initial query inevitably triggers a seemingly endless procession. Second, preschoolers sometimes use questions simply to keep a conversation going. They adore this type of interaction with their parents, and since their ability to introduce mutually interesting topics is still somewhat limited, making constant inquiries becomes their favorite, and perhaps only, means of control in such situations. Third, preschoolers sometimes ask "Why?" as a ploy to stall or resist complying with parental instructions. However, the first reason is far and away the most common motivation behind this behavior. So, as exasperating as it can be at times, be prepared to indulge your preschooler's truly unquenchable thirst for knowledge.

Some of the stories my preschooler tells and the pretend activities she engages in have been getting more dramatic and violent. Is something wrong with her?

Not at all. This is very typical behavior for preschoolers. Perhaps because they are comfortable with the extremes of everything, and probably because they are thrilled by their own imaginative and language skills, preschoolers love to tell stories that are loaded with all sorts of large-scale, high-impact, and often extremely unpleasant events. In other words, violence is present in the stories of many preschoolers not so much because it allows them to blow off serious emotional steam, but rather because it usually makes for good drama. That's a lesson that Hollywood learned a long time ago. By the way, some parents assume that movie and television violence is at the root of this behavior. The fact is that preschoolers usually go far beyond what they see on the screen in their own stories. Moreover, extreme violence was a major part of stories that preschoolers told long before the advent of movies and television. (That does not mean, however, that you should encourage your preschooler to watch violent shows on television. According to the American Academy of Pediatrics, violence on television may contribute to nightmares and may even play a role in promoting aggressive or violent behavior.)

When she's alone, my preschooler talks to herself, but it often seems like she's addressing someone else. Does this mean she has an imaginary friend?

Not necessarily. Preschoolers love to use their ever-increasing language skills. They will often exercise their powers of speech just for the sheer pleasure of doing so as well as to communicate. During solitary play, it is very common for preschoolers to provide a running "play-by-play" commentary of their activities, and they are content to play the parts of both commentator and audience if necessary. By the way, imaginary friends are not unusual during this period either. If your preschooler is addressing someone by name who isn't there or regularly talks about a specific person who doesn't exist, then she probably has created a pal for herself. Imaginary friends typically are the result of a powerful imagination rather than loneliness or some other emotional problem. As intrusive as they may be at times, these imaginary friends usually don't stick around for more than a few months.

Lately, my preschooler has been doing a lot of boasting about her abilities. Is this a problem?

Boasting is very typical among preschoolers, and it rarely constitutes a real problem. For the most part, boasting is the result of a preschooler's natural tendency to exaggerate and go to extremes combined with her interest in exploring her capacities for self-expression. Sometimes, boasting becomes a minor form of competition among preschoolers. It tends to be more of a contest of imaginative and verbal skills, however, than a genuine attempt to impress or induce jealousy. By the way, as Muhammad Ali was fond of saying, "If you really can do it, then it ain't boasting." A preschooler with healthy self-esteem is justifiably proud of her accomplishments and abilities. If no one else acknowledges and applauds her for them, she is very apt to take on the job of doing so herself. In other words, what appears to be questionable behavior in this regard usually is essentially harmless.

My preschooler almost has a fetish about silly words, rhymes, songs, and activities. Is this typical?

It certainly is. Preschoolers love anything and everything that produces laughter, and they are easily entertained. At the beginning of this period, simple incongruity—shoes on the

He'll enjoy doing silly things, especially if they make you laugh as well.

wrong feet or Mommy wearing Daddy's hat—are their main sources of mirth. However, as the months go by, preschoolers realize that they can use their own growing language and imaginative skills to create merriment for both themselves and others. Of course, your preschooler's sense of humor, although abundant, will not be particularly sophisticated at first. Consequently, while she will get a kick out of virtually everything she sees, hears, or does that is offbeat in some way, you may find it difficult to continually share her excitement and enthusiasm for a lot of very "silly" things. Fortunately, although she will be especially thrilled when you react favorably to her comic routines, your preschooler will be quite content to merely make herself merry much of the time. By the end of this period, you may be pleasantly surprised to find that she is saying or doing quite a few things that are genuinely funny on occasion.

To what extent is my preschooler capable of unsupervised play with her peers at this point?

Peer play will probably become a very important part of your preschooler's life during this period. She will become quite adept at all aspects of truly cooperative play, such as sharing, taking turns, and communicating effectively with her peers. She will enjoy making friends, will actively seek the approval of other children, and may identify strongly with a group of which she is a part. Her need to assert personal power and establish possession also diminish during this period. So, in general, unsupervised peer play rarely presents much of a problem in terms of frequent and intense altercations. However, because of their daring and adventuresome spirits, preschoolers sometimes can get into trouble all by themselves, and they often are more likely to when they can enlist or be enlisted by a peer in a joint venture. In other words, when your preschooler is playing with peers, you don't have a lot *more* to worry about than you do when she plays by herself, but you do not have any *less* to worry about either. Therefore, some supervision of play is still a good idea.

Although they often play together nicely, my preschooler and her older brother still get into frequent fights. Will this ever end?

As long as you have two or more children, and especially if they are closely spaced, you probably will have to accept that a certain amount of sibling rivalry will always be present in your home. As the children get older and the differences in their interests and abilities become less significant, it is likely that the bad times may be more than compensated for by the many good times, when they serve as companions and playmates for each other. Furthermore, as they get older, they will adjust to and accept the family circumstances to a greater extent, so you probably will be able to expect fewer—although possibly more intense—confrontations. Keep in mind that a fight for your attention is at the root of most of your children's conflicts. So, at this point, their fights are likely to be cases of "showing off" for your benefit rather than expressions of genuine hostility toward each other.

As long as you have two or more children—especially if they're close in age—you can expect occasional confrontations.

GO EASY ON THE NEIGHBORS

During the first two or three years of their child's life, parents can get spoiled by the fact that they tend to have exclusive control over external influences upon their child's behavior. However, as their child becomes a preschooler, and her world widens to include everyday exposure to other adults and peers, they have to expect that they will not be the only people from whom their child learns. They also need to realize that this sometimes can lead to unpleasant eventualities. It is a rare parent who does not end up asking "Where did she pick that up?" with regularity at this point. If you find yourself in this situation, keep two things in mind. First, no matter how much exposure your preschooler has to other people, you will remain the primary and most powerful force in her life. Whatever behavior she has picked up elsewhere can always be modified and even eliminated eventually through your efforts to provide a more suitable model and channel her into a more acceptable direction. Second, nobody is perfect, and although your preschooler may pick up a few things of which you don't approve, it is likely that she also will pick up many things that are pleasantly benign and possibly extremely beneficial. Isolating your preschooler may solve a few problems, but it probably will cut her off from many more advantages. By the way, it also helps to remember that "nobody is perfect" applies to you as well. There is a good chance that your neighbors are asking "Where did he pick that up?" with just as much regularity as you are.

DAILY CARE BASICS

How can I tell if my preschooler is ready to start toilet training?

It is very important to understand that children are ready to begin toilet training at different times. Some begin to show signs of readiness as early as 20 months, while others are not ready until three years of age or later. Until certain specific signs of readiness (see accompanying list) are apparent, attempts to toilet train your child will be both frustrating and futile. This normal physiologic maturation process should not become a battleground. If training is attempted too early, it often results in an inappropriate focus on the issue and actually may delay the time when the child uses the toilet independently. Once your child demonstrates these signs of readiness, you can begin the process; remember, however, not to rush it.

Give her a chance to get familiar with the potty chair before you begin toilet training.

SIGNS OF READINESS TO TOILET TRAIN

When these signs of readiness appear, you can begin toilet training. Keep in mind that trying to toilet train your child before he demonstrates the necessary signs may very well delay the process. Your preschooler is probably ready to begin toilet training if he:

- Has a dry diaper for increasingly long time periods, which indicates that his bladder is able to store increasing amounts of urine.
- Has bowel movements on a fairly regular schedule.
- Shows a desire and ability to follow instructions.
- Is anxious to be changed from a wet or dirty diaper.
- Tries to copy bathroom activities of other family members.
- Demonstrates to you in a recognizable way (by facial expression; by squatting or running to a particular place, such as his changing table; by actually telling you so; etc.) that urination or a bowel movement is about to occur.
- Has the motor skills to remove and at least partially replace the clothing that must be removed to use the toilet.
- Has the ability to get to the toilet or potty when he needs to "go."

What do I need to do to get ready as well?

Your preliminary tasks fall into two categories—behavioral and mechanical. With regard to the former, it is helpful to allow your preschooler to accompany you when you use the toilet so he will have an appropriate model. Also, start using specific terms for the body parts and functions involved regularly, so your preschooler will know exactly what you are talking about. Finally, talk to your preschooler about the advantages of being toilet trained in a positive, upbeat manner every now and then. With regard to the mechanics of toilet training, you probably will want to purchase a potty chair or adapter seat. A potty chair allows your preschooler to be largely independent, since he will not need you to lift him onto the seat. The fact that it is easily portable can mean a lot in terms of convenience. Make sure that the potty chair is simple to use and clean and that it is stable and has nonskid features to keep it from slipping on a tile floor. An adapter seat, on the other hand, has the advantage of direct flushing, but it may create inconvenience for other family members who will have to remove and replace it. If you purchase one, make sure it fits your toilet securely. You may want to consider purchasing a sturdy footstool as well so that your preschooler can climb up more easily. If your preschooler is older and larger, you may want to train him directly on the regular toilet; but for most, this is problematic.

How should I begin the process of toilet training my preschooler?

The first thing to do is to inform your preschooler of what will be happening. Then, give him several opportunities to practice the various steps involved—removing his clothing, sitting on the potty chair, etc. Once your preschooler is aware of the process, pick a time of day when he usually eliminates, and take him to the toilet. Tell him in a pleasant and reassuring tone using words he can understand and say ("pee" and "BM," for example) that from now on, his waste products will begin going into the toilet instead of into his diapers. Then place him or help him onto the potty chair, and ask him to try eliminating. Never strap him in or in any way make the process seem like punishment, and be sure to stay with him at all times. While he is trying, talk to him, read to him, or in other ways keep him entertained and comfortable. Don't force him to sit on the potty if he is unwilling; keep the time to a minimum (less than five minutes). Praise every bit of progress lavishly—even if it's something as simple as sitting quietly on

An adapter seat with a step stool or a built-in step can make it easier for her to climb up.

the potty chair for more than a few seconds. And be patient. Toilet training rarely is accomplished completely in one session; and if things aren't going well, just forgetting about it for the moment and attempting it again later often is the best solution to whatever problems are arising.

What kinds of problems can I typically expect when toilet training my preschooler?

Quite commonly, preschoolers resist the first attempts at toilet training. If they are pushed, the bathroom becomes a battleground, and the whole experience becomes extraordinarily unpleasant for everyone involved. Therefore, if your preschooler demonstrates that he is not inclined to approach this process with a positive attitude, the easiest thing to do is just wait a couple of weeks and try again. Some preschoolers manage to do very well up to the point where flushing comes in—they may get very upset that something that was a part of them is considered "dirty" and must be gotten rid of. If this occurs with your preschooler, it helps to explain that this is "extra" that he doesn't need. He may feel better if you wait until he leaves the bathroom before you flush, or he may prefer to flush and wave "bye-bye."

Once he is toilet trained, what do I do when my toddler has an accident?

Most accidents of this kind are truly accidents—that is, it is likely that your preschooler will feel worse about them than you will. It therefore is a good idea to just clean up in a matter-of-fact manner, console him as necessary, and encourage him to use the toilet "just to see if there's anything left." Never shame or scold him. If your preschooler has a "deliberate accident" in order to punish you or express his anger over something, be careful not to overreact and give him what he was looking for. Clean up calmly; you may want to take your time so that your preschooler remains uncomfortably wet for a while. It is suggested that you also have him help in or take responsibility for cleaning up so he can realize that accidents are not in his best interest. If accidents start occurring frequently, a medical problem may be involved (see page 254 for more on frequent fecal soiling). On the other hand, your preschooler may be genuinely "regressing" in response to a separation, the arrival of a sibling, or some other emotional disturbance. If you suspect it is a medical problem, consult

You can tell her a story or let her flip through a favorite picture book to keep her entertained while she's on the potty, but try not to let her sit there for more than a few minutes at a time.

your pediatrician. If it is a case of regression, again, don't scold or shame, but have your preschooler help in the clean up, and possibly suspend some of his "big boy" privileges for a while as well. Do what you can to help him work through whatever the real problem is, and let him know that you will be happy to start all over again with him as soon as he is ready.

Although he does fine when he's in the house, my four year old has frequent wetting accidents when he's outside playing. How can I get him to be more careful?

What you are describing is a very common occurrence in children of this age, and although it can be disappointing to you, it will pass in time. To help the situation, you'll need to use positive measures. Start by asking him to take time to go potty before he goes out to play. When he doesn't have accidents, tell him what a big, responsible boy he's getting to be. When an accident does happen, don't get overly upset, but do make him responsible for changing his clothes, cleaning himself up, and putting the soiled garments in the laundry. Peer pressure does wonders in this regard, and usually the embarrassment will motivate him to become more careful. If the problem continues or increases, consult your pediatrician. It may be advisable to have your preschooler screened to make certain everything is normal with his urinary tract.

You can help make hygiene fun for her by being her "hygiene pal."

My preschooler is capable of washing himself and brushing his teeth, but can I trust him to do these jobs properly?

By the end of this period, most preschoolers have mastered most such hygienic activities. However, it is probably not a good idea to let your preschooler carry them out unsuper-vised too often. While he will understand and appreciate the importance of keeping himself clean, you simply can't count on your preschooler keeping this concern in the forefront of his mind and at the top of his priority list all the time. Quite often, he may become fascinated by a particular act or a particular feeling, and as a result, he will wash or brush the same area over and over again and neglect everything else almost completely. Also, he may be in a hurry to hear a special bedtime story, go on a special trip, etc., and as a result, he may "go through the motions" in a big hurry without really doing a very good job. Your trust in him in this regard will gradually become total, but even by five years of age, it is unrealistic to expect that it can be complete.

MAKING HYGIENE FUN

Helping your child to develop good hygiene habits now will help ensure that he'll continue them later on. For your preschooler, hygiene is fun when:

- The time allotted is always an important part of the everyday schedule.
- He is praised by you for having clean teeth, hair, hands, and nails.
- He gets to choose his own new products for hygiene, such as a toothbrush, comb, nail brush, soap dispenser, and cup—all in his favorite colors.
- He has a mirror at his height to watch himself get his face and teeth clean and comb his hair.
- He has a nonskid stool or set of little steps so that he can reach the sink with ease.
- He and his parents can be hygiene pals—washing hands together, brushing teeth together, and combing hair together.

My three and a half year old has been potty trained for a year. Besides using too much toilet paper, he doesn't get himself clean, but he refuses to let me help. Should I insist?

You don't want to discourage him from doing it all by himself. You can offer to help wipe. If he refuses, you might try giving him a sponge bath on days when he's not going to have a full bath to make sure he isn't irritating his bottom by not wiping it clean. To help with the toilet paper, you could put the roll out of his reach and leave him a few sections (be careful not to inconvenience other family members by putting it too far out of their reach). Explain how much he should use and how too much can clog the plumbing. Emphasize that big boys don't want to clog the plumbing.

My uncircumcised son is now three years old. On two occasions, I've had trouble pulling back the foreskin to clean beneath it. What should I do?

Never force the foreskin back if it is not totally separated from the glans. Natural separation will occur over time.

Although in many boys the foreskin may separate completely by age five, in some boys separation is not complete until puberty. If the foreskin has separated from the glans, gently retract it at bath time, and clean whatever portion of the glans is exposed. Do not force it back. Retracting the foreskin should never cause pain; if it does, you are forcing it. As early as possible, teach your son to gently retract the foreskin when he urinates and during baths and showers.

How often does my preschooler need to bathe?

The recommendation is two to three times a week. More frequent bathing can cause dry skin. To keep your preschooler's hands, arms, and face clean between tub baths, you can give him a sponge bath. His bottom may also need a frequent sponge bath, since at this age he may not be adept at wiping himself. Tub baths don't have to be long; a short "in-wash-out" for youngsters is fine. Avoid using bubble bath since it can be drying and irritating to his bottom. If your preschooler prefers to take a shower, that's fine, too. When he gets out of the tub or shower, you can lightly spread a little lotion over his skin

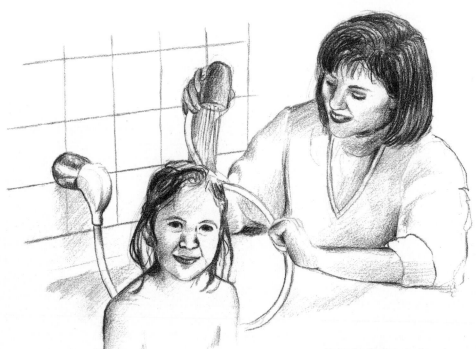

If you bathe her in the tub, you can use a showerhead attachment to help remove soap residue from her skin and rinse shampoo out of her hair.

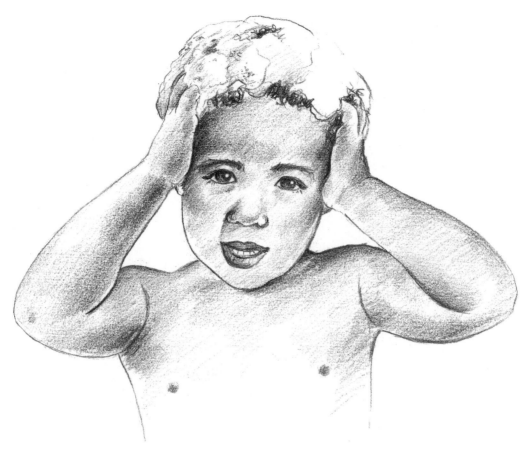

Allowing him to do most of the washing and shampooing may make bath time more enjoyable for him.

before you towel him off to help prevent dryness. Avoid lotions with perfumes, however, as they can cause irritation.

My preschooler suddenly stopped enjoying bath time. What can I do?

Most preschoolers love to take baths and splash around in the water. If your child resists bathing, find out why. It could be that you scrub too hard when you wash him; in that case, ease up. It may be that he doesn't want you to wash him at all and would prefer to do it himself; if so, let him wash himself, and then just lend a hand for the hard-to-reach places. Sometimes the temperature of the bathwater is the problem; let him choose whether the temperature should be warmer or cooler. Shampoo in the eyes or tangled hair is uncomfortable and often the reason a child wants to skip the bathing process

(see the next question for tips on making shampooing easier). Do whatever you can to make bathing or showering a more pleasant and comfortable experience for him.

How often should I shampoo my preschooler's hair?

Unless your child rolls in dirt every day, daily shampooing is not necessary and not recommended; once or twice a week—or whenever it looks and smells grimy—should do it. Dry scalp and dry or damaged hair can result from too much shampooing. On in-between days, you can rinse his hair without washing it if necessary. Even if you wash his hair only once or twice a week, use a mild shampoo, and only shampoo once. Many shampoo instructions say to shampoo twice, but this is unnecessary, especially for children. Be sure to rinse his hair and scalp thoroughly. Use clean water for rinsing, since using bathwater won't get his hair clean enough. If you don't have a shower or if you prefer to bathe your child, there are shower attachments available (the shower head is attached to a rubber hose that fits over the tub faucet) that are ideal for rinsing your preschooler's hair and body. Make certain that the water temperature is comfortable for your child, and avoid rinsing shampoo or water into his eyes. If his hair is very tangled after shampooing, you can use a creme rinse to make combing easier.

How many naps should my preschooler be taking each day? Should I insist that he take them?

Each child is an individual with individual needs. Some children require more sleep than others. In addition, children go through periods when they need increased rest due to growth spurts, increased physical activity, or increased environmental stimulation (such as going on a vacation). Many four year olds still require an afternoon nap, while others have given naps up completely. Preschoolers usually sleep or rest between eight and 11 hours a day. If your child is fatigued in the afternoon, he should be given a chance to take a nap. If he doesn't want a nap, a quiet period with quiet play may suffice. If napping becomes lengthy and pushes back bedtime at night, you'll want to cut down the nap time and probably eliminate it. Still, on occasion, a child will need a nap, and if it's accepted gracefully, fine. If not, try to opt for an earlier bedtime that night. Although parenting should be flexible, children do better with a fairly structured routine. If bedtime is about eight-thirty or nine each night, you should avoid pushing it back an hour or more for special occasions. If you prefer to sleep later in the morning, you can try to manipulate his bedtime, but it may not always work. Like adults, some preschoolers are early to bed and early to rise, some are late to bed and early to rise, and others are late to bed and late to rise. All in all, they're usually adept at getting the necessary amount of sleep that their bodies require. If your child often seems overly tired and cranky, you'll want to try to encourage more rest. Help him avoid activity and excitement just before bedtime. If he doesn't seem to catch up on his sleep, you may want to consult your pediatrician.

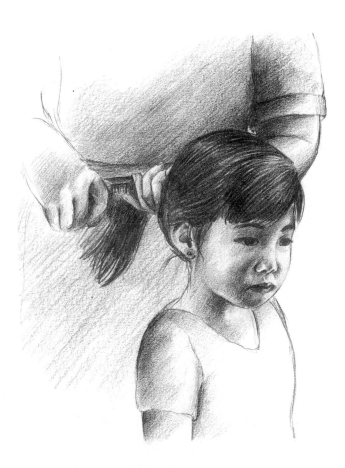

She'll need your help with some washing and grooming tasks.

NUTRITION AND FEEDING

Our water supply does not contain fluoride. Does my preschooler still need to take a fluoride tablet daily?

Your preschooler has probably been taking a fluoride supplement since the first months of her life, and she should continue to take it now. During this time, her primary (deciduous) teeth have been erupting and her secondary teeth have been forming. In the next year or so, the deciduous teeth will loosen and fall out and behind them will be the permanent teeth. This process will continue until the late teens, when the permanent third molars make their appearance. Throughout this process, the teeth are made stronger and more resistant to decay by fluoride. Therefore, if your water supply does not contain fluoride, your preschooler should continue to take one chewable fluoride tablet per day until your pediatrician or dentist recommends stopping (usually sometime during the teen years).

My child gets juice twice a day at school and three times a day at home. Is this okay?

Most juices contain very little except sugar and water and occasionally vitamin C. It is recommended, therefore, that juice be reserved for special treats and snacks. Many preschoolers will drink whatever liquid is given to them when they are thirsty, although what their bodies really need is water. At this age, it is a good idea to get your preschooler used to drinking water when she's thirsty. Try to encourage water as her first choice, and keep the juice intake to a minimum.

Encourage him to make water his first choice of beverage when he's thirsty.

How much milk should my preschooler be drinking each day?

Ideally, children should consume about four servings of dairy products daily. These servings can include milk, yogurt, cheese, or cottage cheese. Ice milk and ice cream can also be served occasionally. Your preschooler should be drinking a minimum of 16 ounces of milk each day and a maximum of 32 ounces. If she's drinking more than a quart of milk daily, she's getting more milk than she requires; try offering her water or other liquids more often when she's thirsty to keep her milk intake within this range.

Is homogenized whole milk (3.8 percent) better for my preschooler than two-percent or skim milk?

There's more butterfat in the whole milk than your preschooler needs. Two-percent milk is the preferred milk to offer your child, although some pediatricians may advise one-percent milk or skim milk under certain circumstances, such as when a child has an elevated cholesterol level or is significantly obese. Consult your pediatrician, and follow his recommendations.

My preschooler is allergic to milk. How can I be sure she's getting enough calcium in other foods?

Foods high in calcium include fortified juices, tofu, broccoli, canned salmon, and sardines. Collard and mustard greens are high in calcium too, but they're not always favorite foods with preschoolers. Other foods with calcium content are soybeans, garbanzo beans, oranges, corn, and wheat bread. If you feel she won't eat enough of these foods to fulfill her calcium requirement, consult your pediatrician. He may advise you to give your preschooler a daily calcium supplement.

My three year old has been picking up the baby's bottle and drinking from it. What should I do about this?

After they are weaned, most children do not like the taste of formula, so chances are your preschooler is feeling a bit jealous of the attention the baby is getting from you. Explain to her that the baby's bottle is not for her. She's beginning to know what is hers and what isn't and can understand this. Point out to her that she's a big girl now and can drink from a cup while her baby brother can't. Let her know that the baby will want to be just like his big sister and drink from the cup as soon as he is able. Don't give her a big reaction, but offer her something to drink in a cup and/or divert her attention to something else. Reassure her about all of her big girl accomplishments and privileges. Make certain to praise and reward her positive behavior and to reserve some special time when you can give her all of your attention.

It's recommended that you offer your preschooler two-percent milk. Whole milk contains more butterfat than he needs, and skim milk may contain too little.

What foods should I avoid offering my preschooler to prevent choking?

Until your child is at least four years of age, you should continue to avoid offering her hot dogs, chunky pieces of raw vegetables and fruits, hard candy, raisins, nuts, and popcorn. Although the molars are usually in by two or three years of age, your preschooler still won't be able to grind foods well, so meat and poultry should still be cut into small pieces for her. And, as before, be sure your child is sitting when she eats meals or snacks, since running around while eating can turn almost any food into a choking hazard.

How many times a day should my preschooler eat or be offered food?

Ideally, a preschooler should be offered three meals and two to three snacks each day. Remember, your child's stomach is smaller than yours, so she'll need to eat more frequently than you will. In addition, most children do not comfortably sit at the table for a lengthy meal. So offer small portions at mealtime, and try to make it a relaxing and pleasant time by not coaxing your preschooler to eat. While you should offer snacks, you should avoid allowing your child to snack all day long; otherwise, she won't want even a small meal. Snacks should be small but nutritious and should be offered far enough away from mealtime to allow the child to become hungry. Snacks and meals should be offered at the table, with your preschooler in her chair or high chair. While your preschooler shouldn't be expected to sit through long meals, she shouldn't be allowed to run around while eating either.

While he should be seated at the table whenever you offer him food, remember that it will still be difficult for him to sit through lengthy meals. Try to keep mealtimes short and pleasant, and praise him when he behaves appropriately at the table.

My child really only eats one meal per day. How can I get her to be a better eater?

Children eat when they are hungry, and if they're growing and developing normally on one meal a day, it's probably adequate. Remember, children eat more on certain days than others, and they increase their intake during a growth spurt. Continue to offer your child three meals and two to three snacks a day. Make certain that what you offer is nutritious so that when she does eat, she'll get important nutrients. Offer her small amounts of a variety of foods, and then leave it up to her as to the quantity she consumes. Anytime you are concerned about your child's weight, consult your pediatrician.

PRUDENT DAILY DIET

Meat or meat substitute (2-3 servings daily)
Single serving suggestions:
1 oz cooked meat, fish, or poultry
1 whole egg (no more than 3 per week)
   or 2 egg whites
½ cup cooked beans or peas
2 tbsp peanut butter spread on bread
   or crackers
2 oz tofu
1 oz high-protein pasta

Dairy products (3-4 servings daily)
Single serving suggestions:
1 cup two-percent milk
1 cup yogurt
1½ oz cheese
½ cup cottage cheese
1 to 1½ cups ice cream (occasionally)

Grains (3-4 servings daily)
Single serving suggestions:
1 slice bread
½ hamburger bun or roll
½ bagel or English muffin
3-4 crackers (whole grain preferred)
½ cup cooked cereal
1 oz cold cereal (not sugary type)
½ cup pasta or rice

Fruits and vegetables (3-4 servings daily)
Single serving suggestions:
½ cup raw or cooked vegetables
   (appropriate for age)
1 cup leafy cooked vegetables
1 whole fruit—soft and/or cooked (apricot,
   banana, pear, apple, plum, peach, fig, etc.)
½ grapefruit or other citrus fruit
½ cup soft cubed melon

The lists above are only guidelines. What is offered and what is eaten is frequently very different. The most important way to evaluate a child's diet is by following her growth and development at routine health maintenance examinations.

How important is breakfast, and how do I get my preschooler to eat it?

Breakfast is a very important meal because your child has gone for eight to ten hours or more without food. Her tummy is empty, and she should be hungry. Many studies have shown that a child's level of energy and functioning throughout the morning is affected by whether or not she had a healthy breakfast. Milk is the preferred beverage at breakfast because it contains protein. The energy boost provided by protein lasts longer than the boost provided by sugar. If your child doesn't like cooked cereal or other traditional—and healthy—breakfast foods, you can offer her a variety of other nonbreakfast foods instead. Whole grain bread or toast with peanut butter or chicken or tuna is nutritious breakfast fare. Bananas and other fruits and fruit juices are wise choices; you might even offer yogurt with fresh fruit. Even leftovers from dinner will do. Allow your child choices, and give her an interesting variety from which to choose. Some preschoolers prefer to have some "wake up" time to run around and play before sitting down to eat. Schedules permitting, breakfast doesn't have to be offered immediately after waking. She can have a choice here, too, such as eating before or after she gets dressed.

My mother insists that children need to take vitamins daily. What kind do you recommend?

There is no reason for a child to take daily vitamins if she's eating a well-rounded diet. However, if there is no fluoride in your water supply, you will need to give her a fluoride supplement. Some of the vitamins on the market appeal to children because of their colors, shapes, and flavors. Keep in mind, however, that vitamin supplements, like drugs, can be dangerous if used improperly. Your child should not learn to think of them as candy or a treat. Therefore, if you feel that you need to offer your child a vitamin supplement, try to choose a plain brand that has been recommended by your pediatrician. Store it as you would any medication—out of your child's reach.

I'm a vegetarian, and I eat a very healthy diet. Is this type of diet healthy for my preschooler, too?

Some very conscientious and health-minded parents have gotten into serious trouble by offering their diets to their growing children. Preschoolers need more fat in their diet (30 percent of their caloric intake) than adults do to maintain normal growth. It's much easier for children to get some of their protein from animal sources, such as meat, fish, poultry, and dairy products. However, if you are careful about the amounts of protein in your vegetarian meals, they may be adequate for your growing and developing child. Since certain grains are poor in protein, you may have to add wheat germ when you serve them as a meal. In general, children shouldn't be on special diets, so for safety's sake, you'll want to discuss your menus with your pediatrician to make certain they are fulfilling your preschooler's nutritional needs.

When should I have my child's cholesterol level checked?

Cholesterol screening is advised at different ages depending upon the judgment of the pediatrician. In some pediatric clinics, routine cholesterol screening is not performed until the child is ten years old. If there is a history of high cholesterol levels and/or cardiovascular disease in your family, however, your pediatrician may want to screen your child at a much earlier age. While growing children require more fat in their diets than adults do, your physician may want to suggest some modifications in your child's daily intake of cholesterol and saturated fat if her cholesterol level is high and the family is considered high risk.

The main part of my preschooler's diet has become macaroni and cheese and bread and margarine. I'm worried about this, but isn't it better than eating nothing?

This intake of macaroni and cheese *is* much better than starving, but children do not starve themselves. Offer your child an interesting variety of nutritious foods daily. She can choose to eat or not, but she should only be allowed to choose from what you offer. Let her choose her favorite macaroni-and-cheese meal occasionally, but don't let her dictate her menu to you. When you offer bread and margarine, serve whole grain bread. Try to be matter-of-fact about meal and snack time. Don't ever plead with your child to eat. If you focus on the amount she eats, eating can become a tug of war between you. Remember, a child isn't good because she eats or bad because she doesn't. Eating isn't good or bad. Your child should choose from the variety of nutritious foods you offer and should eat only when she's hungry.

Encourage her to eat as much as she needs from the variety of nutritious foods you offer each day.

Do you recommend that I cook all of my preschooler's foods without salt?

While you don't have to completely avoid salt when cooking your preschooler's food, you certainly should reduce the amount you add and keep the salt shaker off the table. Likewise, it's a good idea to avoid offering your preschooler salty snacks and salty commercially prepared foods. Once again, you are educating your preschooler's tastes; if she doesn't get used to eating salty foods now, she's not likely to choose them frequently later on.

I have the original cookies-and-ice-cream kid. I know I shouldn't have started this, but how do I get it to stop?

Cookies and ice cream taste very sweet and very good, so of course your preschooler would prefer them to other foods. The point is that parents should determine what food is offered to their child. Children enjoy making choices about meals, and this should be encouraged; however, they should be allowed to choose from the variety of healthy foods offered to them by their parents. You want to help educate your child's tastes toward healthy food choices now and for the future. Limit the cookies and ice cream to special days or special treats. Instead of saying "No cookies today," say "This is what we're having for lunch today." Simply avoid bringing up the cookies and ice cream all together. Try to be "out of cookies" most of the time.

I've heard some confusing statements about the artificial sweetener aspartame. Is it safe for my preschooler?

Aspartame has been extensively tested. So far, the studies have not proven that moderate use of this artificial sweetener is harmful to healthy human beings. As compared to sugar, aspartame is healthier for teeth. However, keep in mind that you want to teach your preschooler to make healthy, nutritious food choices now and in the future. She shouldn't get into the habit of thinking that everything she eats and drinks should taste sweet. In addition, you want to encourage her to choose nutritious foods, regardless of whether they taste sweet or not. So while consuming a limited amount of aspartame in foods is not a problem, you should avoid serving her sweet-tasting but nutritionally poor foods—no matter where the sweet taste comes from.

A WORD ABOUT SUGAR

As many as 20 to 30 percent of school-age children in the United States are overweight. While the quantity of food consumed plays a role in overweight, the caloric content is just as important. Sugar provides empty calories. Preschoolers generally prefer sugary foods and, given the chance, would probably fill up on sweets and leave no room or appetite for nutritious foods. In addition to providing empty calories, sugar plays a role in promoting tooth decay, even in the deciduous (baby) teeth. Therefore, it's best to limit the amount of sugar in your preschooler's diet. While you can use sweets as a special treat, try to avoid using them specifically as a reward; you want to encourage a healthy view of eating and food. Although there are theories linking hyperactivity in children to sugar content in the diet, there has been absolutely no documentation or scientific proof that this is the case. Hyperactive children, like all children and adults, need a healthy, varied diet.

Should I avoid giving my preschooler barbecued food?

A major concern here is the possibility of food poisoning from improper handling of the food before it is cooked. If you're picnicking or barbecuing, make certain that the meat (or poultry or fish) is properly refrigerated until it's cooked, and then cook it thoroughly on the barbecue. Clean your barbecue grill well each time you use it to remove particles of food that may spoil and chemicals that can become a part of your next cookout. In addition, there's some worry about the amount of PAH (polycyclic aroma hydrocarbons) and other possible cancer-causing agents that are produced when food is barbecued. These agents are formed when fat drips onto flame, hot charcoal, lava rocks, and heating elements. The smoke then picks up these agents and deposits them on the food. Some of these agents are also formed on the food itself when the flame touches it. Currently, there is no hard scientific evidence that PAH is harmful to humans in reasonable amounts. As long as you don't barbecue every day, your little one can probably enjoy some barbecued foods. To minimize any potential danger, choose leaner meats; this will cut down on fat drippings. Avoid soft woods as fuel for your barbecue; although they may add a little extra flavor, they also burn at a higher temperature than charcoal, thus producing more PAH. And cover your grill with foil that has holes poked in it to let the fat drip out and keep charring of food to a minimum. The final worry involves the risk of burns from a hot grill, hot utensils, and hot food. Be sure to keep your preschooler away when you're grilling, keep hot utensils out of her reach, and be sure her food is sufficiently cooled to avoid burns.

When barbecuing, make sure your preschooler is at a safe distance from the grill, keep all hot utensils out of her reach, and be sure her food is sufficiently cooled before you serve it.

SAFETY AND HEALTH

Now that my preschooler can understand a lot of my safety instructions, can I ease up on some of my safety precautions?

Naturally, the home of a preschooler need not be as thoroughly safety proofed as the home of an infant or toddler. However, your preschooler's capacity to understand, remember, and follow safety instructions will not be nearly as great at the beginning of this period as it will be toward the end. Therefore, it is a good idea to ease up gradually, monitoring your preschooler carefully to see just how far you can really trust him at each point along the way. It also is a good idea to keep your home "child-oriented" as much as possible for as long as possible. If you really don't need to have corrosive cleansers, surplus medicines, or hazardous equipment lying around, don't invite trouble. Similarly, keeping potentially dangerous substances and items you do need in locked drawers and cabinets is worth the little bit of inconvenience.

Since he's toilet trained, I don't want to continue supervising my preschooler's trips to the bathroom. Will he be okay on his own in there at this point?

By the time your preschooler is toilet trained, he should be able to handle unsupervised visits to the bathroom. However, especially if the bathroom he uses is shared by adults, make sure that hazardous items and substances, such as razors and medicines, are still kept in a securely latched cabinet. Also, see to it that your preschooler understands that trips to the bathroom are for toileting and hygiene. Emphasize that the inside of the toilet is out-of-bounds and that he is not to play with the bathtub faucets. For the sake of your own sanity more so than for your preschooler's safety, you also may want to make sure that he doesn't have access to shampoo bottles, jars of baby powder, and other such things that might result in quite a mess if your preschooler decides to use them as toys.

Since I live in the city, I'd like to teach my preschooler to cross the street by himself as soon as possible. When can I begin?

It is never too soon to start teaching your preschooler how to cross the street properly. Increasingly throughout this period,

He'll probably be able to handle unsupervised visits to the bathroom now, but make sure he understands that it's a place for toileting and hygiene—not play.

he will be able to understand, remember, and follow directions such as "wait for the light to change," "cross only at the corner," "look both ways before you cross," etc. However, even at the end of this period, allowing your preschooler to cross the street by himself just is not a good idea. Again, although you may be able to count on him to not do anything dangerous deliberately, his strong sense of adventure, his capacity to be distracted easily, and other such factors can lead to trouble. In addition, while a preschooler can be expected to learn the basic rules of traffic, he can't really be expected to take into account the many complications created by unsafe drivers who do not follow the rules. Therefore, by all means, start giving your preschooler lessons in this area, but wait another year or two before you start giving him the chance to put them into practice without supervision.

My preschooler has outgrown his car seat. What do I do now?

While every state has a mandatory child-restraint law, the specifics of the laws vary from state to state, so it's wise to check the law in your state to make sure you are complying. Once your preschooler is over four years of age and weighs more than 40 pounds, you may no longer need to keep him in a car seat, but you will have to make sure that he is securely restrained in a booster seat and/or by a standard lap-and-shoulder belt—regardless of whether or not the law requires it. For a while, you probably will have to use a booster seat along with the lap-and-shoulder belt to ensure a proper fit. Keep in mind that the top portion of the belt must pass over your preschooler's shoulder, not his neck. For your child's safety, buckling up is mandatory every time you take him in the car, even for short trips. It is a good idea to keep the doors locked as well. Don't let your preschooler play with sharp objects, such as pens and pencils, while riding in the car, and keep the rear ledge free of objects that might fly forward in the event of a sudden stop. Should any problems arise while you are driving, pull over and stop the car, and don't start moving again until everything is in order.

Once she has outgrown her car seat, she will have to be securely restrained by a standard lap-and-shoulder belt, a securely fastened booster seat, or both. If you use a booster seat, check the manufacturer's instructions for proper use.

I'm tired of fighting with my preschooler to stay in his safety restraint when he's in the car. What can I do?

Some parenting rules are open for discussion and negotiation, and some aren't. There is no negotiation when it comes to wearing a safety restraint in a motor vehicle. It's a safety measure that must be rigidly obeyed. Explain to him that the car will not move if he releases the restraint. If he unbuckles the restraint or otherwise begins to misbehave, stop the car, and get him to rebuckle. Then, leave him at home the next time, and tell him he needs to cooperate in order to ride in the car. When he agrees to comply, try another trip in the car, and be sure to praise him if he behaves appropriately. He'll get the message if you are serious about getting it across to him. If the unbuckling has become a game or test of wills, it's a game you must win now.

Now that he's capable of keeping himself quietly entertained for a while, is it okay to just leave my preschooler in the car for a minute or two while I run into the store?

This seemingly innocent set of circumstances can lead to disaster. A minute or two is an eternity for an active, curious preschooler. The many facets of a typical automobile may very well be irresistible even for the most well-behaved and obedient preschooler. In that short period of time, your preschooler could find the cigarette lighter, he could release the safety brake, he could move the gearshift out of the park position, etc. He also could become impatient and attempt to get out of the car to find you, possibly stepping into traffic as he does so. Furthermore, since you will have to at least keep a window partially open for him, your preschooler will be rather vulnerable for the period that he is in the car and you're not. In other words, in this case, what minor inconvenience you save yourself simply is not worth the risks to your preschooler.

Is it safe to take my preschooler for a ride on my bicycle with me?

Bicycle accidents are a common cause of injury in children. While you don't have to give up on riding with your pre-schooler, you do need to take necessary precautions. Your preschooler must be securely harnessed in a child seat specifi-cally designed for this purpose. Both you and your preschooler must also wear a helmet. In addition, begin teaching your child good bicycle-safety habits as soon as he begins riding with you or riding on his own—even if he's only riding a tricycle. As he graduates to a larger bicycle, you may want to enroll him in a bicycle-safety class. Remember, however, that the best teacher is a parent who knows and practices safe riding techniques.

If you take your preschooler for a ride on your bicycle, she should be securely harnessed in a child seat designed for use on a bicycle, and you should both be wearing a helmet.

I live in a quiet suburb. Is it okay to let my preschooler ride his tricycle unsupervised on the sidewalk?

This probably is not a good idea. Your preschooler's limited sense of responsibility may be too easily overcome by his strong sense of adventure at this point. Although he might be counted upon not to ride into the street deliberately, he may very well do so when distracted, or he may wander off into unfamiliar territory and become disoriented. There are just too many accidents every year involving preschoolers riding or running suddenly in front of unsuspecting motorists on suburban streets to make this sort of activity worth the risk. As an alternative, you might consider blocking off the end of your driveway to create a reasonably large and safe area for your preschooler to pedal around on his own. If you do, just be sure you always look carefully before you back out of the garage.

My preschooler seems extremely fascinated by fire. Is this unusual, and can I do something about it?

Unfortunately, fascination with fire is quite common among preschoolers. It usually seems to be a love/hate relationship. They generally are irresistibly drawn to anything connected with flames, but as soon as things get a little out of hand, they become terrified. Therefore, no matter how responsible your preschooler is becoming, take extra care to make sure that he does not have access to matches, lighters, or any other such items. If a barbecue grill, fireplace, stove, or any other such piece of equipment is in use, make sure that he is not left unsupervised in the area. At this point, you probably can teach your preschooler how to follow a family fire drill, but realize that in case of emergency, you can't count on his memory and rationality overcoming his terror. Good prevention practices are still your preschooler's best protection against fire.

Allowing her to ride her tricycle unsupervised can be dangerous unless she's riding in an enclosed area, such as a fenced-in yard.

ACCIDENTS AS TEACHING TOOLS

Accidents will happen—sometimes you simply have no control over various circumstances surrounding your preschooler's experience. On the other hand, you do have some control over how you react when accidents happen. How you react will have an effect on future incidents for better or for worse. Of course, when your preschooler is injured under any circumstances, your immediate reaction probably will be quite emotional. However, once you've calmed down, it is important for you to remember that any accident can—and should—be used in a positive, constructive manner to teach your preschooler how to avoid getting into similar trouble again. Take the time to talk to him about what happened, how it happened, what his alternatives were, what to watch out for next time, etc. If appropriate, you may consider some form of punishment as well, such as suspending a relevant privilege if the accident occurred because of gross negligence or direct disobedience on his part. But be very careful not to make the accident worse than it already is by overreacting and terrifying your preschooler further. Keep in mind that a cat who jumps on a hot stove once will never jump on a hot stove again—but it also won't jump on a cold stove either. In attempting to keep your preschooler safe, you don't want to scare him into avoiding the world; rather, you want to teach him how to deal with the world in a responsible way.

I've taught my preschooler to swim, and he's good at it. Can I relax a little when he's in the water now?

You can relax a little, but that doesn't mean you can let your preschooler swim unsupervised. In fact, it is not a good idea for anyone—including adults—to go swimming alone. While your preschooler may understand and remember a prohibition about going into the pool by himself, his sense of adventure may get the better of him. Therefore, it is still wise to prevent him from having easy access to a swimming pool or any other body of water that he can get to without your help. Furthermore, to the extent that your preschooler will be engaging in water activities, he should be introduced to appropriate safety rules as well—such as checking for proper depth and absence of obstructions before diving or jumping in. Keep in mind, however, that his natural exuberance at this point may lead to trouble no matter what you teach him, so you can relax a bit—but don't fall asleep!

There's a hill next to my home that is ideal for snow sledding. Can I let my preschooler go down himself, or should I still ride with him?

It depends upon the precise size and location of the hill, as well as upon the condition of the snow at the moment. For example, if the hill is long and steep so that a sled is able to pick up considerable speed, it's probably best if you still ride with your preschooler. Similarly, if the bottom of the hill abuts a busy street or some other hazard, you probably cannot count on your preschooler always being in sufficient control to stay out of danger. Even if the hill is softly sloping and is in a protected area, you have to be careful about icy conditions. A fun ride on fluffy snow can turn into something else entirely when the sled hits a patch of slick ice. By the way, you might consider restricting any solo rides to a saucer-shaped or toboggan-type sled rather than a standard sled with sharp-bladed runners at this point.

I'm scared to death every time my preschooler goes on a jungle gym or other climbing apparatus. Can I trust him to stay within his capacities?

In general, preschoolers are pretty careful during their climbing activities. However, it is always possible that your preschooler's natural enthusiasm or sense of adventure will get

Be sure that the jungle gym he uses is sturdy, well-designed, and properly placed.

him into trouble. Therefore, it is a good idea to make sure that whatever piece of equipment your preschooler is using is sturdy, well-designed, and appropriately placed. For example, if the location is a playground that has an asphalt surface rather than one of grass or sand, the jungle gym should be low and wide so that your preschooler can't get seriously hurt from a fall. On the other hand, you also will have to accept the fact that, to a certain extent, bumps, bruises, and scrapes will be a part of your preschooler's experience. It's okay to be concerned and cautious, but keep in mind that your child will never learn to fly if you don't give him a chance to really spread his wings now and then.

When my preschooler plays with his peers, they sometimes get into fairly serious fights. Can they really hurt each other?

Fights between preschoolers typically involve a lot more barking than biting. Your preschooler and his friends may do a lot of name-calling, wild gesticulating, and even some pushing and shoving during a quarrel, but it is rare that their anger will reach a level that moves them to cause serious injury. However, it is possible that someone could get hurt in a fight, so it is wise to always have an adult reasonably nearby who can step in before a disagreement escalates to the point where it becomes potentially dangerous. You might also consider introducing your preschooler to certain rules about playing with his peers in this regard. For example, you can teach him that wrestling is okay for fun, but fighting of any sort is not the way to handle disputes. You can also teach him that if he's got a real problem, he can ask for adult intervention, but under no circumstances should he ever intentionally seek to injure someone.

I'm afraid of my child being snatched by a stranger, but I also don't want him to fear everyone. How do I handle this?

It is probably a good idea to go easy on this subject at this point. Given your preschooler's tendency to create very dramatic and often very violent fantasies, talking to him about kidnapping and other such dangers is likely to have a much more unpleasant impact than you may have anticipated or desired. Your preschooler's best protection for the time being still will be your supervision. You might consider giving him some general warnings as well, but if you do, try to keep them positive. For example, instead of saying "Don't ever go into a car with a stranger," say something like "You can only go in a car with us or Aunt Sally unless we first give you permission to do otherwise." At the end of this period or possibly a little beyond, your preschooler may be ready to handle a discussion about how most adults are kind and helpful but how some are not.

I've heard that many children are sexually molested by people they know. How can I protect my preschooler from this?

As he proceeds through this period, your preschooler may become increasingly able to handle a discussion about "good touches and bad touches." You can talk to him about hugs and pats that he wants and enjoys, and those that are uninvited and make him feel uncomfortable. You can also teach him to come to you and tell you immediately whenever someone has tried to do the latter. Keep in mind that it is imperative for your child to be very clear about this subject and have total trust in you. Many parents confuse their preschoolers and lose their confidence when they force them to accept a kiss from an unfamiliar aunt or to shake hands with an imposing acquaintance when they really would much rather be hiding behind Mommy or Daddy's leg. Unless you are compassionate under these circumstances, there's a good chance that whatever important instructions you try to impress upon your preschooler will lose their effect through inconsistent application.

I'd like my preschooler to attend day care, but I've read horror stories about what happens in some places. How can I protect my child?

First of all, the number and nature of such day-care incidents tend to be exaggerated a great deal by the media. The overwhelming majority of centers are safe places staffed by competent, caring people. However, it is a good idea to protect your child against the remote possibility of an unpleasant incident. The only way to do that effectively is to know very well who is caring for your child and know exactly what your child does during the day. You can start by checking

references carefully, but in the long run, there is no substitute for getting involved. Volunteer to help out at the center as often as you can so you can really get to know your child's teachers. Drop by unannounced on occasion. Linger a little at drop-off and pick-up times. And most important of all, always get a detailed account of what happened to your child during the day, both from his teacher and from him. In addition to the multitude of other benefits this practice provides, it will give you a chance to establish a sense of routines against which to check gaps and discrepancies.

How can I teach my preschooler to protect himself in case he inadvertently becomes separated from me?

Especially toward the end of this period, you may have success in getting your preschooler to memorize important information such as his last name, his telephone number, his address, the first names of his parents, etc. You'll probably do better if you try to achieve this in a fun atmosphere by making it into a game rather than by taking the chance of frightening him about the subject. You also can teach him to approach a policeman should he ever become separated from you. Many parents make the mistake of introducing their preschoolers to the police as people "who will put you in jail if you do something bad." That makes it very hard for a preschooler to accept the notion that he should approach one of these people voluntarily. Since it is unlikely that your preschooler will be committing any crimes during this period, make sure his first explanation is that "police are people who can help you when you're in trouble."

Will I ever stop worrying about my child's safety?

Of course not. As a parent, it always will be your job to be intensely concerned about your child's well-being. And if you think you're worried now, just wait until he gets his driver's license and starts going out on a dates in a few years. The important things to remember are, first, that growing and learning require a certain amount of risk, and your task is not to eliminate that risk entirely but rather to make it manageable and reasonable; and second, the most effective way to take care of your child from this point on is to start making sure he knows how to take care of himself. You won't always be able to be with him, but the things you teach him about safety will be with him always.

Toward the end of this period, she will probably be able to hold an oral thermometer in her mouth safely.

Can I now take my child's temperature orally?

Most five year olds and many four year olds can hold a thermometer under their tongue for the two minutes it takes to obtain an accurate reading. Ask him to hold the thermometer under his tongue and to close his lips around it while you hold the thermometer. It may be more comfortable for him if you use a rounded-bulb thermometer rather than the type with the longer mercury-filled tip.

What is the "normal" oral temperature for a preschooler?

A normal temperature for a child can be up to 100 degrees Fahrenheit. (The arrow found on most thermometers at 98.6 degrees Fahrenheit does not apply to children.) In children (and often in adults) the normal variation in temperature during a single day can be two or more degrees. A child may awaken with a temperature of 97 degrees Fahrenheit; by the end of the day, however, it may be 99 degrees Fahrenheit or even a little higher. The temperature is usually highest between six and nine in the evening. In addition, it is not unusual for a

child to run a "subnormal" temperature in the healing phase of a viral infection such as the flu. This temperature, usually between 97 and 98 degrees Fahrenheit, often follows several days of fevers over 100 degrees Fahrenheit during the acute phase of the illness. As long as your preschooler feels fine, no further treatment or precautions are necessary.

How can I keep my five year old from giving his three-year-old brother every cold he gets?

In most cases, you can't. A child with a cold is often contagious for one to two days before he has any symptoms. Therefore, all family members are likely to be exposed to that particular virus. If your three year old has not developed antibodies to that virus by previous exposure, he's going to get the cold. It is helpful, however, to make sure that a child with a cold washes his hands frequently and carefully; that dishes, glasses, and utensils are not shared; and that tissues used by the child with the cold are appropriately discarded. Aside from these simple measures, there is little one can do to avoid spreading a cold within a family.

My preschooler frequently gets tummy aches on mornings when I have to go to work and he's scheduled to go to preschool. How do I handle these?

If a tummy ache comes on frequently on days when you are scheduled to work, you need to find out why. You should probably take him to the pediatrician to rule out any physical reason for them. Accompanying symptoms that would be a cause for concern include fever, vomiting, diarrhea, and urinary discomfort. A tummy ache can be a symptom of many conditions and diseases. Among them are appendicitis, gastroenteritis ("stomach flu"), urinary tract infections, dairy product intolerance, and ulcers. It's also important to find out whether or not your child is able to carry out the normal daily activities that he really wants to do. In other words, is he feeling fine when it's too late for you to go to work or too late for him to go to preschool? Fifteen to twenty percent of school-age children will develop a condition called "recurrent abdominal pain" at some point during their school years. It can occur over several months, but the child is pain-free between the episodes. Even if the cause is emotional, the pain can be real. The underlying cause is often stress and unresolved fear or anxiety. The child exhibiting this pain needs to be screened to reassure him that he's really okay, too. Children often need help to identify and face situations and experiences in order for them to grow emotionally and intellectually. The tummy aches may be a symptom of separation anxiety or a fear of a new experience like preschool. We need to help children adjust to preschool and kindergarten. They need to be discouraged from avoiding preschool due to minor complaints or minor illnesses. A child should be returned to his school situation as soon as possible. Allowing avoidance behavior to continue almost always makes the situation worse. Enlist the help of your child's teacher and pediatrician to work things through so your child can comfortably adjust to his changing environment.

How can I tell if my child's injury is a sprain or a broken bone?

Unless you have X-ray vision—or unless the bone is obviously deformed—you can't. If the bone appears to be deformed (not in its usual position or not straight), medical consultation is necessary. The amount of pain your child is experiencing is also often a good indication. If the pain is severe enough to keep the child from resting or sleeping, it is a good idea to

Bumps, scrapes, and bruises are all a part of growing up, but if you're ever worried about an injury your child has sustained, consult your pediatrician.

have the injury examined by a physician. If the child is fairly comfortable, applying a cold pack will help control the swelling. Immobilize the affected area using a splint or sling or by having the child rest with the affected part elevated. Re-evaluate the injured part at frequent intervals as the swelling goes down to help determine if medical attention is necessary. In any case, if you are worried, consult a physician.

What do I do if one of my child's teeth gets broken or knocked out?

If a tooth is knocked out, find it, place it in some liquid (milk or the child's own saliva is preferable), and contact the pedodontist (children's dentist) immediately. If the tooth or teeth are merely loose, observe them for a few hours or a day or two. If they remain loose, consult a pedodontist. If a large piece of a tooth has been chipped off, if there is a red dot visible inside a broken tooth, if your child is in extreme pain, or if you can't stop the bleeding from an injury to the mouth, consult your pedodontist immediately. If you cannot reach your pedodontist, contact your pediatrician.

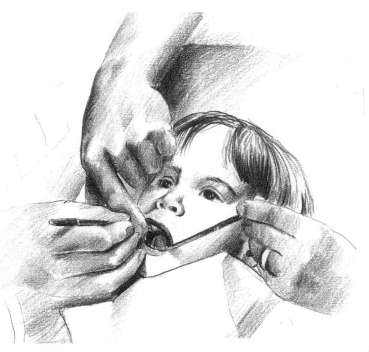

If one of your child's teeth gets knocked out, recover it, place it in some liquid, and contact your child's dentist immediately; there may be a chance that the tooth can be saved.

How do children get scabies? Are they caused by dirty surroundings?

Scabies is a skin condition caused by a small insect (mite) that burrows into the skin to lay eggs. The rash is characterized by small, itchy, red bumps and/or raised streaks. The major symptom is itching. Children get scabies from direct contact with another person with the disease. It spreads most easily in areas where people are in close contact for extended periods. It is not caused by dirty surroundings. There are effective treatments once the proper diagnosis is made. These treatments are available by prescription only, so if you suspect scabies, consult your pediatrician.

My preschooler's best friend has ringworm. Should I keep them from playing together?

Ringworm is a superficial infection of the skin; it can also affect the hair and nails. It was given its descriptive name because many of the skin lesions look like "rings" (a round red area with clearing in the center). It is usually acquired from contact with an animal that has similar lesions or areas of red skin where the hair has fallen out. Ringworm is not considered to be contagious from person to person so it is not necessary to isolate the child, especially after treatment has been initiated.

Is there a way to prevent pinworms?

Pinworms are tiny organisms that look like wiggly white or tan thread; they're about a quarter of an inch long. Their life cycle is very simple. The microscopic eggs get onto the hands or toys of a child, usually through contact with an infected playmate. The child puts his hands or the toys in his mouth, and the pinworm eggs are swallowed and then mature in the child's intestine. The adult worms reside in the lower part of the large intestine. The adult female crawls out and deposits eggs in the skin folds around the anus, usually at night. This causes intense itching. When the child scratches, the eggs get onto his fingers, and the cycle starts again. Pinworm infestation rarely causes symptoms other than rectal itching. If your child is complaining about rectal itching and you suspect pinworms, examine the anal region two to three hours after his bedtime. If you notice the worms, report the condition to your pediatrician. If you are unable to see the worms but still suspect pinworms as the cause, your pediatrician can do a microscopic examination of material from around the anus to reveal the worms or the eggs. There are excellent medications to eliminate the infection, and your pediatrician can prescribe the appropriate one. The only way to avoid reinfection with pinworms is to practice meticulous hand-washing techniques and to keep an infected child away from other children until treatment is complete. While this infestation is a nuisance, it is not dangerous.

My three year old usually goes two to three days without having a bowel movement. Is this normal?

This pattern can be perfectly normal. If there are no symptoms of abdominal pain or straining during bowel movements and if the bowel movements are not hard and dry, you should not be concerned. Many perfectly healthy children go days between bowel movements. If your child is complaining of abdominal pain or discomfort, if he is experiencing pain or discomfort with the passing of the stool, or if the stools are hard and dry, consult your pediatrician. Try to do so before your child starts to voluntarily withhold stools because of the discomfort; this can develop into a physical and emotional problem for your child and for the family (see the following question for more on this problem).

My four year old has been toilet trained for more than a year, but lately he has been constantly soiling his pants with stool. Could this be a medical problem?

The most common cause of fecal soiling in children who are toilet trained is "paradoxical" diarrhea. It results when a child holds stool for days at a time, and the stool becomes firm, dry, and large. The origin of this condition is usually a bowel movement that is accompanied by pain while it is being passed. The child, fearing that subsequent stools will also be painful, holds back the stool and refuses to have a bowel movement. The stool accumulates at the end of the large intestine and becomes firm, dry, and even more difficult to pass. Liquid stool from above works its way around the firm, dry stool and leaks out of the anus, resulting in fecal soiling of the pants and paradoxical diarrhea. This is a condition which requires medical attention and supervision over a period of time to correct. If you suspect that your child has this condition, consult your pediatrician for advice and treatment.

How can I keep my child from getting poison ivy?

Poison ivy, poison oak, and poison sumac are all in the family called "rhus dermatitis." In sensitive individuals, direct contact with the plants causes a red, itchy, and sometimes weeping skin rash that lasts one to two weeks. Oral antihistamines and topical medications can be used to treat the symptoms. Sometimes systemic (oral or injectable) steroids are prescribed. The rash is not contagious from person to person. It occurs only in children and adults who have had direct contact with the plant leaves or, occasionally, with the smoke when the plants are burned. One other source of contact is the fur of pets who get the oil from the leaves onto their coats and then come in contact with the child. If you suspect that your child has been exposed to poison oak, ivy, or sumac, remove his clothes and shoes, and wash everything (including shoes and shoelaces) in warm, soapy water. Give him a shower immediately, and shampoo his hair. To avoid further episodes, be sure that you and your child know what the plants look like (see the illustrations on the following page), and avoid contact whenever possible. Also, have your child wear clothing and footwear that cover his legs and feet when he is in areas where such plants may be found.

My preschooler had a severe reaction to a bee sting. What can I do to protect him in the future?

Whenever the reaction to a sting is systemic—that is, it is more than a local reaction at the site of the sting—immediate medical evaluation is indicated. If your child has already experienced one severe reaction, your pediatrician (or a pediatric allergist) can test your child for sensitivity to stinging insects (honeybee, wasp, yellow jacket, hornet, bumblebee, etc.) and determine if hyposensitization is necessary. If so, your child will be started on a series of injections to gradually decrease the reaction if your child should be stung again. In the meantime, you should have a "bee sting kit" with you at all times. This kit should contain an antihistamine to be given by mouth and a syringe with adrenaline (epinephrine) to inject in the event of a reaction to another sting. Specific instructions for the use of such a kit will be provided by your pediatrician. You can also decrease the probability of future stings by avoiding areas where bees are likely to congregate, such as clover fields, gardens, orchards in bloom, etc. Be sure your child's feet are always covered whenever he is outdoors. Avoid perfumed soaps and lotions, since they tend to attract these insects. Keep in mind, too, that insect repellents are often not effective against these stinging insects.

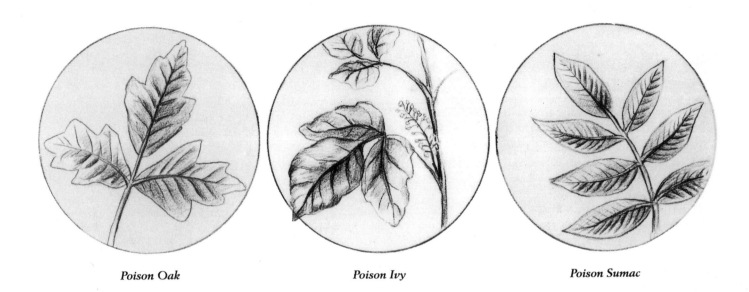

Poison Oak   *Poison Ivy*   *Poison Sumac*

The best way to help prevent your child from having a reaction to poison oak, poison ivy, or poison sumac is to teach him what the plants look like so that he can steer clear if he sees them.

How and when can I tell if my child is hyperactive?

Relative to older children, most preschoolers could be called hyperactive. Their behavior can be impulsive, their attention spans are short, and they are generally always on the go. As mentioned previously, this normal behavior commonly leads parents to fear that their child is "hyperactive." The danger here is that a child will be labeled as "hyperactive" because his parents have a low level of tolerance or patience, rather than because the child has an abnormally high energy level. So you need to be patient and cautious. By the time your child reaches school age, these characteristics should be gradually decreasing in frequency and severity. If the impulsiveness and short attention span make it difficult for the child to perform in school and/or if he can't seem to calm down even if he wants to, you should consult your pediatrician. She will help you determine if what you are observing is normal development or if your child requires further evaluation for the syndrome known as "attention deficit disorder with hyperactivity" or ADHD. Keep in mind that this syndrome is relatively rare.

My three year old has knock knees and is pigeon toed. Will he outgrow this?

Many children at this age do not have straight legs or feet; for the vast majority of them, the apparent problems will correct themselves as the child matures and develops. During routine well-child examinations, the pediatrician will examine your child's feet and legs. If there is a significant problem, your pediatrician will refer you and your child to a specialist.

My five year old will be starting kindergarten soon. Does he need any special shots or tests?

Many school districts make a prekindergarten exam mandatory. Even if yours doesn't, it's wise to take him in for a medical checkup before he enters school. During the visit, his height, weight, and general health and development will be checked and a complete physical examination and any appropriate laboratory tests will be done. The DTP booster and polio vaccines will be given, and a test for tuberculosis may also be performed.

How often should I have my child's vision tested?

It is important to have your child's vision tested any time you suspect there is a problem. One way that you can help detect a possible problem is by playing "vision games" with your child; compare your vision with that of your child by identifying distant objects and asking your child to do the same. You should also pay attention to whether your child's eyes appear aligned and whether both eyes move together when the child is looking at something. During routine medical checkups, the pediatrician will examine your child's eyes as part of the total physical examination. Testing of visual acuity can be accurately done by age five in most pediatric offices. The prekindergarten checkup is also a good time for formal vision screening. By the age of five, a child's vision should be at least 20/30, with no more than a two-line difference between what each eye can read on a standard eye chart. If the pediatrician suspects a problem during routine checks or formal screenings, consultation with an ophthalmologist or pediatric ophthalmologist will be advised. If you suspect there is something wrong with your child's vision in between checkups, however, you should contact your pediatrician. After the prekindergarten screening, your child's vision will be screened by your pediatrician at each subsequent medical examination; often, it is also checked at school.

The prekindergarten checkup is a good time for formal vision screening. If you are ever worried about your child's eyes or vision, however, consult your pediatrician.

ON BEING A PARENT

What can I do to feed my preschooler's desire for adventure?

Indulging your preschooler's desire for adventure is incredibly easy, as long as you remember how new and exciting almost everything will be for her. Simply planning to include your preschooler in any basic excursions around town will solve a lot of problems in this regard. Taking her past a construction site, letting her watch the people in the bank as they go about their business, visiting the train station, and other such things will be as exciting to your preschooler as going to the zoo or an amusement park. Also, to the extent that it is appropriate, join in and enhance the adventures that your preschooler creates for herself. For example, if she is playing "pirate," she probably will enjoy having you as a member of her crew. You might suggest using your bed as a boat and supply other suitable props as the story unfolds.

When my preschooler exaggerates a great deal or even lies on occasion, how should I respond?

Keep in mind that exaggerations and lies are part of the behavioral repertoire of a normal preschooler, so try not to worry too much about this, and avoid making a big deal out of it. In fact, if what is involved is largely unimportant, the best thing to do is to just let it pass. In situations where you feel that your preschooler's statements are distinctly inappropriate, it is a good idea to talk to her about the need to be accurate and to tell the truth. Let her know that you disapprove of her behavior in such instances, but understand her natural inclinations in this regard and refrain from punishing her severely. By supplying a good role model for her, praising her when she is accurate and truthful, and being patient, you will see the bulk of this problem resolved within a few months.

If you are employed outside the home, a great way to feed your preschooler's desire for adventure is to show him your workplace and let him see some of the things you do when you "go to work."

How should I react when my preschooler starts getting really silly? It can be terribly annoying at times.

As is the case with most annoying behaviors, the easiest way to eliminate it is to simply ignore it. If your preschooler gets the clear sense that you are not reacting either positively or negatively and, in fact, aren't even noticing what she's doing, she probably will diminish her efforts fairly quickly. However, you might try to keep in mind that on most occasions, your preschooler is not attempting to annoy you—she really gets a lot of pleasure out of silly things at this point. Therefore, you might consider not only accepting her silliness, but joining in as well. You may be surprised by how easily you can be silly as well. This is likely to bring an incredible amount of enjoyment to your preschooler—and possibly provide you with a lot more fun than you imagined as well.

Sometimes my preschooler gets very angry and calls me awful names. Should I allow her to do this?

It helps to remember that this sort of behavior is typical of preschoolers. Therefore, your best bet probably is to simply ignore it and not give her the satisfaction she is seeking. Overreacting and giving her a lot of negative attention will only give her the notion that name-calling is a powerful tool. Stay calm, see if you can discover the real root of her anger, and help her deal with it in an appropriate manner. By the way, it also helps to remember that your preschooler loves being silly at this point. If she angrily calls you a "stupid potato head," you might try turning it around, and in a pleasant and joking fashion call her "a crazy zucchini head." Her delight in your comeback may overwhelm her momentary ire, and instead of an unpleasant confrontation, the situation may turn into a fun interaction.

Lately, it seems as if I'm having constant confrontations with my preschooler. Am I doing something wrong?

Constant confrontations probably stem from two basic sources. The first is lack of awareness concerning what you can realistically expect from your preschooler. Perhaps it is the case that she is not doing what you want her to do because she is either incapable of doing so or simply not inclined at this point. By adjusting your expectations to her true ability levels, and by working with the natural interests and preferences of preschoolers, you may be able to avoid many confrontations. The second is a tendency that many parents have to let their preschooler know when she's doing something wrong, but not necessarily inform her when she's doing something right. If the only attention that your preschooler can count on getting from you is negative attention, then she is more likely to exhibit behavior that will produce it.

PRACTICE WHAT YOU PREACH

Teaching your preschooler proper safety procedures will be a lot easier and more effective if you remember to practice what you preach. Keep in mind that during this period, your preschooler will be trying to "be like you" as much as she can, and you will be able to use her imitative inclinations to great advantage. For example, if you always buckle your seat belt before putting the car in motion, if you always put on a helmet before picking up a baseball bat, if you always cross the street at the corner, etc., your verbal instructions to your preschooler will be powerfully reinforced. Of course, there will be a number of instances where it will be necessary for you to do something that your preschooler is prohibited from doing—lighting the barbecue grill, for example. However, if you routinely divide the world into things that adults are allowed to do and other things that children are required to do, you will give your preschooler the impression that ignoring proper safety procedures is a privilege that comes with age. As a result, you may find yourself having to constantly remind her to heed your instructions; and when you are not around, you can expect that she will attempt to "act like a grown-up" more often than she will follow your previous warnings. On the other hand, by setting good examples for her, you can help ensure that when she tries to "be like you," she'll be acting safely.

If you can remember to give her praise and encouragement when she's being good, you may see many of these confrontations disappear.

When my preschooler directly disobeys me or otherwise engages in intolerable behavior, what's the most effective way to discipline her at this point?

In general, particularly at the beginning of this period, temporary isolation usually works very well. A good idea is to use a special "time out" chair and require your preschooler to sit in it for a specific length of time—a minute for each year of age is a suitable rule of thumb. It helps to use a mechanical kitchen timer so she can focus on her "sentence" rather than become overly anxious. As your preschooler gets older, you also might try to use the suspension of privileges or something else that is directly tied to her misbehavior. You should also make an effort to explain to her why what she did was wrong. Remember, "discipline" should be more "education" than "punishment," so what you do should be immediate and should provide your preschooler with a clear sense of logical consequences. For example, if she leaves her toys on the stairs, you might prohibit her from playing with those items for a while; or, if she hits a playmate, you might restrict her to solitary play for a time.

When I'm on the phone, my preschooler sometimes gets impatient for my attention and does everything she can to interrupt. How should I handle this situation?

First, it helps to understand where your preschooler is coming from and to avoid as many unnecessary confrontations as possible. If your preschooler is counting on your attention during a particular part of the day, waiting a long time for you to finish a phone call can be very hard for her. Expecting her to be infinitely patient in such situations is unrealistic. Therefore, to the extent that it is appropriate, try to schedule your more lengthy phone calls during her nap period or later in the evening. If a long call is necessary, and your preschooler refuses to cease interrupting, then employing a disciplinary procedure, such as a stint in a "time out" chair, may be appropriate. In any event, try not to "give in" to her demands for attention, as that will serve to encourage her interruptive activities. And don't forget to praise your preschooler at times when you talk on the phone and she doesn't interrupt. By the

way, keeping a special toy or game close to the phone is a good idea. You may be able to avoid a confrontation simply by providing her with an alternate activity that will keep her busy until you're done.

How should I respond when my preschooler starts asking me things like where babies come from and why her body is different from her brother's?

The "how" part is easy—be unembarrassed, straightforward, and truthful. The "what" is a little more complicated. What you tell your preschooler about sex and related issues should be based on what she is capable of understanding and what she is willing to accept. The best place to start is with your preschooler's questions—let them be your guide. Explain things simply, clearly, and specifically, and monitor your preschooler's reactions to see if what you're saying is getting through and making sense to her. By the way, don't be surprised if she doesn't accept your explanations in total at this point. Some preschoolers simply are not ready to relate to various concepts that are involved, and they may prefer to stick with their own notions—such as the idea that babies are purchased at the supermarket—instead. If this is the case with your preschooler, don't push it, and try again when she asks at a future date.

If your preschooler wants to know where babies come from, keep your answers simple—and let her questions be your guide.

How should I respond when I catch my preschooler playing "doctor"?

Showing curiosity about bodies and their parts is totally normal behavior for a preschooler. To a child, one part of the body is very much the same as another part until they receive adult implications about them. If you catch your child playing "doctor," it's best not to overreact; you don't want your child to feel that she is "good" or "bad" for being curious about these things. Redirect her activities and discuss "polite" or "acceptable" behavior, but stay away from good and bad. Discuss private parts with her using terms she can understand, and explain how she should not allow others to touch her there, and that if anyone does, she should tell you immediately. Try to be upbeat and matter-of-fact in your explanations, using her questions as a guide. You want to encourage her to feel good about her body, but you also want her to learn about modesty, privacy, and acceptable behavior.

When we go to the local pool, I take my four-and-a-half-year-old son into the ladies' locker room to shower with me. Is it still okay to allow a child of this age to bathe with the opposite-sex parent?

The answers to questions regarding modesty and nudity depend largely upon your philosophy and comfort zone rather than on some absolute right or wrong. At four and a half years of age, your son is aware of his male identity. He's still establishing what that means and will continue to do so for a decade or two. In our society, some boys of this age would resent being taken into the ladies' locker room, and others would not care at all. You have to make the choice between taking him in with you or sending him alone to the men's locker room; at this age, it's not recommended that he go into the men's locker room by himself. So if your son feels uncomfortable or embarrassed when you take him into the ladies' locker room, you'll have to make another arrangement, such as inviting your husband or an older male sibling or friend to come along on your outings to the pool. If your son doesn't mind going into the ladies' locker room with you, you can continue to take him, unless his presence makes the other women uncomfortable; after all, you want to teach your son about considerate and polite behavior as well. The bathing together, itself, is also a matter of comfort zones and philosophy, even if it's done in the privacy of your own home. When it becomes uncomfortable for either one of you, put an end to the practice.

I'm concerned about the amount of time my preschooler spends rubbing herself. Should I put a stop to it?

It's normal to rub wherever and whenever it feels good. Part of your job as a parent, however, is to teach your child what is acceptable behavior in our society and what isn't. You probably only need to be concerned about this "rubbing" if it seems to be the only thing that comforts her. If she rubs herself continually instead of finding other satisfactory and entertaining activities, then it's too much. Have a "what is polite behavior" conversation. Plan to help divert her attention and focus to more interesting things when she begins rubbing. Try not to pay too much attention to this activity, however, or she may use it to command your attention whenever she wants. Usually, peer pressure takes care of this behavior at preschool. You'll want to find out if she is rubbing at school and discuss this with her teachers. Enlist their cooperation in helping to divert her attention to other things. If the "rubbing" doesn't seem to be diminishing, discuss it with your pediatrician and have your preschooler examined to make sure there is no physical cause for the activity.

My preschooler bites her nails. Should I put bitter-tasting stuff on them to get her to stop?

Putting bitter stuff on her nails to curtail nail biting is not likely to work. You can talk to your child and tell her why she shouldn't bite her nails, such as that "it can spread germs" or "it can hurt the fingers"; but this usually doesn't work either. Like thumb sucking, nail biting may simply be a comfort habit for her—something she does when she feels stressed. And, as with thumb sucking, it's better to simply ignore it. You can help her to quit the habit on her own by helping her keep her nails smooth and filed. With girls, putting nail polish on the nails can help her feel grown up and may discourage her from biting her nails. Be sure to praise her and tell her how nice her nails look when she doesn't bite them. If she's biting the nails to the point of causing bleeding, consult your pediatrician.

I don't want my preschooler to become addicted to television. Is this a potential problem at this point?

Now that their language, intellectual, and memory skills have grown to the point where they can recognize characters and follow plots, preschoolers do become very interested in television programs as well as in stories that are read to them. However, television is only one of many activities that fascinate preschoolers, so it is rare that they become engrossed to the point of largely excluding everything else—unless, of course, they have few other opportunities and options available. The real danger is that watching television provides an opportunity for relatively quiet, passive entertainment. While preschoolers certainly enjoy this sort of thing from time to time, their parents often find it irresistibly appealing and really appreciate the break it provides them. Consequently, the television tends to be used more and more to keep the preschoolers occupied, and the parents fail to keep pace in providing and encouraging other types of activities. In other words, as long as you do not become addicted to your preschooler watching television and as long as you provide and encourage other entertainment options as well, there is no reason to believe that she will want to do it any more or less than anything else she enjoys doing. For advice on teaching your child good television viewing habits, see the following question.

What can I do to help encourage good television viewing habits for the future?

Television, like many other aspects of your child's environment, has the potential to be either a positive or negative force in your child's development. Television programs geared to the interests and mental capacities of your child can be both entertaining and educational. Programs such as *Sesame Street* and *Mister Rogers' Neighborhood* (both on PBS) can introduce your child to new places, people, and animals and can even help her learn to count and spell. On the other hand, much of what is shown on television is geared to an adult audience and can be confusing, inappropriate, and even detrimental to your child. For instance, many studies suggest that watching violence on television can contribute to violent or aggressive behavior in children. In addition, excessive television viewing—regardless of the content—can contribute substantially to obesity in children (and probably in adults as well) because time spent in front of the tube is not spent on more strenuous physical activity. So while television is inherently neither good nor bad, the effect it has on your child

One of the best ways to help ensure that television plays a beneficial role in your children's development is to choose and watch programs with them. Viewing shows together allows you to explain confusing scenes and screen out inappropriate material.

depends, to a great extent, on how it is used. And this is where you, as a parent, can play a major role. Indeed, the American Academy of Pediatrics issued a policy statement on "Children, Adolescents, and Television" in 1990 that emphasizes the need for parents to teach good television viewing habits to their children very early in life. Your involvement can help turn television into a beneficial tool rather than a hindrance. The following steps can help you take an active part in determining what role television plays in your child's development.

1. Provide alternatives to television viewing. Encourage your child to engage in physical activities instead of watching television. For quiet play, provide her with puzzles, books, and arts-and-crafts supplies. Whenever possible, include her in your daily chores and errands.
2. Limit the amount of time spent watching television. The American Academy of Pediatrics recommends that you limit your child's viewing time to one to two hours daily.
3. Plan in advance the programs to watch. Try sitting down together on Sunday to decide what programs you'll watch for the rest of the week. Don't be afraid to turn off the set if a selected program does not turn out to be appropriate.
4. Watch television together. Plan to watch the selected programs together so that you can answer her questions and explain confusing or disturbing scenes. Expand on what is shown by talking with her, planning "field trips," or providing her with pertinent books or other materials. If she was fascinated by a scene involving the mailman, take her to your local post office or supply her with some envelopes and cancelled stamps to play with.
5. Set a good example. Remember, your child wants to be like you. Your lessons about television are likely to have less impact if she sees you watching for hours on end or if the set is constantly left on as background noise.

My neighbors have their child on a busy schedule of classes and special programs that I can't afford. How can I compensate for my preschooler's lack of learning opportunities?

There's nothing for which you need to compensate. The notion that a busy schedule of classes and programs provides a preschooler with a lot of special learning opportunities is erroneous. There is no evidence whatsoever that children who have these extraordinary experiences gain any lasting advantages. On the contrary, there is a growing body of evidence to suggest that they often suffer severe stress reactions, loss of interest in learning, and other signs of early "burnout." As long

---

DON'T FORGET TO ENJOY YOUR PRESCHOOLER

Raising children inevitably involves a certain number of problems. The responsibilities of parenthood also bring a certain number of pressures to bear on mothers and fathers. Parents can easily be overcome by these problems and pressures. This is especially true during the preschool period, as the physical and mental capacities of their child grow to impressive—and often imposing—levels, and as their child starts taking substantial steps away from the relative security of home toward the challenge—and sometimes uncertainty—of the outside world. Therefore, it is important for you to keep in mind that this is also a period when being a parent can be extremely pleasurable and rewarding. You can't forget to take the time and make the effort to simply enjoy your preschooler. Your preschooler will be looking at many things for the very first time, and if you allow yourself to look at these things through her eyes, they will become just as new and exciting for you. Your preschooler will be exercising her imagination and engaging in a variety of silly behaviors, and if you allow yourself to join in on her activities, you will be able to experience the simple fascination and fun of "being a kid" yourself. It is your responsibility to be your preschooler's guardian, teacher, and disciplinarian, but it also is your privilege to be her cohort, playmate, and friend.

as your preschooler is happy, busy, and getting lots of love and attention from you at home, you can be assured that she probably is making the most of her potential. Although your neighbor's child may display some apparently impressive behaviors, you can be confident that your preschooler is getting the kind of sensible, solid educational foundation that will enable her to equal and probably surpass the other child's performance in the long run.

Is there an especially effective way to informally teach my preschooler?

As always, it is a good idea to serve as a "consultant" rather than as an "instructor" most of the time. Motivation on the part of the pupil is a key ingredient of success, so make sure that whatever "lessons" you are providing serve to expand and elaborate upon what your preschooler is intensely interested in at the moment. Following her lead—by responding to her questions and monitoring her reactions—will be far more pleasant and productive than pursuing some formal agenda. Also, be careful not to push your preschooler past her abilities. For instance, even if she shows a strong interest in tying her own shoelaces, she simply may not be able to get the hang of it easily. Waiting and then trying again a few weeks later is likely to result in success, whereas drilling her on the procedure over and over probably will not enable her to learn it any faster and may very well be counterproductive.

Your preschooler doesn't need a lot of classes and programs as long as he is happy and busy at home, gets lots of love and attention from you, and has a chance to spend time with other children and adults from time to time.

Now that she's talking all the time, is it still important that I make an effort to talk a lot to my preschooler?

It certainly is. First of all, language learning advances at a significant rate during this period, and your preschooler requires good grammatical models and constant vocabulary input. In addition, having conversations with you will be among your preschooler's favorite activities, and it would be a shame to deprive her of one of her most reliable sources of enjoyment. Finally, talking to your preschooler inevitably will involve listening to her as well, and this gives you an excellent chance to get a clear picture of what's going on in her mind. In dealing with your preschooler on a daily basis and in helping her develop to the full extent of her potential, it is important that you have the best information available about her interests, abilities, and preferences—and there is no better source of such information than your preschooler herself.

Sometimes my preschooler asks me a question and I don't know the answer. Should I make something up?

Certainly not. There is nothing wrong with letting your preschooler know that you are human and don't know everything. In addition, not being honest sets a poor model for your preschooler, and any untruths you tell may very well come back to haunt you later on. What you can do, if possible and appropriate, is to invite your preschooler to join you in an attempt to find an answer to her question. Consulting various reference books in your home or, better yet, taking a trip to the local library will be an adventure that can be extremely enjoyable as well as educational for your preschooler. By the way, it helps to keep in mind that your preschooler has a lot of questions about a lot of things, and a particular stumper may be more important to you than it is to her. So, later on, when you've finally discovered the answer, don't be surprised if your preschooler has already forgotten about her question and moved on to other interests.

Occasionally, my preschooler refuses to even try a new task that I'm confident she can do. How can I motivate her?

There is no motivator for preschoolers like success. If your preschooler balks at a particular task, perhaps the best thing to do is to see if you can break it down into smaller, simpler components; then, give her an opportunity to succeed step-by-step until she has mastered the entire process. You also might try "getting her into the mood" by having her perform other tasks that she enjoys doing and letting her soak up your praise for her accomplishments. It is possible that the task in question may be invoking some fear in your preschooler that is not obvious. Therefore, if she persistently refuses to make an attempt, it might be a good idea to talk to her about it and gently probe for an underlying reason for her distress. In any event, don't push. Waiting patiently and then trying again at a later date may be all that is required.

I'd like my preschooler to start reading, writing, and doing arithmetic as soon as possible. How can I stimulate her to do these things?

There is no method that has been proven to be effective in "stimulating" children to learn these things before they are ready. The best thing that you can do is expose your pre-

You can't get him to start reading or doing arithmetic before he's ready, but you can be sure that he has easy access to books, crayons, pencils, and other materials.

schooler to books, pencils, and other materials in a pleasant, easy-going atmosphere, and patiently wait for her own motivation to kick in. Too many parents misguidedly push too hard in these directions, often with disastrous results. Their efforts usually are completely futile at best, and very counterproductive at worst. What's more, even in cases where they seem to manage some success, the results simply are not worth the risks. Early ability in these areas does not correlate in any way with later performance during the elementary years. Even children who eventually are identified as "gifted" typically did not learn these skills during this period.

My school district doesn't offer free nursery school. Is this an essential experience for my preschooler?

Nursery school is one of those "nice but certainly not essential" elements of the preschool period. A good nursery school can provide your preschooler with an assortment of play materials and a ready supply of playmates. Consequently, if you can find one that is convenient and affordable, you probably can count on your preschooler having a good time and getting many good learning opportunities. On the other hand, there is no reason to believe that she won't be able to get an equal amount of enjoyment and education in your home and neighborhood without this kind of formal experience. Sometimes children who attend nursery school learn some special routines—such as walking single file, raising hands, etc. that definitely come in handy later on in school; but children who are not exposed to these routines beforehand ordinarily have little trouble picking them up later on. If your child does not have access to other children of her age in the neighborhood, then enrolling her in nursery school or some form of play group can help provide her with experiences that may make the transition to kindergarten a bit easier. By the way, there is no "type" of nursery school that has proven advantages over any other, so a safe, friendly environment staffed by warm, caring, upbeat people should be the first and foremost thing to look for if you decide to enroll your preschooler.

How will I know when my preschooler is really ready to begin kindergarten?

You will not know your preschooler is ready if your in-laws or someone else says she's ready. You will not know if she's ready

MAKING THE GUILT GO AWAY

Suffering guilt is as inevitable a part of parenting as changing diapers and kissing boo-boos. No matter how proficient you are at child rearing, there will be times when you convince yourself that you have done something wrong, you have not done something you should have done, you are doing too much, or not doing enough. A certain amount of guilt can be considered healthy, in that it helps prod you to become the best parent you can be. However, if it becomes chronic, the condition can be quite uncomfortable and counterproductive. If you find yourself heading over the edge in this regard, it probably would help to join a parent support group. Undoubtedly, you will learn that no one does a perfect job of parenting. There are no guaranteed answers for every situation, and we all make mistakes. The important thing is to learn from them and simply try to do better next time around. Furthermore, as time goes by, you will learn that children are a lot less fragile and a lot more forgiving than we tend to give them credit for. Many of the horrible errors for which you are blaming yourself probably won't even be noticed by your child. Even if your child does notice, it is likely that you will go on punishing yourself for months after she has forgotten completely about them. When you do make a mistake in behavior or response, apologize to your child. Remember, it's okay to kick yourself once in a while, but make sure the kick moves you forward and doesn't leave you languishing in the past.

if your neighbor's child of the same age is ready. And, you will not know if she's ready by looking at the calendar. The time for a child to start kindergarten is when she is "behaviorally" ready to do so. Behavioral age does not always correlate with chronological age, and preschoolers vary widely in this regard. Many school districts offer prekindergarten screening services to help parents determine how easily their child will adjust to a kindergarten setting. If your district does not offer such services, and even if they do, it might be wise to visit a kindergarten class, observe what goes on, and then assess how well the situation fits with your child's current level of interests and abilities. If you are unsure, it is better to err on the side of starting too late rather than starting too early. Starting her in kindergarten before she is ready may result in consistent failure and loss of self-esteem, and she may end up having problems in school from that point on.

I've been told to buy my preschooler a pet so she can learn responsibility. Is this a good idea?

This may not be a bad idea, as long as you don't expect your preschooler to take on more responsibility than she actually is able to handle at this point. The care and feeding of a dog, for example, involves many things for which a preschooler may very well not be ready. So unless you are willing to assume the bulk of the responsibilities, obtaining a pet of this sort will only lead to unpleasantness and resentment. If you want your preschooler to have primary responsibility for the pet, perhaps it would be better to start with a fish, frog, or some other terrarium creature that does not require a lot of complicated attention. You might even consider beginning your preschooler's lessons in responsibility with something as simple as a plant. Of course, you can buy your preschooler a pet without assuming that she will take immediate and primary responsibility for caring for it. Your preschooler probably will derive a lot of pleasure and many learning opportunities from a dog or cat, and acquiring a sense of the responsibilities involved can come gradually.

My preschooler became fascinated with his friend's toy-soldier set, but I prefer that he doesn't play with war toys. Is there an appropriate alternative?

It is very likely that your preschooler has become "hooked" on the fun of manipulating the little figures and imagining all

If you want her to see what it's like to be responsible for taking care of a pet, you might be wise to start out with a fish or other terrarium creature.

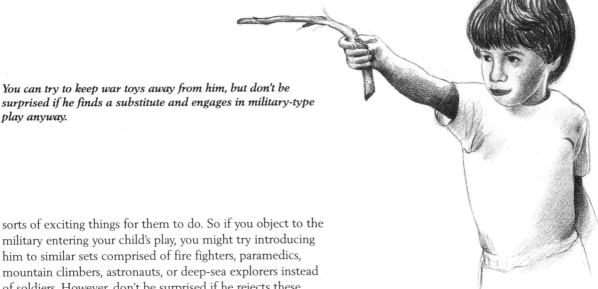

You can try to keep war toys away from him, but don't be surprised if he finds a substitute and engages in military-type play anyway.

sorts of exciting things for them to do. So if you object to the military entering your child's play, you might try introducing him to similar sets comprised of fire fighters, paramedics, mountain climbers, astronauts, or deep-sea explorers instead of soldiers. However, don't be surprised if he rejects these alternatives or even uses the alternative figures as substitute soldiers. Preschoolers are very prone to engage in dramatic and sometimes violent fantasies, and as a result, war toys and games have powerful appeal. You can encourage your preschooler to channel his energies elsewhere, but be careful not to give him the impression that you disapprove of his using his imagination in general by criticizing him harshly for engaging in militaristic activities.

Is there any way I can at least minimize the fighting and rivalry between my preschooler and her siblings?

Keep in mind that the primary source of the rivalry is competition for your attention. Therefore, you would be wise to make every attempt to give each child a significant amount of special, individual attention every day. This can be a walk around the block, a story session, a cookie-baking lesson, whatever. Also, there will be many times when your children will be getting along, playing together nicely, and serving as excellent companions for each other; it is critical that you don't forget to give them a lot of positive attention at such times. Finally, since some of their confrontations will concern issues of material possessions, to the extent possible, see to it that each child is provided with a sufficient supply of her own individual items. Forcing siblings to share or take turns is likely to be futile, causing more resentment and rivalry than settling anything.

It looks like we won't be able to avoid getting a divorce. How can we make this as easy as possible for our preschooler?

Divorce is almost always painful and confusing for preschoolers to a certain extent, but most specialists on the subject agree that staying together strictly for the sake of the children usually does more harm than good in the long run. On the other hand, they also agree that staying civil for the sake of the children is essential. When a mother and father act out their anger, resentment, and other such emotions through attempts to control the children, major problems are practically inevitable. A child who becomes trapped in a parental tug-of-war or is forced or even encouraged to "choose" one parent over the other suffers immensely. Therefore, regardless of the relationship between you and your spouse, it is a good idea to make every effort to enable your preschooler to maintain a strong, positive relationship with both of you. Reassure her that what is happening is not her fault in any way, and that even though one or the other parent may be leaving, this does not mean that she will be losing a mother or father. Your preschooler is likely to be concerned about practical matters, so be prepared to answer any and all questions regarding where she will live, when she will be able to see the absent parent, etc. And most important of all, see to it that she understands that just because her parents no longer love each other, it doesn't mean that they love her any less.

My preschooler needs minor surgery. How do I prepare her for an overnight stay in the hospital?

No matter what you do, a hospital stay may still be upsetting for your preschooler to a certain extent—although you probably will have a tougher time handling the situation than she will. As time allows, you can prepare your preschooler by explaining as much about the procedure as possible and answering any and all questions she has to the best of your ability. You might consider providing her with a pretend doctor's kit so she can go through some simple routines with her stuffed animals and dolls. Reading special story books on the subject may help as well. Some hospitals even have educational "tours" for children prior to a planned hospital stay. Once your preschooler is admitted to the hospital, see to it that she has several permitted items from home to serve as a bridge—a favorite blanket, coloring book, toy, etc. Spend as much time as you can with her, and ask if you can be the adult who handles nonmedical routines such as feeding and bathing. And, if possible, give your preschooler a chance to explore and become familiar with her temporary surroundings and the people with whom she will come in contact so that she will not feel so much like a stranger in a strange land.

To help prepare her for a planned stay in the hospital, try providing her with a pretend doctor's kit so she can play "hospital" with her dolls.

My preschooler is adopted. When and how should I tell her about this?

There is no set time or manner for handling this situation. Usually, it is best to wait until a preschooler shows some interest in the subject. However, if you are concerned about her suffering confusion or embarrassment as a result of someone else informing her inappropriately, you might consider introducing the subject with a special story book. Explain the circumstances of her adoption to your preschooler in an honest, straightforward fashion, using her questions to guide you in adjusting your explanation to her level of understanding. The key things to convey are how much you wanted her, how much you have loved her from the day of the adoption, and how you will continue to love her always. Avoid using phrases like "even though you are adopted" or anything else that implies that there is something inherently second-class about an adoptive relationship, even if that obviously is not your intention. And be prepared for your preschooler to come back with another round of more sophisticated questions at a later date.

I'm a single, working mother and am finding it hard to have enough energy left for my child at the end of the day. How can I spend quality time with my preschooler with this schedule?

It's very difficult to work all day and still have enough energy left to spend with an active preschooler. Keep in mind, however, that spending quality time with your child in the evening doesn't have to mean hours of chasing her around the house, playing ball, and doing other physical activities. You can reserve those types of activities for weekends or for days when you're not quite so tired. Spending quality time with your child at the end of the day can simply mean sharing some time with her alone, without other people and, hopefully, without the phone or door bell ringing. It can be quiet time when you talk to her about how her day was, what she did, how she feels, etc. or read her a bedtime story and help her get ready for bed. Your preschooler is old enough to understand that parents have to do a lot of things. She's more likely to be accepting of the situation, however, if she can really count on special time with you alone. You can even allow your child to choose some outing or treat once a week or on the weekend. As long as you let her know that you consider her special and always save some time for her alone, you'll be giving her quality time.

SELECTING TOYS AND EQUIPMENT

Isn't my preschooler old enough at this point to select his own playthings?

Your preschooler certainly is now old enough to have distinct preferences regarding playthings and to communicate those preferences to you clearly and effectively. Unlike an infant or toddler, he is likely to see something at a friend's house or on television and say "I want one of those." He is even likely to be more than willing to help prepare a list for his birthday or for holidays. However, his powers of perception and communication are still far greater than his capacities for sound judgment and restraint. He may know what he wants, but he may not always know what is best for him or what fits into the family finances. Therefore, while choosing toys for your child is no longer a task you must do by yourself, it also is not yet a task that your preschooler can be trusted to do by himself. For the next few years, this will be a "collaborative" effort involving your child making requests and you exercising a fair measure of guidance and control.

Is a large outdoor gym set a good investment for my preschooler at this point?

This depends upon the state of your family finances. An item of this sort surely would be appropriate and appealing at this point, but it certainly should not be considered a necessity—especially if your preschooler has access to good equipment at the local park or at his nursery school. If you do decide to invest in an outdoor gym set, make sure it is safe and sturdy. If possible, obtain one that offers a variety of activities—swinging, ladder climbing, tunnel crawling, and see-sawing. Durability also is a consideration, as you will want a relatively expensive item such as this to last several years. The models made of high-quality wood are generally more costly than their metal counterparts, but they don't rust and generally tend to hold up better over the long haul.

Won't my preschooler now be bored with a simple sandbox or wading pool?

Probably not. Although these pieces of equipment will remain basically the same, your preschooler's interest and abilities will

If you decide to purchase an outdoor gym set for your preschooler, look for one that is safe, sturdy, and durable and that offers a variety of activities.

change dramatically over the course of this period. Most noticeably, his play will now start to include peers to a great extent, and this will add a whole new dimension to sand and water activities. Also, as his imagination becomes more active, he probably will be able to keep himself entertained for long periods of time taking jungle-river journeys, building elaborate castles, etc. Consequently, it is not likely that you will have to replace these items at this point. You may, however, want to consider adding new accessories on occasion to help facilitate your preschooler's growing inclination to play with his friends and his fantasies.

What can I do to keep my preschooler entertained during long trips in the car?

There are a number of basic items that are especially suitable for these circumstances. Small snap-together blocks are particularly appropriate for car trips in that they allow your preschooler to build rather elaborate structures yet they will hold their place and shape going over bumps and around turns. Crayons and paper will provide long periods of enjoyment. You might want to consider a coloring book as well, in case your preschooler's fatigue begins to interfere with his free-form creativity after a while. Many coloring books come with a section containing simple connect-the-dots puzzles, which your preschooler probably will find quite appealing, especially toward the end of this period. Keep in mind, however, that toys are likely to be your preschooler's secondary source of entertainment. Now that his mental and communication capacities are so advanced, his primary interest probably will be in talking to you about the trip itself and/or in playing games like "find an out-of-state license plate" or "count the yellow cars."

My preschooler is a real little athlete, and I don't think he'll be satisfied with sponge and wiffle bats and balls for long. When can I let him use real sports equipment?

Keep in mind that the greatest motivator for your preschooler will be success. Therefore, it is important that you keep his play equipment well matched not only to his interests, but to his abilities as well. If your preschooler exhibits a desire to move beyond sponge and wiffle bats and balls, for example, the next step does not have to be "the real thing" necessarily. If you provide him with a regulation bat and ball, it is very

possible that he will experience a fair amount of frustration, thereby placing his original enthusiasm in jeopardy. Fortunately, when it comes to sports equipment, there are many intermediate alternatives available. Therefore, it might be a good idea to move your preschooler up gradually from "pretend" to "junior" and eventually to "real" so that his enthusiasm has a good chance to grow with his abilities. As soon as you feel your preschooler is ready to handle them, there's no harm in introducing him to various pieces of real sports equipment—as long as you introduce him to the rules of safety that go along with them beforehand. For instance, before you allow your preschooler to use a real bat, see to it that he has learned to make sure no one is standing nearby when he swings it. If you allow him to use a hard ball, see to it that he has learned to wear a batting helmet whenever he stands at the plate. By the way, with any play involving balls, it is important to constantly remind your preschooler not to chase a ball into the street or attempt to recover it from a hazardous area. Let him know that playing "real" sports has its rewards, but it also comes with responsibilities.

Philosophically, I don't object to my preschooler playing with a toy gun, but I've heard that they present a lot of safety problems. Is this true?

It certainly is if the toy gun shoots a projectile of any sort. Many such items fire rubber-tipped darts, which can be extremely dangerous if the tips fall off or are pulled off. Even with the tip secured, these darts can cause serious damage if aimed at certain parts of the body, such as the eyes. The same is true for guns that shoot seemingly safe objects such as table-tennis balls. In general, it is probably not a good idea to provide your preschooler with a gun that shoots anything, except, perhaps, water. Maybe late in this period you might consider introducing some more complex items, but be sure to teach your preschooler that these are special toys with special rules, and that he is never to aim them at anything other than inanimate targets.

My preschooler says he loves the elaborate battery-operated toys he sees in the store. Is the play value of these items worth the price?

Probably not. Although such items will thoroughly entrance your preschooler for a short period of time, it is doubtful that

Providing her with a variety of nontoxic art supplies—such as watercolor paints, brushes, clay, crayons, paper, and glue—can keep her entertained and allow her to express her creativity.

they will be able to sustain his interest for very long. Many parents have given in to the impassioned pleas of their preschooler to purchase one of these expensive items, only to watch it collect dust after it is brought home. Keep in mind that the play value of any toy increases with the number of things that your preschooler can do with it, not with the number of things it does all by itself. A battery-operated robot, for example, may do a lot of impressive things, but once it has run through its repertoire, that's it. On the other hand, something as simple as a small rubber ball can be a baseball, a basketball, and a bowling ball as well as a cannon ball and a wrecking ball. What's more, in combination with other simple items, that small rubber ball can be someone's head, a hood ornament for a car, a Christmas-tree ornament, and a limitless number of other things.

My preschooler is very creative. What can I give him to bring out his artistic talent?

There is an almost limitless number of "art" supplies appropriate for preschoolers, and your preschooler's use of these materials is likely to be limitless as well. Watercolor paints, finger paints, crayons or markers, simple and safe scissors, paper, nontoxic glue, and modeling clay or play dough all will be suitable and appealing to a certain extent. It will be up to you to determine where your preschooler's particular preferences lie in this regard. For example, some preschoolers are very visual in their creative activities, and they appreciate a wide variety of paints and crayons. Others are very tactile, and they appreciate greater variety in the color and texture of their clay. Keep in mind that your preschooler's likes and dislikes may not remain constant, so as you feed into one avenue of expression, don't forget to make other avenues available as well from time to time.

My preschooler plays with a wide variety of materials, especially arts-and-crafts supplies. Do I still have to be concerned about him putting everything into his mouth?

During this period, your preschooler will pretty much stop using his mouth as an exploratory organ, and he will become increasingly less likely to put anything and everything into his

MONEY-SAVING TIPS

Buying toys for preschoolers, although easier than doing so for infants and toddlers, is still a hit-or-miss proposition to a certain extent. Even with your preschooler communicating his preferences and you providing sound judgment and appropriate guidance, it is very possible that a given item simply will not turn out to be the long-term success that everyone expected it to be. Of course, your percentage of "hits" will be getting better as your child gets older. Unfortunately, the cost of your "misses" will be increasing as well. Toy libraries, therefore, are still a good resource, but many are not willing to handle the considerably more expensive and complex items that preschoolers desire and require. As an alternative, you might consider becoming a regular visitor—and perhaps vendor—at garage sales, flea markets, etc. Because the interests and abilities of preschoolers are so varied, one child's "too boring" or "too frustrating" toy may be another child's "favorite" plaything. Rather than having a lot of families possessing a lot of toys that are getting very little or no play time, these outlets allow the "misses" to be put back into circulation. There, they may very well become "hits" that cost relatively little money and enable the original purchaser to recoup at least some of the original investment. If you do take this strongly recommended route, just remember to be extra careful about checking for safety considerations. Federal regulations do not apply to resales. If an item has been repaired or repainted, there is no guarantee that it will be as durable or that the paint used was nontoxic, so investigate and choose wisely.

mouth. However, from time to time, he may absent-mindedly suck on the end of a paintbrush or a part of some other toy. In addition, like a lot of preschoolers, he may be curious about certain foodlike substances, especially crayons and paste, and will want "to see what they taste like." Consequently, while his playthings no longer represent the choking hazard they did during infancy and toddlerhood, your preschooler still may be at risk when it comes to ingesting poisonous substances. Therefore, make sure whatever materials he is using are nontoxic, just in case they end up in his mouth.

After seeing a professional puppet show, my preschooler asked me to buy him puppets. Is it possible to make suitable ones instead?

It certainly is. Even by the end of this period, sophisticated puppets like marionettes will be beyond the abilities of your preschooler. Simple hand puppets, however, will be appropriate and greatly appreciated. You can start out with something as easy as painting a face on an old mitten. You then might move on to an old glove with different faces painted on the tip of each finger. Eventually, you may consider taking a small paper bag, filling it with rags or newspaper, painting a face on it, and then fastening it to an ice-cream stick or small dowel rod. Armed with a few such items, and having a large cardboard carton or even just a table with a sheet over it for a drape, your preschooler will have a sufficient cast and an adequate theater for his own puppet-show productions.

Will these new "pop-up" books be more appealing to my preschooler than the standard picture and story books?

They probably will have a certain amount of appeal as novelties, but in the long run, it is doubtful that your preschooler will get a significant degree of additional enjoyment from these items. His imagination is pretty powerful at this point, so seeing something presented in three dimensions certainly isn't necessary and may actually be a distraction on occasion. It also should be noted that this feature generally adds to the cost of a book and usually decreases the book's durability, resulting in a substantial decrease in investment value. Therefore, rather than relying on a gimmick to capture your preschooler's attention, it is likely to be considerably more sensible to simply make sure that you choose books on specific subjects that hold a particular fascination for him.

Are there any toys I can provide for my preschooler to encourage his interest in how machines work?

Fortunately, there are some toys that are very appropriate for this purpose, and they are extremely appealing to most preschoolers. Generically, they are referred to as "marble run" or "mousetrap" toys. They consist of interlocking poles and ramps that can be put together to form an elaborate track for rolling marbles. The more sophisticated versions include levers, wheels, and other such devices as well. It may not be until the end of this period that your preschooler will be able to assemble more than the simplest version. However, once he has mastered this sort of device, he is likely to get many hours of enjoyment out of constructing a custom-made "machine" and watching how it "works" as the marble proceeds along its path and triggers the various mechanisms. By the way, marbles can constitute a choking hazard, so make sure your preschooler can be trusted not to put them in his mouth before you leave him alone with a toy of this sort.

You can introduce more complex puzzles as his interests and abilities dictate.

What level of complexity will my preschooler be able to handle with regard to puzzles?

Throughout this period, preschoolers vary a great deal with regard to their desire to play with puzzles, their ability to concentrate on this type of task, and their tolerance for frustration. In other words, there are no "typical" patterns for puzzle play, so it will be necessary for you to observe your preschooler carefully and determine precisely what his needs and desires are. It is a good idea to start off this period with puzzles that contain only about five pieces. Once your preschooler has successfully mastered that level, you can try introducing more complex puzzles gradually as his interests dictate. You probably should avoid purchasing more than one or two puzzles of similar complexity, however; your preschooler won't mind doing the same puzzle over and over again, and his abilities in this area may advance rapidly. When he is ready for a new one, it probably should contain at least two or three pieces more than the previous puzzle.

There are a variety of toys available that may appeal to and encourage her interest in how machines work.

Will my preschooler enjoy mechanical creative toys like an Etch-A-Sketch® or a spin-art machine?

As he moves through this period, such toys will become increasingly appropriate and appealing for your preschooler. The important thing to remember is that your preschooler will get the most out of such items only when he is capable of using them without a lot of help from you. It may not be until the middle of this period that he becomes adept at manipulating the knobs of an Etch-A-Sketch® accurately, and it may not be until the very end of the period that he can master a simple spin-art machine all by himself. Prior to these points, your preschooler may get several minutes of entertainment out of watching you use such items, but it will be later on that he really gets hours of enjoyment from being "creative" with them himself.

My preschooler loves to play with blocks. Should I be "upgrading" these materials as he gets older?

When it comes to large blocks, the only "upgrading" that may be necessary will involve adding to the number of pieces available to your preschooler, since his forts, roads, corrals, garages, and the like will probably become larger. Providing him with suitable alternative materials, such as shoe boxes, plastic tubs, wrapped rolls of paper towels or toilet paper, and toilet-paper tubes, also will be a good idea. On the other hand, you may want to consider "upgrading" both the number and the complexity of his small blocks as he attempts to create more realistic structures. When building a house for his dolls or a garage for his cars, for example, your preschooler may now require—or at least desire—a greater variety of shapes to work with. However, it is important to remember that "upgrading" in this regard should involve increasing rather than decreasing your preschooler's opportunities to use his imaginative and creative skills. In other words, adding pieces that enable him to build a chimney is far preferable to adding a single piece that already is a chimney.

My preschooler has a very active imagination. Will I go broke trying to supply adequate materials for his "pretend" activities?

The bulk of the raw materials that your preschooler will use in his pretend activities consist of "experiences" rather than

You can help provide fuel for his role-play activities by involving him in your chores whenever safe and practical.

"things." The depth and detail of his role-play and fantasy games come from what he has been exposed to previously, not from what is presently in front of him. Therefore, you will find that it is very easy and inexpensive to keep up with your preschooler in this regard. By supplying him with one simple red towel, you may very well give him everything he needs to play Superman, bullfighter, Betsy Ross, fashion model, Arab chieftain, and several other roles. With one simple toy truck, he may have everything he needs to take a trip to Grandma's house, build a city, go on a hayride, and partake in any number of fantasies. Of course, as he gets older, your preschooler may desire—and may even require—more "realism" in certain items. Still, you will be surprised at how resourceful he can be and how satisfied he will be using primarily the products of his own mind.

Whenever I do something around the house, my preschooler wants to do it too. Should I let him use "real" things or restrict him to special "play" sets?

Through the course of this period, your preschooler probably will become increasingly disenchanted with "play" sets. There will be times when he will be satisfied with them. However, when his goal is to participate in some activity with you, he will want to feel that he is really doing something. Of course, considerations of both safety and practicality enter into any decision regarding how often you will be able to allow your preschooler to use "real" equipment. However, it is nice to know that it won't take much to satisfy your preschooler at this point. For instance, in setting the table, he probably will be happy to do the napkins while you do the forks, knives, and glassware. In repairing the garage door, he probably will be content to rub a piece of sandpaper back and forth while you do the drilling (be sure he is a safe distance away and cannot reach any dangerous equipment). And, when taking a trip in the car, he probably will be thrilled to hold the map while you do the driving.

As soon as we return from the doctor's office, zoo, or supermarket, my preschooler wants to set up the same thing at home. Will he really be satisfied with just a few pieces of relevant equipment?

He certainly will. Moreover, those pieces of relevant equipment do not necessarily have to come from special sets. For

Encourage him to help with safe chores. If you make a sandwich for him to eat when he goes over to his friend's house, let him wrap it up and put it in his pack.

SEXISM IN TOYLAND

As noted earlier, gender differences in play preferences tend to start showing up during toddlerhood. Now, during the preschool period, they are likely to become rather pronounced. To a certain extent, your reactions to your preschooler's choices will remain a primary factor in this regard. However, at this point, you should be aware that your preschooler will be subject to a number of additional influences. Toy manufacturers often are lax when it comes to depicting both boys and girls on boxes containing certain toys, and their advertising agents sometimes are even more lax about this when it comes to making commercials. Consequently, even though your preschooler may be "turned on" by a particular type of toy, he may be "turned off" to it when he sees only children of the opposite sex playing with it on the box or commercial. Furthermore, while you may be very careful about your own remarks about proper sex roles, your preschooler may receive negative feedback about his toy selections from his peers. His need to "conform to the group" won't be nearly as strong as it will be during adolescence, but "boyness" and "girlness" are among the very few ways in which young children can establish identity easily. Therefore, being "proper" in his choice of playthings, according to the standards set by his playmates, may be quite important to your preschooler. In any event, it probably is wise to avoid making a fuss over the whole thing at this time. In another year or two, your child will have had more experience and will be less hung up on some of the issues involved. You, in turn, will have better success in convincing him to stick with his own choices regardless of what he sees or hears from outside sources.

example, a turkey baster will make a perfectly acceptable hypodermic needle, a laundry basket turned upside down will serve very well as a cage, and an old calculator will be a more than adequate cash register. The only really "special" thing your preschooler may require to a certain extent is you. If you can take a little time to participate in his role-play and fantasy games as a client, animal, customer, colleague, or whatever, and especially if you provide suggestions and elaborations along the way, your preschooler's activities will be that much richer and more enjoyable for him—and probably just as fascinating and fun for you.

Lately, my preschooler has become frustrated with his toy camera and record player, but I'm not ready to let him use mine. How do I manage a compromise?

Fortunately, there now are a number of "starter" cameras and record players on the market. These items are simple to use, safe, durable, and take "real" pictures or play "real" records. Of course, the quality of their performance is nowhere near what you expect from your own equipment, but the price is considerably lower. Since it is the fact that they are "real" that is of primary importance to your preschooler, he probably won't mind the below-par quality of the picture or sound. Keep in mind, however, that these junior versions won't satisfy your preschooler forever, especially if he really gets "hooked" on photography, music, or whatever. Therefore, particularly toward the end of this period, as his interests and abilities warrant, you might consider relaxing some of your strict prohibitions against his using your equipment. Give him a chance to at least "get the feel" of using some more sophisticated items under your supervision.

Is my preschooler still too young for board games?

Board games require that a preschooler have a certain level of both intellectual and social skills, so it may not be until the middle or end of this period that your preschooler is really ready. Keep in mind that he not only will need the capacity to master the rules and moves involved, he also will need the capacity to wait his turn and accept losing as well as winning. The ability to lose graciously may be the last to kick in—some preschoolers often try to change the rules or otherwise "cheat" or even quit playing rather than acknowledge defeat. In the beginning, it's best to stick with very simple games that are based on shape recognition or color matching instead of reading. Once your preschooler is able to recognize basic numbers regularly, you might consider introducing him to dominoes or even to a deck of cards—many five year olds can master and enjoy a game of "Go Fish" or "War."

I keep all of my preschooler's toys in a large chest in his room, but he sometimes has trouble finding and getting things out on his own. Is there a better storage system?

You have several options available. First, you might consider storing your preschooler's toys in a few different areas around the house. Since he will not play with everything in the same place, there's no need for everything to be in one location. Having small storage areas strategically located in various rooms will make his toys more accessible—and may enable him to be more enthusiastic and effective at clean-up time. In addition, it is a good idea to store toys on shelves as opposed to inside large containers. This eliminates your preschooler's need to struggle with a lot of items he doesn't want in order to get the one he does want—a process which often results in "dumping" the whole thing out. Since your preschooler probably won't have a lot of clothes that need to be hung at this point, you might consider building a few extra shelves into his closet to accommodate his toy needs. To the extent that

containers are necessary, small ones—such as milk crates—are ideal. Finally, as your preschooler's toys become more complex and contain many pieces, it helps to hang a shoe bag so the pouches can be used to organize and hold things that otherwise would be difficult to keep track of and retrieve.

I'm buying a bed for my preschooler, and I thought a bunk bed would be fun and sensible in the long run. Are they safe?

If you're planning on having more than one child, or even if you expect your preschooler to have friends sleep over regularly, a bunk bed may be a good idea in that it will save valuable floor space. Besides, most children like bunk beds. Of course, your preschooler's first bed should be easy for him to climb into and out of. If you confine him to the bottom at first, a bunk bed need not be an immediate problem in this regard. Unfortunately, bunk beds are inherently hazardous to a certain extent, so if you do purchase one, make sure that the top portion has a sturdy safety rail. Make sure your preschooler understands that the top bed is for sleeping and not for playing upon. If possible and practical, you might consider getting a bunk bed with a detachable ladder rather than a built-in one. That way, you can remove it during play time and install it only when it's time for sleep.

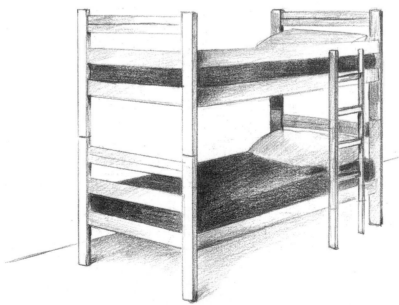

If you're planning on getting a bunk bed for your preschooler, look for one that has a sturdy safety rail on the top bunk.

GLOSSARY

Accommodation: The continuing process of adjusting to one's environment.

Allergen: An environmental substance that causes an allergic response in a sensitive individual.

Allergy: A state of sensitivity to a particular environmental substance, or allergen. An allergic reaction is the body's response, directed by the immune system, to exposure to an allergen.

Animism: The belief that anything that moves is alive.

Appendicitis: An inflammation of the appendix (a small pouch at the juncture of the small and large intestines).

Areola: The pink or brown circular area of skin around the breast nipple.

Assimilation: The process of incorporating new experiences and information into one's consciousness.

Asthma: A respiratory disorder characterized by unpredictable periods of breathlessness and wheezing; often an allergic disorder.

Attachment behavior: An outward expression of a young child's need to re-establish contact and reaffirm the bond with the primary caregiver. Attachment behavior is most often displayed when the child is confronted with unfamiliar circumstances.

Attention deficit disorder with hyperactivity (ADHD): A relatively rare syndrome marked by developmentally inappropriate inattention, impulsivity, and restlessness. A child with ADHD may have learning problems and impaired visual/spacial coordination. Thorough medical evaluation must be done before the diagnosis of ADHD can be made. Care must be taken to distinguish a true disorder from the normal overexuberance of a young child.

Bonding: The development of a deep emotional attachment between parent and child.

Botulism: A severe form of food poisoning. It is caused by a toxin produced by a bacteria often found in improperly canned or preserved food.

Bronchitis: A respiratory disease characterized by inflammation and swelling of the bronchi (the main airways connecting the windpipe and the lungs).

Chicken pox: A common, highly contagious disease, primarily of childhood, caused by the zaricella zoster virus. Symptoms include an itchy rash with blisters, fever, and mild coldlike symptoms. Chicken pox is usually a relatively mild disease in childhood.

Circumcision: Partial removal of the foreskin of the penis.

Colic: Repeated episodes of inconsolable crying, possibly due to abdominal discomfort, in a baby who previously was not especially fussy.

Concussion: An injury to the brain (usually temporary) caused by a violent jar or shock, such as a blow to the head.

Congenital: Present at the time of birth or before.

Conjunctivitis: A redness or pinkness of the white portion of the eye that often accompanies a cold. The infection may be caused by the same virus that caused the cold or may be due to a secondary bacterial infection. *Also called* pinkeye.

Cradle cap: A common form of seborrheic dermatitis in infants that causes the scalp to appear yellowish, scaly, and crusted.

Croup: An inflammation and swelling of the larynx or trachea, usually caused by a virus.

Cruising: The act of taking steps while holding onto supports, such as furniture.

Deciduous teeth: The first set of twenty teeth, which usually begin to erupt at about six months of age. *Also called* baby teeth *or* primary teeth.

Diaphragm: The muscle dividing the abdominal and chest cavities that is used in breathing.

Diphtheria: A sudden, severe, and highly contagious disease caused by bacteria. It primarily affects the tonsils, upper airways, and larynx (voice box). Complications may include inflammation of the heart muscle, which sometimes results in heart failure. Diphtheria can be prevented by immunization with the diphtheria-tetanus-pertussis (DTP) or diphtheria-tetanus (D-T) vaccine.

Epiglottitis: A life-threatening bacterial infection of the epiglottis (the "lid" over the opening of the larynx) and surrounding tissue. Symptoms include rapidly increasing difficulty in breathing, drooling, partial protrusion of the tongue, difficulty swallowing, and high fever.

Eustachian tube: A thin, hollow tube that connects the middle ear with the upper part of the throat and equalizes the air pressure in the middle ear with the air pressure outside the body.

Expressive language development: The process of acquiring the ability to use the spoken word.

Febrile convulsion: A seizure related to a sudden elevation of body temperature.

Fontanel: A soft, membrane-covered area on a baby's head where the skull bones have not yet come together. *Also called* soft spot.

Gastroenteritis: An inflammation of the lining of the stomach and the intestines. Among the causes are viral or bacterial infection, food poisoning, and allergic reaction. Symptoms include nausea, vomiting, abdominal discomfort, and diarrhea.

Hyperactivity: *See* attention deficit disorder with hyperactivity.

Hyposensitization: A treatment involving the administration of increasingly large doses of an allergen to gradually build tolerance to the allergen in a sensitive individual.

Immunity: The body's ability to resist infection. Active immunity is acquired by vaccination against a disease or by recovery from a previous infection. Passive immunity, which is only temporary, is acquired from antibodies obtained either from the mother (such as through breast-feeding) or by injection of serum from an immune person or animal who has active immunity.

Interpersonal awareness: Knowledge of one's self as an individual who is separate and distinct from other human beings.

Large muscle skills: Ability to perform movements—such as sitting, crawling, climbing, jumping, and walking—that require coordination of the large muscles. *Also called* gross motor skills.

Larynx: Voice box.

Measles: A highly contagious viral disease that is spread from person to person in airborne droplets of moisture from an infected person's respiratory system. The disease is marked by fever, coldlike symptoms, and a rash of dark red spots that begins on the face and neck and spreads to the torso, arms, and legs. Possible complications include pneumonia and inflammation of the brain. Measles can be prevented by immunization with the measles vaccine, which is usually given as part of the measles-mumps-rubella (MMR) vaccine.

Meningitis: A very serious disease that involves inflammation and infection of the membranes that cover the brain and spinal cord.

Middle ear infection: A common form of ear infection, also called otitis media, that affects the part of the hearing mechanism between the eardrum and the inner ear.

Mumps: A moderately contagious viral infection that affects the salivary glands. Symptoms include fever, headache, loss of appetite, and swelling of the glands in the neck. Possible complications include meningitis, inflammation of the brain, and permanent deafness. Mumps can be prevented by immunization with the mumps vaccine, which is usually given as part of the measles-mumps-rubella (MMR) vaccine.

Negativism: A normal stage of personality development during which a toddler expresses a growing capacity for independence and self-assertiveness by routinely refusing to comply with instructions and requests.

Night terror: A sudden feeling of extreme fear that awakens a sleeping child. Episodes are marked by screaming, inconsolable fear, and panic, but the child generally does not remember such episodes in the morning.

Object permanence: The ability to retain an image of an item or person in mental form even when that item or person is removed from direct contact with the senses.

Paradoxical diarrhea: Frequent passage of liquid stool that results when a child withholds stool, often because of a previous painful bowel movement.

Parallel play: A type of play generally displayed by toddlers in which each engages in a separate activity in close proximity to the other without actually sharing or interacting.

Pertussis: Whooping cough.

Pinkeye: Conjunctivitis.

Pinworms: An infection by tiny, white or tan, wormlike parasites called pinworms. The infection begins when the microscopic pinworm eggs get on a child's hands, usually through the sharing of toys or utensils with an infected child. The child puts the hands in the mouth, and the eggs are ingested. The eggs mature in the intestine. The female pinworm lays her eggs in the child's anal region at night, which causes itching. When the child scratches the anal region, the eggs get on the hands, and the cycle continues until treated.

Play value: The degree to which a toy or object suits the interests and abilities of a child at a particular stage in development.

Pneumonia: An inflammation of the lungs caused by a virus, bacteria, other microscopic organisms, or inhaled irritants.

Polio: Poliomyelitis. A highly contagious disease caused by a poliovirus. The disease occurs most often in children and can involve the spinal cord, causing paralysis. Poliomyelitis can be prevented by immunization with the polio vaccine.

Prehension: Visually directed reaching.

Premature: Refers to birth that occurs before the thirty-seventh week of pregnancy.

Prickly heat: A mild skin condition caused by temporary blockage of the sweat gland openings in the skin. It occurs when a child is overheated.

Realism: A toddler's inability to distinguish dreams from reality.

Receptive language development: The process of acquiring the ability to understand the spoken word.

Ringworm: A fungal infection of the skin that causes red, scaly, itchy, ring-shaped lesions on the skin.

Rooting: A reflexive turning of the head when the cheek is touched.

Roseola: A disease marked by high fever that lasts two to four days and goes away. It is followed by the appearance of a transient red rash. It occurs most commonly during the first three years of life.

Rubella: A contagious viral disease marked by fever, mild coldlike symptoms, swollen lymph nodes, and a red rash. The disease is usually mild in children; however, if a pregnant woman contracts rubella during early pregnancy, her baby may be born with severe birth defects. Rubella can be prevented through immunization with the rubella vaccine, which is usually given as part of the measles-mumps-rubella (MMR) vaccine. *Also called* German measles.

Scabies: A contagious skin infection caused by small insects called mites, which burrow into the skin and lay eggs, causing an itchy, red rash.

Seborrhea, seborrheic dermatitis: A skin condition causing redness, scaling, and sometimes itching. Dandruff and cradle cap are mild forms of seborrhea.

Sensorimotor: Relating to the first stage of development in which basic information about the world is gathered through the senses and physical movements.

Small muscle skills: Ability to perform movements—such as picking up and manipulating small objects—that require precise coordination of the small muscles. *Also called* fine motor skills.

Steady staring: An apparently passive state during which a baby or toddler actually is taking in a substantial amount of environmental stimuli through the eyes.

Stranger anxiety: A temporary phenomenon, common during the second half of the first year of life, in which a baby expresses extreme discomfort about being in the company of unfamiliar adults.

Sudden infant death syndrome (SIDS):   The sudden, unexpected, and unexplained death of an apparently healthy and normal infant during sleep. It occurs most often during the second and third months of life. The cause is unknown.

Tetanus: A serious infection caused by a bacterium that invades an open wound. It affects the central nervous system, causing severe, painful muscle contractions. Tetanus can be prevented by immunization with the diphtheria-tetanus-pertussis (DTP) or diphtheria-tetanus (D-T) vaccine.

Tonic neck reflex: A natural response in the newborn that results in the "fencer's pose." When the newborn is in a faceup position and the head is turned to one side, the arm on that side will extend while the arm on the opposite side will bend.

Trachea: Windpipe.

Transitional object: A toy, blanket, or other such item that provides a feeling of security as a baby moves from complete helplessness to early independence.

Tuberculosis: A contagious bacterial infection that usually affects the lungs but may also affect other body parts including the spine, kidneys, and digestive tract.

Tympanic membrane: Eardrum.

Umbilical granuloma: A gray mass of tissue that develops where the umbilical cord separates. Treatment may require cauterization.

Vaccine: A solution containing dead or weakened microorganisms or specially treated toxins that, when introduced into the body, stimulates the production of antibodies, creating immunity to a disease.

Visually directed reaching: The ability to use the hands under the direction of the eyes.

Water intoxication: Severe overhydration that can result in nausea, vomiting, weakness, tremors, and sometimes even seizures and death.

Whooping cough: A disease, primarily affecting children, due to bacterial infection. Symptoms include inflammation of the mucous membranes of the air passages, excessive secretion of mucus, mild fever, and attacks of explosive coughing followed by gasping breaths (which produce the characteristic whooping sound). The disease can be prevented by immunization with the diphtheria-tetanus-pertussis (DTP) vaccine. *Also called* pertussis.

INDEX

A

abdominal pain, 252
abduction, child, 50, 249-250
abstract concepts and preschoolers, 216-217
accommodation, 13
acetaminophen
 administration, 125
 for fever, 54, 123, 124, 184, 185
 to minimize side effects of immunization, 122
 for teething pain, 57
acne, infant, 56-57
activity center, 139-140, 144
ADHD. *See* attention deficit disorder with hyperactivity.
adoption, explaining to child, 268
adultomorphism, 21
adventure and preschoolers, 224, 248, 257
airplane travel with baby, 50
allergies, 190
 to bee stings, 254
 and breast-feeding, 37
 to cow's milk, 238
 to formula, 37
 and introduction of solid foods, 46-47, 111
anger in children, 258
animism, 152
antibiotics, 124, 185, 186
arithmetic, stimulating preschooler to begin, 264-265
art supplies, 145, 207, 271-272
aspirin, 57, 185
assimilation, 13
attachment behavior, 93-94, 157, 196
attention deficit disorder with hyperactivity (ADHD), 255
attention span, 97, 192, 194, 204, 225, 255

B

babbling, 22, 90
baby bottles. *See also* bottle-feeding; formula.
 in bed, 42-43, 171
 giving, 42-43
 sterilizing, 40-41, 107
 warming, 42
baby-sitters, 67-69
balloon play, 139
balls, 203-204
barbecued food, 243
bathing, parent with child, 165, 260
bathing baby
 sponge bath, 27-29
 toys for, 78, 141
 tub bath, 28, 30

bathing preschooler, 234-236
bathing toddler, 165-166
bedtime routine, 167
bee stings, 254
belly button. *See* umbilical cord.
bicycle riding, 246-247
birthmarks, 57
birth order, 93
biting, 199
bladder control, 149, 213-214
blocks, 207, 208, 274
boasting, 227
bonding, 10, 40, 42
bones, broken, 252-253
books
 introducing to baby, 65-66, 137
 for preschoolers, 272
 for toddlers, 204-205
booster seat in car, 245
boredom
 in babies, 64, 81
 in parents, 136
 in toddlers, 156
bottle-feeding. *See also* baby bottles; formula.
 and bonding, 40, 42
 and propping, 42-43, 109, 171
 techniques, 40-43
 and weaning, 108-109
 and weight gain, 42, 45-46, 109
bottles. *See* baby bottles.
botulism. 46, 111. *See also* food poisoning.
bowed legs, 60
bowel control, development of, 149, 213-214
bowel movements. *See also* paradoxical diarrhea; stools.
 frequency in children, 254
 in newborns, 44
breakfast, importance of, 240
breast-feeding
 advantages of, 36
 and allergies, 37
 breast care during, 39-40
 and drug abuse, 38
 and medications, 38
 and mother's diet, 37-38
 positions for, 36-37
 techniques, 36-40
 and weaning, 107-108
 and weight gain, 39
 and working mothers, 36-37, 43
breast milk
 adequacy of, 38-39
 expressing, 36-37

breasts, enlargement of, in newborn, 58
bubble play, 139
bunk beds, safety of, 277
burping, 44-45
busy boxes, 139-140, 144
butterfly bandage, 184

C

car, leaving child alone in, 246
cardiopulmonary resuscitation, 51
car safety, 50, 79, 121, 181, 245-246
car seats
    selecting, 79
    use of, 50, 79, 121, 181, 245
car trips
    entertaining baby during, 78
    entertaining preschooler during, 270
cats and babies, 49
chicken pox, 187-188
childproofing. *See* safety; safety proofing.
choking. *See* foods to avoid.
cholesterol, 241
circumcision
    pros and cons, 59
    treatment following, 28
classes. *See also* gymnastics; swimming classes.
    for preschoolers, 262-263
clay, 145. *See also* art supplies.
climbing, 86, 118, 142
clothing
    baby
        basic needs, 35
        care of, 35
        safety factors, 35
    toddler, laundering, 166
cold, common
    preventing the spread of, 251
    protecting baby from, 54
    treatment for, 54, 123-124, 185-186
cold compresses, 184
colic, 56
concussion, 184
confrontations
    avoiding, with toddler, 196
    with preschooler, 258
conjunctivitis, 186
constipation, 42, 191
convulsions, febrile, 186
cough, 124, 186
CPR. *See* cardiopulmonary resuscitation.
cradle cap, 28, 58, 127
crawling, 23, 84, 85, 92, 129
creativity, 226, 271
crib death (SIDS). *See* sudden infant death syndrome.

crib gyms, 76-77
cribs
    and climbing out, 102-103, 167-169
    selecting, 78
critical periods, 215
croup, 56, 124
cruising, 85
crying. *See also* colic.
    in newborns, 18
    reasons for, 63-64
cup, introducing, 107-109, 171
cuts, treatment for, 184

D

day care
    and child abuse, 250
    and contagious illness, 183
    and discipline, 200-201
    guilt concerning, 69
    readiness for, 201
    and safety concerns, 69, 183, 250
    selecting, 69-70
    and social skills, 201
day care providers, baby's attachment to, 135
dental emergencies, 253
dental hygiene, 104, 166, 233
depression, postpartum, 61
development. *See also* language development;
      motor development.
    birth to six months, 10-16
    one year to two and a half years, 148-155
    physical, 67, 142
    and premature babies, 89
    sensorimotor, 13-14, 67
    six months to one year, 84-91
    two and a half years to five years, 212-220
diapering, 24-27, 100
    cloth diapers, 24-27
    costs, 24-25
    and diaper rash, 24-26, 100
    diaper service, 24
    disposable diapers, 25-27
    toys to use during, 78
diarrhea, 44, 112, 191. *See also* bowel movements;
      paradoxical diarrhea.
diet
    mother's, during breast-feeding, 37-38
    prudent, for children, 172, 240
    vegetarian, safety of, for children, 240-241
diphtheria-tetanus-pertussis vaccine, 55, 122,
    188-189
discipline
    and preschoolers, 259
    and toddlers, 197-200

divorce, 267
doctor, when to call, 51-52, 124-125, 191
dogs
    and babies, 49
    and toddlers, 180
dreams, 152
dressing baby, 34, 101
    for indoors, 33
    for outdoors, 33, 35
dressing herself/himself, preschooler, 222
drooling, 57
DTP vaccine. *See* diphtheria-tetanus-pertussis vaccine.

E

ear infections
    causes of, 43, 127
    symptoms of, 126
    treatment of, 127, 187
ears. *See also* hearing.
    care of, 31, 126
    placement of tubes in, 187
eating habits
    establishing good, 239-240
    and food jags, 222, 241
    picky, 173
    poor, 174-175
eating nonfood items, toddlers, 157
education of baby, 131-132
eggs, 174
    introducing, 46
emergencies
    dental, 253
    fire prevention, 51
    preparation for, 48, 51
emotional support, child's need for, 154-155
energy level in preschoolers, 223-224
epiglottitis, 124
exercise and toddlers, 169
exploring
    birth to six months, 20-21
    one year to two and a half years, 156
    six months to one year, 92-95, 130-131
    two and a half years to five years, 224
eye-hand coordination, 14-15
eyes. *See also* vision.
    examination of, 187

F

fantasy activities, 160-161, 195, 208-209, 227, 275-276
fast foods, 175
father
    and child-rearing, 62-63
    role of, 62

fat in baby's diet, 111-112
feeding baby. *See also* bottle-feeding; breast-feeding.
    and cleanups, 112
    with the family, 113
    and messes, 96-97
    solids, 42, 46-47, 109-113
    who wants to feed herself/himself, 47
feeding schedule for baby, 43
feet, pigeon-toed, 255
fencer's pose, 11-12, 75
fever. *See also* temperature.
    assessing severity of, 122-123
    and convulsions, 186
    treatment for, 123
fingernails. *See* nails.
finger paints, 145
fire, fascination with, 247
fire drills, 183
fireplace safety, 118-119
fire safety, 247
flu, 185-186
fluoride, 45, 107, 237
fontanels, 11, 28, 31
food, baby. *See also* solids.
    and loose stools, 112
    preparing homemade, 110-111
food allergies, 238
food poisoning, 243. *See also* botulism.
foods to avoid
    birth to six months, 46-47
    one year to two and a half years, 172-173
    six months to one year, 111-112
    two and a half years to five years, 239
football carry
    in bathing, 29
    in breast-feeding, 37
formula. *See also* baby bottles; bottle-feeding.
    and allergies, 37
    preparing, 40-42
    and traveling, 107
    and weight gain, 42, 109
furniture and equipment, baby, 78-81, 139

G

games
    for baby, 143
    board, 276-277
    for toddlers, 204
gender differences, 91
genitals. *See also* circumcision.
    care of, in newborn, 28
gifts, selecting, for baby, 140
grammar and preschoolers, 217
growth. *See* development.

guilt in parents, 265
guns, toy, 270
gymnastics classes, 142
gym set, 269

H

hair
    in newborns 10-11
    shampooing, 235-236
handling baby, 24-25
head
    injury to, 184
    in newborns, 11
hearing
    in newborn, 12
    testing baby's, 60, 126
hemophilus influenza type B vaccine, 122, 189
HiB vaccine. *See* hemophilus influenza type B vaccine.
hiccups, 59
honey, dangers of, 46
hospital stay, preparing child for, 268
humidifier, 124
humor and preschoolers, 227-228
hygiene, 233
hyperactivity, 97, 160, 223-224, 255
hyposensitization, 254

I

ibuprofen, 185
illnesses
    common cold, 54, 123-124, 185-186, 251
    and day care, 183
    flu, 185-186
    noting symptoms of, 51-52
imaginary friend, 227
imitative behavior, 99, 160-161
immunization
    reactions to, 55, 122, 188-189
    schedule of, 55, 255-256
independence, toddler's struggle for, 154-155
individuality in preschoolers, 223
infections, secondary, 185-186
injury
    to baby, 121
    first aid for, 184
    head, 184
intercom, 48, 119
ipecac, syrup of, 184

J

juice, 109, 237
jump seats, 80

K

kindergarten, readiness for, 265-266
kitchen safety, 114-115, 177
knock knees, 255

L

language development. *See also* speech development.
    and bilingual parents, 193-194
    expressive, 153
    one year to two and a half years, 153-154, 159-160, 193-194
    receptive, 89-90, 132-133
    six months to one year, 90, 98-99, 132-133
    stimulating, in baby, 65, 132
    stimulating, in toddler, 193-194
    two and a half years to five years, 217-218, 263
lanugo, 10
large muscle skills, development of, 142, 205, 212
layette, 35
learning
    birth to six months, 13-15
    six months to one year, 87-90, 129-132
leash, toddler, 182
legs, development of, 60
lies, children telling, 152, 257
lisping, 218

M

massage, baby, 66
math, assessing readiness for, 218-219
measles-mumps-rubella vaccine, 189
medical supplies, recommended, 52-54, 184
medication, prescription, 185
medication for baby
    administering, 125
    over-the-counter, 124-125
memory
    birth to six months, 15
    one year to two and a half years, 151
    six months to one year, 89
    two and a half years to five years, 217
meningitis, 122
microwave ovens and baby foods, 42
middle ear infections. *See* ear infections.
milk, cow's
    adding chocolate to, 175
    allergy to, 238
    best type for baby, 109
    best type for preschooler, 238
    best type for toddler, 174-175
    ensuring adequate intake, 237
"mine," when toddler says, 159
mirrors, 75

misbehavior, 99
MMR vaccine. *See* measles-mumps-rubella vaccine.
mobiles, 74
moral values, development of, 152-153
motivation of preschoolers, 264
motor development
    large muscle, 142, 205, 212
    small muscle, 87, 149-150, 207, 212-213
mouth, putting objects into, 95, 105
muscle control and baby, 19
muscle tone in newborn, 11
musical toys, introducing, 144-145

N

nails
    biting, 260
    trimming, 32
name-calling by preschooler, 258
naming baby, 67
naps, 167, 221, 236
    changing patterns in, 167, 221, 236
    giving up, 167
    length of, 101-102
    number of, 156
negativism, 157, 158, 196-197
neonatal imitation, 16
newborns
    communication by, 15
    individual differences in, 13
    memory in, 15
    physical appearance, 10-12
    reflexes, 12-13, 16
    senses, 12-17
    sleep patterns, 17
    temperament in, 19
    thinking and cognitive development in, 12-16
nightmares, 221
night terrors, 221
night waking, 17, 134, 168-169
"no"
    effective use of, 133-134
    when toddler says, 157, 158, 196-197
nose drops, 54
nursery school, 265
nursing. *See* breast-feeding.

O

object permanence, 20, 88-89
outings, 103-104
out-of-doors
    play, 144
    safety, 119-120
overprotectiveness, 71, 121

P

pacifiers, 42
paradoxical diarrhea, 254
parallel play, 163
parent support groups, 71
pediatrician, when to call, 51-52, 124-125, 191
peek-a-boo, 143
penis. *See also* circumcision.
    care of uncircumcised, 234
personality traits, development of, 155
pets, 49, 266
pinkeye, 186
pinworms, 253-254
plants, poisonous, 118
play
    dress-up, 179-180
    fantasy, 160-161, 195, 208-209, 227, 275-276
playground equipment
    safety of, 248-249
    selecting, for purchase, 269
play groups, 163
playing. *See also* parallel play.
    alone, 160
    with peers, 209, 228, 249
playpens, 103, 130-131
play sets, 209, 275-276
poisoning, first aid for, 184
poison ivy, 254
polio vaccine, 189
pool safety, 120, 181, 248
potty chair, selecting, 231
prehension. *See* visually directed reaching.
premature babies, development in, 89
pretending and violence, 227
prickly heat rashes, 128
privacy, 222-223
pulling up, 98
punishment, preschoolers' perception of, 220
puppets, 272
push and pull toys, 143
puzzles, 205, 225, 273

R

rashes. *See also* diapering and diaper rash.
    around the mouth, 190-191
    and childhood illnesses, 128
rational thought, 150-151, 214
rattles, 76
reading
    assessing readiness for, 218-219
    to baby, 65-66
    stimulating preschooler to begin, 264-265
    to toddler, 194-195

realism, 152
rebellion in toddlers, 157-159
reflexes, 12-13, 16
rights
    baby's, 136
    parents', 136
ringworm, 253
rituals
    modifying, 196
    recognizing, 197
    toddlers' need for, 161
role-playing, 195-196, 208-209
rolling over, 11
rooting, 12
roseola, 188

S

safety
    bathroom, 116, 165, 178, 244
    bathtub, 165
    bedroom, 115-116
    and bicycle riding, 246-247
    and childproofing, 114-119
    and crossing the street, 244-245
    at day care, 69
    around fireplaces, 118-119
    guidelines for infants' furniture and equipment, 78-81
    at home, 48, 114-119, 177-180
    out-of-doors, 119-120, 180-181
    and parental concern, 71, 250
    around toilets, 93
    and toys, 72-73, 122
    around water, 120, 180-181, 248
    when visiting others, 122, 170
safety proofing, 114-119, 133, 177
salt, 242
sandboxes, 269-270
scabies, 253
schedules
    feeding, 43
    sleeping, 101-102
school
    anxiety about, 252
    immunizations needed before starting, 255-256
seborrheic dermatitis. *See* cradle cap.
security objects, 144, 226
self-esteem, development of, 91, 135-136, 220
sensorimotor development, 13-14, 87, 150
separation anxiety, 135, 219-220
sex education and preschoolers, 259-260
sexual abuse, protecting child from, 250
sexual relations following childbirth, 62
shoes, baby, 106
shopping with baby, 50

siblings
    and baby's safety, 49, 121
    and confrontations, 161-162, 182, 228, 267
    and jealousy, 49, 95, 121, 161-162, 200
    spacing of, 201
SIDS. *See* sudden infant death syndrome.
silly behavior and preschoolers, 227-228, 257-258
singing to baby, 66
single parents, 63, 268
sitting up, 11
skim milk. *See* milk, cow's.
skin, newborn, 10
sledding, 248
sleep. *See also* naps.
    best position for, 32-33
    birth to six months, 17
    one year to two and a half years, 156
    in parents' room, 32
    six months to one year, 92
    two and a half years to five years, 221, 236
sleeping through the night, 108-109, 134-135, 169
sleep problems
    nightmares, 221
    night terrors, 221
    night waking, 17, 134, 168-169
    for parents, 61
small muscle skills, development of, 87, 149-150, 207, 212-213
smiling in newborns, 15
smoking and baby's health, 55-56
snacking, 175
social awareness, 15, 21-22
social skills and day care, 201
soft drinks, 174
soft spots, 11, 28-31
solid food
    allergic reaction to, 46-47
    introducing, 42, 46-47, 109-113
spacing children, 201
spanking, 198-199
speech. *See also* language development.
    communication prior to onset of, 98
    onset of, 90, 153-154
spitting up, 44
spoiling a baby, 64
sports equipment, 270
sprains, 252-253
stairs
    beginning to climb, 86
    and safety, 118, 130, 142
staring, 23, 97
stools
    and constipation, 191
    and diarrhea, 44, 112, 191
stork bites, 57
stranger anxiety, 91, 135

stuttering, 218
sucking, 18-19
  on feet and toes, 22
  on hands and fingers, 22
sudden infant death syndrome (SIDS), 52
sugar, 242
sun, protecting baby from, 106, 127-128
sunglasses, baby, 106
superbaby syndrome, 193
surgery, preparing child for, 268
swaddling, 32-33
swimming classes
  and babies, 120
  and toddlers, 181
swimming pool, taking baby into, 120
swings, infant, 80

T

tantrums, 198
tear duct, blocked, 57
teeth
  cleaning, 104, 166, 233
  decay in, from bottle use, 42-43
  development of, 11
  and fluoride, 45, 104
  injury to, 253
teething, 57, 166
television watching
  and baby, 22-23
  and nightmares, 227
  and preschoolers, 260-262
temperament, 19
temperature. *See also* fever.
  normal, 251
  taking orally, 251
  taking rectally, 52-53
  when to take, 122-123
thumb-sucking, 47, 199
"time out" as method of discipline, 259
toenails. *See* nails.
toilet, baby's fascination with, 92-93
toilet training
  and accidents, 223, 232-233
  how to begin, 231-232
  and independence, 234, 244
  preparing for, 231
  readiness for, 164, 213-214, 230-231
tonic neck reflex, 11-12
toy library, 203
toys
  age recommendations for, 73
  birth to six months
    cleaning, 35, 105-106
    homemade, 72-74

    safety of, 72-73
    selecting, 72-78
  and gender issues, 209, 276
  homemade, 72
  one year to two and a half years, 203-209
    household items as, 203-209
    safety of, 203
  six months to one year
    household items as, 137-139
    safety of, 138-141
    selecting, 139-145
  storage of, 139, 277
  two and a half years to five years
    mechanical, 273-274
    safety of, 270
    selecting, 269-277
  war, 266-267
toys of older siblings, dangers to baby, 122
transitional objects, 144
tricycle riding, 247
tuberculosis test, 189
tummy aches, 252

U

umbilical cord, care of, 31
umbilical granuloma, 31

V

vaccination. *See* immunization.
vaginal discharge in newborn girls, 58
vaporizer, 54, 124
vernix, 10
vision
  development of, in newborn, 12, 59-60
  testing, 256
visually directed reaching, 14, 20
vitamin supplements, 45, 107, 240

W

walkers, 81
walking, 85-86, 129, 148-149
"walking reflex," 16
war toys, 266-267, 270
water, offering, to baby, 45
water intoxication, 120, 181
weaning, 171
weight, excessive, in baby, 42, 45-46, 109
"why," when preschooler asks, 227
window safety, 119
working parents and day care, 69-71
writing, stimulating preschooler
  to begin, 264-265